Scott Foresman-Addison We
enVisionMATH
Florid

Authors

Randall I. Charles
Professor Emeritus
Department of Mathematics
San Jose State University
San Jose, California

Janet H. Caldwell
Professor of Mathematics
Rowan University
Glassboro, New Jersey

Mary Cavanagh
Executive Director of Center for
Practice, Research and Innovation
in Mathematics Education (PRIME)
Arizona State University
Mesa, Arizona

Dinah Chancellor
Mathematics Consultant,
Carroll ISD, Southlake, Texas
Mathematics Consultant,
Kerrville, ISD, Kerrville, Texas

Juanita V. Copley
Professor Emeritus, College of Education
University of Houston
Houston, Texas

Warren D. Crown
Professor Emeritus of Mathematics Education
Graduate School of Education
Rutgers University
New Brunswick, New Jersey

Francis (Skip) Fennell
Professor of Education
McDaniel College
Westminster, Maryland

Alma B. Ramirez
Sr. Research Associate
Math Pathways and Pitfalls WestEd
Oakland, California

Kay B. Sammons
Coordinator of Elementary Mathematics
Howard County Public Schools
Ellicott City, Maryland

Jane F. Schielack
Professor of Mathematics
Associate Dean for Assessment and
Pre K-12 Education, College of Science
Texas A&M University
College Station, Texas

William Tate
Edward Mallinckrodt Distinguished
University Professor in Arts & Sciences
Washington University
St. Louis, Missouri

John A. Van de Walle
Professor Emeritus, Mathematics Education
Virginia Commonwealth University
Richmond, Virginia

Consulting Mathematicians

Edward J. Barbeau
Professor of Mathematics
University of Toronto
Toronto, Canada

Sybilla Beckmann
Professor of Mathematics
Department of Mathematics
University of Georgia
Athens, Georgia

David Bressoud
DeWitt Wallace Professor of Mathematics
Macalester College
Saint Paul, Minnesota

Gary Lippman
Professor of Mathematics and Computer Science
California State University East Bay
Hayward, California

Glenview, Illinois • Boston, Massachusetts • Chandler, Arizona • Upper Saddle River, New Jersey

Consulting Authors

Charles R. Allan
Mathematics Education Consultant
(retired)
Michigan Department of Education
Lansing Michigan

Stuart J. Murphy
Visual Learning Specialist
Boston, Massachusetts

Grant Wiggins
Researcher and Educational Consultant
Hopewell, New Jersey

Center Activities Author

Ruth I. Champagne
Mathematics Education Specialist
FRIENDLY MATH, LLC
Chicago, Illinois

ELL Consultant/Reviewers

Jim Cummins
Professor
The University of Toronto
Toronto, Canada

Alma B. Ramirez
Research Associate
Math Pathways and Pitfalls WestEd
Oakland, California

Florida Reviewers

Ralph Blose
Curriculum Support Specialist
Miami-Dade County

Lynda Cihanowic
Teacher
Okaloosa County

Janice Demers
Teacher
Pinellas County

Carmen Elliott
Teacher
Brevard County

David Hyers
Teacher
Nassau County

Noreen Kraebel
Math Resource Specialist
Pasco County

Susan Petrek
Math Resource Specialist
Osceola County

Virginia Sanchez
Teacher
Miami-Dade County

Anita Saunders
Math and Science Coach
Collier County

Gay Street
Math Coach
Marion County

ISBN-13: 978-0-328-44656-8

ISBN-10: 0-328-44656-4

3 4 5 6 7 8 9 10 V042 16 15 14 13 12 11 10

Topic Titles

Florida

Grade 4
Big Ideas and Supporting Ideas

Big Idea 1 Develop quick recall of multiplication facts and related division facts and fluency with whole number multiplication.
Benchmarks: **MA.4.A.1.1, MA.4.A.1.2**

Big Idea 2 Develop an understanding of decimals, including the connection between fractions and decimals.
Benchmarks: **MA.4.A.2.1, MA.4.A.2.2, MA.4.A.2.3, MA.4.A.2.4**

Big Idea 3 Develop an understanding of area and determine the area of two-dimensional shapes.
Benchmarks: **MA.4.G.3.1, MA.4.G.3.2, MA.4.G.3.3**

Supporting Ideas Algebra
Benchmarks: **MA.4.A.4.1, MA.4.A.4.2, MA.4.A.4.3**

Supporting Ideas Geometry and Measurement
Benchmarks: **MA.4.G.5.1, MA.4.G.5.2, MA.4.G.5.3**

Supporting Ideas Number and Operations
Benchmarks: **MA.4.A.6.1, MA.4.A.6.2, MA.4.A.6.3, MA.4.A.6.4, MA.4.A.6.5, MA.4.A.6.6**

K–5 Math Strand Colors

- Number and Operations
- Algebra
- Geometry and Measurement
- Data Analysis
- **Problem Solving**

Topic 1

Numeration

Supporting Ideas Number and Operations MA.4.A.6.1

Scott Foresman-Addison Wesley
enVisionMATH™
Florida

Florida Contents

Equations

 Supporting Ideas **Algebra** MA.4.A.4.1, MA.4.A.4.2

Decimals and Numeration

Big Idea 2 MA.4.A.2.1, MA.4.A.2.2, MA.4.A.2.4

Fractions

Big Idea 2 MA.4.A.2.4

Supporting Ideas **Number and Operations** MA.4.A.6.3, MA.4.A.6.4

Problem-Solving Handbook

Use this Problem-Solving Handbook throughout the year to help you solve problems.

Don't give up!

Everybody can be a good problem solver!

There's almost always more than one way to solve a problem!

Pictures help me understand!

Explaining helps me understand!

Problem-Solving Process

Read and Understand

What am I trying to find?
- Tell what the question is asking.

What do I know?
- Tell the problem in my own words.
- Identify key facts and details.

Plan and Solve

What strategy or strategies should I try?

Can I show the problem?
- Try drawing a picture.
- Try making a list, table, or graph.
- Try acting it out or using objects.

How will I solve the problem?

What is the answer?
- Tell the answer in a complete sentence.

Strategies
- Show What You Know
  - Draw a Picture
  - Make an Organized List
  - Make a Table
  - Make a Graph
  - Act It Out/ Use Objects
- Look for a Pattern
- Try, Check, Revise
- Write an Equation
- Use Reasoning
- Work Backward
- Solve a Simpler Problem

Look Back and Check

Did I check my work?
- Compare my work to the information in the problem.
- Be sure all calculations are correct.

Is my answer reasonable?
- Estimate to see if my answer makes sense.
- Make sure the question was answered.

Using Bar Diagrams

Use a bar diagram to show how what you know and what you want to find are related. Then choose an operation to solve the problem.

Problem 1

Carrie helps at the family flower store in the summer. She keeps a record of how many flower bouquets she sells. How many bouquets did she sell on Monday and Wednesday?

Carrie's Sales

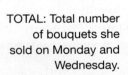

Days	Bouquets Sold
Monday	19
Tuesday	22
Wednesday	24
Thursday	33
Friday	41

Bar Diagram

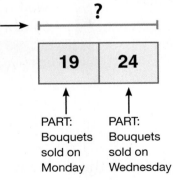

TOTAL: Total number of bouquets she sold on Monday and Wednesday.

?

| 19 | 24 |

PART: Bouquets sold on Monday   PART: Bouquets sold on Wednesday

19 + 24 = ▢

Think I can add to find the total.

Problem 2

Kim is saving to buy a sweatshirt from the college her brother attends. She has $18. How much more money does she need to buy the sweatshirt?

Bar Diagram

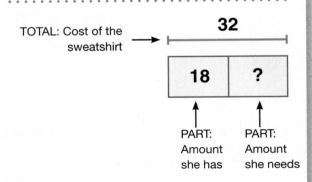

TOTAL: Cost of the sweatshirt

32

| 18 | ? |

PART: Amount she has   PART: Amount she needs

32 − 18 = ▢

Think I can subtract to find the missing part.

Pictures help me understand!

Problem 3

Tickets to a movie on Saturday cost only $5 each no matter what age you are. What is the cost of tickets for a family of four?

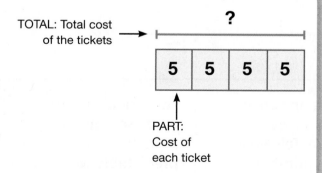

Bar Diagram

TOTAL: Total cost of the tickets → ?

| 5 | 5 | 5 | 5 |

↑ PART: Cost of each ticket

4 × 5 = ▨

 I can multiply because the parts are equal.

Problem 4

Thirty students traveled in 3 vans to the zoo. The same numbers of students were in each van. How many students were in each van?

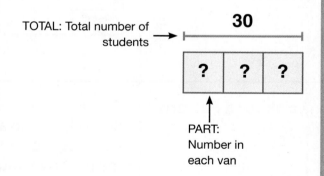

Bar Diagram

TOTAL: Total number of students → **30**

| ? | ? | ? |

↑ PART: Number in each van

30 ÷ 3 = ▨

 I can divide to find how many are in each part.

Problem-Solving Handbook

xiii

Problem-Solving Strategies

Strategy	Example	When I Use It
Draw a Picture	The race was 5 kilometers. Markers were at the starting line and the finish line. Markers showed each kilometer of the race. Find the number of markers used.	Try drawing a picture when it helps you visualize the problem or when the relationships such as joining or separating are involved.

Start Line — Finish Line

Start Line — 1 km — 2 km — 3 km — 4 km — Finish Line

Strategy	Example	When I Use It
Make a Table	Phil and Marcy spent all day Saturday at the fair. Phil rode 3 rides each half hour and Marcy rode 2 rides each half hour. How many rides had Marcy ridden when Phil rode 24 rides?	Try making a table when: • there are 2 or more quantities, • amounts change using a pattern.

Rides for Phil	3	6	9	12	15	18	21	24
Rides for Marcy	2	4	6	8	10	12	14	16

Strategy	Example	When I Use It
Look for a Pattern	The house numbers on Forest Road change in a planned way. Describe the pattern. Tell what the next two house numbers should be.	Look for a pattern when something repeats in a predictable way.

3   6   10   15   ?   ?

Strategy	Example	When I Use It
Make an Organized List	How many ways can you make change for a quarter using dimes and nickels?	Make an organized list when asked to find combinations of two or more items.

1 quarter =
1 dime + 1 dime + 1 nickel
1 dime + 1 nickel + 1 nickel + 1 nickel
1 nickel + 1 nickel + 1 nickel + 1 nickel + 1 nickel

Strategy	Example	When I Use It
Try, Check, Revise	Suzanne spent $27, not including tax, on dog supplies. She bought two of one item and one of another item. What did she buy? $8 + $8 + $15 = $31 $7 + $7 + $12 = $26 $6 + $6 + $15 = $27	Use Try, Check, Revise when quantities are being combined to find a total, but you don't know which quantities.

Dog Supplies Sale!
Leash $8
Collar $6
Bowls $7
Medium Beds $15
Toys $12

Strategy	Example	When I Use It
Write an Equation	Maria's new CD player can hold 6 discs at a time. If she has 204 CDs, how many times can the player be filled without repeating a CD? Find $204 \div 6 = n$.	Write an equation when the story describes a situation that uses an operation or operations.

Even More Strategies

Strategy	Example	When I Use It
Act It Out	How many ways can 3 students shake each other's hand?	Think about acting out a problem when the numbers are small and there is action in the problem you can do.
Use Reasoning	Beth collected some shells, rocks, and beach glass. **Beth's Collection** 2 rocks 3 times as many shells as rocks 12 objects in all How many of each object are in the collection?	Use reasoning when you can use known information to reason out unknown information.
Work Backward	Tracy has band practice at 10:15 A.M. It takes her 20 minutes to get from home to practice and 5 minutes to warm up. What time should she leave home to get to practice on time? Time Tracy leaves home **?** ← 20 minutes ← Time warm up starts ← 5 minutes ← Time practice starts **10:15**	Try working backward when: • you know the end result of a series of steps, • you want to know what happened at the beginning.

Strategy	Example	When I Use It

I can think about when to use each strategy.

Solve a Simpler Problem

Each side of each triangle in the figure at the left is one centimeter. If there are 12 triangles in a row, what is the perimeter of the figure?

I can look at 1 triangle, then 2 triangles, then 3 triangles.

          perimeter = 3 cm

          perimeter = 4 cm

   perimeter = 5 cm

Try solving a simpler problem when you can create a simpler case that is easier to solve.

Make a Graph

Mary was in a jump rope contest. How did her number of jumps change over the five days of the contest?

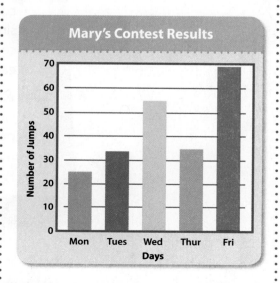

Mary's Contest Results

Make a graph when:
- data for an event are given,
- the question can be answered by reading the graph.

Writing to Explain

Here is a good math explanation.

Writing to Explain What happens to the area of the rectangle if the lengths of its sides are doubled?

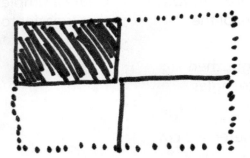

■ = $\frac{1}{4}$ of the whole rectangle

The area of the new rectangle is 4 times the area of the original rectangle.

Tips for Writing Good Math Explanations....

A good explanation should be:
- correct
- simple
- complete
- easy to understand

Math explanations can use:
- words
- pictures
- numbers
- symbols

This is another good math explanation.

Explaining helps me understand!

Writing to Explain Use blocks to show 13 × 24.
Draw a picture of what you did with the blocks.

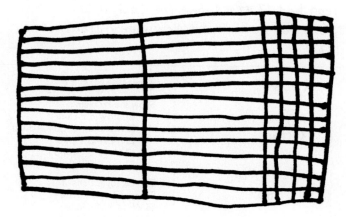

First we made a row of 24 using
2 tens and 4 ones. Then we made
more rows until we had 13 rows.
Then we said 13 rows of 2 tens is
13 × 2 tens = 26 tens or 260.
Then we said 13 rows of 4 ones is
13 × 4 = 52 . Then we added the parts.
260 + 52 = 312   So, 13 × 24 = 312.

Problem-Solving Recording Sheet

Name __Jane__

Teaching Tool
1

Problem-Solving Recording Sheet

Problem:
On June 14, 1777, the Continental Congress approved the design of a national flag. The 1777 flag had 13 stars, one for each colony. Today's flag has 50 stars, one for each state. How many stars were added to the flag since 1777?

Find?

Number of stars added to the flag

Know?

Original flag
13 stars

Today's flag
50 stars

Strategies?

Show the Problem
☑ Draw a Picture
☐ Make an Organized List
☐ Make a Table
☐ Make a Graph
☐ Act It Out/Use Objects

☐ Look for a Pattern
☐ Try, Check, Revise
☑ Write an Equation
☐ Use Reasoning
☐ Work Backwards
☐ Solve a Simpler Problem

Show the Problem?

50

13	?

Solution?

I am comparing the two quantities.
I could add up from 13 to 50. I can also subtract 13 from 50. I'll subract.

$$\begin{array}{r} 50 \\ -\ 13 \\ \hline 37 \end{array}$$

Answer?

There were 37 stars added to the flag from 1777 to today.

Check? Reasonable?

$37 + 13 = 50$ so I subtracted correctly.

$50 - 13$ is about $50 - 10 = 40$
40 is close to 37. 37 is reasonable.

Here's a way to organize my problem-solving work.

Name ___Benton___

Problem-Solving Recording Sheet

Problem:

Suppose your teacher told you to open your math book to the facing pages whose page numbers add to 85. To which two pages would you open your book?

Find?

Two facing page numbers

Know?

Two pages.
Facing each other.
Sum is 85.

Strategies?

Show the Problem
- ☑ Draw a Picture
- ☐ Make an Organized List
- ☐ Make a Table
- ☐ Make a Graph
- ☐ Act It Out/Use Objects

- ☐ Look for a Pattern
- ☑ Try, Check, Revise
- ☑ Write an Equation
- ☐ Use Reasoning
- ☐ Work Backwards
- ☐ Solve a Simpler Problem

Show the Problem?

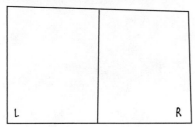

L + R = 85
L is 1 less than R

Solution?

I'll try some numbers in the middle.
40 + 41 = 81, too low
How about 46 and 47?
46 + 47 = 93, too high
Ok, now try 42 and 43.
42 + 43 = 85.

Answer?

The page numbers are 42 and 43.

Check? Reasonable?

I added correctly.
42 + 43 is about 40 + 40 = 80
80 is close to 85.
42 and 43 is reasonable.

Numeration

1 Baby the snake weighed 403 pounds in 2003. Was Baby the heaviest snake living in captivity? You will find out in Lesson 1-4.

2 About how many people visit the Brevard Zoo in Melbourne, Florida, each year? You will find out in Lesson 1-5.

3 The African continent has an area of 11,608,000 square miles. Is it the largest continent on Earth? You will find out in Lesson 1-4.

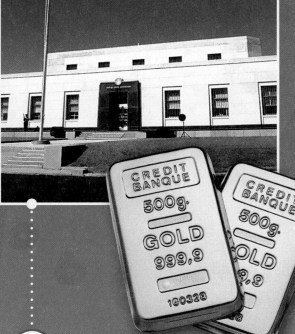

4

How much gold is stored in Fort Knox? You will find out in Lesson 1-2.

Review What You Know!

Vocabulary

Choose the best term from the box.

> • digit   • period
> • compare   • number line
> • even   • odd

1. A group of three digits in a number separated by a comma is a ?.

2. A ? is a line that shows numbers in order using a scale.

3. The number 8 is an ? number.

4. The number 5 is an ? number.

Comparing Numbers

Compare each set of numbers using >, <, or =.

5. 13 ◯ 10   **6.** 7 ◯ 7   **7.** 28 ◯ 29

8. 14 ◯ 5   **9.** 43 ◯ 34   **10.** 0 ◯ 1

11. 52 ◯ 52 **12.** 13 ◯ 65 **13.** 22 ◯ 33

Place Value

Tell if the underlined digit is in the ones, tens, or hundreds place.

14. 34<u>6</u>   **15.** <u>1</u>7   **16.** 9<u>2</u>1

17. <u>1</u>06   **18.** 3<u>3</u>   **19.** <u>4</u>7

20. <u>2</u>17   **21.** <u>3</u>20   **22.** 81<u>0</u>

23. 1,00<u>6</u>   **24.** <u>9</u>99   **25.** 1,4<u>0</u>5

26. Writing to Explain How does using commas to separate periods help you read large numbers?

Topic Essential Questions

• How are greater numbers read and written?

• How can whole numbers be compared and ordered?

• How can sums and differences be estimated?

Lesson
1-1

MA.4.A.6.1 Use and represent numbers through millions in various contexts, including estimation of relative sizes of amounts or distances.

Representing Numbers

What are some ways to write numbers in the thousands?

Jill is 3,241 feet above sea level. There are different ways to represent 3,241.

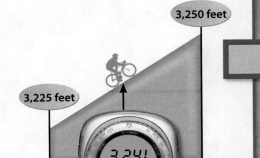

3,250 feet

3,225 feet

3.241 feet

Another Example **How do you read and write numbers in the thousands?**

Another bicycle racer is 5,260 feet above sea level. Write 5,260 in standard form, expanded form, and word form.

When writing a number in <u>standard form,</u> write only the digits: 5,260.

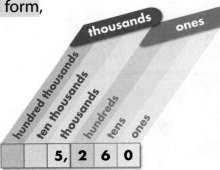

thousands   ones

hundred thousands | ten thousands | thousands | hundreds | tens | ones

| | | 5, | 2 | 6 | 0 |

<u>Each group of 3 digits starting from the right forms a</u> period.

A number in expanded form <u>is written as the sum of the values of the digits:</u> 5,000 + 200 + 60 + 0.

Use periods in the place-value chart to <u>write the number in words or</u> word form: five thousand, two hundred sixty.

Explain It

1. Explain why the value of 5 in 5,264 is 5,000.

2. Is the expanded form for 5,260 the same as for 5,206? Explain.

You can represent numbers using place-value blocks.

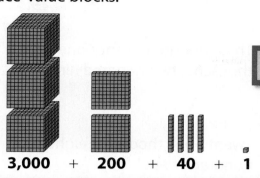

3,000 + **200** + **40** + **1**

You can represent numbers on a number line.

3,241

3,200　　　3,250　　　3,300

Guided Practice*

Do you know HOW?

In **1** through **4**, write the word form, and tell the value of the red digit in each number.

1. 15,324   **2.** 135,467

3. 921,382   **4.** 275,206

In **5** and **6**, write the expanded form.

5. 42,158   **6.** 63,308

Do you UNDERSTAND?

7. If Jill climbed 100 feet more, how many feet above sea level would she be?

8. What is the value of the 2 in 3,261? the 3? the 1?

9. Write one hundred one thousand, eleven in standard form.

Independent Practice

Leveled Practice In **10** through **13**, write each number in standard form.

10.

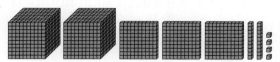

11.

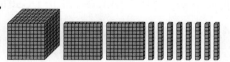

12.

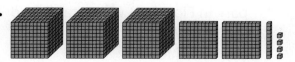

13.

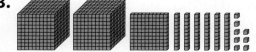

In **14** and **15**, write each number in standard form.

14. Eighty-three thousand, nine hundred two

15. Three hundred twenty-one thousand, two hundred nine

In **16** and **17**, write each number in expanded form.

16. Four hundred ninety-seven thousand, three hundred thirty-two

17. Twenty-one thousand, eight hundred seven

In **18** and **19**, write each number in word form.

18. 300,000 + 8,000 + 20 + 9

19.

20. Reasoning The pedometer below counts the number of steps you walk. It can show 5 digits. What is the greatest number it can show?

21. A town library has 124,763 books and 3,142 DVDs. This year, they bought 1,000 books and 2,000 DVDs. How many books does the library have now?

  A 5,142 books   **C** 125,763 books

  B 23,142 books   **D** 134,763 books

22. Number Sense Which digit is in the same place in all three numbers below? Name the place-value position.

574,632   24,376   204,581

23. Reasoning What is the greatest 4-digit number you can write? What is the least 4-digit number?

Critical Thinking

24. A city counted 403,867 votes in the last election. Write this number in word form.

25. Social Studies Everglades National Park is the largest national park in Florida. It was established in 1947. What is this number in expanded form?

Mixed Problem Solving

The Egyptians created a number system that used symbols, or hieroglyphs. The chart to the right shows the symbols and their equivalent numbers.

1–9	10	100
I	∩	@
strokes	heelmark	coil
1,000	10,000	100,000
lotus plant	bent finger	tadpole

Data

Description	Symbol	Number
Hieroglyphs are drawn with the greater number in front of the lesser number.	∩∩∩I	31
Hieroglyphs can be read from left to right.	@@@∩∩ III II	525
If the symbols are stacked, the greater number is on top.		214,419

1. Write 217 in word form and with hieroglyphs.

2. Use hieroglyphs to draw the greatest 5-digit number.

3. Which number will take less time to write with hieroglyphs, 9 or 100? Explain your answer.

4. Use hieroglyphs to draw the number one greater than 349.

5. It is believed that the Egyptian number system was created around 3000 B.C. Use hieroglyphs to represent this number.

6. Hieroglyphs can also be read from right to left. What number is represented by IIII∩∩⇊ ?

Lesson

1-2

MA.4.A.6.1 Use and represent numbers through millions in various contexts, including estimation of relative sizes of amounts or distances.

Millions

What are some ways to write numbers in the millions?

From 2001 through 2005, 356,039,763 fans attended professional baseball games. Write the expanded form and word form for 356,039,763. Use a place-value chart to help.

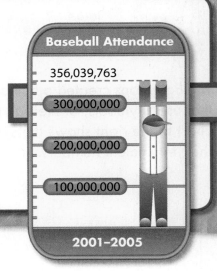

Baseball Attendance

356,039,763

300,000,000

200,000,000

100,000,000

2001-2005

Guided Practice*

Do you know HOW?

In **1** and **2**, write the number in word form. Then, tell the value of the red digit in each number.

1. 75,600,295

2. 249,104,330

In **3** through **6**, write the number in expanded form.

3. 6,173,253

4. 75,001,432

5. 16,107,320

6. 430,290,100

Do you UNDERSTAND?

7. What is the value of the 5 in 356,039,763?

8. What is the value of the 9 in 356,039,763?

9. Between 1996 and 2000, 335,365,504 fans attended games. Which digit is in the millions place in 335,365,504?

Independent Practice

In **10** through **12**, write each number in standard form.

10. 300,000,000 + 40,000,000 + 7,000,000 + 300,000 + 10,000 + 6,000 + 20 + 9

11. 900,000,000 + 20,000,000 + 6,000,000 + 20,000 + 4,000 + 10

12. 80,000,000 + 1,000,000 + 600,000 + 20,000 + 900 + 40 + 8

In **13** through **16**, write the number in word form. Then, tell the value of the red digit in each number.

13. 7,915,878

14. 23,341,552

15. 214,278,216

16. 334,290,652

For another example, see Set A on page 26.

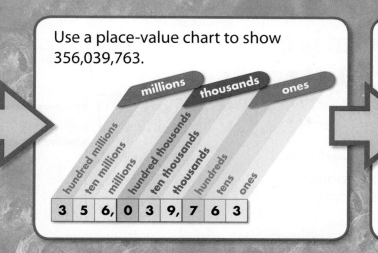

Use a place-value chart to show 356,039,763.

millions thousands ones

hundred millions | ten millions | millions | hundred thousands | ten thousands | thousands | hundreds | tens | ones

3 5 6, 0 3 9, 7 6 3

There is a 3 in the hundred millions place. Its value is 300,000,000.

Expanded Form: 300,000,000 + 50,000,000 + 6,000,000 + 30,000 + 9,000 + 700 + 60 + 3

Word Form: Three hundred fifty-six million, thirty-nine thousand, seven hundred sixty-three

In **17** through **20**, write the number in expanded form. Then, tell the value of the red digit in each number.

17. 7,330,968 **18.** 30,290,447 **19.** 133,958,840 **20.** 309,603,114

Problem Solving

21. Writing to Explain Which number will take less time to write in expanded form, 800,000,000 or 267,423?

22. Write the expanded form of 123,456,789 and 987,654,321. Which digit has the same value in both numbers?

23. In 2005, seventy-four million, nine hundred fifteen thousand, two hundred sixty-eight fans attended baseball games. Which choice shows this number in standard form?

A 74,015,268 **C** 74,905,268

B 74,900,268 **D** 74,915,268

24. Write the standard form of a 9-digit number with a 5 in the millions place and a 9 in the tens place.

a Write a number that is ten million more than the number you chose.

b Write a number that is one million less than the number you chose.

25. Social Studies The vault at Fort Knox holds 147,300,000 ounces of gold. Write the number that is one million more.

Critical THINKING

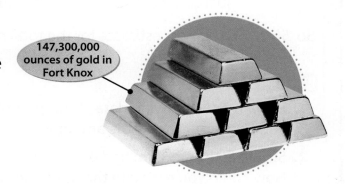

147,300,000 ounces of gold in Fort Knox

MA.4.A.6.1 Use and represent numbers through millions in various contexts, including estimation of relative sizes of amounts or distances.

Estimating Relative Amounts and Distances

How can you estimate an unknown distance?

Mrs. Vale asked her students to estimate the distance around their classroom. Is the distance closer to 50 feet, 100 feet, or 150 feet?

?

?

Another Example How can you estimate an unknown amount?

Dan wanted to estimate the number of seats in a football stadium. Is the total number of seats in this stadium closer to 15,000 seats, 50,000 seats, or 150,000 seats?

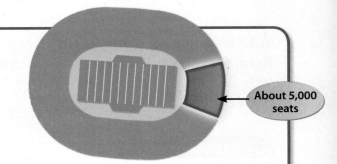

About 5,000 seats

Step 1 Use a known amount to estimate an unknown amount. One section of the stadium has about 5,000 seats.

Step 2 Estimate the number of known amounts in the entire stadium. The stadium has 10 sections about the same size as the region shown above.

Step 3 Use the known amount to estimate the total. Skip count by 5,000 ten times.

5 thousand, 10 thousand, 15 thousand, 20 thousand, 25 thousand, 30 thousand 35 thousand, 40 thousand, 45 thousand, 50 thousand

So, 50,000 is the best estimate for the total number of seats in the stadium.

Explain It

1. Explain how knowing data about part of an unknown amount can help you figure out the whole amount.

2. Suppose the stadium had 6 sections and each section had 4,856 seats. How could you estimate the total number of seats?

Step 1

Use a known distance to estimate an unknown distance.

You know each big step is about 3 feet.

It takes about 10 steps to walk the length of the shorter wall.

$$3 + 3 + 3 + 3 + 3 + 3 + 3 + 3 + 3 + 3 = 30 \text{ feet}$$

It takes about 14 big steps to walk the length of the longer wall.

$$3 + 3 + 3 + 3 + 3 + 3 + 3 + 3 + 3 + 3 + 3 + 3 + 3 + 3 = 42 \text{ feet}$$

Step 2

Use the known distance to estimate the total.

Add the lengths of two shorter walls.

$$30 + 30 = 60$$

Add the lengths of the two longer walls.

$$42 + 42 = 84$$

Add: $60 + 84 = 144$

144 feet is closest to 150 feet.

So, 150 feet is the best estimate of the distance around the classroom.

Guided Practice*

Do you know HOW?

In **1** and **2**, estimate the relative distance.

1. An unsharpened pencil is about 7 inches long. Use an unsharpened pencil to estimate the distance around your desktop. Is the distance closer to 15 inches, 95 inches, or 300 inches?

2. Is the distance around your math book closer to 10 inches, 50 inches, or 100 inches? Estimate to decide.

Do you UNDERSTAND?

3. In the example above, what known distance was used to estimate the unknown total?

4. What known amount might you use to estimate the total number of students in your school?

Independent Practice

In **5** through **7**, use the picture to estimate the unknown amount.

5. How can the known data help you estimate how many beans the jar can hold?

6. Would the jar hold about 1,000, 2,500, or 5,000 beans? Explain.

7. Suppose you fill the jar with marbles. It takes 198 marbles to reach the same level as the beans in the jar to the right. Estimate how many marbles the jar can hold.

There are 481 beans in the jar.

For **8** and **9**, use the map of Florida at the right.

8. **Reasoning** The distance between Orlando and Tampa is about 85 miles. Is the distance between Tampa and Miami closer to 100 miles, 300 miles, or 1,000 miles? Explain.

9. **Estimation** How can you use the map and the known distance between Orlando and Tampa to estimate the distance from Orlando to Lake Okeechobee?

10. **Reasonableness** A city parking garage has six levels. Each level has 312 parking spaces. Over 10,000 vehicles are expected to need parking spaces for an event. Will the parking garage be able to hold over 10,000 vehicles? Explain.

Critical THINKING

11. The Mote Aquarium in Sarasota, Florida, has a 135,000-gallon shark habitat. What is the value of the digit 3?

   A 30   **C** 30,000

   B 3,000   **D** 300,000

For **12** and **13** use the picture of Palm Park at the right.

12. The area in the upper right of the picture shows where trees will be planted. What fraction shows about how much of Palm Park will have trees?

13. **Number Sense** New park benches will be installed about 100 yards apart along the sidewalks. The total length of the sidewalks is 1,000 yards. Which is the best estimate of the number of new benches Palm Park will have?

   F 150   **H** 30

   G 50   **I** 10

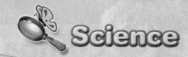

Mixed Problem Solving

The length of one year on a planet is the total time for the planet to make one complete trip around the Sun.

Length of Year	
Planet	**Length of Year** (in Earth days)
Mercury	88
Venus	225
Earth	365
Mars	687
Jupiter	4,330
Saturn	10,756
Uranus	30,687
Neptune	60,190

1. About how many fewer Earth days is a year on Mercury than a year on Earth?

2. About how many more Earth days is a year on Mars than a year on Earth?

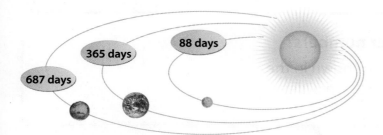

3. Which planet has a digit 6 with a value of sixty thousand in the length of its year?

4. Which planet has a year that is about six thousand Earth days more than Jupiter's?

5. Which space object listed in the table at the right has an average surface temperature closest to Earth's?

Space Object	Average Surface Temperature
Mercury	332°F
Earth	59°F
The Moon	0°F
Venus	867°F

6. Write the average surface temperatures in order from least to greatest.

7. **Strategy Focus** Solve. Use the strategy Make an Organized List.

   Meg's favorite planet has at least 5 letters in its name. The length of its year is less than 10,000 Earth days. List all the planets that fit these clues.

MA.4.A.6.1 Use and represent numbers through millions in various contexts, including estimation of relative sizes of amounts or distances.

Comparing and Ordering Numbers

How do you compare numbers?

Africa and Asia are the two largest continents on Earth. The land area of Africa is 11,608,000 square miles. The land area of Asia is 17,212,000 square miles. Which continent is larger?

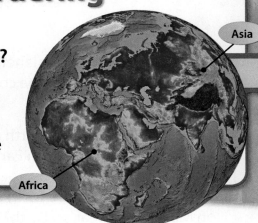

Asia

Africa

Another Example How do you order numbers?

The areas of 3 continents on Earth are shown in the table at the right. Which shows the areas in order from **least** to **greatest**?

A 9,450,000; 4,010,000; 6,890,000

B 4,010,000; 9,450,000; 6,890,000

C 6,890,000; 9,450,000; 4,010,000

D 4,010,000; 6,890,000; 9,450,000

Continent	Areas (in square miles)
Europe	4,010,000
North America	9,450,000
South America	6,890,000

Data

Step 1 Plot the numbers on a number line.

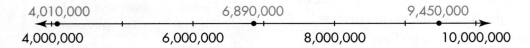

Step 2 Order the numbers. On a number line, numbers to the right are greater.

Reading from left to right: 4,010,000; 6,890,000; 9,450,000

The correct choice is **D**.

Explain It

1. Describe how you would order the continents' areas using place value.

2. **Reasonableness** How can you rule out choices A and C as the correct answer?

Use place value to compare numbers.

Write the numbers, lining up places. Begin at the left and compare.

11,608,000
17,212,000

The ten millions digit is the same in both numbers.

The first place where the digits are different is the millions place. Compare.

11,608,000
17,212,000

1 million < 7 millions, so 11,608,000 < 17,212,000.

The symbol > means is greater than, and the symbol < means is less than.

The land area of Asia is greater than the land area of Africa.

Guided Practice*

Do you know HOW?

In **1** through **4**, copy and complete by writing > or < for each ◯.

1. 12,643 ◯ 12,801

2. 6,519 ◯ 6,582

3. 111,785 ◯ 111,731

4. 6,703 ◯ 6,699

In **5** and **6**, order the numbers from least to greatest.

5. 3,107,502   2,906,793   2,906,723

6. 80,371   15,048   80,137

Do you UNDERSTAND?

7. Writing to Explain Why would you look at the hundreds place to order these numbers?

105,232,463

105,232,482

105,232,947

8. Compare the area of Europe and of South America. Which is greater?

Independent Practice

In **9** through **16**, copy and complete by writing > or < for each ◯.

9. 221,495 ◯ 210,388

10. 52,744 ◯ 56,704

11. 138,752 ◯ 133,122

12. 4,937 ◯ 4,939

13. 22,873 ◯ 22,774

14. 1,912,706 ◯ 1,913,898

15. 412,632 ◯ 412,362

16. 999,999,999 ◯ 9,990,999

In **17** through **20**, copy and complete the number lines.
Then use the number lines to order the numbers from greatest to least.

17. 27,505   26,905   26,950

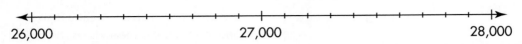

26,000   27,000   28,000

18. 3,422,100   3,422,700   3,422,000

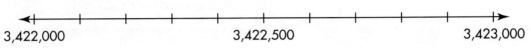

3,422,000   3,422,500   3,423,000

19. 7,502   7,622   7,523   7,852

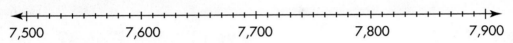

7,500   7,600   7,700   7,800   7,900

20. 3,030 3,033 3,003

3,000   3,050

In **21** through **28**, write the numbers in order from least to greatest.

21. 57,535 576,945 506,495

22. 18,764 18,761 13,490

23. 25,988 25,978 25,998

24. 87,837 37,838 878,393

25. 43,783 434,282 64,382

26. 723,433 72,324 72,432

27. 58,028 85,843 77,893

28. 274,849,551 283,940,039 23,485,903

Problem Solving

29. Estimation Aaron added 57 and 20 and said the answer is greater than 100. Is Aaron correct?

30. Number Sense Write three **Critical THINKING** numbers that are greater than 780,000 but less than 781,000.

31. Reasoning Could you use only the millions period to order 462,409,524, 463,409,524, and 463,562,391?

32. Describe how to order 7,463, 74,633, and 74,366 from least to greatest.

33. **Science** In 2003, the heaviest snake living in captivity was a Burmese python named Baby. An average Anaconda snake weighs 330 pounds. Which snake weighs more?

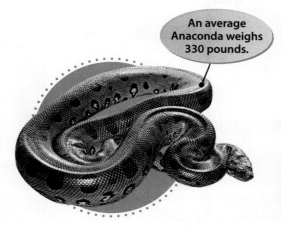

An average Anaconda weighs 330 pounds.

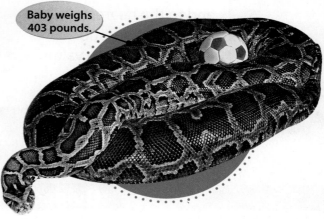

Baby weighs 403 pounds.

34. Which list of numbers is in order from least to greatest?

A	1,534	1,576	1,563
B	18,732	18,723	18,765
C	234,564	234,568	234,323
D	383,847	383,848	383,849

35. **Social Studies** How much greater is the land area of China than Japan?

Country	Land Area (square kilometers)
Japan	377,835
China	9,600,000

36. The chart below shows the number of game cards owned by the top collectors in one school. Which student had the most cards?

F	Shani	H	Ariel
G	Lin	I	Jorge

Collector	Number of cards
Shani	3,424
Ariel	3,443
Lin	2,354
Jorge	2,932

37. **Social Studies** The Atlantic Ocean has an area of 33,420,000 square miles. This area is between which numbers?

A   33,400,000 and 33,440,000

B   33,000,000 and 33,040,000

C   33,100,000 and 33,419,000

D   33,430,000 and 33,500,000

MA.4.A.6.1 Use and represent numbers through millions in various contexts, including estimation of relative sizes of amounts or distances.

Rounding Numbers

How can you round numbers?

Round 293,655,404 to the nearest thousand and to the nearest hundred thousand. You can use place value to round numbers.

304,691,952

293,655,404

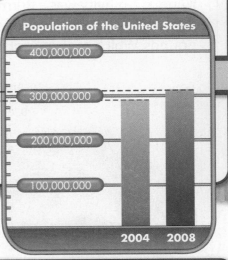

Population of the United States

400,000,000
300,000,000
200,000,000
100,000,000

2004   2008

Guided Practice*

Do you know HOW?

In **1** through **6**, round each number to the place of the underlined digit.

1. 128,955

2. 85,639

3. 9,924

4. 1,194,542

5. 160,656

6. 149,590

Do you UNDERSTAND?

7. Writing to Explain Explain how to round a number when 7 is the digit to the right of the rounding place.

8. In 2008, the population of the United States was 304,691,952. Round 304,691,952 to the nearest hundred thousand.

Independent Practice

Leveled Practice In **9** through **28**, round each number to the place of the underlined digit.

9. 493,295

    ▓▓▓,000

10. 39,230

    ▓▓,000

11. 77,292

    ▓▓,▓▓0

12. 54,846

    ▓0,000

13. 4,028

14. 6,668,365

15. 453,280

16. 17,909

17. 1,406

18. 55,560

19. 21,679

20. 3,417,547

21. 117,821

22. 75,254

23. 9,049

24. 1,666,821

25. 2,420

26. 9,000,985

27. 9,511

28. 73,065

For another example, see Set D on page 27.

Round 293,655,404 to the nearest thousand.

thousands place

293,65̲5,404

If the digit to the right of the rounding place is 5 or more, add 1 to the rounding digit. If it is less than 5, leave the rounding digit alone.

293,65̲5,000

Since 4 < 5, leave the rounding digit as is. Change the digits to the right of the rounding place to zeros.

So, 293,655,404 rounds to 293,655,000.

Round 293,655,404 to the nearest hundred thousand.

hundred thousands place

293,6̲55,404

The digit to the right of the rounding place is 5.

293,7̲00,000

Since the digit is 5, round by adding 1 to the digit in the hundred thousands place.

So, 293,655,404 rounds to 293,700,000.

Problem Solving

For **29** and **30**, use the table at the right.

29. For each zoo in the chart, round the attendance to the nearest hundred thousand.

30. Reasoning Which zoo had the greatest number of visitors?

Zoo Attendance

Data		
Nashville Zoo	:	546,429
Philadelphia Zoo	:	1,244,000
Oregon Zoo	:	1,503,565
Brevard Zoo	:	328,973

31. Number Sense Write four numbers that round to 700 when rounded to the nearest hundred.

32. Reasoning Write a number that, when rounded to the nearest thousand and hundred, will have a result that is the same.

Critical THINKING

33. Jonas read that about 1,760,000 people will graduate from high school in the next four years. Jonas thinks this number is rounded to the nearest ten thousand. What would the number be if it were rounded to the nearest hundred thousand?

34. Liz had attended class every day since she started school as a kindergartner. She said she had been in school for about 1,000 days. What could the actual number of school days be if she rounded to the nearest ten?

THINK SOLVE EXPLAIN

35. When rounded to the nearest ten thousand, which number would be rounded to 120,000?

    A 123,900   **C** 128,770

    B 126,480   **D** 130,000

36. A fruit market sold 3,849 apples, 3,498 oranges, and 3,894 pears in one day. Which of these numbers is the greatest?

MA.4.A.6.1 Use and represent numbers through millions in various contexts, including estimation of relative sizes of amounts or distances.

Estimating Sums and Differences

How can you estimate sums and differences?

The Empire State Building was completed in 1931. From ground to tip, it measures 1,250 feet. At the top of the building is an antenna and lightning rod that measures 204 feet. Estimate the total height of the structure.

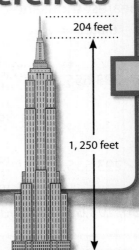

204 feet

1, 250 feet

Guided Practice*

Do you know HOW?

In **1** through **6**, estimate each sum or difference.

1.
$$
\begin{array}{r}
563 \rightarrow \blacksquare00 \\
+\ 375 \rightarrow \underline{\blacksquare00} \\
\end{array}
$$

2.
$$
\begin{array}{r}
288 \rightarrow \blacksquare\blacksquare0 \\
-\ 171 \rightarrow \underline{\blacksquare\blacksquare0} \\
\end{array}
$$

3. 645 + 253

4. 262 − 132

5. 952 − 402

6. 398 + 121

Do you UNDERSTAND?

7. **Writing to Explain** In the first example above, why can't you round both numbers to the nearest thousand?

8. The Statue of Liberty was completed in 1886. About how many years later was the Empire State Building completed than the Statue of Liberty?

Independent Practice

In **9** through **16**, estimate by rounding to the nearest ten.

9.
$$
\begin{array}{r}
542 \\
+\ 27 \\
\end{array}
$$

10.
$$
\begin{array}{r}
281 \\
-\ 172 \\
\end{array}
$$

11.
$$
\begin{array}{r}
5,001 \\
-\ 1,999 \\
\end{array}
$$

12.
$$
\begin{array}{r}
6,324 \\
+\ 77 \\
\end{array}
$$

13. 738 + 741

14. 895 − 305

15. 755 − 344

16. 586 + 278

In **17** through **24**, estimate by rounding to the nearest hundred.

17.
$$
\begin{array}{r}
368 \\
+\ 137 \\
\end{array}
$$

18.
$$
\begin{array}{r}
918 \\
+\ 391 \\
\end{array}
$$

19.
$$
\begin{array}{r}
5,317 \\
+\ 1,734 \\
\end{array}
$$

20.
$$
\begin{array}{r}
778 \\
+\ 95 \\
\end{array}
$$

21. 423 + 196

22. 891 + 223

23. 1,724 − 731

24. 551 − 249

*For another example, see Set E on page 27.

Round each number to the nearest hundred.

$$1{,}250 \longrightarrow 1{,}300$$
$$+\ \ 204 \longrightarrow +\ \ 200$$
$$\overline{ \quad 1{,}500}$$

The total height is about 1,500 feet.

The answer is reasonable because the total height is greater than the height of the Empire State Building.

The Washington Monument was completed in 1884. About how many years after was the Empire State Building completed?

$$1{,}931 \longrightarrow 1{,}930$$
$$-\ 1{,}884 \longrightarrow -\ 1{,}880$$
$$\overline{\phantom{-\ 1{,}884} \quad 50}$$

Round each number to the nearest ten. Show rounding to subtract.

The Empire State Building was completed about 50 years later.

Problem Solving

25. Kala bought a board game for $24, a key ring for $3, and a book for $8. How much money did she spend?

26. Theo was born in the year 2004. One of his older sisters was born in 1992. Rounding to the nearest ten, about how many years younger is Theo?

Critical THINKING

27. This year, 35,658 people ran in a marathon. Last year, 8,683 fewer people ran. About how many people ran last year?

28. During swimming practice, Juan swam 15 laps and Ted swam 9 laps. How many more laps did Juan swim than Ted?

29. The table to the right shows the number of students per grade.

  a About how many students are in Grades 3, 4 and 5?

  b About how many students are in Grades 4 and 6?

Data

Grade	Number of Students
3	145
4	152
5	148
6	149

30. Alex sold 86 tickets to a school talent show on Thursday and 103 tickets on Friday. About how many tickets to the talent show did Alex sell in all?

  A About 100

  B About 200

  C About 300

  D About 400

31. Sandy read 235 pages of a book. She had 192 more pages to read before she was done. How many pages were there in the book?

?	
235	192

MA.4.A.6.1 Use and represent numbers through millions in various contexts, including estimation of relative sizes of amounts or distances.

Draw a Picture and Write an Equation

The mass of a human brain is how much greater than the mass of a chimpanzee brain?

Average Masses of Brains	
House cat	30 grams
Chimpanzee	420 grams
Human	1,350 grams
Dolphin	1,500 grams

The human brain has a mass of 1,350 grams.

Guided Practice*

Do you know HOW?

Solve. Draw a picture to help you.

1. In one week, Sandy earned $36 from her babysitting job. She got $15 more for doing her chores. How much money did Sandy earn?

? money earned in all

$36	$15

Do you UNDERSTAND?

2. How can you show that 930 grams is a reasonable answer for the question asked above?

3. **Write a Problem** Write a problem using the table at the top.

Independent Practice

Solve. Draw a picture to help you.

4. The American Kennel Club® lists 17 breeds of herding dogs and 26 breeds of terriers. Find the total number of breeds of herding dogs and terriers.

5. Using the information in Problem 4, write an equation to find how many more breeds of terriers than herding dogs there are.

Stuck? Try this....

- What do I know?
- What diagram can I use to help understand the problem?
- Can I use addition, subtraction, multiplication, or division?
- Is all of my work correct?
- Did I answer the right question?
- Is my answer reasonable?

*For another example, see Set F on page 27.

What do I know? The average mass of a chimpanzee brain is 420 grams. The average mass of a human brain is 1,350 grams.

What am I asked to find? The difference between the masses

Draw a picture.

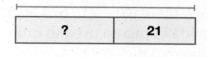

1,350 grams

420	?

Write an equation. Use subtraction to solve.

$1{,}350 - 420 = \boxed{}$

The human brain has a mass that is 930 grams more than the chimpanzee brain.

---

6. Four cities are on the same road that runs east to west. Fleming is west of Bridgewater, but east of Clinton. Union is between Fleming and Bridgewater. It is 21 miles from Fleming to Union. It is 55 miles from Clinton to Union. How far is it from Clinton to Fleming?

Critical THINKING

55 miles

?	21

For **7** through **9**, use the table to the right.

7. There are about 200 more species of animals in the Minnesota Zoo than in the Phoenix Zoo. About how many species of animals are in the Minnesota Zoo?

8. About how many more species are in the Indianapolis Zoo than the Phoenix Zoo?

9. How can you find the number of species of animals at the Miami Metro Zoo?

THINK SOLVE EXPLAIN

Name of Zoo	**Approximate Number of Species**
Phoenix	200
Minnesota	
Miami Metro	▢
Indianapolis	360
Total Species	2,260

Data

10. A parking lot had a total of 243 cars in one day. By 6:00 A.M., there were 67 cars in the lot. In the next hour, 13 more cars joined these. How many more cars would be parked in the lot by the end of the day?

243 cars in all

67	13	?

11. A shoe store sold 162 pairs of shoes. The goal was to sell 345 pairs. How many pairs of shoes did they NOT sell?

345 pairs of shoes

162	?

1 Which of the following is another way to write the number 10,220? (1–1)

A. one thousand, two hundred twenty

B. ten thousand, twenty-two

C. ten thousand, two hundred two

D. ten thousand, two hundred twenty

2 In 2002, there were 719,674 acres of Florida farmland used to grow oranges. What is 719,674 rounded to the nearest ten thousand? (1–5)

F. 720,000

G. 719,000

H. 710,000

I. 700,000

3 The table shows the land areas of four states. Which state has the least land area? (1–4)

A. Montana

B. Oklahoma

C. Oregon

D. Wyoming

State	Land Area (square miles)
Montana	147,042
Oklahoma	68,898
Oregon	98,381
Wyoming	97,814

Data

4 Florida has about sixteen million, three hundred thousand acres of forested land. Which is another way to write this number? (1-2)

F. 16,300

G. 16,000,300

H. 16,300,000

I. 163,000,000

5 There were 16,807,534 passengers that flew out of the Orlando Airport in 2006. Which number is less than 16,807,534? (1–4)

A. 16,907,534

B. 16,807,645

C. 16,807,543

D. 16,807,529

6 Which number best represents point *P* on the number line? (1–1)

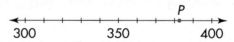

F. 378

G. 382

H. 388

I. 392

7 In the number 951,427,308, which digit is in the ten millions place? (1–2)

A. 5

B. 4

C. 2

D. 0

8 A total solar eclipse took place in 1777 over what is now Florida. The next total solar eclipse over Florida will occur in 2045. Which number sentence shows the best way to estimate the number of years between the two eclipses? (1–6)

F. $2000 - 1800 = 200$

G. $2100 - 1800 = 300$

H. $2045 - 1777 = 268$

I. $2050 - 2000 = 50$

9 Dara's book has 323 pages. She has read 141 pages. Which diagram models how to find the number of pages she has left to read? (1–7)

A.
?	
323	141

B.
323
141	?

C.
141
323	?

D.
323
141	141	?

10 The U.S. Constitution has 4,543 words, including the signatures. What is 4,543 rounded to the nearest hundred? (1–5)

F. 4,000

G. 4,500

H. 4,540

I. 4,600

11 Manuel has 60 minutes to get to karate class. It takes him 27 minutes to ride his bike to class and 10 minutes to change into his karate uniform. How much time does he have before he must leave his house? (1–7)

60 minutes
27	10	?

A. 20

B. 21

C. 23

D. 97

12 The table shows the number of tickets sold to a play.

Data

Tickets Sold	
Thursday	320
Friday	282
Saturday	375

Estimate the total number of tickets sold. (1–6)

13 There are 52 marbles in the jar so far. Estimate how many marbles it would take to fill the entire jar. Explain your thinking. (1–3)

THINK
SOLVE
EXPLAIN

Set A, pages 4–6, 8–9

Use a place-value chart to write the expanded form and word form of 26,500,070.

Expanded form:
20,000,000 + 6,000,000 + 500,000 + 70

Word form: twenty-six million, five hundred thousand, seventy

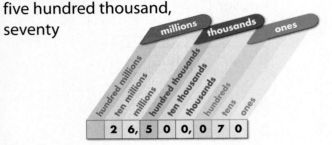

Remember that periods can help you read large numbers.

Use place-value charts to write each number in expanded form and word form.

1. 7,549   **2.** 27,961

3. 321,209   **4.** 80,452

5. 6,792,365   **6.** 15,164,612

Set B, pages 10–12

Estimate the distance around a calculator. Is it closer to 15 inches, 25 inches, or 50 inches?

Use a known distance to help you estimate unknown distances.

A paper clip is about 1 inch long.

The distance around the calculator is about 12 paper clips.

12 is closest to 15.

So, 15 inches is the best estimate.

Remember to use a known amount or distance to make a good estimate.

Solve.

1. Estimate the distance from your classroom door to the principal's office door. Use strides, floor tiles, or other known distances.

2. Estimate the distance around a novel. Is it closer to 2 inches, 20 inches, or 80 inches?

Set C, pages 14–17

45,423 ◯ 44,897

Use place value to compare. Start comparing from the left. Look for the first digit that is different.

45,423   44,897

      5 > 4

So, 45,423 > 44,897.

Remember that a number line can be used to compare numbers.

Write > or < for each ◯.

1. 11,961 ◯ 12,961

2. 735,291,000 ◯ 735,291,001

Order the numbers from greatest to least.

3. 22,981   14,762   21,046

Set D, pages 18–19

Round 346,764,802 to the nearest hundred thousand.

hundred thousands place

↓

346,<u>7</u>64,802   The digit to the right of the rounding place is 6.

346,<u>8</u>00,000   Since 6 > 5, round by adding 1 to the digit in the hundred thousands place.

So, 346,764,802 rounds to 346,800,000.

Remember to look at the number to the right of the rounding place. Then change the digits to the right of the rounding place to zeros.

Round each number to the place of the underlined digit.

1. 166,<u>7</u>42   **2.** 7<u>6</u>,532

3. <u>5</u>,861   **4.** 2,43<u>2</u>,741

5. <u>1</u>32,505   **6.** <u>2</u>57,931

Set E, pages 20–21

Estimate   1,579
          + 1,248

Round each number to the nearest hundred.

1,579 rounds to 1,600.

1,248 rounds to 1,200.

Add   1,600
       + 1,200
        2,800

Remember you can round numbers to the nearest hundred or thousand when estimating sums and differences.

Estimate each sum or difference.

1. 473 + 465   **2.** 8,352 − 3,421

3. 586 − 483   **4.** 4,094 + 246

5. 1,440 − 933   **6.** 748 − 392

7. 981 + 193   **8.** 725 + 635

Set F, pages 22–23

Cathy spent $8 on lunch. She bought a sandwich, a fruit cup, and a milk at the snack bar. She spent a total of $6 on the sandwich and milk. How much did the fruit cup cost?

What do I know?   Cathy had $8. Cathy bought a sandwich, a milk, and a fruit cup. Cathy spent $6 on the sandwich and the milk.

What am I being asked to find?   The amount of money Cathy spent on the fruit cup

$8	
$6	?

$8 − $6 = $2

Cathy spent $2 on the fruit cup.

Remember to draw a picture to help you solve a problem.

Draw a picture and write an equation to solve.

1. Luz had collected a total of 393 tokens from the games at Funland. To win a large stuffed animal, 500 tokens were needed. How many more tokens does Luz need to win the large stuffed animal?

Recalling Multiplication Facts

1 Do you think all starfish have five arms? You will find out in Lesson 2-1.

2 The manatee is Florida's state marine mammal. What is the length of a baby manatee? You will find out in Lesson 2-3.

3

Mark Twain is a famous author. Do you know what his name means? You will find out in Lesson 2-4.

4

Temari balls are special decorations that represent long-lasting friendships and loyalty. Where did this art form originate? You will find out in Lesson 2-5.

Topic Essential Questions

- How can patterns and properties be used to find some multiplication facts?
- How can unknown multiplication facts be found by breaking them apart into known facts?

Review What You Know!

Vocabulary

Choose the best term from the box.

- breaking apart
- factor
- product
- multiples

1. In the number sentence $8 \times 3 = 24$, 8 is a __?__ .

2. In the number sentence $2 \times 6 = 12$, 12 is a __?__ .

3. $191 + 67 = (191 + 9) + 58$ is an example of using the __?__ strategy.

Skip Counting

Find the term that comes next in the list.

4. 10, 12, 14, 16, ▢

5. 5, 10, 15, 20, 25, ▢

6. 3, 6, 9, 12, ▢

7. 12, 16, 20, 24, ▢

8. 6, 12, 18, 24, ▢

9. 8, 16, 24, 32, ▢

10. 7, 14, 21, 28, ▢

11. 9, 18, 27, 36, ▢

Multiplication

Copy each array and circle equal groups of 3.

12.

13.

14. Writing to Explain Henry is thinking of a whole number. He multiplies the number by 5, but the result is less than 5. What number is Henry thinking about? Explain.

Lesson
2-1

MA.4.A.1.1 Use and describe various models for multiplication in problem-solving situations, and demonstrate recall of basic multiplication and related division facts with ease.

Patterns for Facts

What are the patterns for multiples of 2, 5, and 9?

A <mark>multiple</mark> is the product of any two whole numbers.

○ multiples of 2

□ multiples of 5

△ multiples of 9

1	②	3	④	⑤	⑥	7	⑧	△9	⑩
11	⑫	13	⑭	15	⑯	17	⑱	19	⑳
21	㉒	23	㉔	25	㉖	△27	㉘	29	㉚
31	㉜	33	㉞	35	㊱	37	㊳	39	�40

Guided Practice*

Do you know HOW?

In **1** and **2**, skip count to find the number that comes next.

1. 20, 25, 30, ▨   **2.** 36, 45, 54, ▨

In **3** through **6**, find the product.

3. 9×1 **4.** 2×8

5. $\begin{array}{r} 5 \\ \times\ 4 \\ \hline \end{array}$ **6.** $\begin{array}{r} 4 \\ \times\ 2 \\ \hline \end{array}$

Do you UNDERSTAND?

7. In the chart above, what pattern do you see for the numbers that have both red circles and green squares?

8. How do you know that 13 is not a multiple of 2? Explain using the pattern for multiples of 2.

9. Felix is sorting socks. He has 9 pairs of socks. How many socks does he have in all?

Independent Practice

In **10** through **24**, find each product.

10. 2×6 **11.** 5×3 **12.** 5×2 **13.** 5×8 **14.** 9×7

15. $\begin{array}{r} 2 \\ \times\ 7 \\ \hline \end{array}$ **16.** $\begin{array}{r} 5 \\ \times\ 7 \\ \hline \end{array}$ **17.** $\begin{array}{r} 9 \\ \times\ 3 \\ \hline \end{array}$ **18.** $\begin{array}{r} 9 \\ \times\ 6 \\ \hline \end{array}$ **19.** $\begin{array}{r} 2 \\ \times\ 4 \\ \hline \end{array}$

20. $\begin{array}{r} 2 \\ \times\ 3 \\ \hline \end{array}$ **21.** $\begin{array}{r} 5 \\ \times\ 9 \\ \hline \end{array}$ **22.** $\begin{array}{r} 5 \\ \times\ 6 \\ \hline \end{array}$ **23.** $\begin{array}{r} 2 \\ \times\ 1 \\ \hline \end{array}$ **24.** $\begin{array}{r} 5 \\ \times\ 5 \\ \hline \end{array}$

DIGITAL Animated Glossary
www.pearsonsuccessnet.com

For another example, see Set A on page 44.

To find multiples of 2, skip count by 2s.

(2),(4),(6),(8),
(10),(12),(14),(16)...

All multiples of 2 are even numbers.

To find multiples of 5, skip count by 5s.

| 5 | 10 | 15 | 20 |,
| 25 | 30 | 35 | 40 | ...

All multiples of 5 have a 0 or 5 in the ones place.

To find multiples of 9, skip count by 9s.

9, 18, 27, 36,
45, 54, 63, 72 ...

The digits of multiples of 9 add to 9 or a multiple of 9.

For 99, for example, 9 + 9 = 18, and 18 is a multiple of 9.

Problem Solving

25. 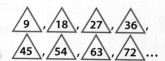 **Science** While most species of starfish have 5 arms, some species can have up to 40 arms. How many arms do 9 starfish have

    a if each starfish has 6 arms?

    b if each starfish has 7 arms?

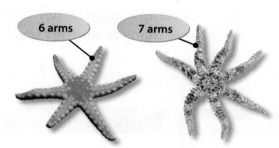

6 arms   7 arms

26. In wheelchair basketball, players use sports chairs that have 2 large wheels and 3 small wheels. If there are 5 players, how many

    a large wheels do the sports chairs have?

    b small wheels do the sports chairs have?

    c wheels do the sports chairs have in all?

27. Jody is working on her model train. She adds 9 pieces of track. Each piece of track is attached with 4 screws. How many screws does she need in all?

    A 18 screws   **C** 54 screws

    B 36 screws   **D** 72 screws

28. Geometry Each pentagon shown below has 5 sides. How many sides are there in all? Skip count by 5s to find the answer. Then, write the multiplication sentence.

29. Which is equal to 9 dollars and 9 nickels?

    F $9.09   **H** $9.45

    G $9.36   **I** $9.54

30. Number Sense Write a 3-digit *Critical THINKING* number that when rounded to the nearest ten or the nearest hundred, the answer is the same.

Lesson 2-2

MA.4.A.1.1 Use and describe various models for multiplication in problem-solving situations, and demonstrate recall of basic multiplication and related division facts with ease.

Multiplication Properties

How can properties help you multiply?

Multiplication properties can help you remember basic facts.

Commutative Property of Multiplication
Two numbers can be multiplied in any order and the product will be the same.

3 groups of 2 (6 in all)

2 groups of 3 (6 in all)

$3 \times 2 = 2 \times 3$

Guided Practice*

Do you know HOW?

In **1** through **4**, find the product.

1. 0×5

2. 1×6

3.
$$\begin{array}{r} 1 \\ \times\ 0 \\ \hline \end{array}$$

4.
$$\begin{array}{r} 1 \\ \times\ 9 \\ \hline \end{array}$$

In **5** and **6**, copy and complete.

5. $4 \times 7 = 7 \times \blacksquare$

6. $6 \times 3 = \blacksquare \times 6$

Do you UNDERSTAND?

7. When you multiply any number by one, what is the product?

8. In a soccer tournament, Matt's team scored zero goals in each game. They played a total of 6 games. Write a multiplication sentence to show how many goals they scored in all.

Independent Practice

In **9** through **18**, find the product.

9. 1×5

10. 7×0

11. 3×9

12. 0×8

13. 0×3

14.
$$\begin{array}{r} 4 \\ \times\ 0 \\ \hline \end{array}$$

15.
$$\begin{array}{r} 9 \\ \times\ 4 \\ \hline \end{array}$$

16.
$$\begin{array}{r} 2 \\ \times\ 7 \\ \hline \end{array}$$

17.
$$\begin{array}{r} 5 \\ \times\ 6 \\ \hline \end{array}$$

18.
$$\begin{array}{r} 1 \\ \times\ 1 \\ \hline \end{array}$$

In **19** through **22**, find the missing number.

19. $4 \times 5 = \blacksquare \times 4$

20. $7 \times 1 = 1 \times \blacksquare$

21. $0 \times 6 = \blacksquare \times 0$

22. $9 \times 8 = \blacksquare \times 9$

Animated Glossary
www.pearsonsuccessnet.com

Zero Property of Multiplication	Identity Property of Multiplication
Zero Property of Multiplication <u>The product of any number and zero is zero.</u>	**Identity Property of Multiplication** <u>The product of any number and one is that number.</u>

2 groups of 0

$2 \times 0 = 0$

1 group of 7

$1 \times 7 = 7$

Problem Solving

For **23** and **24**, use the table at the right.

23. Annie has 6 packages of tennis balls. How many packages of golf balls would Annie need so that she has an equal number of golf balls and tennis balls?

24. If Annie and her three friends each bought 1 package of baseballs, how many baseballs do they have in all?

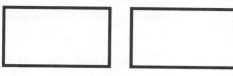

Type of Ball	Number in each Package
Baseball	1
Tennis Balls	3
Golf Balls	6

25. Writing to Explain How do you know that $9 \times 8 = 8 \times 9$ without finding the products?

26. Reasoning Andy scored 4 goals in each of 3 soccer games. His friend Bob scored 3 goals in each of 4 soccer games. Who scored more goals, Andy or Bob? Explain.

Critical THINKING

27. Mrs. Grayson has 27 students in her class. She wants to rearrange the desks in equal groups. If the desks are in 9 groups of 3 desks now, what is another way that she could arrange the desks?

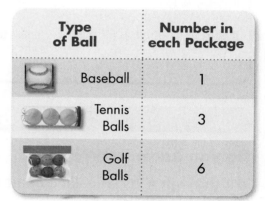

Tip *Use a multiplication property.*

  A   3 groups of 9 desks   **C**   5 groups of 6 desks

  B   2 groups of 13 desks   **D**   4 groups of 7 desks

MA.4.A.1.1 Use and describe various models for multiplication in problem-solving situations, and demonstrate recall of basic multiplication and related division facts with ease.

Using Known Facts: 3 and 4 as Factors
How can you break apart facts?

Darnel is replacing the wheels on 8 skateboards. How many wheels does he need in all?

Use the Distributive Property to break apart facts into simpler problems.

Each skateboard has 4 wheels.

Other Examples

Find 3×6.

$3 \times 6 = (2 \times 6) + (1 \times 6)$ Break the first factor, 3, into 2 + 1.

$12 + 6 = 18$

Guided Practice*

Do you know HOW?

In **1** through **4**, use breaking apart to find each product.

1. $3 \times 4 = (1 \times 4) + (\;\;\; \times 4) = \;\;\;$

2. $4 \times 7 = (2 \times 7) + (\;\;\; \times 7) = \;\;\;$

3.   3
    $\times\, 3$

4.   4
    $\times\, 6$

Do you UNDERSTAND?

5. In Exercise 4, find 4×6 by breaking apart the 6.

6. On Friday, Darnel received a box of skateboard wheels from the factory. The box contained 9 sets of 4 wheels. How many wheels were there in all?

Independent Practice

Leveled Practice In **7** through **18**, use breaking apart to find each product.

7. $9 \times 4 = (5 \times 4) + (\;\;\; \times 4) = \;\;\;$

8. $8 \times 3 = (4 \times 3) + (4 \times \;\;\;) = \;\;\;$

9.   2
   $\times\, 3$

10.   0
   $\times\, 4$

11.   4
   $\times\, 4$

12.   8
   $\times\, 4$

13.   5
   $\times\, 4$

14. 3×5

15. 3×6

16. 4×7

17. 4×9

18. 3×7

Animated Glossary
www.pearsonsuccessnet.com

DIGITAL

*For another example, see Set C on page 44.

One Way

Find 8 × 4. Break apart 4 into 2 + 2.

(8 × 2) + (8 × 2)
16 + 16 = 32
So, 8 × 4 = 32.

Darnel needs 32 wheels in all.

Another Way

Find 8 × 4. Break apart 8 into 3 + 5.

3 × 4 = 12

5 × 4 = 20

12 + 20 = 32
So, 8 × 4 = 32.

Darnel needs 32 wheels in all.

Problem Solving

19.  **Science** The manatee is an endangered sea mammal. A mother manatee, pictured to the right, is three times as long as her baby. How long is the baby manatee?

 *3 × ? = 12*

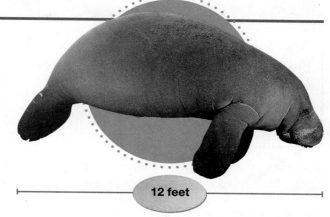

12 feet

20. Jacob, Hannah, and their mom went to the movies. Each ticket cost $7. They also each spent $2 on snacks. How much money did they spend at the movies?

21. THINK SOLVE EXPLAIN Vicki scored 6 two-point baskets and 6 one-point free throws. Li scored 6 three-point baskets. Explain how you know each girl scored the same total.

22. 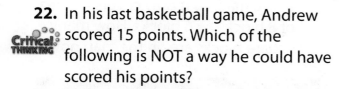 In his last basketball game, Andrew scored 15 points. Which of the following is NOT a way he could have scored his points?

A 5 three-point shots

B 3 three-point shots in the first half and 2 three-point shots in the second half

C 3 two-point shots and 2 one-point free throws

D 5 two-point shots and 5 one-point free throws

23. **Science** A botanist is growing a four-petal pawpaw shrub. He counted 9 flowers on the shrub. Which uses breaking apart to find the total number of petals on the pawpaw?

F (5 × 4) + (4 × 4)

G (9 × 4) + (9 × 4)

H (5 + 4) × (4 + 4)

I (9 + 4) × (9 + 4)

MA.4.A.1.1 Use and describe various models for multiplication in problem-solving situations, and demonstrate recall of basic multiplication and related division facts with ease.

Using Known Facts: 6, 7, and 8 as Factors

Are there different ways to break apart a fact?

Mrs. White's class drew a map of their town. The map is 6 blocks by 6 blocks. How many square blocks are on the map?

Other Examples

Find 7×8.
Break the first factor, 7, into $5 + 2$.

$7 \times 8 = (5 \times 8) + (2 \times 8)$

$40 + 16 = 56$

Find 8×8.
Break the first factor, 8, into $5 + 3$.

$8 \times 8 = (5 \times 8) + (3 \times 8)$

$40 + 24 = 64$

Guided Practice*

Do you know HOW?

In **1** through **4**, use breaking apart to find each product.

1. $6 \times 8 = (6 \times 4) + (6 \times \boxed{}) = \boxed{}$

2. $7 \times 3 = (7 \times 1) + (\boxed{} \times 2) = \boxed{}$

3. 7×9 **4.** 8×8

Do you UNDERSTAND?

5. Writing to Explain In the example at the top, how can $3 \times 6 = 18$ help you find 6×6?

6. Two streets are added to one side of the map, so it now covers an area of 8 blocks by 6 blocks. How many square blocks are on the map now?

Independent Practice

Leveled Practice In **7** through **22**, use breaking apart to find each product.

7. $8 \times 6 = (8 \times 1) + (8 \times \boxed{}) = \boxed{}$

8. $5 \times 7 = (5 \times \boxed{}) + (5 \times 1) = \boxed{}$

9. $7 \times 6 = (7 \times \boxed{}) + (7 \times 4) = \boxed{}$

10. $4 \times 8 = (4 \times 5) + (4 \times \boxed{}) = \boxed{}$

11. $6 \times 9 = (6 \times 5) + (6 \times \boxed{}) = \boxed{}$

12. $7 \times 8 = (\boxed{} \times 4) + (7 \times 4) = \boxed{}$

*For another example, see Set D on page 45.

What You Show

Find 6 × 6.

You can break apart the first factor or the second factor.

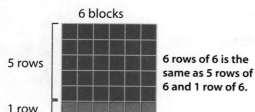

6 blocks

5 rows

1 row

6 rows of 6 is the same as 5 rows of 6 and 1 row of 6.

What You Write

Break apart 6 into 5 + 1.

$6 \times 6 = (5 \times 6) + (1 \times 6)$

$30 + 6 = 36$

So, 6 × 6 = 36.

There are 36 square blocks on the map.

---

13. 6 × 6   **14.** 7 × 5   **15.** 8 × 7   **16.** 4 × 6   **17.** 3 × 7

18. 9 × 3   **19.** 8 × 9   **20.** 4 × 4   **21.** 6 × 3   **22.** 7 × 7

Problem Solving

23. For the chessboard shown below, write a multiplication sentence to find the total number of

   a red pieces.

   b squares with pieces.

   c squares on the board.

24. Joe, Vicki, and Tom took a hiking vacation. They traveled the distances shown in the table below. Who walked the farthest?

Critical THINKING

   A Joe   **C** Vicki

   B Tom   **D** They all walked the same distance.

Hiker	Distance walked
Joe	9 miles each day for 8 days.
Vicki	8 miles each day for 4 days and 4 miles each day for 8 days.
Tom	7 miles each day for 5 days then 5 miles each day for 7 days.

Data

25. **Literature** Mark Twain's name is taken from riverboat slang. "Mark twain" means "Mark two," for 2 fathoms. One fathom is equal to 6 feet. How many feet does Mark Twain's name stand for?

Mark Twain

Recalling Multiplication Facts

What are some strategies that can be used to find products?

Sunnyside Summer Camp has 7 tents where the campers will stay. Five campers are assigned to each tent. If all of the tents are full, how many campers are at the camp?

What are the different ways to find 7×5?

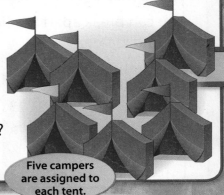

Five campers are assigned to each tent.

MA.4.A.1.1 Use and describe various models for multiplication in problem-solving situations, and demonstrate recall of basic multiplication and related division facts with ease.

Guided Practice*

Do you know HOW?

For **1** through **4**, use strategies to find each product.

1. 4×8

2. 5×9

3. $\begin{array}{r} 6 \\ \times\ 4 \\ \hline \end{array}$

4. $\begin{array}{r} 7 \\ \times\ 7 \\ \hline \end{array}$

Do you UNDERSTAND?

5. Explain how you would use a fact you know to find 6×7.

6. How could you use patterns to find 8×5?

Independent Practice

For **7** through **31**, use strategies to find each product.

7. 3×8

8. 5×4

9. 6×6

10. 4×7

11. 5×5

12. 6×7

13. 8×6

14. 9×3

15. 4×4

16. 2×9

17. $\begin{array}{r} 7 \\ \times\ 9 \\ \hline \end{array}$

18. $\begin{array}{r} 9 \\ \times\ 3 \\ \hline \end{array}$

19. $\begin{array}{r} 8 \\ \times\ 8 \\ \hline \end{array}$

20. $\begin{array}{r} 5 \\ \times\ 3 \\ \hline \end{array}$

21. $\begin{array}{r} 7 \\ \times\ 4 \\ \hline \end{array}$

22. $\begin{array}{r} 8 \\ \times\ 9 \\ \hline \end{array}$

23. $\begin{array}{r} 9 \\ \times\ 7 \\ \hline \end{array}$

24. $\begin{array}{r} 4 \\ \times\ 6 \\ \hline \end{array}$

25. $\begin{array}{r} 5 \\ \times\ 6 \\ \hline \end{array}$

26. $\begin{array}{r} 8 \\ \times\ 7 \\ \hline \end{array}$

27. $\begin{array}{r} 3 \\ \times\ 6 \\ \hline \end{array}$

28. $\begin{array}{r} 8 \\ \times\ 5 \\ \hline \end{array}$

29. $\begin{array}{r} 9 \\ \times\ 9 \\ \hline \end{array}$

30. $\begin{array}{r} 2 \\ \times\ 8 \\ \hline \end{array}$

31. $\begin{array}{r} 6 \\ \times\ 9 \\ \hline \end{array}$

*For another example, see Set E on page 45.

Use patterns to find 7×5.	Use the Commutative Property.	Use known facts to find unknown facts.
5, 10, 15, 20, 25, 30, 35 Seven 5s are 35. So, $7 \times 5 = 35$.	7×5 is the same as 5×7. 5 groups of 7 are 35. So, $7 \times 5 = 35$.	7×5 $(5 \times 5) + (2 \times 5)$ $25 + 10 = 35$ There are 35 campers at camp if all of the tents are full.

Problem Solving

32. Writing to Explain Carla says that she can use the fact $3 \times 6 = 18$ to find 7×6. Is she correct? Explain.

33. Reasoning Kim says he can use the Commutative Property to find 8×8. Is he correct? Explain.

Critical THINKING

34. Barb has 9 vases. She wants to put 8 tulips in each vase. Use the diagram below to help you find how many tulips Barb will need.

? tulips needed in all

8	8	8	8	8	8	8	8	8

↑
Tulips in each vase

35. **Social Studies** Arches and Bryce Canyon are two national parks in Utah. Bryce Canyon is 35,835 acres in area and Arches is 76,679 acres in area. How many acres greater is Arches?

A   41,844

B   41,244

C   40,944

D   40,844

36. **Art** The art of Temari originated in China and was brought to Japan over one thousand years ago. Kaneko arranges her Temari balls into 3 rows with 8 balls in each row. What is another way she can arrange all of her Temari balls into equal groups?

MA.4.A.1.1 Use and describe various models for multiplication in problem-solving situations, and demonstrate recall of basic multiplication and related division facts with ease.

Problem Solving

Draw a Picture and Write an Equation

A stegosaurus was 5 times as long as a velociraptor. If a velociraptor was 6 feet long, how long was a stegosaurus?

Stegosaurus: ? feet long

Velociraptor: 6 feet long

Guided Practice*

Do you know HOW?

Solve. Write an equation to help you.

1. Manuel has a collection of coins, all of which are nickels and quarters. He has 8 nickels and three times as many quarters.

   a How many quarters does he have?

   b How many coins does Manuel have in all?

Do you UNDERSTAND?

2. How did the picture in the example above help you to write an equation?

3. A ceratosaurus was 5 times the length of a microvenator. A microvenator was 4 feet long. Use this information to write a problem you can solve by writing an equation. Then solve.

Independent Practice

4. **Science** For the science fair, Joe made a model of a microraptor, one of the smallest dinosaurs ever discovered. He made his model 8 inches long. The actual dinosaur was 3 times the length of Joe's model. How long was the microraptor?

? inches in all

| Microraptor | 8 | 8 | 8 | 3 times as long |
| Model | 8 | | | |

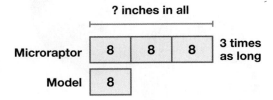

Stuck? Try this....

- What do I know?
- What diagram can I use to help understand the problem?
- Can I use addition, subtraction, multiplication, or division?
- Is all of my work correct?
- Did I answer the right question?
- Is my answer reasonable?

*For another example, see Set F on page 45.

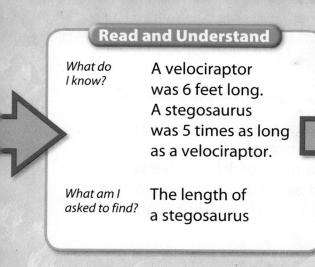

What do I know? A velociraptor was 6 feet long. A stegosaurus was 5 times as long as a velociraptor.

What am I asked to find? The length of a stegosaurus

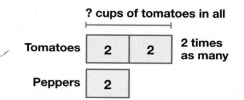

Draw a picture.

Write a number sentence.

Multiply: $5 \times 6 = 30$

A stegosaurus was 30 feet long.

---

5. Carmen's recipe calls for three times as many carrots as peas. If Carmen uses 2 cups of peas, how many cups of carrots will she use?

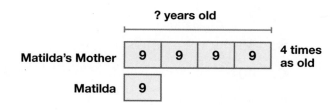

? cups of carrots in all

| Carrots | 2 | 2 | 2 | 3 times as many |
| Peas | 2 | | | |

6. Rae's recipe calls for twice as many tomatoes as peppers. She uses 2 cups of peppers. How many cups of tomatoes will she use in all?

? cups of tomatoes in all

| Tomatoes | 2 | 2 | 2 times as many |
| Peppers | 2 | | |

7. THINK SOLVE EXPLAIN Marley, Jon, and Bart swim a relay race. Jon swims two more laps than Marley. Bart swims twice as many laps as Marley. If Marley swims 3 laps, how many laps do they swim all together? Explain.

8. Critical THINKING Jack's dog has a rectangular pen. The length is two feet longer than the width. The width is 6 feet. Write an equation to find the perimeter. What is the perimeter of the pen?

9. Matilda is 9 years old. Her mother is 4 times as old as she is. Use the model below to find the age of Matilda's mother.

? years old

| Matilda's Mother | 9 | 9 | 9 | 9 | 4 times as old |
| Matilda | 9 | | | | |

10. Think About the Process Four relay team members run an equal part of an 8-mile race. Which equation could you use to find how far each member runs?

A $4 + \blacksquare = 8$

B $4 \times \blacksquare = 8$

C $4 + 4 + 4 + 4 = \blacksquare$

D $2 \times 2 = \blacksquare$

1 Which is NOT a way to find 6 × 7? (2-5)

A. (3 × 7) + (4 × 7)

B. (3 × 7) + (3 × 7)

C. (5 × 7) + 7

D. 7 × 6

2 Grant made 4 flags for the school play. Each flag had 1 white star. How many white stars did Grant make? (2-2)

F. 5

G. 4

H. 3

I. 0

3 Which is a way to find 7 × 8? (2-4)

A. (7 × 5) + (7 × 2)

B. (4 × 8) + (3 × 8)

C. (7 × 5) + (8 × 1)

D. (5 × 8) + (2 × 7)

4 Each flower has 5 petals.

If Stephanie counted the petals in groups of 5, which list shows numbers she could have named? (2-1)

F. 12, 15, 18, 30

G. 15, 20, 34, 40

H. 15, 20, 25, 30

I. 10, 12, 14, 16

5 Elizabeth bought 3 packages of buttons. Each package had 6 buttons. Which number sentence can be used to find the total number of buttons Elizabeth bought? (2-3)

A. 6 − 3 = ▨

B. 3 + 6 = ▨

C. 3 × ▨ = 6

D. 3 × 6 = ▨

6 Sue collected 5 rocks. Angie collected 4 times as many rocks as Sue. Which number sentence shows how many rocks Angie collected? (2-6)

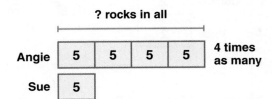

F. 4 + 5 = 9

G. 5 − 4 = 1

H. 4 × 5 = 20

I. 5 × 5 = 25

7 Gina made an invitation for each of her 8 friends. She used 4 stickers on each invitation. How many stickers did Gina use in all? (2-4)

A. 32

B. 35

C. 40

D. 42

8 Trevor's display case has 6 shelves. Each shelf displays 8 golf balls. Which number sentence shows how many golf balls are displayed in the case? (2-6)

? golf balls in all					
8	8	8	8	8	8

↑
Golf balls on each shelf

F. $6 + 8 = 14$

G. $6 - 3 = 3$

H. $6 \times 8 = 48$

I. $8 \times 8 = 64$

9 Luis counted all the wheels on the 8 bicycles in the bike rack at the park. If he counted the wheels in groups of 2, which list shows numbers he could have named? (2-1)

A. 8, 10, 12, 15

B. 10, 12, 14, 16

C. 12, 15, 16, 18

D. 10, 15, 20, 25

10 The Mendez family replaced tile on their kitchen counter. A 9×4 array of tiles fit the area. How many tiles did they use? (2-3)

F. 13

G. 27

H. 34

I. 36

11 Which number makes the number sentence true? (2-2)

$6 \times 2 = \blacksquare \times 6$

A. 0

B. 1

C. 2

D. 6

12 Which is a way to break apart 4×8? (2-3)

F. $(4 \times 8) + (4 \times 8)$

G. $(2 \times 5) + (2 \times 3)$

H. $(2 \times 4) + (2 \times 4)$

I. $(2 \times 8) + (2 \times 8)$

13 Before touring Kickapoo Cavern State Park, the 4th graders were put into 6 groups of 9 students. Which is a way to find 6×9? (2-4)

A. $(6 \times 5) + (6 \times 4)$

B. $(6 \times 9) + (6 \times 9)$

C. $(3 \times 5) + (3 \times 4)$

D. $(3 \times 8) + (3 \times 1)$

14 It takes Dave 7 minutes to paint one section of a fence. How many minutes would it take him to paint 3 sections? (2-4)

15 THINK SOLVE EXPLAIN Explain how you could use a pattern to find 5×6. (2-5)

Set A, pages 30–31

Find 2 × 8.

When you multiply a number by 2, the product is always even.

2 × 8 = 16

When you multiply a number by 5, the product always ends in 0 or 5.

5 × 2 = 10

Remember you can solve some multiplication problems by using patterns of multiples.

1. 6 × 5 **2.** 9 × 8
3. 9 × 6 **4.** 2 × 3
5. 2 × 7 **6.** 5 × 7
7. 9 × 5 **8.** 2 × 5
9. 5 × 8 **10.** 9 × 3
11. 9 × 9 **12.** 5 × 3

Set B, pages 32–33

Find 9 × 0.

When you multiply any number by 0, the product is 0.

9 × 0 = 0

When you multiply any number by 1, the product is the original number.

6 × 1 = 6

Remember you can change the order of the factors when you multiply.

1. 5 × 0 **2.** 8 × 5
3. 0 × 8 **4.** 1 × 6
5. 1 × 9 **6.** 7 × 2
7. 1 × 5 **8.** 9 × 6
9. 7 × 1 **10.** 0 × 7
11. 0 × 190 **12.** 9 × 4

Set C, pages 34–35

Find 3 × 9 using breaking apart.

3 groups of 9 = 3 groups of 5 + 3 groups of 4

3 × 9 = (3 × 5) + (3 × 4)
15 + 12
27

Remember you can use breaking apart to remember multiplication facts.

1. 3 × 8 **2.** 4 × 9
3. 4 × 2 **4.** 3 × 6
5. 3 × 7 **6.** 4 × 6
7. 4 × 8 **8.** 3 × 5

Set D, pages 36–37

What are two ways to break apart 8×7?

Break apart the first factor as $4 + 4$.

$$8 \times 7 = (4 \times 7) + (4 \times 7)$$
$$28 + 28$$
$$56$$

Break apart the second factor as $5 + 2$.

$$8 \times 7 = (8 \times 5) + (8 \times 2)$$
$$40 + 16$$
$$56$$

Remember you can break apart either factor to find a multiplication fact.

1. 7×6 **2.** 8×8

3. 9×8 **4.** 6×9

5. 6×7 **6.** 7×5

7. 6×8 **8.** 9×7

Set E, pages 38–39

Use known facts to find unknown facts.

6×9 is 5×9 and 9 more.

$$45 + 9 = 54$$

So, $6 \times 9 = 54$.

Remember you can use patterns, the Commutative Property, or known facts to find unknown facts.

1. 4×5 **2.** 9×4

3. 7×2 **4.** 6×3

5. 5×8 **6.** 9×7

7. 6×7 **8.** 8×9

Set F, pages 40–41

Marisol has 8 pennies in her collection. She has four times as many quarters as pennies. How many coins are in Marisol's collection?

? quarters in all

quarters | 8 | 8 | 8 | 8   4 times as many

pennies | 8

$4 \times 8 = 32$ quarters

Add 8 pennies to find how many coins are in Marisol's collection.

$32 + 8 = 40$ coins in all

Remember you can draw a picture to help you write an equation.

Draw a picture and write an equation to solve.

1. The length of Mel's basement is 9 times the length of a broom. The length of a broom is 3 feet. What is the length of the basement?

Division Meanings and Facts

1

Gouramis go to the surface of a fish tank to breathe air directly. How many gouramis can you keep in a 15-gallon tank? You will find out in Lesson 3-1.

2

When did people start riding carousels in the United States? You will find out in Lesson 3-5.

Review What You Know!

3 What kind of shells did some Native American tribes use to make jewelry? You will find out in Lesson 3-2.

4 How many calories does the average fourth-grade student burn jumping rope each minute? You will find out in Lesson 3-4.

Vocabulary

Choose the best term from the box.

- divisor
- quotient
- multiple
- product
- factor
- division

1. In the number sentence $9 \times 5 = 45$, 45 is the _?_.

2. The number you divide by is the _?_.

3. The answer in a division problem is the _?_.

Multiplication Facts

Find each product.

4. 5×3	**5.** 7×2	**6.** 6×8
7. 8×0	**8.** 1×4	**9.** 2×8
10. 5×7	**11.** 3×6	**12.** 4×4
13. 4×5	**14.** 4×8	**15.** 2×6

Addition and Subtraction Facts

Write a subtraction fact for each addition fact.

16. $8 + 8 = 16$ **17.** $4 + 7 = 11$

18. $6 + 6 = 12$ **19.** $9 + 5 = 14$

20. Write a subtraction fact for the array below.

21. Writing to Explain Explain how you could subtract $146 - 51$ using mental math.

Topic Essential Questions

- What are different meanings of division?
- How can unknown division facts be found by thinking about a related multiplication fact?

Lesson

3-1

MA.4.A.6.2 Use models to represent division as:
• the inverse of multiplication;
• as partitioning;
• as successive subtraction.
Also MA.4.A.1.1

Division as Repeated Subtraction

How can you divide to find the number of groups?

Terri has collected 15 snow globes from around the world. She wants to display them in groups of 5. How many groups will she make?

15 snow globes

5 | ? groups →

Snow globes in each group

Guided Practice*

Do you know HOW?

In **1** and **2**, use repeated subtraction to help you divide.

1. Gina is hanging 9 suncatchers on her windows. She puts 3 suncatchers on each window. How many windows will have suncatchers?

2. Mr. Rios has 20 students in his gym class. He separates the class into teams of 4 students. How many teams will there be?

Do you UNDERSTAND?

3. Explain how you could use repeated addition to check the answer to the example above.

4. Terri now has 18 snow globes in her collection. She decides to place them in groups of 3. How many groups will she make?

Independent Practice

Leveled Practice In **5** through **10**, divide using repeated subraction. Use diagrams to help.

5. Kobe counted 21 pelican eggs. If each nest has 3 eggs, how many nests are there?

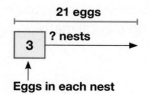

21 eggs

3 | ? nests →

Eggs in each nest

6. Meg has 36 beads. Each bracelet has 9 beads. How many bracelets does she have?

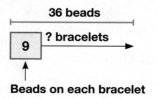

36 beads

9 | ? bracelets →

Beads on each bracelet

For another example, see Set A on page 66.

What You Show

Use repeated subtraction to find the number of groups.

$$15 - 5 = 10$$
$$10 - 5 = 5$$
$$5 - 5 = 0$$

You subtract 5 three times.

What You Write

There are three groups of 5 in 15.

15 snow globes

5	5	5

Terri will make 3 groups.

---

7. There are 28 dancers in a dance recital. For the final dance, they will stand in rows with 7 dancers each. How many rows will there be?

8. Claire has 30 stickers that she wants to share with her friends. Each friend will get 5 stickers. How many friends will receive stickers?

9. Jena is making apple pies. She has 24 apples. Eight apples will go into each pie. How many pies will Jena make?

10. A dog trainer has 10 puppies signed up for training class. He divides them into classes with 5 puppies in each. How many classes will he be teaching?

Problem Solving

In **11** and **12**, use the picture at the right.

11. Ramon has 27 baseball cards in his collection. He places the same number of cards on each page. How many pages will he need for all of his cards?

12. Writing to Explain Debbie's baseball card collection has 5 pages of cards. She places the same number of cards on each page. Who owns more cards, Ramon or Debbie? Explain your answer.

Critical THINKING

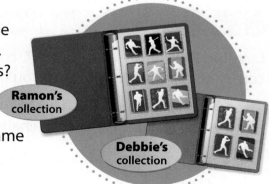

Ramon's collection

Debbie's collection

13. Ray collects toy cars and stores them in special boxes that hold 6 cars each. He had a total of 36 cars. Today he got 12 more cars. How many boxes will Ray need to store all of his cars now?

    A 2 boxes   **C** 8 boxes

    B 6 boxes   **D** 10 boxes

14. A fish store clerk tells you that 3 gallons of water are needed for each gourami in a fish tank. How many fish can you keep in a 15-gallon tank?

MA.4.A.6.2 Use models to represent division as:
• the inverse of multiplication;
• as partitioning;
• as successive subtraction.
Also MA.4.A.1.1

Using Models to Divide: Sharing

When do you divide?

A museum wants to display a collection of 24 gems on four shelves, placing the same number of gems on each shelf. How many gems will be on each shelf?

Choose an Operation Think about sharing. Divide to find the number in each group.

24 gems on 4 shelves

Guided Practice*

Do you know HOW?

In **1** and **2**, draw pictures to help you divide.

1. You put 18 people into 3 rows. How many people are in each row?

2. Rocco is putting 14 drawings into 2 art binders. How many drawings are in each binder?

Do you UNDERSTAND?

3. What do the 4 boxes in the diagram above represent?

4. Sixteen players came to soccer practice. They formed four teams with the same number of players per team. How many players were on each team?

Independent Practice

Leveled Practice In **5** through **7**, copy and complete the diagrams to help you divide.

5. Kevin is arranging 12 chairs in 3 equal groups. How many chairs are in each group?

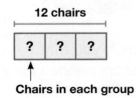

12 chairs

| ? | ? | ? |

↑
Chairs in each group

6. Toby has 14 baseball caps. He sorts them into 2 equal groups. How many baseball caps are in each group?

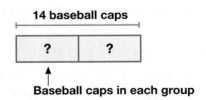

14 baseball caps

| ? | ? |

↑
Baseball caps in each group

7. The class yearbook has 16 pictures shown on 4 pages. How many pictures are on each page?

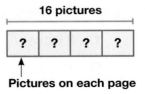

16 pictures

| ? | ? | ? | ? |

↑
Pictures on each page

For another example, see Set A on page 66.

Think of sharing the gems equally among the 4 shelves. How many gems are on each shelf?

24 gems

| 6 | 6 | 6 | 6 |

↑
Gems on each shelf

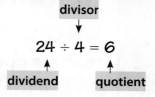

divisor
↓
$24 \div 4 = 6$
↑   ↑
dividend   quotient

Each shelf should have 6 gems.

In **8** and **9**, draw pictures to solve each problem.

8. Jeff puts 25 quarters into 5 equal groups. How many quarters are in each group?

9. There are 30 stuffed bears in a gift shop arranged in 5 equal rows. How many bears are in each row?

Problem Solving

10. Dentalia shells were used by some Native American tribes to make jewelry. A craftsperson has 24 dentalia shells. She uses 8 shells for each necklace. How many necklaces can she make?

11. There are 18 students on the playground. They want to make 2 equal teams for a kickball game. How many students will be on each team?

   A   9   **C**   11

   B   10   **D**   12

12. Snooty the Manatee was born in 1948 at the Miami Aquarium. How old was Snooty in 2008?

13. Geometry A rectangular wading pool is 10 feet wide and 15 feet long. What is the perimeter of the wading pool?

   F   25 feet   **H**   100 feet

   G   50 feet   **I**   150 feet

14. Reasoning An aquarium has 7 more sharks than rays. It has 3 fewer rays than dolphins. If the aquarium has 7 dolphins, how many sharks does it have?

Critical THINKING

15. Trisha and 5 of her friends shared 18 pancakes equally. How many pancakes did each person receive?

18 pancakes

| ? | ? | ? | ? | ? | ? |

↑
Pancakes each received

MA.4.A.6.2 Use models to
represent division as:
• the inverse of multiplication;
• as partitioning;
• as successive subtraction.
Also MA.4.A.1.1

Relating Multiplication and Division

How are operations related?

Operations that undo each other are inverse operations. Multiplying by 3 and dividing by 3 are inverse operations.

How many pockets are on each sheet?

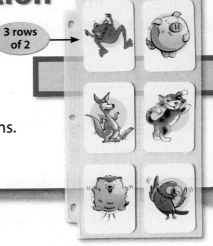

3 rows of 2

Guided Practice*

Do you know HOW?

In **1** and **2**, copy and complete each fact family.

1. $8 \times \square = 32$

$32 \div \square = 4$

$32 \div \square = \square$

$\square \times \square = 32$

2. $6 \times 9 = \square$

$54 \div \square = 9$

$54 \div 9 = \square$

$9 \times \square = \square$

In **3** and **4**, write the fact family for each set of numbers.

3. 3, 6, 18

4. 5, 7, 35

Do you UNDERSTAND?

5. Why are there four number sentences in the example above?

6. Is $2 \times 6 = 12$ part of the fact family from the example above?

7. Why is $3 + 3 = 6$ NOT in the fact family of 2, 3, and 6?

8. If you know $7 \times 9 = 63$, what division facts do you know?

Independent Practice

Leveled Practice In **9** through **12**, copy and complete each fact family.

9. $5 \times \square = 35$

$35 \div 5 = \square$

$\square \times \square = 35$

$35 \div \square = \square$

10. $9 \times \square = 72$

$72 \div 9 = \square$

$\square \times \square = 72$

$72 \div \square = \square$

11. $3 \times \square = 18$

$18 \div 3 = \square$

$\square \times \square = 18$

$18 \div \square = \square$

12. $4 \times \square = 32$

$32 \div 8 = \square$

$\square \times \square = 32$

$32 \div \square = \square$

Animated Glossary
www.pearsonsuccessnet.com

A **fact family** <u>shows all the related multiplication and division facts for a set of numbers.</u> You can use fact families to help you remember division facts.

This is the fact family for 2, 3, and 6:

$2 \times 3 = 6$ $\qquad$ $6 \div 2 = 3$

$3 \times 2 = 6$ $\qquad$ $6 \div 3 = 2$

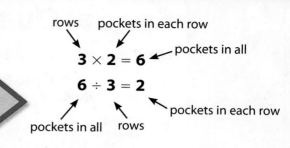

rows$\quad$pockets in each row

$3 \times 2 = 6 \leftarrow$ pockets in all

$6 \div 3 = 2$

pockets in all$\quad$rows$\quad$pockets in each row

Each has 6 pockets.

In **13** through **24**, write a fact family for each set of numbers.

13. 7, 8, 56 $\qquad$ **14.** 2, 8, 16 $\qquad$ **15.** 6, 7, 42 $\qquad$ **16.** 6, 6, 36

17. 3, 8, 24 $\qquad$ **18.** 7, 4, 28 $\qquad$ **19.** 6, 5, 30 $\qquad$ **20.** 5, 8, 40

21. 4, 4, 16 $\qquad$ **22.** 9, 3, 27 $\qquad$ **23.** 1, 7, 7 $\qquad$ **24.** 8, 6, 48

Problem Solving

25. **Social Studies** Use the table at the right. How many state quarters were released after eight years?

United States State Quarters	
First quarters released	1999
Number of new quarters each year	5

26. In the fact family for the numbers 3, 7, 21, which symbol can NOT be used?

A $\times$

B $\div$

C $=$

D $+$

27. Josh practices his drums two hours each day. How many hours will he have practiced after seven days?

F 7 hours

G 10 hours

H 14 hours

I 16 hours

28. Write the fact family that has 9 as a factor and 45 as a product.

Critical THINKING

29. Why does the fact family for 64 and 8 have only two number sentences?

THINK SOLVE EXPLAIN

Lesson
3-4

MA.4.A.1.1 Use and describe various models for multiplication in problem-solving situations, and demonstrate recall of basic multiplication and related division facts with ease. **Also MA.4.A.6.2**

Special Quotients

How can you divide with 1 and 0?

A sandwich is cut into 8 pieces. How many people can have 1 piece each? Find $8 \div 1$.

1 group of 8

8 **people** can have 1 piece of sandwich

Dividing by 1

Think What number times 1 equals 8?

$1 \times 8 = 8$

So, $8 \div 1 = 8$.

Rule: Any number divided by 1 is itself.

Guided Practice*

Do you know HOW?

In **1** through **8**, use multiplication facts to help you divide.

1. $9 \div 9$ **2.** $5 \div 1$

3. $0 \div 4$ **4.** $7 \div 1$

5. $0 \div 3$ **6.** $1 \div 1$

7. $2 \div 1$ **8.** $6 \div 6$

Do you UNDERSTAND?

9. What multiplication sentence can help you find $0 \div 8$?

10. What multiplication sentence can help you find $8 \div 8$?

11. Writing to Explain If none of the sandwich is left, how many pieces can 4 people have?

Independent Practice

In **12** through **15**, use multiplication facts to help you divide.

12. $1\overline{)3}$ **13.** $8\overline{)0}$ **14.** $2\overline{)0}$ **15.** $4\overline{)4}$

In **16** through **27**, copy and complete by writing >, <, or = for each $\bigcirc$.

16. $7 \div 7 \bigcirc 2 \div 2$ **17.** $0 \div 5 \bigcirc 3 \div 1$ **18.** $4 \div 1 \bigcirc 4 \div 4$

19. $6 \div 6 \bigcirc 0 \div 4$ **20.** $9 \div 1 \bigcirc 4 \div 1$ **21.** $3 \div 3 \bigcirc 6 \div 1$

22. $0 \div 3 \bigcirc 0 \div 8$ **23.** $0 \div 5 \bigcirc 5 \div 5$ **24.** $8 \div 1 \bigcirc 6 \div 1$

25. $0 \div 9 \bigcirc 0 \div 7$ **26.** $0 \div 1 \bigcirc 1 \div 1$ **27.** $7 \div 1 \bigcirc 0 \div 6$

1 as a Quotient

To find 8 ÷ 8, think 8 times what number equals 8?

$$8 \times 1 = 8$$

So, 8 ÷ 8 = 1.

Rule: Any number (except 0) divided by itself is 1.

Dividing 0 by a Number

To find 0 ÷ 8, think 8 times what number equals 0?

$$8 \times 0 = 0$$

So, 0 ÷ 8 = 0.

Rule: 0 divided by any number (except 0) is 0.

Dividing by 0

To find 8 ÷ 0, think 0 times what number equals 8?

There is no such number.

Rule: You cannot divide by 0.

Problem Solving

28. The average fourth-grade student can burn 7 calories each minute jumping rope. How many minutes would a fourth-grade student have to jump rope to burn 35 calories?

29. Tony's family is driving 70 miles to a fair. They have already traveled 30 miles. They are traveling at a speed of 40 miles per hour. How many more hours will it take them to complete the rest of the trip?

30. On a trip to the beach, the Torrez family brought 5 beach balls for their 5 children.

   a If the beach balls are divided equally among the children, how many beach balls will each child get?

   b If the children give the 5 balls to 1 parent, how many balls will the parent have?

31. In one season, a baseball team will practice 4 times a week. If there are 36 practices, how many weeks will the team practice in the season?

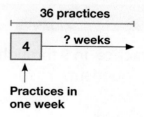

32. Write a Problem Write a word problem in which 3 is divided by 3 and another problem in which 3 is divided by 1.

34. Number Sense Write a fact family in which 9 is the product of two numbers.

33. Algebra If ☐ ÷ 4 = 0, what do you know about ☐?

   A ☐ cannot equal 0.

   B ☐ must equal 0.

   C ☐ must equal 1.

   D ☐ must equal 4.

MA.4.A.6.2 Use models to
represent division as:
• the inverse of multiplication;
• as partitioning;
• as successive subtraction.
Also MA.4.A.1.1

Using Multiplication Facts to Find Division Facts: 2, 3, 4, 5

How does multiplication help you divide?

Matt wants to buy 20 super bouncy
balls to give as prizes. How many
packs does Matt need to buy?

Choose an Operation Divide to
find the number of equal groups.

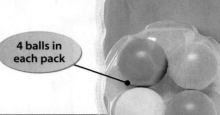

4 balls in
each pack

Guided Practice*

Do you know HOW?

In **1** through **6**, use multiplication facts
to help you divide.

1. $12 \div 2$ **2.** $40 \div 5$

3. $24 \div 4$ **4.** $27 \div 3$

5. $4\overline{)36}$ **6.** $3\overline{)21}$

Do you UNDERSTAND?

7. What multiplication fact could
you use to help you find $45 \div 5$?

8. Matt has 18 super bouncy balls
to put in 3 bags. He puts the
same number in each bag. What
multiplication fact can you use
to find the number of balls in
each bag?

Independent Practice

Leveled Practice In **9** through **25**, use multiplication facts to help
you find the quotient.

9. ○○○○○
○○○○○
○○○○○

☐ $\times 5 = 15$ $15 \div$ ☐ $= 5$

10. ○○○○○○
○○○○○○

☐ $\times 6 = 12$ $12 \div$ ☐ $= 6$

11. $3\overline{)27}$ **12.** $3\overline{)12}$ **13.** $4\overline{)16}$ **14.** $5\overline{)10}$ **15.** $2\overline{)14}$

16. $3\overline{)24}$ **17.** $4\overline{)32}$ **18.** $2\overline{)18}$ **19.** $5\overline{)35}$ **20.** $2\overline{)16}$

21. $5\overline{)30}$ **22.** $2\overline{)12}$ **23.** $4\overline{)24}$ **24.** $5\overline{)40}$ **25.** $5\overline{)25}$

For another example, see Set D on page 67.

How many groups of 4 are in 20?

$20 \div 4 = $ ▢

Change this to a multiplication sentence:

What number times 4 equals 20?

▢ $\times 4 = 20$ $5 \times 4 = 20$

There are two ways to write division facts.

$$20 \div 4 = 5$$

or

$$4\overline{)20}\,^{5}$$

Matt needs to buy 5 packs of bouncy balls.

Problem Solving

For **26** and **27**, use the table at the right.

26. On a field trip to Gatorland, Shana spends $24 in the gift shop. Which item can Shana buy the most of? Explain.

THINK
SOLVE
EXPLAIN

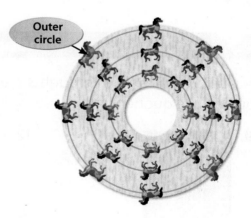

Price List	
Postcard packs	$3
Rubber alligator	$6
Gator puzzle	$8

Data

27. How many rubber alligators can Shana buy if she uses all of her money?

28. **Social Studies** People started riding carousels in the United States in 1835. The carousel drawing, at the right, has a total of 24 horses with an equal number of horses on each circle. Write a division fact you can use to find the number of horses on the outer circle.

Critical
THINKING

Outer circle

29. Carson plays a card word game. She gives the same number of cards to each of 4 players. If there are 28 cards in all, how many cards does each player get?

30. The total lunch bill for five people is $34. They add a $6 tip and split the bill evenly. How much is each person's equal share of the total bill?

  A $6   **C** $10

  B $8   **D** $12

3-6

MA.4.A.6.2 Use models to represent division as:
• the inverse of multiplication;
• as partitioning;
• as successive subtraction.
Also MA.4.A.1.1

Using Multiplication Facts to Find Division Facts: 6, 7, 8, 9

How can you use multiplication to divide?

Malik has 56 oil-based paint tubes. How many sets of paint tubes does Malik have?

Choose an Operation Divide to find the number of equal groups.

8 paint tubes in each set

Guided Practice*

Do you know HOW?

In **1** through **6**, use multiplication facts to help you divide.

1. $27 \div 9$ **2.** $64 \div 8$

3. $56 \div 7$ **4.** $42 \div 6$

5. $9\overline{)63}$ **6.** $9\overline{)81}$

Do you UNDERSTAND?

7. What multiplication fact could you use to help you find $36 \div 9$?

8. Malik now has a total of 72 paint tubes. What multiplication fact can you use to find the number of sets he will have?

Independent Practice

Leveled Practice In **9** through **30**, use multiplication facts to help you find the quotient.

9. 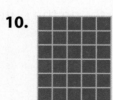 $7 \times \boxed{} = 42$ $42 \div 7 = \boxed{}$ **10.** $8 \times \boxed{} = 40$ $40 \div 8 = \boxed{}$

11. $7\overline{)49}$ **12.** $6\overline{)48}$ **13.** $7\overline{)21}$ **14.** $9\overline{)36}$ **15.** $6\overline{)36}$

16. $8\overline{)24}$ **17.** $6\overline{)30}$ **18.** $9\overline{)18}$ **19.** $7\overline{)35}$ **20.** $7\overline{)56}$

21. $7\overline{)42}$ **22.** $8\overline{)64}$ **23.** $6\overline{)24}$ **24.** $9\overline{)54}$ **25.** $9\overline{)72}$

26. $8\overline{)16}$ **27.** $7\overline{)28}$ **28.** $8\overline{)40}$ **29.** $7\overline{)63}$ **30.** $6\overline{)54}$

*For another example, see Set D on page 67.

How many groups of 8 are in 56?

$56 \div 8 = \square$

Change this to a multiplication sentence:

What number times 8 equals 56?

$\square \times 8 = 56$ $7 \times 8 = 56$

There are two ways to write division facts.

$$56 \div 8 = 7$$

or

$$7$$
$$8\overline{)56}$$

Malik has 7 sets of paint tubes.

Problem Solving

For **31** and **32**, use the table at the right.

31. For one circus act, 6 clowns juggle the same number of rings. If all the rings are used in the act, how many rings does each clown juggle?

32. During another circus act, clowns juggle balls and bowling pins. Each clown juggles 8 items. How many clowns can perform in the act?

Juggling Item	Total Number Needed Per Act
Balls	28
Bowling Pins	36
Rings	30

33. Number Sense Quinn is thinking of two numbers. The product of the numbers is 24. The sum of the numbers is 10. What are the numbers?

Critical THINKING

34. Sarah biked 73 miles in two days. She biked 39 miles the first day. How many miles did she bike the second day?

35. Trevor has 48 solar panels on his roof. He has 8 panels in each row. How many rows of solar panels does Trevor have on his roof?

  A 4 rows   **C** 8 rows

  B 6 rows   **D** 9 rows

36. Reasoning The answer to a division problem is 1. What do you know about the divisor and the dividend?

37. A group of hikers spent 7 days hiking a 63-mile-long trail. Each day they hiked the same distance. How many miles did they hike each day?

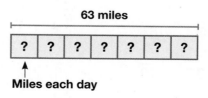

MA.4.A.1.1 Use and describe various models for multiplication in problem-solving situations, and demonstrate recall of basic multiplications and related division facts with ease.

Recalling Division Facts

How can you find the quotient?

If 56 members of a marching band march in rows of 7, how many rows are there?

Choose an Operation Divide to find the number of rows of band members.

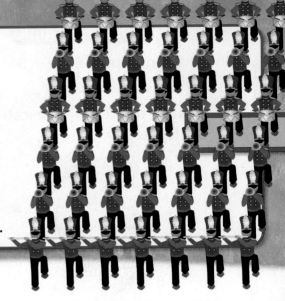

Guided Practice*

Do you know HOW?

In **1** through **6**, find the quotient.

1. $35 \div 7$

2. $18 \div 3$

3. $42 \div 6$

4. $54 \div 9$

5. $4\overline{)32}$

6. $5\overline{)20}$

Do you UNDERSTAND?

7. The band director decided to arrange the marching band in rows of 8. How many rows will there be?

8. Why can you multiply to check your answer in the example above?

Independent Practice

Leveled Practice In **9** through **40**, find the quotient. Multiply to check your answer.

9. $27 \div 3 = \blacksquare$
$3 \times \blacksquare = 27$

10. $40 \div 8 = \blacksquare$
$8 \times \blacksquare = 40$

11. $42 \div 6 = \blacksquare$
$6 \times \blacksquare = 42$

12. $63 \div 7 = \blacksquare$
$7 \times \blacksquare = 63$

13. $5 \div 5 = \blacksquare$

14. $32 \div 4 = \blacksquare$

15. $72 \div 9 = \blacksquare$

16. $28 \div 7 = \blacksquare$

17. $32 \div 8 = \blacksquare$

18. $10 \div 2 = \blacksquare$

19. $0 \div 8 = \blacksquare$

20. $81 \div 9 = \blacksquare$

21. $1\overline{)8}$

22. $5\overline{)15}$

23. $6\overline{)54}$

24. $5\overline{)35}$

25. $7\overline{)49}$

26. $3\overline{)21}$

27. $9\overline{)36}$

28. $5\overline{)25}$

29. $9\overline{)18}$

30. $6\overline{)6}$

31. $7\overline{)35}$

32. $9\overline{)81}$

33. $3\overline{)21}$

34. $5\overline{)45}$

35. $6\overline{)12}$

36. $1\overline{)6}$

37. $2\overline{)10}$

38. $7\overline{)7}$

39. $9\overline{)27}$

40. $4\overline{)16}$

For another example, see Set D on page 67.

Find 56 ÷ 7.

56 members

7 | **? number of rows** →

Number of band members in each row

There are 8 rows of band members.

Check your answer using inverse operations.

$8 \times 7 = 56$ Multiply to check your answer.

The answer checks.

Problem Solving

41.  **Science** A clutch is the total number of eggs laid at one time. A green turtle lays two clutches of eggs on the beach. Use the picture at the right to find how many eggs the green turtle laid in all.

One clutch has 107 eggs and the other clutch has 110 eggs.

42. The Volusia-Flagler Turtle Patrol protects sea turtle nests in Volusia County and Flagler County in Florida. They are sending 5 groups to patrol 25 miles of beach. If each group patrols the same length of beach, how many miles of beach will each group patrol?

   A 5 miles   **C** 10 miles

   B 6 miles   **D** 125 miles

43. **Number Sense** Can you write a fact family using the numbers 4, 6, and 28? Explain why or why not.

 Critical THINKING

44. **Write a Problem** Write a division story for $45 \div 5 = 9$.

45. A chorus with 27 members is having a concert. Can the students stand in 4 equal rows if 3 members are absent for the night of the concert? Explain your reasoning.

THINK SOLVE EXPLAIN

46. Which equation can help you solve $24 \div 3 = \square$?

   F $4 \times 6 = 24$

   G $24 - 3 = 21$

   H $3 \times 8 = 24$

   I $24 + 3 = 27$

MA.4.A.1.1 Use and describe various models for multiplication in problem-solving situations, and demonstrate recall of basic multiplication and related division facts with ease. Also MA.4.A.6.2

Problem Solving

Draw a Picture and Write an Equation

Ruben's scout troop is making 4 milk-jug birdfeeders. Each birdfeeder will use the same number of wooden dowels. If they have 24 dowels in all, how many dowels will be used for each feeder?

24 dowels

Guided Practice*

Do you know HOW?

Solve. Write an equation to help you.

1. Tina put 32 flowers into eight bouquets. How many flowers were in each bouquet if each had the same number of flowers?

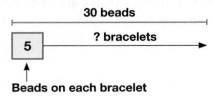

32 flowers in all

| ? | ? | ? | ? | ? | ? | ? | ? |

↑
Flowers in each bouquet

Do you UNDERSTAND?

2. How did the picture in Problem 1 help you to write an equation?

3. How many birdfeeders could Ruben's scout troop make with 36 dowels?

4. **Write a Problem** Write a problem about sharing items that you can solve by drawing a picture. Then solve.

Independent Practice

Solve. Write an equation to help you.

5. Kylie bought a bag of 30 beads to make bracelets. Each bracelet requires 5 beads. How many bracelets can Kylie make?

30 beads

| 5 | ? bracelets → |

↑
Beads on each bracelet

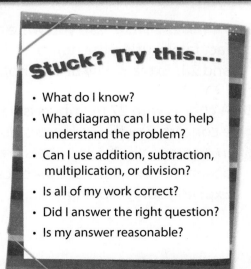

Stuck? Try this....

• What do I know?
• What diagram can I use to help understand the problem?
• Can I use addition, subtraction, multiplication, or division?
• Is all of my work correct?
• Did I answer the right question?
• Is my answer reasonable?

*For another example, see Set E on page 67.

Read and Understand

What do I know?	There are 24 dowels. There are 4 birdfeeders. Each birdfeeder has the same number of dowels.
What am I asked to find?	The number of dowels for each birdfeeder

Plan and Solve

Draw a picture.

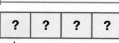

24 dowels

?	?	?	?

↑
Dowels for each birdfeeder

Write a number sentence.

Divide: $24 \div 4 = \square$

$24 \div 4 = 6$

There are 6 dowels for each birdfeeder.

Look Back and Check

Check the answer by multiplying.

Each birdfeeder has 6 dowels. There are 4 birdfeeders.

$4 \times 6 = 24$

The answer checks.

6. Sheena is packing 18 paperweights in boxes. She packs them in 6 boxes with the same number of paperweights in each box. How many paperweights are in each box?

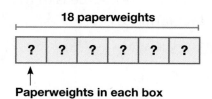

18 paperweights

?	?	?	?	?	?

↑
Paperweights in each box

7. Jodi is bundling newspapers. She has 54 newspapers and puts 6 newspapers in each bundle. How many bundles does Jodi make?

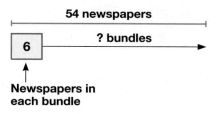

54 newspapers

? bundles

6

↑
Newspapers in each bundle

Use the bar graph at the right for **8** and **9**.

8. How much more money did Katie save in September than in October?

9. Katie used the money she saved in November and December to buy her mother a present. How much did she spend?

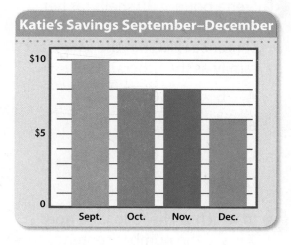

10. **Draw It** Manny is going camping with friends. He packed 30 sandwiches. How many sandwiches can Manny and his friends eat each day if they go camping for 5 days and eat the same number of sandwiches each day?

11. Jenna bought 36 pencils to give to her friends before the first day of school. If each friend received 6 pencils, how many friends did Jenna buy pencils for?

1 Kent uses 8 nails to make each birdhouse. So far, he has used 24 nails. Which number sentence can be used to find the number of birdhouses he has made so far? (3-6)

A. $24 + 8 = 32$

B. $24 - 8 = 16$

C. $24 \times 8 = 192$

D. $24 \div 8 = 3$

2 Which symbol makes the number sentence true? (3-4)

$0 \div 9 \bigcirc 6 \div 6$

F. $\times$

G. $=$

H. $<$

I. $>$

3 Sierra bought 30 shells for her 6 hermit crabs. Which number sentence is NOT in the same fact family as the others? (3-3)

A. $6 \times 5 = 30$

B. $5 \times 6 = 30$

C. $30 \div 5 = 6$

D. $5 \times 30 = 150$

4 In which of the following does 7 make the number sentence true? (3-6)

F. $35 \div \blacksquare = 7$

G. $28 \div \blacksquare = 4$

H. $48 \div \blacksquare = 8$

I. $20 \div \blacksquare = 5$

5 Three friends have 27 water balloons to share equally. How many water balloons will each friend get? (3-2)

27 water balloons

| ? | ? | ? |

Water balloons each friend gets

A. 9

B. 8

C. 6

D. 3

6 Which number sentence is in the same fact family as $63 \div 9 = \blacksquare$? (3-3)

F. $63 \times 9 = \blacksquare$

G. $\blacksquare \times 9 = 63$

H. $\blacksquare - 9 = 63$

I. $9 + \blacksquare = 63$

7 Which number makes the number sentence true? (3-5)

$40 \div \blacksquare = 8$

A. 7

B. 6

C. 5

D. 4

8 Which number sentence is true? (3-4)

F. $4 \div 4 = 0$

G. $7 \div 1 = 1$

H. $2 \div 2 = 2$

I. $0 \div 8 = 0$

9 Which number makes both number sentences true? (3-7)

$4 \times \boxed{} = 32$

$32 \div 4 = \boxed{}$

A. 9

B. 8

C. 7

D. 6

10 Olivia has 48 daisies and 6 vases. Which number sentence shows how many daisies she can put in each vase if she puts the same number in each vase? (3-8)

48 daisies

?	?	?	?	?	?

↑
Daisies in each vase

F. $48 - 6 = 42$

G. $48 + 6 = 54$

H. $48 \div 6 = 8$

I. $6 \times 48 = 288$

11 Tammy made 10 friendship rings to share equally among 5 of her friends. How can she find how many rings to give each friend? (3-2)

A. Divide the number of rings by 5.

B. Add the number of rings 5 times.

C. Subtract the number of rings from 5.

D. Multiply the number of rings by 5.

12 Mrs. Warren bought 3 packages of pencils for her students. Each package had 6 pencils. Which number sentence is in this fact family? (3-3)

F. $2 \times 3 = 6$

G. $6 - 3 = 3$

H. $3 + 6 = 9$

I. $18 \div 3 = 6$

13 Mason bought a package of 20 wheels. Each model car needs 4 wheels. How many cars can he make? (3-1)

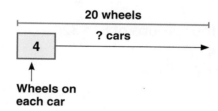

20 wheels

? cars

4

↑
Wheels on each car

14 Mr. Nessels bought 14 apples to feed his horse. He wants to give the horse the same number of apples each day for 7 days. How many apples will the horse get each day? Show your work and explain how you found the number of apples. (3-6)

THINK
SOLVE
EXPLAIN

Set A, pages 48–49, 50–51

James is placing 8 tangerines into each box. If he has a total of 32 tangerines, how many boxes can James fill?

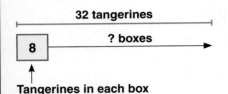

Use repeated subtraction to find the number of boxes.

$$32 - 8 = 24$$
$$24 - 8 = 16$$
$$16 - 8 = 8$$
$$8 - 8 = 0$$

Subtract 8 four times.

There are four groups of 8 in 32.
$$32 \div 8 = 4$$
So, James can fill 4 boxes.

Remember you can think about sharing equally to divide.

Use the diagram to help you divide.

1. There are 15 chairs in 3 equal groups. How many chairs are in each group?

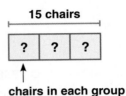

2. The soccer club has 28 balls for all the teams to share equally. If each team gets 7 balls, how many teams are there?

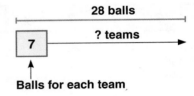

Set B, pages 52–53

Francine places 12 dolls on 3 shelves with the same number of dolls on each shelf.

shelves   dolls on each shelf

$$3 \times \boxed{} = 12 \leftarrow \text{dolls in all}$$

Use the fact family for 3, 4, and 12 to find how many dolls are on each shelf.

$$3 \times 4 = 12 \qquad 12 \div 3 = 4$$

$$4 \times 3 = 12 \qquad 12 \div 4 = 3$$

There are 4 dolls on each shelf.

Remember a fact family shows all of the related facts for a set of numbers.

Copy and complete each fact family.

1. $5 \times \boxed{} = 40$ $\boxed{} \div 5 = 8$

   $8 \times 5 = \boxed{}$ $\boxed{} \div 8 = \boxed{}$

2. $7 \times 9 = \boxed{}$ $\boxed{} \div 7 = 9$

   $9 \times \boxed{} = 63$ $63 \div \boxed{} = 7$

3. $6 \times 2 = \boxed{}$ $\boxed{} \div 6 = 2$

   $2 \times \boxed{} = 12$ $12 \div \boxed{} = 6$

Set C, pages 54–55

Find 6 ÷ 6 and 6 ÷ 1.

Any number divided by itself, except 0, is 1.
So, 6 ÷ 6 = 1.

Any number divided by 1 is that number.
So, 6 ÷ 1 = 6.

Remember zero divided by any number is zero, but you cannot divide by zero.

Compare. Use >, <, or = for each $\bigcirc$.

1. 8)8 $\bigcirc$ 3)3   **2.** 1)7 $\bigcirc$ 6)0

3. 1)7 $\bigcirc$ 1)4   **4.** 2)0 $\bigcirc$ 9)0

5. 1)8 $\bigcirc$ 1)5   **6.** 2)0 $\bigcirc$ 1)2

Set D, pages 56–57, 58–59, 60–61

Find 24 ÷ 4.

What number times 4 equals 24?

▨ × 4 = 24

6 × 4 = 24

So, 24 ÷ 4 = 6.

Find 81 ÷ 9.

What number times 9 equals 81?

▨ × 9 = 81

9 × 9 = 81

So, 81 ÷ 9 = 9.

Remember to use multiplication facts to help you divide.

Divide. Then check your answer.

1. 5)30   **2.** 2)18

3. 7)28   **4.** 9)81

5. 8)56   **6.** 8)48

Set E, pages 62–63

What do I know? Mrs. Collins has 36 pairs of scissors. She puts the same number of scissors in each of 6 drawers. How many pairs of scissors are in each drawer?

What am I being asked to find? The number of scissors in each drawer

Draw a picture.

Divide to find the number of scissors in each drawer.

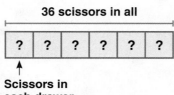

36 scissors in all

↑
Scissors in each drawer

36 ÷ 6 = ▨

36 ÷ 6 = 6

There are 6 pairs of scissors in each drawer.

Remember to draw a picture to help you write an equation.

Draw a picture and write an equation to solve.

1. Winnie buys 20 bookmarks for herself and three of her friends. Each person received the same number of bookmarks. How many bookmarks did they each receive?

Number Sense: Multiplying by One-Digit Numbers

1 The bald eagle was named the United States national emblem in 1782. About how long is the wingspan of an adult female bald eagle? You will find out in Lesson 4-5.

2 How many gallons of air does a student breathe each school day? You will find out in Lesson 4-2.

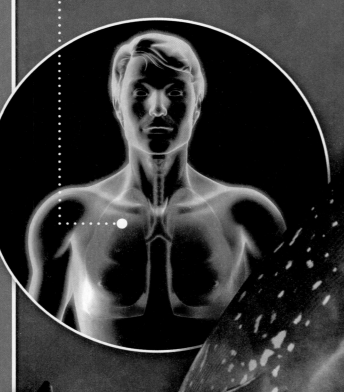

3 How long was the longest blue whale? You will find out in Lesson 4-3.

4

How many passengers can fit in 7 cabins on the London Eye Ferris Wheel? You will find out in Lesson 4-4.

Topic Essential Questions

- How can some products be found mentally?
- How can products be estimated?

Review What You Know!

Vocabulary

Choose the best term from the box.

> • multiples   • factor
> • arrays   • product

1. When you multiply numbers, you find the _?_ .

2. In the number sentence $8 \times 6 = 48$, 8 is a _?_ .

3. The numbers 5, 10, 15, and 20 are all _?_ of 5.

Multiplication Facts

Find each product.

4. 3×4 5. 7×3

6. 6×5 7. 2×8

8. 4×6 9. 9×5

10. 7×7 11. 8×9

Rounding

Round each number to the nearest ten.

12. 16   13. 82   14. 35

15. 53   16. 24   17. 49

18. 78   19. 73   20. 97

Round each number to the nearest hundred.

21. 868   22. 499   23. 625

24. 167   25. 341   26. 772

27. 919   28. 552   29. 809

30. **Writing to Explain** Explain how to round 745 to the hundreds place.

MA.4.A.1.2 Multiply multi-digit whole numbers through four digits fluently, demonstrating understanding of the standard algorithm, and checking for reasonableness of results, including solving real-world problems.

Arrays and Multiplying by 10 and 100

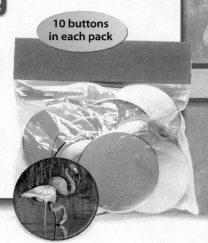

10 buttons in each pack

How can you multiply by 10 and 100?

Addition and multiplication are related.

4×5 can be written as $5 + 5 + 5 + 5$.

Use this idea to multiply by 10 and 100.

How many photo buttons can Dara make if she buys 4 packs of 10 buttons?

Guided Practice*

Do you know HOW?

In **1** and **2**, find each product.

1. 5×10

2. 1×100

Do you UNDERSTAND?

3. Which product is greater: 4×10 or 4×100? Draw a picture to show how you know.

4. How many photo buttons could Dara make if she bought five packs of 100 buttons?

Independent Practice

Leveled Practice For **5** through **8**, find each product.

5. 6×10

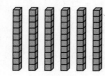

6. 3×100

7. 2×10

8. 4×100

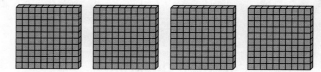

Find 4 × 10.

$4 \times 10 = 10 + 10 + 10 + 10$
$= 40$
$4 \times 10 = 40$

Dara can make 40 photo buttons.

Dara found a website that sells packs of 100 buttons. How many buttons will she have if she buys two packs of 100 buttons?

Find 2 × 100.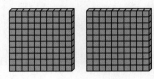

$2 \times 100 = 100 + 100$
$= 200$
$2 \times 100 = 200$

Dara will have 200 buttons.

For **9** through **12**, draw an array and find each product.

9. 9×10 **10.** 7×100 **11.** 8×10 **12.** 6×100

Problem Solving

13. Reasoning Give three whole number values for ▨ to solve the equation below.

$$▨ \times 10 = ▨ 0$$

14. Cheryl has earned $37 babysitting. She needs $65 to buy a skateboard. How much more money does Cheryl need to earn?

15. Miki has 6 bags of balloons with 8 balloons in each bag. Karen has 4 bags of balloons with 10 balloons in each bag. Who has more balloons? Explain how you know.

THINK
SOLVE
EXPLAIN

16. Luis has 4 rolls of pennies. There are 100 pennies in each roll. How many pennies does Luis have?

A 40   **C** 400

B 104   **D** 4,100

17. The sabal palm is Florida's state tree. A sabal palm leaf can be up to 12 feet long and up to 6 feet wide. How many times as long can the leaf be as it is wide?

18. Jim is counting the number of sabal palms in his neighborhood. There are six neighbors who have 10 palms each and one neighbor with 7 palms. How many total palms are in Jim's neighborhood?

The sabal palm leaf can be up to 12 feet long.

MA.4.A.1.2 Multiply
multi-digit whole numbers
through four digits
fluently, demonstrating
understanding of the
standard algorithm, and
checking for reasonableness
of results, including solving
real-world problems.

Lesson

4-2

Multiplying by Multiples of 10 and 100

What is the rule when you multiply by multiples of 10 and 100?

You can use basic multiplication facts to multiply by multiples of 10 and 100. Find 3×50.

150 in all

Guided Practice*

Do you know **HOW**?

In **1** through **6**, use basic facts to help you multiply.

1. 7×70 **2.** 2×700

3. 3×20 **4.** 9×800

5. 7×50 **6.** 8×500

Do you **UNDERSTAND**?

7. How many zeros will be in the product for 5×200? Explain how you know.

8. **Reasonableness** Peter said the product of 4×500 is 2,000. Bob said it is 200. Who is correct?

Independent Practice

Leveled Practice In **9** through **32**, find each product.

9. $3 \times 7 = \blacksquare$ **10.** $6 \times 4 = \blacksquare$ **11.** $8 \times 5 = \blacksquare$ **12.** $2 \times 8 = \blacksquare$

$3 \times 70 = \blacksquare$ $6 \times 40 = \blacksquare$ $8 \times 50 = \blacksquare$ $2 \times 80 = \blacksquare$

$3 \times 700 = \blacksquare$ $6 \times 400 = \blacksquare$ $8 \times 500 = \blacksquare$ $2 \times 800 = \blacksquare$

13. 4×20 **14.** 7×40 **15.** 70×2 **16.** 8×60 **17.** 3×40

18. 5×500 **19.** 3×600 **20.** 9×700 **21.** 600×6 **22.** 300×9

23. 5×40 **24.** 200×6 **25.** 9×50 **26.** 900×4 **27.** 80×3

28. 8×70 **29.** 2×90 **30.** 300×4 **31.** 7×600 **32.** 800×5

*For another example, see Set B on page 86.

Find 3 × 50.

Multiply by the digit in the tens place.

Multiply:
3 × 5 = 15

Write one zero after 15.

3 × 5$\underline{0}$ = 15$\underline{0}$

So, 3 × 50 = 150.

Find 3 × 500.

Multiply by the digit in the hundreds place.

Multiply:
3 × 5 = 15

Write two zeros after 15.

3 × 5$\underline{00}$ = 1,5$\underline{00}$

So, 3 × 500 = 1,500.

When the product of a basic fact ends in zero, the answer will have an extra zero.

6 × 5 = 30

6 × 50 = 300

6 × 500 = 3,000

Problem Solving

In **33** and **34**, use the table to the right.

33. Tina visited Funland with her mom and a friend. They chose Plan C. How much did they save on the two children's tickets by buying combined tickets instead of buying separate tickets?

34. Aimee's scout troop has 8 girls and 4 adults. How much did the troop pay for tickets to the amusement park?

Funland Ticket Prices		
Plans	Adult	Child
Plan A Waterpark	$30	$20
Plan B Amusement Park	$40	$30
Plan C Combined A + B	$60	$40

Data

35. **Science** A fourth grader breathes about 50 gallons of air per hour. Shana, a fourth grader, arrives at school at 8:00 A.M. and leaves at 3:00 P.M. How many gallons of air does she breathe at school?

Critical THINKING

36. Without calculating the answer, tell which has the greater product, 4 × 80 or 8 × 400. Explain how you know.

THINK SOLVE EXPLAIN

37. Last year, the fourth graders at Summit School collected 500 cans of food for the food drive. This year's fourth graders want to collect two times as many cans. How many cans do this year's fourth graders hope to collect?

  A 250 cans   **C** 1,000 cans

  B 500 cans   **D** 10,000 cans

38. Ted, Jason, and Angelina are trying to raise 200 dollars for a local shelter. Ted raised 30 dollars. Jason raised 90 dollars. How much money does Angelina need to raise in order to reach their goal?

$200		
$30	$90	?

MA.4.A.1.2 Multiply multi-digit whole numbers through four digits fluently, demonstrating understanding of the standard algorithm, and checking for reasonableness of results, including solving real-world problems.

Breaking Apart to Multiply

How can you use breaking apart to multiply with greater numbers?

A parking lot has the same number of spaces in each row. How many spaces are in the lot?

Choose an Operation Multiply to find the total for an array.

24 parking spaces in each row

4 rows

Other Example

Find 3×145.
Break apart 145 into 100, 40, and 5.

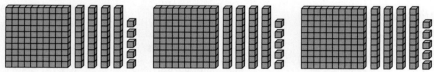

$3 \times 145 = (3 \times 100) + (3 \times 40) + (3 \times 5)$

$= 300 + 120 + 15$ Add the partial products.

$= 435$

So, $3 \times 145 = 435$.

Guided Practice*

Do you know HOW?

In **1** and **2**, copy and complete. You may use place-value blocks or drawings to help.

1. 4×36

$4 \times 30 = \blacksquare$

$4 \times 6 = \blacksquare$

$\blacksquare + \blacksquare = \blacksquare$

2. 5×127

$5 \times 100 = \blacksquare$

$5 \times 20 = \blacksquare$

$5 \times 7 = \blacksquare$

$\blacksquare + \blacksquare + \blacksquare = \blacksquare$

Do you UNDERSTAND?

3. In the parking lot example above, what two groups is the array broken into?

4. The buses at a bus garage are parked in 4 equal rows. There are 29 buses in each row. How many buses are parked at the garage?

5. Writing to Explain Why can you break apart numbers to multiply without changing the product?

Animated Glossary, eTools
www.pearsonsuccessnet.com

For another example, see Set C on page 86.

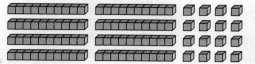

Step 1

Use an array to show 4 × 24.

Break apart 24 into 20 and 4.

Think of 4 × 24 as

(4 × 20) + (4 × 4).
      | |
     80   16

Step 2

Add each part to find the total.

$$80 + 16 = 96$$

80 and 16 are called partial products because they are parts of the product.

$4 \times 24 = 96$

There are 96 spaces in the parking lot.

Independent Practice

In **6** through **15**, find each product. You may use place-value blocks or drawings to help.

6. 3 × 19   **7.** 4 × 131   **8.** 6 × 23   **9.** 5 × 325   **10.** 2 × 254

11. 3 × 49   **12.** 6 × 27   **13.** 5 × 143   **14.** 7 × 35   **15.** 4 × 462

Problem Solving

16. Mia is buying two chairs that cost $46 each. The tax on each chair is $5. What is the total cost?

17. Walt wants to buy shelves that cost $168 each. If he has $500, can he buy three shelves? Explain.

THINK SOLVE EXPLAIN

18. Helen walked 5 miles every day for 37 days. Show breaking apart to find how many miles Helen walked in all.

19. Class A checks out 15 books from the school library each week. Class B checks out 8 fewer books than Class A each week. How many books do both Class A and Class B check out in 6 weeks?

Critical THINKING

20. **Science** The longest blue whale on record was about 18 scuba divers in length. Use breaking apart to estimate the length of the blue whale.

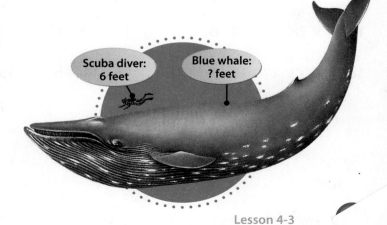

Scuba diver: 6 feet

Blue whale: ? feet

MA.4.A.1.2 Multiply multi-digit whole numbers through four digits fluently, demonstrating understanding of the standard algorithm, and checking for reasonableness of results, including solving real-world problems.

Using Mental Math to Multiply

What are some ways to multiply mentally?

Evan rode his bicycle for 18 miles each day for 3 days. How many miles did he ride his bicycle in all?

Find 3×18 mentally.

18 miles per day

DAY 1 | **DAY 2** | **DAY 3**

Guided Practice*

Do you know HOW?

In **1** through **4**, use compensation to find each product mentally.

1. 33×4 **2.** 9×83

3. 6×104 **4.** 2×394

Do you UNDERSTAND?

5. Writing to Explain Why were three groups of two subtracted instead of added in the example above?

6. Explain how to use mental math to multiply 4×56.

Independent Practice

Leveled Practice In **7** through **20**, use compensation to find each product.

7. 5×17 Substitute: $5 \times \boxed{} = 100$ Adjust: $\boxed{} - 15 = \boxed{}$

8. 3×295 Substitute: $3 \times \boxed{} = 900$ Adjust: $\boxed{} - 15 = \boxed{}$

9. 7×29 Substitute: $7 \times \boxed{} = 210$ Adjust: $210 - \boxed{} = \boxed{}$

10. 5×102 Substitute: $5 \times \boxed{} = 500$ Adjust: $500 + \boxed{} = \boxed{}$

11. 7×28 **12.** 61×8 **13.** 106×5 **14.** 64×3 **15.** 2×599

16. 4×23 **17.** 3×195 **18.** 44×6 **19.** 5×109 **20.** 9×52

DIGITAL   Animated Glossary www.pearsonsuccessnet.com

*For another example, see Set D on page 87.

Use compensation to find 3×18.

Substitute a number for 18 that is easy to multiply.

3×18

$3 \times 20 = 60$

Now adjust. Subtract 3 groups of 2.
$60 - 6 = 54$ So, $3 \times 18 = 54$.

Evan rode his bicycle 54 miles in all.

With compensation you choose numbers close to the numbers in the problem to make the computation easier and then adjust the answer for the numbers chosen.

Evan rode his bicycle 405 miles each month for 3 months. How many miles did he ride in all?

Substitute a number for 405 that is easy to multiply.

3×405

$3 \times 400 = 1,200$

Now adjust. Add 3 groups of 5.

$1,200 + 15 = 1,215$ So, $3 \times 405 = 1,215$.

Evan rode his bicycle 1,215 miles in all.

Problem Solving

For **21** and **22**, use the table to the right.

21. To raise money, the high school band members sold items shown in the table. Use mental math to find how much money the band raised in all.

Item	Cost	Number Sold
Caps	$9	36
Mugs	$7	44
Pennants	$8	52

22. How much more do 9 caps cost than 9 pennants?

23. Writing to Explain Ashley and 3 friends bought tickets to a musical. The cost of each ticket was 43 dollars. How much did the tickets cost in all? Explain how you found the answer.

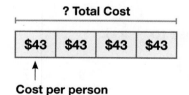

? Total Cost

| $43 | $43 | $43 | $43 |

↑
Cost per person

24. A store clerk is stacking soup cans on shelves. If he puts 110 cans on each shelf, how many cans will be on 4 shelves?

A   106

B   440

C   444

D   510

25. Using the picture at the right, how many passengers can 7 cabins hold on the London Eye Ferris Wheel?

Each cabin can hold up to 25 people.

MA.4.A.1.2 Multiply multi-digit whole numbers through four digits fluently, demonstrating understanding of the standard algorithm, and checking for reasonableness of results, including solving real-world problems.

Using Rounding to Estimate

How can you use rounding to estimate when you multiply?

Hoover School is holding a walk-a-thon. Any class that raises more than $500 earns a prize. Mr. Hector and Mrs. Alan both want to know if their class will earn a prize.

Class	Blocks Walked	Pledges per Block
Mr. Hector's	193	$4
Mrs. Alan's	115	$3

Guided Practice*

Do you know HOW?

In **1** through **8**, estimate each product.

1. 6×125

2. 39×5

3. 538×3

4. 7×314

5. 2×97

6. 4×261

7. 63×6

8. 9×48

Do you UNDERSTAND?

9. Is the estimate for Mr. Hector's class more or less than the actual answer? Explain how you know.

10. Mrs. Alan's class walked 70 more blocks. Estimate to see if her class will now get a prize.

Independent Practice

Leveled Practice In **11** through **34**, estimate each product.

11. 7×34 is close to $7 \times \blacksquare$.

12. 6×291 is close to $6 \times \blacksquare$.

13. 41×9 is close to $\blacksquare \times 9$.

14. 814×3 is close to $\blacksquare \times 3$.

15. 117×4

16. 3×86

17. 9×476

18. 34×6

19. 7×77

20. 52×9

21. 46×5

22. 3×287

23. 6×131

24. 602×9

25. 394×2

26. 77×8

27. 2×863

28. 44×8

29. 303×5

30. 486×7

31. 719×5

32. 6×609

33. 219×4

34. 54×8

*For another example, see Set E on page 87.

Mr. Hector's Class	Mrs. Alan's Class
Estimate 4 × 193 using rounding.	Estimate 3 × 115 using rounding.

Mr. Hector's Class
Estimate 4 × 193 using rounding.

$$4 \times 193$$
↓ Round 193 to 200.
$$4 \times 200 = 800$$

Mr. Hector's class raised more than 500 dollars.

His class has earned a prize.

Mrs. Alan's Class
Estimate 3 × 115 using rounding.

$$3 \times 115$$
↓ Round 115 to 100.
$$3 \times 100 = 300$$

Mrs. Alan's class has raised about 300 dollars.

This is not enough to earn a prize.

Problem Solving

35. Sam and his 2 brothers want to fly to Miami. One airline offers a round-trip fare of $319. Another airline has a round-trip fare of $389. About how much will Sam and his brothers save by buying the less expensive fare?

36. **Science** An adult female bald eagle has a wingspan that is about 7 feet long. If there are 12 inches in one foot, how long would you estimate a female bald eagle's wingspan is in inches?

37. Ellie estimates that the product of 211 and 6 is 1,800. Is this estimate reasonable? Why or why not?

THINK
SOLVE
EXPLAIN

38. **Number Sense** Which has more pencils, 3 packs with 40 pencils or 40 packs with 3 pencils? Explain.

Critical
THINKING

In **39** through **41**, use the bar graph at the right.

39. The students at Spring Elementary voted on a school mascot. Which mascot has about 4 times as many votes as the unicorn?

   A Lion   **C** Dragon

   B Owl   **D** Bear

40. Which mascot had the least number of votes?

41. **Estimation** Explain how you could estimate the number of students who voted on a school mascot. Then give your estimate.

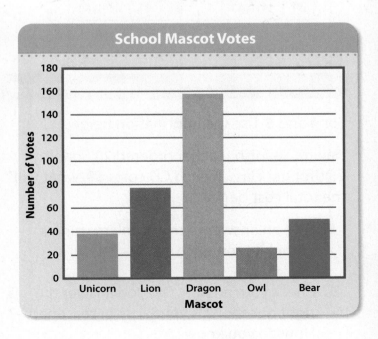

School Mascot Votes

Lesson
4-6

MA.4.A.6.6 Estimate and describe reasonableness of estimates; determine the appropriateness of an estimate versus an exact answer. Also MA.4.A.1.2

Problem Solving

Reasonableness

Karen glued sequins onto her project. She used 7 rows with 28 sequins in each row. How many sequins did Karen glue in all?

After you solve a problem, check whether your answer is reasonable. Ask yourself: Did I answer the right question? Is the calculation reasonable?

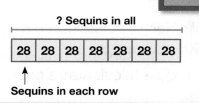

? Sequins in all

| 28 | 28 | 28 | 28 | 28 | 28 | 28 |

↑
Sequins in each row

Guided Practice*

Do you know HOW?

Solve and make an estimate to show that your answer is reasonable.

1. A fish store has 8 empty tanks. After a delivery, the store put 41 fish in each tank. How many fish were in the delivery?

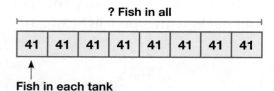

? Fish in all

| 41 | 41 | 41 | 41 | 41 | 41 | 41 | 41 |

↑
Fish in each tank

Do you UNDERSTAND?

2. How could Karen use mental math to multiply 7 and 28?

3. **Write a Problem** Write and solve a problem that would have an answer near 80. Use an estimate to show that your answer is reasonable.

Independent Practice

For **4** and **5**, use the information below.

Dawn's Spanish teacher ordered 20 Spanish CDs for her class. If each CD costs $9, what will the total cost be?

4. Give an answer to the problem using a complete sentence.

5. Check your answer. Did you answer the right question? Is your answer reasonable? How do you know?

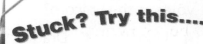

Stuck? Try this....

- What do I know?
- What diagram can I use to help understand the problem?
- Can I use addition, subtraction, multiplication, or division?
- Is all of my work correct?
- Did I answer the right question?
- Is my answer reasonable?

80   *For another example, see Set F on page 87.*

Reasonable

There were 196 sequins in all.

Estimate: 7 × 30 = 210

The answer is reasonable because 210 is close to 196.

The right question was answered and the calculation is reasonable.

Not reasonable

There were 140 sequins in all.

Estimate: 7 × 20 = 140

The answer is not reasonable because 140 is not close to 196.

The right question was answered, but the calculation is not reasonable.

For **6** through **9**, use the data table at the right and the information below.

A plane increases its height at a rate of 400 feet per second.

6. How high will the plane be after 5 seconds?

7. What number sentence can you use to solve Problem 6?

8. Did you answer the right question?

9. Is your answer reasonable? How do you know?

Elapsed Seconds	Increase in Height	Height
1 sec	400 ft	400 ft
2 sec	400 ft	800 ft
3 sec	400 ft	1,200 ft
4 sec	400 ft	1,600 ft
5 sec	400 ft	
6 sec	400 ft	2,400 ft

For **10** through **12**, use the data table at the right.

10. About how much money does an American family spend in 8 weeks to feed a child who is 11 years old?

11. In four weeks, about how much more money does a family spend to feed a child who is 8 years old than a child who is 3 years old?

12. Is your answer for Problem 11 reasonable? How do you know?

Money Spent by an American Family to Feed a Child	
Age of Child	Weekly Amount
1–2 years	$27
3–5 years	$31
6–8 years	$42
9–11 years	$49

For **13** through **16**, use the chart at the right.

13. How many stickers does Mr. Richardson have on rolls?

Mr. Richardson's Stickers

On sheets	♥ ♥ ♥
On rolls	♥ ♥ ♥ ♥
In boxes	♥

Each ♥ = 10 stickers

14. How many more stickers on sheets does Mr. Richardson have than stickers in boxes?

15. Is your calculation for Problem 14 reasonable? How do you know?

16. How many stickers does Mr. Richardson have in all?

For **17** through **20**, use the chart at the right.

17. How many miles does a police officer walk in 4 weeks?

Kind of Job	Distance Walked in 1 Week
Doctor	16 miles
Mail carrier	21 miles
Nurse	18 miles
Police officer	32 miles

18. How many miles does a nurse walk in 6 weeks?

19. How many miles does a mail carrier walk in 7 weeks?

20. How many miles does a doctor walk in 3 weeks?

Think About the Process

21. Which of the following uses the Distributive Property to solve 4×9?

Critical THINKING

A $4 \times 9 = (3 \times 3) + (1 \times 6)$

B $4 \times 9 = (4 \times 9) + (4 \times 9)$

C $4 \times 9 = (2 \times 9) + (2 \times 9)$

D $4 \times 9 = (2 \times 3) + (2 \times 6)$

22. Which of the following correctly uses compensation to solve 2×38?

F (2×40) and $80 - 2$

G (2×30) and $60 + 8$

H (2×40) and $80 - 4$

I (2×40) and $80 + 4$

Multiplying with Mental Math

Use 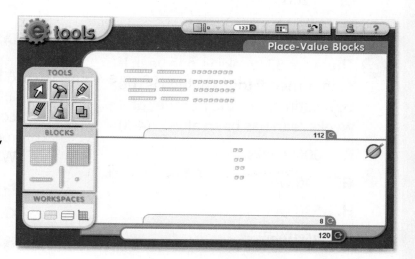 **e tools** Place-Value Blocks.

Explain how to use compensation to find 4 × 28.

Step 1 Go to the Place-Value Blocks eTool. Select the two-part workspace. 30 is the closest number to 28 that is easy to multiply. Click on the horizontal long block. Then click in the top workspace to show 4 rows with 3 longs in each row, or 4 × 30.

Step 2 Click on the hammer tool icon. Then click on the last long in each row to break each into ten ones. Use the arrow tool to select two ones from the first group, and move them to the bottom workspace. Do the same for the last two ones in each row.

To find 4 × 28, find 4 × 30 = 120 and subtract 4 × 2 = 8.

So, 120 − 8 = 112.

Practice

Use compensation to find each product mentally.

1. 3 × 19	**2.** 4 × 499	**3.** 2 × 67	**4.** 6 × 29
5. 4 × 38	**6.** 3 × 47	**7.** 3 × 29	**8.** 4 × 899
9. 2 × 49	**10.** 3 × 58	**11.** 4 × 109	**12.** 2 × 39
13. 3 × 107	**14.** 3 × 28	**15.** 4 × 47	**16.** 2 × 48
17. 4 × 37	**18.** 4 × 48	**19.** 3 × 57	**20.** 3 × 198
21. 2 × 47	**22.** 3 × 402	**23.** 4 × 67	**24.** 4 × 58

1 Mrs. Ortiz can make 50 tortillas out of one batch of dough. If she makes 4 batches of dough, how many tortillas can she make? (4-2)

A.   8

B.   20

C.   200

D.   2,000

2 There are 52 weeks in one year. If Jean turned 9 today, which is the best estimate of the number of weeks Jean has been alive? (4-5)

F.   600 weeks

G.   540 weeks

H.   530 weeks

I.   450 weeks

3 Which shows one way to use breaking apart to find 7×32? (4-3)

A. $(7 \times 30) + (7 \times 2)$

B. $(7 \times 30) - (5 \times 2)$

C. $(2 \times 30) + (3 \times 2)$

D. 30×7

4 A factory produces 295 cars in one week. How many cars does the factory produce in 4 weeks? (4-4)

F.   885

G.   1,180

H.   1,200

I.   1,220

5 Which shows another way to find $10 + 10 + 10$? (4-1)

A. $10 \times 10 \times 10$

B. 3×100

C. 3×10

D. 3×1

6 A bike loop is 8 miles long. Ed rode around the loop 18 times. He used compensation to find how far he rode. First, he multiplied $20 \times 8 = 160$. What should Ed do next? (4-4)

F. $160 + 8 = 168$

G. $160 - 8 = 152$

H. $160 + 16 = 176$

I. $160 - 16 = 144$

7 Susanna's school has 5 grades with an average of 48 students in each grade. Which is a reasonable number of students in Susanna's school? (4-6)

A. 205, because 5×48 is about $5 \times 40 = 200$

B. 240, because 5×48 is about $5 \times 50 = 250$

C. 285, because 5×48 is about $5 \times 60 = 300$

D. 315, because 5×48 is about $6 \times 50 = 300$

8 Ivan gets $22 a month for completing his chores. Which is the best estimate for the amount of money Ivan would have, if he saved all the money for 6 months? (4-5)

  F. $200

  G. $180

  H. $120

  I. $100

9 Which shows another way to find 100 + 100 + 100 + 100? (4-1)

  A. 4×1

  B. 4×10

  C. 4×100

  D. $100 \times 100 \times 100 \times 100$

10 Mrs. Henderson bought 4 boxes of facial tissues. Each box has 174 tissues. Which number sentence shows the best way to use rounding to estimate the total number of tissues? (4-5)

  F. $4 \times 200 = 800$

  G. $4 \times 100 = 400$

  H. $4 + 200 = 204$

  I. $4 + 100 = 104$

11 Which shows how to use breaking apart to find 5×17? (4-3)

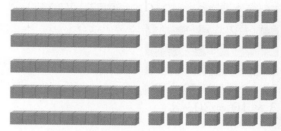

  A. $(5 \times 1) + (5 \times 7)$

  B. $(5 \times 10) - (5 \times 1)$

  C. $(5 \times 10) + (5 \times 7)$

  D. 5×15

12 Ali ran for 19 minutes 7 days in a row. How many minutes did Ali run? (4-4)

  F. 175 minutes

  G. 147 minutes

  H. 140 minutes

  I. 133 minutes

13 A gallon of paint can cover about 400 square feet of wall space. About how many square feet of wall space will 3 gallons cover? (4-2)

14 Nia has 5 piles of paper clips. There are 79 paper clips in each pile. She says she has 3,995 paper clips in all. Is her answer reasonable? Explain why or why not. (4-6)

THINK
SOLVE
EXPLAIN

Set A, pages 70–71

Use arrays to multiply by 10 and 100.

Find 3 × 10.

3 × 10 = 10 + 10 + 10

3 × 10 = 30

Find 3 × 100.

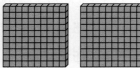

3 × 100 = 100 + 100 + 100

3 × 100 = 300

Remember you can think of multiplication as repeated addition.

Find the product.

1. 5 × 10	**2.** 2 × 100
3. 6 × 100	**4.** 4 × 10
5. 7 × 10	**6.** 8 × 100
7. 9 × 100	**8.** 8 × 10

Set B, pages 72–73

Use basic multiplication facts to multiply by multiples of 10 and 100.

Find 4 × 60.   Find 4 × 600.

Multiply 4 × 6 = 24.   Multiply 4 × 6 = 24.

Write one zero after 24. Write two zeros after 24.

4 × 60 = 240   4 × 600 = 2,400

Remember when the product of a basic fact ends in zero, the answer will have an extra zero.

Find the product.

1. 8 × 60	**2.** 3 × 40
3. 6 × 50	**4.** 5 × 300
5. 700 × 4	**6.** 2 × 900
7. 80 × 8	**8.** 400 × 5

Set C, pages 74–75

Use breaking apart to find 2 × 123.

Think of 123 as 100 + 20 + 3.

2 × 123 = (2 × 100) + (2 × 20) + (2 × 3)

            = 200 + 40 + 6

            = 246

Remember you can use place-value blocks or drawings to help you multiply.

Find the product.

1. 4 × 73	**2.** 2 × 59
3. 6 × 135	**4.** 3 × 281
5. 7 × 25	**6.** 5 × 146
7. 8 × 42	**8.** 5 × 354

Set D, pages 76–77

Use compensation to find 2 × 297.

First substitute 300 for 297 and find
2 × 300 = 600.

Then adjust by subtracting 2 groups of 3.

600 − 6 = 594

So, 2 × 297 = 594.

Remember to check your answers for reasonableness.

Find the product.

1. 6 × 13　　　**2.** 3 × 46

3. 5 × 397　　**4.** 6 × 72

5. 6 × 203　　**6.** 4 × 499

Set E, pages 78–79

Use rounding to estimate 9 × 83.

Round 83 to 80.

9 × 83

9 × 80 = 720

So, 9 × 83 is about 720.

Remember to round a two-digit number to the nearest ten and a three-digit number to the nearest hundred.

Estimate each product.

1. 8 × 76　　　**2.** 493 × 3

3. 96 × 5　　　**4.** 678 × 6

5. 707 × 4　　　**6.** 57 × 3

Set F, pages 80–82

Ty wants to buy 100 roses to make centerpieces. He will use 5 roses in each of 11 vases. Is the number of roses he wants to buy reasonable?

What do I know? Ty wants to buy 100 roses.

He will use 5 roses in each of 11 vases.

What am I asked to find? Is it reasonable for Ty to buy 100 roses?

Estimate to determine reasonableness.

11 rounds to 10, and 10 × 5 = 50.

50 is not close to 100, so the number of roses Ty wants to buy is not reasonable.

Remember to use rounding to estimate.

Solve.

1. Mitch earned $88 delivering newspapers. He worked for 11 hours and earned $8 an hour. Is the amount Mitch earned reasonable? Explain.

2. Joan needs 9 packs of envelopes and each pack costs $4. She estimates that she will spend a total of $72 on envelopes. Is that estimate reasonable? Explain.

Developing Fluency: Multiplying by One-Digit Numbers

1 How many years were in one full cycle of the Aztec calendar? You will find out in Lesson 5-2.

2 How many miles long is the Appalachian Trail? You will find out in Lesson 5-5.

Vocabulary

Choose the best term from the box.

> • product • factor
> • array • rounding

1. You multiply numbers to find a __?__.

2. A(n) __?__ shows the number of objects in rows and columns.

3. When you estimate to the nearest 10 or 100, you may use __?__.

3 How far can a jerboa jump? You will find out in Lesson 5-1.

4 A memory card can be used to store images. What year was the first memory card sold? You will find out in Lesson 5-6.

Multiplication Facts

Find each product.

4. 4×8 5. 2×9

6. 9×5 7. 6×8

8. 6×4 9. 6×6

10. 8×5 11. 9×9

Rounding

Round each number to the nearest hundred.

12. 164   13. 8,263   14. 351

15. 527   16. 2,498   17. 9,634

18. 7,892   19. 472   20. 119

Round each number to the nearest thousand.

21. 8,685   22. 4,991   23. 62,549

24. 167,241   25. 77,268   26. 34,162

27. 1,372   28. 9,009   29. 919,263

30. **Writing to Explain** Explain how to round 625,608,149 to the millions place.

Topic Essential Questions

• How can arrays be used to find products?

• What is a standard procedure for multiplying multi-digit numbers?

MA.4.A.1.2 Multiply multi-digit whole numbers through four digits fluently, demonstrating understanding of the standard algorithm, and checking for reasonableness of results, including solving real-world problems.

Arrays and Using an Expanded Algorithm

Hands-On
place-value blocks

How can you record multiplication?

A store ordered 2 boxes of video games. How many games did the store order?

Choose an Operation Multiply to join equal groups.

Each box contains 16 video games.

Another Example How do you record multiplication when the product has three digits?

Gene played his new video game 23 times each day for 5 days. How many times did he play his video game in 5 days?

   A   18

   B   28

   C   115

   D   145

Choose an Operation Since 5 equal groups of 23 are being joined, you will multiply. Find 5×23.

What You Show

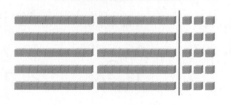

What You Write

$$
\begin{array}{r}
23 \\
\times \quad 5 \\
\hline
15 \\
+ \ 100 \\
\hline
115
\end{array}
$$

Gene played his video game 115 times in 5 days. The correct choice is **C**.

Explain It

1. Explain how the partial products, 15 and 100, were found in the work above.

2. Reasonableness How can an estimate help you eliminate choices above?

Build an array to show 2×16.

$2 \times 10 = 20$ $2 \times 6 = 12$

$20 + 12 = \mathbf{32}$

What You Write

Here is one way to record multiplication.

$$
\begin{array}{r}
16 \\
\times\ \ 2 \\
\hline
12 \quad \leftarrow \text{Partial} \\
+\ 20 \quad \leftarrow \text{Products} \\
\hline
32
\end{array}
$$

The store ordered 32 games.

Guided Practice*

Do you know HOW?

In **1** and **2**, use place-value blocks or draw pictures to build an array for each. Copy and complete the calculation.

1. $2 \times 34 =$ 🔲

$$
\begin{array}{r}
34 \\
\times\ \ 2 \\
\hline
 \\
+\ \\
\hline

\end{array}
$$

2. $3 \times 18 =$ 🔲

$$
\begin{array}{r}
18 \\
\times\ \ 3 \\
\hline
 \\
+\ \\
\hline

\end{array}
$$

Do you UNDERSTAND?

Use the array and the calculation shown for Problem 3.

$$
\begin{array}{r}
14 \\
\times\ \ 3 \\
\hline
12 \\
+\ 30 \\
\hline
42
\end{array}
$$

3. What calculation was used to give the partial product 12? 30?

Independent Practice

Leveled Practice In **4** and **5**, use place-value blocks or draw pictures to build an array for each. Copy and complete the calculation.

4.

$$
\begin{array}{r}
27 \\
\times\ \ 3 \\
\hline
 \\
+\ \\
\hline

\end{array}
$$

5.

$$
\begin{array}{r}
22 \\
\times\ \ 4 \\
\hline
 \\
+\ \\
\hline

\end{array}
$$

eTools
www.pearsonsuccessnet.com

Leveled Practice In **6** through **15**, copy and complete the calculation. Draw a picture to help.

6. 26
× 5

+

7. 19
× 3

+

8. 24
× 2

+

9. 21
× 4

+

10. 24
× 3

+

11. 22
× 8

12. 17
× 3

13. 24
× 8

14. 16
× 5

15. 23
× 7

Problem Solving

Use the table at the right for **16** and **17**.

16. Estimation Emma wants to put 3 smiley stickers on each of her note cards. Use estimation to decide if one roll of smileys has enough stickers for 42 note cards.

17. How many more stickers are in 3 rolls of dog stickers than in 3 rolls of star stickers?

A	50	C	100
B	75	D	150

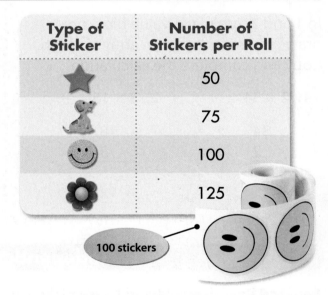

Type of Sticker	Number of Stickers per Roll
⭐	50
🐕	75
🙂	100
🌸	125

100 stickers

18. Large tables in the library have 8 chairs and small tables have 4 chairs. How many students can sit at 3 large tables and 5 small tables if each seat is filled?

F	20 students	H	44 students
G	36 students	I	52 students

19. Writing to Explain Tim called 3 × 20 and 3 × 4 *simple calculations*. Explain what he meant.

Critical THINKING

20. **Science** A jerboa can jump 25 times its body length. How many inches can this jerboa jump?

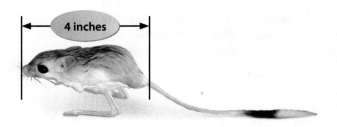

4 inches

Find the product.

1. 7×2 **2.** 4×5 **3.** 6×8 **4.** 9×7

5. 4×8 **6.** 0×1 **7.** 3×6 **8.** 8×8

9. 3×3 **10.** 6×7 **11.** 5×7 **12.** 9×4

Find the quotient.

13. $81 \div 9$ **14.** $4\overline{)12}$ **15.** $56 \div 7$ **16.** $2\overline{)10}$ **17.** $54 \div 6$

18. $5\overline{)20}$ **19.** $0 \div 8$ **20.** $3\overline{)21}$ **21.** $24 \div 6$ **22.** $9\overline{)27}$

23. $63 \div 9$ **24.** $8\overline{)64}$ **25.** $18 \div 3$ **26.** $5\overline{)5}$ **27.** $81 \div 9$

Error Search Find each product or quotient that is not correct. Write it correctly and explain the error.

28. $8 \div 1 = 8$ **29.** $4 \times 4 = 16$ **30.** $0 \div 5 = 5$ **31.** $9 \times 6 = 53$

32. $12 \div 2 = 6$ **33.** $25 \div 5 = 5$ **34.** $5 \times 3 = 15$ **35.** $24 \div 3 = 6$

36. $7 \times 7 = 42$ **37.** $18 \div 2 = 8$ **38.** $12 \div 6 = 2$ **39.** $28 \div 7 = 4$

Number Sense

Estimating and Reasoning Write whether each statement is true or false. Explain your answer.

40. The product of 1 and 34,654 is 34,654.

41. The quotient of 8 divided by 0 is not possible.

42. The sum of 52,128 and 21,179 is less than 70,000.

43. The difference of $8{,}853 - 1{,}978$ is greater than 8,000.

44. The product of 2 and a number will always be even.

45. The product of 6 and 7 is 6 less than 36.

MA.4.A.1.2 Multiply multi-digit whole numbers through four digits fluently, demonstrating understanding of the standard algorithm, and checking for reasonableness of results, including solving real-world problems.

Connecting the Expanded and Standard Algorithms

What is a common way to record multiplication?

A small school bus holds 24 passengers. A small jet holds 4 times as many passengers. How many passengers does the small jet hold?

Find 4×24.

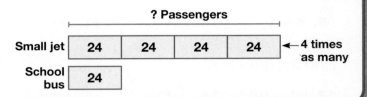

Guided Practice*

Do you know HOW?

In **1** through **6**, find each product two ways. First use the expanded algorithm, and then use the standard algorithm.

1. 5×17

2. 3×43

3. 4×56

4. 6×62

5.
$$\begin{array}{r} 29 \\ \times\ 3 \\ \hline \end{array}$$

6.
$$\begin{array}{r} 88 \\ \times\ 2 \\ \hline \end{array}$$

Do you UNDERSTAND?

7. Mara used the expanded algorithm shown to the right. Is she correct? Explain.

$$\begin{array}{r} 24 \\ \times\ 4 \\ \hline 80 \\ +\ 16 \\ \hline 96 \end{array}$$

8. A ferry can carry 16 cars. How many cars can the ferry carry in 5 trips?

Independent Practice

In **9** through **24**, find each product. Use either method.

9. 6×38

10. 4×47

11. 8×42

12. 5×64

13. 7×26

14. 9×33

15. 2×76

16. 4×29

17.
$$\begin{array}{r} 17 \\ \times\ 9 \\ \hline \end{array}$$

18.
$$\begin{array}{r} 61 \\ \times\ 3 \\ \hline \end{array}$$

19.
$$\begin{array}{r} 45 \\ \times\ 7 \\ \hline \end{array}$$

20.
$$\begin{array}{r} 83 \\ \times\ 5 \\ \hline \end{array}$$

21.
$$\begin{array}{r} 23 \\ \times\ 5 \\ \hline \end{array}$$

22.
$$\begin{array}{r} 18 \\ \times\ 8 \\ \hline \end{array}$$

23.
$$\begin{array}{r} 53 \\ \times\ 3 \\ \hline \end{array}$$

24.
$$\begin{array}{r} 37 \\ \times\ 7 \\ \hline \end{array}$$

For another example, see Set A on page 112.

Expanded Algorithm

Find the partial products.

```
   24
 ×  4
 ─────
   16  ←—— Partial
 + 80  ←—— Products
 ─────
   96
```

The jet can hold 96 passengers.

Standard Algorithm

First, multiply the ones. Regroup if needed.

```
   1
   24      4 × 4 ones = 16 ones
 ×  4      Regroup 16 ones
 ─────     as 1 ten 6 ones.
    6
```

Then, multiply the tens. Add any extra tens.

```
   1
   24      4 × 2 tens = 8 tens
 ×  4      There is 1 extra ten.
 ─────     8 tens + 1 ten = 9 tens
   96
```

The jet can hold 96 passengers.

Problem Solving

25. A speedboat holds 12 adults and 6 children. How many people in all can go on 4 speedboat rides?

26. Number Sense Vera created a large design using 68 tiles. If she doubles her design and then doubles it again, how many tiles will she use in all?

Critical THINKING

27. Estimation In 2008, a Florida surfer set a world record for stand up paddle surfing. In 24 hours, he paddled 49 miles. About how far did he go each hour?

28. Luis recycles aluminum cans. His goal was to recycle 10,000 cans by May 1. He recycled 3,789 cans in March and 5,068 cans in April. How many cans is Luis over or under his goal? Explain how you found your answer.

THINK SOLVE EXPLAIN

29. 🌐 **Social Studies** In the Aztec calendar, each year has a number from 1 to 13. It also has one of four signs: house, rabbit, reed, or flint. It takes 4 × 13 years to go through one complete cycle of years. How many years are in one cycle?

30. Belle used 286 pages of newspaper to make a volcano of papier-mâché. What is this number rounded to the nearest hundred?

A 200   **C** 290

B 280   **D** 300

31. 🔍 **Science** Eucalyptus trees grow in Southern Florida. How much taller would a fast-growing eucalyptus tree be after 7 years?

A fast-growing eucalyptus can grow about 11 feet each year.

MA.4.A.1.2 Multiply multi-digit whole numbers through four digits fluently, demonstrating understanding of the standard algorithm, and checking for reasonableness of results, including solving real-world problems.

Multiplying 2-Digit by 1-Digit Numbers

What is a common way to record multiplication?

How many T-shirts with the saying, *and your point is...* are in 3 boxes?

Choose an Operation Multiply to join equal groups.

Saying on T-shirt	Number of T-shirts per Box
Trust Me	30 T-shirts
and your point is...	26 T-shirts
I'm the princess that's why	24 T-shirts
Because I said so	12 T-shirts

Another Example Does the common way to record multiplication work for larger products?

Mrs. Stockton ordered 8 boxes of T-shirts with the saying, *I'm the princess that's why*. How many of the T-shirts did she order?

Choose an Operation Since you are joining 8 groups of 24, you will multiply. Find 8×24.

Step 1 Multiply the ones. Regroup if necessary.

$$\begin{array}{r} 3 \\ 24 \\ \times\ \ 8 \\ \hline 2 \end{array}$$

$8 \times 4 = 32$ ones
Regroup 32 ones as 3 tens 2 ones.

Step 2 Multiply the tens. Add any extra tens.

$$\begin{array}{r} 3 \\ 24 \\ \times\ \ 8 \\ \hline 192 \end{array}$$

8×2 tens $= 16$ tens
16 tens + 3 tens $= 19$ tens
or 1 hundred 9 tens

Mrs. Stockton ordered 192 T-shirts.

Explain It

1. **Reasonableness** How can you use estimation to decide if 192 is a reasonable answer?

2. In the example above, do you multiply 8×2 or 8×20? Explain.

Step 1

Multiply the ones.
Regroup if needed.

$$
\begin{array}{r}
{\scriptstyle 1} \\
26 \\
\times \quad 3 \\
\hline
8
\end{array}
$$

Step 2

Multiply the tens.
Add any extra tens.

$$
\begin{array}{r}
{\scriptstyle 1} \\
26 \\
\times \quad 3 \\
\hline
78
\end{array}
$$

There are 78 T-shirts
in 3 boxes.

Step 3

Estimate to check
reasonableness.

3×26 is about
$3 \times 30 = 90$

The answer is
reasonable
because 78
is close to 90.

Guided Practice*

Do you know HOW?

In **1** through **8**, find each product.
Estimate to check reasonableness.

1. $\quad 15 \\ \underline{\times \ 5}$
2. $\quad 28 \\ \underline{\times \ 3}$

3. $\quad 34 \\ \underline{\times \ 7}$
4. $\quad 43 \\ \underline{\times \ 4}$

5. 5×70
6. 5×78

7. 3×24
8. 3×79

Do you UNDERSTAND?

9. Explain how you would estimate the answer in Exercise 3.

10. Carrie bought 8 boxes of T-shirts with the saying *Because I said so.* How many T-shirts did Carrie buy?

11. Writing to Explain Explain how the answer to Exercise 5 can be used to find the answer to Exercise 6.

Independent Practice

In **12** through **19**, find each product.
Estimate to check reasonableness.

12. $\quad 12 \\ \underline{\times \ 6}$
13. $\quad 18 \\ \underline{\times \ 7}$
14. $\quad 72 \\ \underline{\times \ 5}$
15. $\quad 49 \\ \underline{\times \ 8}$

16. $\quad 31 \\ \underline{\times \ 4}$
17. $\quad 52 \\ \underline{\times \ 6}$
18. $\quad 79 \\ \underline{\times \ 7}$
19. $\quad 87 \\ \underline{\times \ 7}$

In **20** through **27**, find each product.
Estimate to check reasonableness.

20. 9×23 **21.** 6×51 **22.** 4×29 **23.** 8×42

24. 3×64 **25.** 5×56 **26.** 6×83 **27.** 4×47

Problem Solving

28. Use the diagram to the right. How many floors does the Purple-Tower Hotel have?

   A 60   **B** 70   **C** 105   **D** 1,010

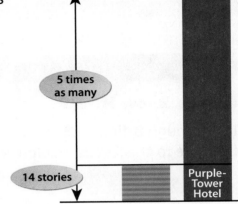

29. Estimation It takes 286 rolls of tape to make a car sculpture out of boxes. What is this number rounded to the nearest hundred?

   F 200   **H** 300

   G 280   **I** 380

30. **Think About the Process** Katie made 24 rag dolls. She gave away 8 of them as gifts. Which expression gives the number of rag dolls Katie had left?

   A $24 + 8$ **C** $24 - 8$

   B 24×8 **D** $24 \div 8$

31. A skateboard speed record of almost 63 miles per hour (about 92 feet per second) was set in 1998. At that speed, about how many feet would the skateboarder travel in 6 seconds?

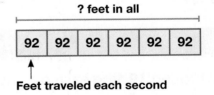

For **32** and **33**, use the table to the right.

32. What is the average length fingernails will grow in one year?

   F 60 mm   **H** 40 mm

   G 50 mm   **I** 5 mm

Average Rate of Growth in Millimeters per Month	
Fingernails	5 mm
Hair	12 mm

33. How much longer will hair grow in six months than fingernails will grow in six months?

Algebra Connections

Multiplication and Number Sentences

Remember that a number sentence has two numbers or expressions connected by <, >, or =. Estimation or reasoning can help you tell if the left side or right side is greater.

Copy and complete. Write <, >, or = in the circle. Check your answers.

Example: 7 × 52 ◯ 7 × 60

Think *Is 7 groups of 52 more than 7 groups of 60?*

Since 52 is less than 60, the left side is less. Write "<".

7 × 52 ⊙ 7 × 60

 Remember

> is greater than   < is less than   = is equal to

1. 5 × 71 ◯ 5 × 70   **2.** 8 × 30 ◯ 8 × 35   **3.** 2 × 90 ◯ 89 + 89

4. 4 × 56 ◯ 200   **5.** 6 × 37 ◯ 37 × 6   **6.** 190 ◯ 9 × 25

7. 3 × 33 ◯ 100   **8.** 80 ◯ 4 × 19   **9.** 10 × 10 ◯ 9 × 8

10. 1 × 67 ◯ 1 + 67   **11.** 2 + 34 ◯ 2 × 34   **12.** 6 × 18 ◯ 7 × 20

For **13** and **14**, copy and complete the number sentence below each problem. Use it to help explain your answer.

13. A red tray holds 7 rows of oranges with 8 oranges in each row. A blue tray holds 8 rows of oranges with 5 oranges in each row. Which tray holds more oranges?

____ × ____ ◯ ____ × ____

14. Look at the hats below. Mr. Fox bought 2 brown hats. Mrs. Lee bought 3 green hats. Who paid more for their hats?

____ × ____ ◯ ____ × ____

15. Write a Problem Write a problem using the hats at the right.

$60 $30 $10 $40

MA.4.A.1.1 Use and describe various models for multiplication in problem-solving situations, and demonstrate recall of basic multiplication and related division facts with ease.

Problem Solving

Try, Check, and Revise

Wilma bought supplies for her dog at the pet store. She spent a total of $27 not including tax. She bought two of one item in the chart and one other item. What did she buy?

Dog Toy: $8

Dog Supplies	
Leash	$12
Collar	$6
Bowl	$7
Medium Bed	$15
Toy	$8

Guided Practice*

Do you know HOW?

Use Try, Check, and Revise to solve this problem. Write the answer in a complete sentence.

1. Annie and Matt spent a total of $29 on a gift. Annie spent $7 more than Matt. How much did each spend?

Do you UNDERSTAND?

2. How do you know that two beds cost too much?

3. **Write a Problem** Write a problem using the Try, Check, and Revise strategy.

Independent Practice

Use Try, Check, and Revise to solve the problems. Write the answer in a complete sentence.

4. Lana's mom brought 27 cartons of orange juice and grape juice to the park. There were twice as many cartons of orange juice as there were of grape juice. How many of each kind did she bring?

5. In football, a team can score 2, 3, 6, 7, or 8 points. The Terriers scored 3 times and had 19 points. How did they score their points?

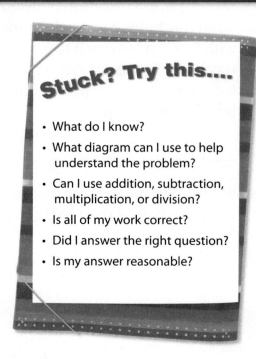

Stuck? Try this....

- What do I know?
- What diagram can I use to help understand the problem?
- Can I use addition, subtraction, multiplication, or division?
- Is all of my work correct?
- Did I answer the right question?
- Is my answer reasonable?

Make a reasonable first try.

Two beds cost too much.

Try one bed. Then try two of the smaller priced items, like the toy.

Check using the information given in the problem.

2 × $8 = $16

$16 + $15 = $31

That's too high, but it is close.

Revise. Use your first try to make a reasonable second try.

The first try was $4 too high. If you keep the bed, you need to come down $4 total or $2 for each item.

Try two collars.

2 × $6 = $12

$12 + $15 = $27

Wilma bought two collars and one medium bed.

For **6** through **8**, use the data at the right.

6. Trent spent $16, before tax, at Fun Town. He bought 3 different items. What did he buy?

7. Alicia spent $14, before tax, on 3 items at Fun Town. Two of her three items were the same. What did she buy?

8. Rich spent $32, before tax, at Fun Town. He bought two of one item and two of another item. What did Rich buy?

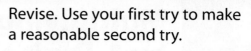

Fun Town	
Jump Rope	$2
Skateboard	$26
Basketball	$9
Football	$6
Baseball	$5
Bat	$10

9. Mr. Mill took all of the tires off the old bicycles and tricycles in his garage. He got 12 tires off 5 cycles. How many of each type of cycle did he have?

10. Linda earned $8 per hour and Susan earned $10 per hour. Linda and Susan worked the same number of hours. Linda earned $72. How much did Susan earn?

11. If Chuck's Sports sold 12 fishing poles each week, how many fishing poles would be sold in four weeks?

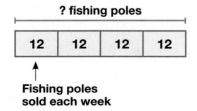

? fishing poles

| 12 | 12 | 12 | 12 |

Fishing poles sold each week

12. Tennessee has 53 state parks. Florida has 3 times as many state parks as Tennessee. How many state parks does Florida have?

A 24   **C** 115

B 105   **D** 159

MA.4.A.1.2 Multiply multi-digit whole numbers through four digits fluently, demonstrating understanding of the standard algorithm, and checking for reasonableness of results, including solving real-world problems.

Multiplying 3- and 4-Digit by 1-Digit Numbers

How do you multiply larger numbers?

Juan guessed that the large bottle had 3 times as many pennies as the small bottle. What was Juan's guess?

Choose an Operation Multiply to find "3 times as many."

264 pennies

Other Example

Find $3 \times 2{,}746$.

Step 1

Multiply the ones. Regroup if necessary.

$$\begin{array}{r} 1 \\ 2{,}746 \\ \times 3 \\ \hline 8 \end{array}$$

Step 2

Multiply the tens. Add any extra tens. Regroup if necessary.

$$\begin{array}{r} 1\,1 \\ 2{,}746 \\ \times 3 \\ \hline 38 \end{array}$$

Step 3

Multiply the hundreds. Add any extra hundreds. Regroup if necessary.

$$\begin{array}{r} 2\,1\,1 \\ 2{,}746 \\ \times 3 \\ \hline 238 \end{array}$$

Step 4

Multiply the thousands. Add any extra thousands. Regroup if necessary.

$$\begin{array}{r} 2\,1\,1 \\ 2{,}746 \\ \times 3 \\ \hline 8{,}238 \end{array}$$

Guided Practice*

Do you know HOW?

In **1** and **2**, find each product. Estimate to check for reasonableness.

1. $\begin{array}{r} 519 \\ \times \quad 4 \\ \hline \end{array}$

2. $\begin{array}{r} 3{,}378 \\ \times \quad 2 \\ \hline \end{array}$

Do you UNDERSTAND?

3. Number Sense In the example at the top, 3×6 tens is how many tens?

4. A band performed 4 sold-out shows. All 2,428 seats in the theater were filled for each show. How many fans saw the 4 shows?

Independent Practice

In **5** through **12**, find each product. Estimate to check reasonableness.

5. $\begin{array}{r} 423 \\ \times \quad 2 \\ \hline \end{array}$

6. $\begin{array}{r} 3{,}942 \\ \times \quad 4 \\ \hline \end{array}$

7. $\begin{array}{r} 6{,}271 \\ \times \quad 3 \\ \hline \end{array}$

8. $\begin{array}{r} 159 \\ \times \quad 5 \\ \hline \end{array}$

9. 2×125

10. $3 \times 3{,}196$

11. 4×265

12. $5 \times 4{,}129$

Step 1	**Step 2**	**Step 3**

Step 1

Multiply the ones. Regroup if needed.

$$\begin{array}{r} \overset{1}{26}4 \\ \times \quad 3 \\ \hline 2 \end{array}$$

3 × 4 ones = 12 ones or 1 ten 2 ones

Step 2

Multiply the tens. Add any extra tens. Regroup if needed.

$$\begin{array}{r} \overset{1\ 1}{26}4 \\ \times \quad 3 \\ \hline 92 \end{array}$$

(3 × 6 tens) + 1 ten = 19 tens or 1 hundred 9 tens

Step 3

Multiply the hundreds. Add any extra hundreds.

$$\begin{array}{r} \overset{1\ 1}{26}4 \\ \times \quad 3 \\ \hline 792 \end{array}$$

(3 × 2 hundreds) + 1 hundred = 7 hundreds

Juan's guess was 792 pennies.

Problem Solving

In **13** through **15**, find the weight of the animal.

13. Horse **14.** Rhino **15.** Elephant

Bear: Weighs 836 pounds

Horse: Weighs 2 times as much as the bear

Rhino: Weighs 5 times as much as the bear

Elephant: Weighs 9 times as much as the bear

Use the table a the right for **16** and **17**.

16. Estimation About how much did Dr. Sims spend if he bought 3 flat-screen TVs for his office?

Electronics Sale	
Digital Camera	$295
Laptop Computer	$1,075
Flat-Screen TV	$1,650

17. Number Sense Which costs more—2 laptop computers or 4 digital cameras? Use number sense to decide.

Critical THINKING

18. 🌐 **Social Studies** The Appalachian Trail is 2,174 miles long. If Andy hiked the entire trail one time, how many miles did he hike?

A 1 mile   **B** 1,087 miles   **C** 2,174 miles   **D** 4,348 miles

MA.4.A.1.2 Multiply multi-digit whole numbers through four digits fluently, demonstrating understanding of the standard algorithm, and checking for reasonableness of results, including solving real-world problems.

Multiplying by 1-Digit Numbers

What are the steps to record multiplication?

Paying for the damage to cars from potholes can be costly. The table shows some of the repair costs.

Repairs Due to Pothole Damage

Item	Cost
Shock Absorber	$69 each
Tires	$135 each
Paint	$1,450 per coat

Guided Practice*

Do you know HOW?

In **1** through **6**, find each product. Estimate to check reasonableness.

1. 5×188 **2.** 8×135

3. 6×276 **4.** 3×329

5. $\begin{array}{r} 1,450 \\ \times \quad 4 \\ \hline \end{array}$ **6.** $\begin{array}{r} 48 \\ \times \quad 9 \\ \hline \end{array}$

Do you UNDERSTAND?

7. A road repair crew can usually fix 825 potholes each week. How many potholes can they fix in 6 weeks?

8. Writing to Explain A tire shop sells 3 tires at $175 each and includes a fourth tire for free. Is this more or less expensive than buying 4 tires at $135 each? Explain.

Independent Practice

In **9** through **28**, find each product. Estimate to check reasonableness.

9. 6×77 **10.** 5×83 **11.** 4×62 **12.** 7×89

13. 3×245 **14.** 9×318 **15.** 2×736 **16.** 8×314

17. $4 \times 4,347$ **18.** $6 \times 2,716$ **19.** $7 \times 1,287$ **20.** $3 \times 1,942$

21. $\begin{array}{r} 195 \\ \times \quad 4 \\ \hline \end{array}$ **22.** $\begin{array}{r} 58 \\ \times \quad 7 \\ \hline \end{array}$ **23.** $\begin{array}{r} 426 \\ \times \quad 5 \\ \hline \end{array}$ **24.** $\begin{array}{r} 1,123 \\ \times \quad 3 \\ \hline \end{array}$

25. $\begin{array}{r} 2,617 \\ \times \quad 6 \\ \hline \end{array}$ **26.** $\begin{array}{r} 985 \\ \times \quad 8 \\ \hline \end{array}$ **27.** $\begin{array}{r} 3,265 \\ \times \quad 4 \\ \hline \end{array}$ **28.** $\begin{array}{r} 2,134 \\ \times \quad 9 \\ \hline \end{array}$

For another example, see Set D on page 113.

What is the total cost for 3 new shock absorbers?

Estimate:
3 × $69 is about
3 × 70 = 210

$$\begin{array}{r} \overset{2}{69} \\ \times\ \ 3 \\ \hline 207 \end{array}$$

Three shocks cost $207.

What is the total cost for 4 new tires?

Estimate:
4 × $135 is about
4 × 125 = 500

$$\begin{array}{r} \overset{1\,2}{135} \\ \times\ \ \ 4 \\ \hline 540 \end{array}$$

Four tires cost $540.

What is the total cost for two coats of paint?

Estimate:
2 × $1,450 is about
2 × 1,500 = 3,000

$$\begin{array}{r} \overset{1}{1,450} \\ \times\ \ \ \ 2 \\ \hline 2,900 \end{array}$$

Two coats of paint cost $2,900.

Problem Solving

29. Elaine rents a car for 5 days. It costs $44 a day to rent the car, $7 a day for insurance, and $35 to fill the car up with gas. How much does it cost Elaine to rent the car in all?

30. Estimation A fundraiser was held at Ella School. The first day $188 was collected, $201 was collected the second day, and $79 was collected on the third day. About how much money was collected in all?

31. Geometry What is the perimeter of the rectangle below?

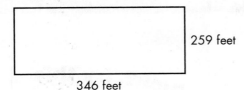

259 feet

346 feet

32. Reasoning Mr. Tran would like to buy a new sofa that costs $934. He can pay the total all at once, or he can make a $125 payment each month for 8 months. Which plan costs less? Explain.

Critical THINKING

33. The first memory card was sold in 1998. How many images can 7 memory cards hold?

? images

| 491 | 491 | 491 | 491 | 491 | 491 | 491 |

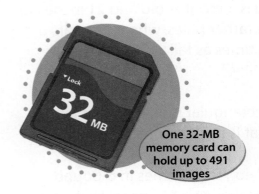

▼Lock

32 MB

One 32-MB memory card can hold up to 491 images

Lesson
5-7

MA.4.A.1.2 Multiply multi-digit whole numbers through four digits fluently, demonstrating understanding of the standard algorithm, and checking for reasonableness of results, including solving real-world problems.

Problem Solving

Missing or Extra Information

A pocket bike is smaller than an average-sized family car. The length of a pocket bike is 38 inches, the height is 19 inches, and the weight is 39 pounds. The length of the family car is five times the length of the pocket bike. How long is the family car?

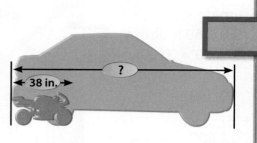

Guided Practice*

Do you know HOW?

Solve. Tell if there is extra or missing information.

1. A sturdy dog crate weighs 29 pounds. It costs $68. Wendy has 3 dogs. How much will she spend on crates if she buys one for each dog?

Do you UNDERSTAND?

2. What operation was needed to solve Problem 1? Tell why.

3. **Write a Problem** Write a problem that has extra or missing information.

Independent Practice

For **4** through **6**, decide if each problem has extra or missing information. Solve if possible.

4. Niki is 3 months old and 21 inches tall. Her father Miles, who is 25 years old, is 3 times as tall as Niki. How tall is Miles?

5. A rectangular pool is 45 feet long. What is its perimeter?

6. Dry dog food comes in 6-pound bags that cost $15 each. How many pounds of food are there in 7 bags?

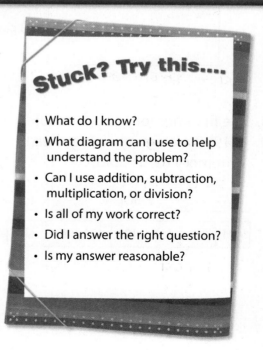

Stuck? Try this....

- What do I know?
- What diagram can I use to help understand the problem?
- Can I use addition, subtraction, multiplication, or division?
- Is all of my work correct?
- Did I answer the right question?
- Is my answer reasonable?

106 *For another example, see Set E on page 113.*

Draw a diagram to show what you know and what you want to find.

? length

Length of car	38	38	38	38	38	5 times as long

Length of bike	38

Is there extra information that is not needed to solve this problem?

Yes, the height and weight of the pocket bike are not needed.

Is there missing information that is needed to solve this problem?

No, all of the information I need is given in the problem.

$5 \times 38 = 190$

The average family car is 190 inches long.

---

7. In 1990, a high-school class in Indiana made a very large yo-yo. It weighed 6 times as much as a student who weighed 136 pounds. What was the weight of the yo-yo?

? pounds

Yo-yo	136	136	136	136	136	136	6 times as much

Student	136

For **9** and **10**, use the picture at the right.

9. What is the perimeter of the park?

10. If the length of the park was increased by 10 feet, what is the new perimeter?

11. At a large dog show, there were 45 entries for each of the breeds in the chart at the right. What is the total number of dogs in this show?

12. A chihuahua weighs 6 pounds. The standard adult height of a Great Pyrenees is about 27 inches. What is the weight of the Great Pyrenees dog?

8. Yo-yos first appeared in the United States in 1866, but the name "yo-yo" was first used 50 years later. It is probably from a Filipino word for "come-come" or "to return." In what year did the toy get the "yo-yo" name?

? year

1866	50

45 feet

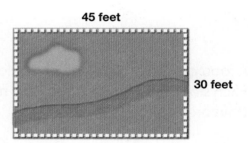

30 feet

Breed of Dog

Hound

Working

Terrier

Gundog

Pastoral

Utility

Toy

Great Pyrenees Weighs 17 times as much

Chihuahua Weighs 6 pounds

For **13** and **14**, use the table at the right.

13. What would the total cost be for 3 round-trip tickets to Hawaii?

 The prices in the table are for one way!

14. How much less does a one-way ticket to Orlando cost than a one-way ticket to Chicago?

Destination	One-Way Price
Chicago	$296
Los Angeles	$349
Orlando	$189
Hawaii	$625

For **15** and **16**, use the chart to the right.

15. Use the data to the right. How much more is a ton of dimes worth than a ton of pennies?

16. How much would three tons of pennies be worth?

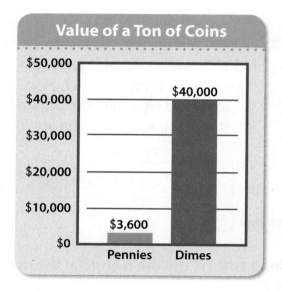

Value of a Ton of Coins

$50,000

$40,000 — $40,000

$30,000

$20,000

$10,000

$3,600

$0

Pennies   Dimes

17. A food cart on an airplane has 6 slots. Each slot holds 2 food trays. How many trays are in 8 food carts?

Critical THINKING

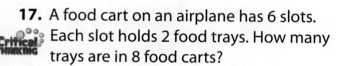

? trays in one cart

| 2 | 2 | 2 | 2 | 2 | 2 |

Trays in each slot

Think About the Process

18. A pocket bike costs 5 times as much as a 10-speed bicycle. If the bicycle costs $150, which expression gives the cost of the pocket bike?

Critical THINKING

    A $150 - 5$ **C** $150 + 5$

    B 150×5 **D** $150 \div 5$

19. Tickets for a movie cost $10 for an adult and $6 for a child. Wally is buying tickets for 2 adults and 1 ticket for a child. Which expression can be used to find the total?

    F $10 + 10 + 10$ **H** $10 + 6$

    G $10 + 6 + 6$ **I** $10 + 10 + 6$

Operations on a Calculator

Jamie made 4 trips between Foster and Andersonville this summer. Each trip was 379 miles. How many miles were the 4 trips in all?

Step 1 Draw a picture and choose an operation for the first question.

? miles in all

| 379 | 379 | 379 | 379 |

Multiply 4 × 379.

Step 2 Press: 4 × 379 ENTER =

Display: *1516*

Jamie's four trips were 1,516 miles in all.

In September, Jamie traveled 379 miles from Andersonville to Foster, 244 miles from Foster to Leyton, and 137 miles from Leyton back to Andersonville. How many miles did Jamie travel in September?

Step 1 Draw a picture and choose an operation for the second question.

? miles in all

| 379 | 244 | 137 |

Add 379 + 244 + 137.

Step 2 Press: 379 + 244 + 137 ENTER =

Display: *760*

Jamie traveled 760 miles in September.

Practice

For each problem, draw a picture, choose an operation, and solve.

1. How much farther did Jamie travel from Andersonville to Foster than from Foster to Leyton?

2. How many miles would Jamie travel if she went from Andersonville to Leyton and back to Andersonville?

1 Part of the calculation for 3×26 is shown below. What is the missing partial product? (5-1)

A. 8
B. 18
C. 20
D. 60

$$\begin{array}{r} 26 \\ \times\ 3 \\ \hline \blacksquare\blacksquare \\ +\ 60 \\ \hline 78 \end{array}$$

2 A factory produced 275 cars in one week. How many cars could the factory produce in 4 weeks? (5-5)

F. 880 cars
G. 1,000 cars
H. 1,100 cars
I. 8,300 cars

3 The table lists prices of sports gear.

Sports Gear	Price
Inline skates	$45
Catcher's mitt	$37
Hockey stick	$18
Knee pads	$9

Denise spent $54 on two different items. What did Denise buy? (5-4)

A. Catcher's mitt and knee pads
B. Knee pads and inline skates
C. Hockey stick and inline skates
D. Two catcher's mitts

4 In 2008, the state of Florida had 23 congressional districts. If each district office employed 5 clerks, how many clerks were there for all the districts? (5-2)

F. 105
G. 108
H. 115
I. 155

5 There were 42 people at the Jones family reunion last July in Orlando. There were twice as many children as adults at the reunion. How many children attended the reunion? (5-4)

A. 14
B. 21
C. 24
D. 28

6 Which problem best describes the array modeled below? (5-1)

F. $30 + 12$
G. 4×13
H. 3×14
I. 3×10

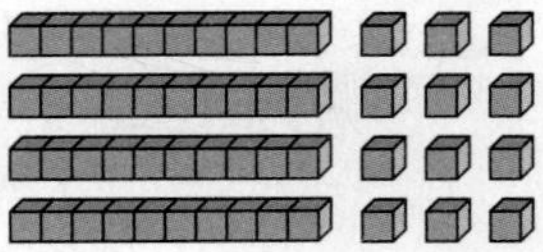

7 Florida has 14 deepwater ports. Each port is run by 6 directors. How many directors run Florida's ports in all? (5-2)

A. 184
B. 102
C. 84
D. 70

8 Kai owns a rental shop at a beach club. Last year, Kai bought 6 used water vehicles for $3,179 each. How much did Kai spend? (5-6)

F. $3,185

G. $18,624

H. $19,074

I. $19,474

9 The lighthouse at Egmont Key, Florida, is 76 feet tall and has 99 stairs. The Vehicle Assembly Building (VAB) is one of the largest buildings in the world, covering 8 acres. The doors of the VAB at the Kennedy Space Center are as tall as 6 lighthouses. Which is NOT extra information if you want to find the height of the VAB doors? (5-7)

A. The lighthouse is 76 feet tall.

B. The lighthouse has 99 stairs.

C. The VAB is one of the largest buildings in the world.

D. The VAB covers 8 acres.

10 Mr. Tyler lives in Miami, Florida. He travels to Richmond, Virginia, 4 times each month for business. The distance there and back is 2,658 kilometers. What is the total distance of Mr. Tyler's business trips each month? (5-5)

F. 5,316 kilometers

G. 5,406 kilometers

H. 10,432 kilometers

I. 10,632 kilometers

11 Seven students took a bus to Key West. The round-trip tickets cost $45 per student. They stayed for a few nights at a campground at a cost of $5 per student each night. Which missing information is needed to find the total amount each student spent on the camping trip? (5-7)

A. How many students went

B. How far it is to Key West

C. How many nights they camped

D. How many hours the trip took

12 A radio station played a new hit song 34 times a day for 4 days. What partial products would you use to find how many times the song was played in all? (5-1)

F. 8 and 120

G. 16 and 12

H. 16 and 70

I. 16 and 120

13 There are 1,576 seats in each section of a stadium. How many seats are there in 5 sections of the stadium? (5-6)

14 Liz drinks 28 liters of water each month. How many liters of water does Liz drink in 5 months? Explain each step you took to find your answer. (5-3)

THINK
SOLVE
EXPLAIN

Set A, pages 90–92, 94–95

Find 6 × 22.

```
   22
 ×  6
   12
 + 120
   132
```

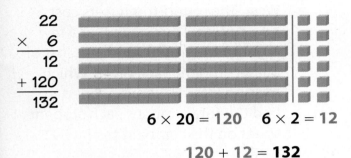

$6 \times 20 = 120 \quad 6 \times 2 = 12$

$120 + 12 = \mathbf{132}$

Remember to regroup when needed.

Find each product using the expanded algorithm or the standard algorithm.

1. 28 × 6	**2.** 28 × 3	
3. 75 × 5	**4.** 53 × 4	
5. 88 × 2	**6.** 21 × 6	

Set B, pages 96–98

Find 8 × 24.

Step 1

Multiply the ones. Regroup if needed.

```
  3
 24
× 8
  2
```

Step 2

Multiply the tens. Add any extra tens.

```
  3
 24
× 8
 192
```

Remember to check your answer with an estimate.

Find each product.

1. 18 × 2	**2.** 48 × 5
3. 33 × 6	**4.** 97 × 7

Set C, pages 100–101

Dan spent $73 on 4 items at the store. Two of his items were the same. What did he buy?

Kids Mart

Video game	$16
Shoes	$33
Sports hat	$12

Try two video games, one pair of shoes, and one hat.

$32 + $33 + $12 = $77

That's too high, but it is close.

Revise. Try two sports hats, one video game, and one pair of shoes.

$24 + $16 + $33 = $73

Dan bought 1 video game, 1 pair of shoes, and 2 sports hats.

Remember to revise if your answer doesn't check.

Use Try, Check, and Revise to solve the problem.

1. Terry, Corey, and Chris together made 20 baskets in a basketball game. Terry made 5 more baskets than Corey. Chris made 3 times as many baskets as Corey. How many baskets did they each make?

Reteaching

Set D, pages 102–103, 104–105

Find 768 × 6.

Step 1

Multiply the ones. Regroup if necessary.

$$
\begin{array}{r}
\overset{4}{76}8 \\
\times\quad 6 \\
\hline
8
\end{array}
$$

Step 2

Multiply the tens. Add any extra tens. Regroup if necessary.

$$
\begin{array}{r}
\overset{4\;4}{76}8 \\
\times\quad 6 \\
\hline
08
\end{array}
$$

Step 3

Multiply the hundreds. Add any extra hundreds.

$$
\begin{array}{r}
\overset{4\;4}{76}8 \\
\times\quad 6 \\
\hline
4,608
\end{array}
$$

Remember to check your answer with an estimate.

Find each product.

1. $\begin{array}{r} 239 \\ \times\quad 4 \\ \hline \end{array}$
2. $\begin{array}{r} 148 \\ \times\quad 5 \\ \hline \end{array}$

3. $\begin{array}{r} 4{,}233 \\ \times\quad 6 \\ \hline \end{array}$
4. $\begin{array}{r} 937 \\ \times\quad 7 \\ \hline \end{array}$

5. $\begin{array}{r} 3{,}261 \\ \times\quad 4 \\ \hline \end{array}$
6. $\begin{array}{r} 1{,}250 \\ \times\quad 8 \\ \hline \end{array}$

Set E, pages 106–108

An orchard has 3 times as many apple trees as cherry trees. If there are 63 orange trees and 52 cherry trees, how many apple trees are there?

What do I know?

There are 63 orange trees and 52 cherry trees. There are 3 times as many apple trees as cherry trees.

What am I being asked to find?

The number of apple trees

	? apple trees in all			
Number of apple trees	52	52	52	3 times as many
Number of cherry trees	52			

Choose an Operation Multiply when you want to find "times as many."

$3 \times 52 = 156$

There are 156 apple trees.

The number of orange trees was extra information.

Remember some problems do not have enough information to solve.

Tell if there is extra information or if there is missing information. Solve if you have enough information.

1. Todd read 35 pages of his book on Saturday. He read for 10 minutes on Sunday. How many pages did Todd read over the weekend?

2. Molly bought 150 sheets of paper and 5 notebooks. She put 50 sheets in her math folder, 25 sheets in her science folder, 25 sheets in her social studies folder, and 40 sheets in her reading folder. How many sheets did Molly have left?

Number Sense: Multiplying by Two-Digit Numbers

1

In 1858, a telegraph cable connected Europe and America for the first time. How long was the cable? You will find out in Lesson 6-4.

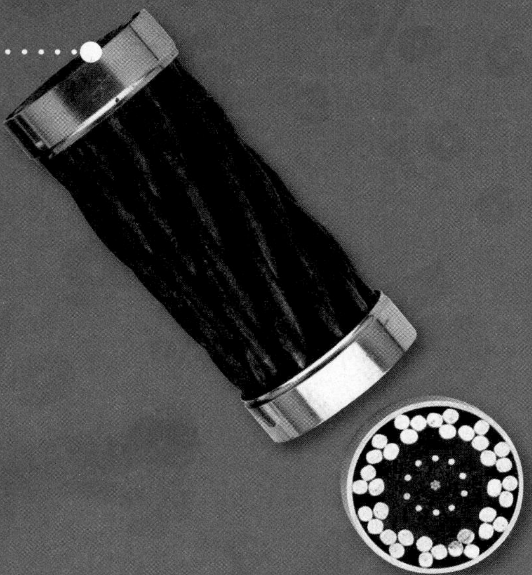

2

How many times per second do the world's fastest drummers hit their drums? You will find out in Lesson 6-2.

3

How much water might you use while brushing your teeth? You will find out in Lesson 6-2.

4

One man balanced 75 drinking glasses on his chin. What was the capacity of the drinking glasses he balanced? You will find out in Lesson 6-1.

Topic Essential Questions

- How can greater products be found mentally?
- How can greater products be estimated?

Review What You Know!

Vocabulary

Choose the best term from the box.

- equation
- product
- factors
- round

1. A(n) __?__ is another word for a number sentence.

2. One way to estimate a product is to __?__ each number.

3. A(n) __?__ is the answer to a multiplication problem.

4. In the equation $9 \times 5 = 45$, 9 and 5 are both __?__.

Multiplication Facts

Find each product.

5. 3×9
6. 5×6
7. 4×8
8. 6×9
9. 7×4
10. 9×8

Rounding

Round each number to the nearest hundred.

11. 864
12. 651
13. 348
14. 985
15. 451
16. 749

Multiplying Three Factors

Writing to Explain Write an answer to the question.

17. Gina wants to multiply $9 \times 2 \times 5$. How can Gina group the factors to make it easier to multiply?

MA.4.A.1.2 Multiply multi-digit whole numbers through four digits fluently, demonstrating understanding of the standard algorithm, and checking for reasonableness of results, including solving real-world problems.

Arrays and Multiplying 2-Digit Numbers by Multiples of 10

How can you use a model to multiply?

Max's Moving Company has boxes for packing books. If each box holds 24 books, how many books would fit into 10 boxes?

Choose an Operation Multiply to join equal groups.

24 Books

Another Example **What is another way to use a model to multiply?**

Mrs. Harrigan ordered 30 boxes of glasses for her restaurant. Each box holds 16 glasses. How many glasses did she order?

Step 1

To find 30 × 16, use a grid to draw a model. On the grid draw an array with 30 rows of 16. Break apart 16 into 10 and 6.

Step 2

Add to find the total.

$$\begin{array}{r} 300 \\ +\ 180 \\ \hline 480 \end{array}$$

30 × 16 = 480

Mrs. Harrigan ordered 480 glasses.

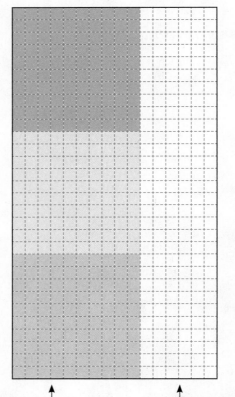

↑ 30 groups of 10 = 300   ↑ 30 groups of 6 = 180

Explain It

1. Explain how you found the product for 30 groups of 6.

2. Mrs. Harrigan also orders 30 boxes of plates. There are 25 plates in each box. How many plates did she order?

Use a model to find 10×24.

10 groups of 20 = 200   10 groups of 4 = 40

Add to find the total.

$$\begin{array}{r} 200 \\ + \quad 40 \\ \hline 240 \end{array}$$

$10 \times 24 = 240$

240 books will fit into 10 boxes.

Guided Practice*

Do you know HOW?

For **1** through **6**, draw a model to find each product.

1. 10×18 **2.** 20×15

3. 10×27 **4.** 20×12

5. 20×23 **6.** 30×21

Do you UNDERSTAND?

7. Draw a model to show 40×16. Then use the model to find the product.

8. There are 30 boxes on one of Max's moving trucks. If each box weighs 36 pounds, how much do the boxes weigh all together?

Independent Practice

Leveled Practice In **9** through **14**, use models to find each product.

9. 10×22 **10.** 10×13

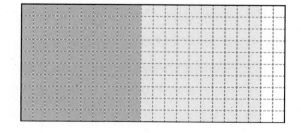

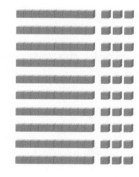

11. 20×35 **12.** 20×41 **13.** 30×29 **14.** 40×37

Independent Practice

In **15** through **22**, find each product. Use models to help.

15. 30 × 18

16. 40 × 22

17. 50 × 11

18. 40 × 25

19. 30 × 39

20. 50 × 15

21. 40 × 15

22. 60 × 21

Problem Solving

23. In the first 3 months of the year, the electronics store sold 1,446 cameras. They sold 486 cameras in January and 385 cameras in February. How many cameras did they sell in March?

24.  **Science** The American bison is the heaviest land mammal in North America. They live in groups of up to 20 bison. How many bison could there be in 12 groups?

25. Writing to Explain Miranda says that 30 × 26 is greater than 20 × 36. Is she correct? Explain how you know.

26. Draw a Diagram Show how you can find 30 × 15 by drawing an array.

For **27**, use the picture at the right.

27. The 2001 record for balancing drinking glasses was 75 glasses. How many total fluid ounces could all of the glasses contain?

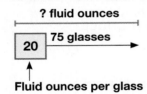

? fluid ounces

| 20 | 75 glasses → |

Fluid ounces per glass

Each glass holds 20 fluid ounces.

28. How many ones blocks do you need to model 20 × 17 ?

A 34

B 37

C 170

D 340

29. **Think About the Process** Which of the following shows how to use the Distributive Property to find 3 × 46?

F (3 × 40) + (3 × 6)

G (3 × 46) + (3 × 46)

H (1 × 4) + (2 × 6)

I (3 × 4) + (3 × 6)

Perfect Squares

Use Counters.

The first three perfect square numbers are 1, 4, and 9. They are called perfect squares because they name square shaped arrays.

Use arrays to find the next perfect square.

●   ●●   ●●●
          ●●   ●●●
                     ●●●

$1 \times 1 = 1$ $2 \times 2 = 4$ $3 \times 3 = 9$

Step 1   Go to the Counters eTool. Select the array workspace icon. ▦ Pull the resize button in the upper right corner of the rectangle to make an array that has 3 rows and 3 columns of counters. Increase the number of rows and columns until you see the next square shaped array, or perfect square. The total number of counters is shown in the odometer at the bottom of the page.

Step 2   The array shows that 16 is a perfect square.

Use the array to write the multiplication fact for the perfect square. There are 4 rows and 4 columns, which is 4×4.

Practice

For **1** through **6**, find the multiplication fact for each perfect square.

1. 36   **2.** 64   **3.** 25

4. 100   **5.** 49   **6.** 81

MA.4.A.1.2 Multiply multi-digit whole numbers through four digits fluently, demonstrating understanding of the standard algorithm, and checking for reasonableness of results, including solving real-world problems.

Using Mental Math to Multiply 2-Digit Numbers

How can you multiply by multiples of 10?

How many adults under 65 visit the Sunny Day Amusement Park in 20 days? How many children visit the park in 30 days? How many adults 65 and over visit the park in 50 days?

Average Number of Visitors Each Day

Adults under 65: **60**

Adults 65 and over: **40**

Children: **80**

Guided Practice*

Do you know HOW?

In **1** through **8**, use basic facts and patterns to find the product.

1. 30×10 **2.** 50×10

3. 20×10 **4.** 60×20

5. 20×20 **6.** 70×10

7. 40×50 **8.** 80×50

Do you UNDERSTAND?

9. When you multiply 60×50, how many zeros are in the product?

10. In cold weather, fewer people go to Sunny Day Amusement Park. November has 30 days. If the park sells 30 tickets each day in November, how many would they sell for the whole month?

Independent Practice

For **11** through **34**, multiply using mental math.

11. 30×30 **12.** 10×60 **13.** 50×30 **14.** 80×40

15. 20×70 **16.** 70×90 **17.** 40×20 **18.** 40×30

19. 70×40 **20.** 20×30 **21.** 60×40 **22.** 60×90

23. 70×80 **24.** 30×80 **25.** 60×60 **26.** 70×30

27. 50×50 **28.** 30×90 **29.** 90×40 **30.** 30×60

31. 20×50 **32.** 80×30 **33.** 60×80 **34.** 50×90

*For another example, see Set B on page 130.

Adults under 65 in 20 Days	Children in 30 Days	Adults 65 and over in 50 Days
To multiply 20 × 60, use a pattern. **2 × 6 = 12** **20 × 6 = 120** **20 × 60 = 1,200** 1,200 adults under 65 visit the park in 20 days.	The number of zeros in the product is the total number of zeros in both factors. **30 × 80 = 2,400** 1 zero 1 zero 2 zeros 2,400 children visit the park in 30 days.	If the product of a basic fact ends in zero, include that zero in the count. **5 × 4 = 20** **50 × 40 = 2,000** 2,000 adults 65 and over visit the park in 50 days.

Problem Solving

35. 🎵 **Music** The world's fastest drummer can hit the drum 20 times in one second. How many times can the drummer hit the drum in 30 seconds?

36. THINK SOLVE EXPLAIN Explain why the product of 50 and 80 has three zeros when 50 has one zero and 80 has one zero.

37. Use the picture below. You might use about 2 gallons of water while brushing your teeth. How many cups of water might you use while brushing your teeth?

There are 16 cups in 1 gallon.

38. Critical THINKING Of every 30 minutes of television air time, about 8 minutes show TV commercials. If 90 minutes of television is aired, how many minutes of commercials will be played?

A 8 minutes   **C** 38 minutes

B 24 minutes   **D** 128 minutes

39. If in one year a city recorded a total of 97 rainy days, how many of the days did it NOT rain?

365 days in one year	
97	?

Using Rounding to Estimate

How can you use rounding to estimate?

The workers at Mrs. Piper's apple grove picked 87 dozen apples. There are 12 apples in one dozen. About how many apples did the workers pick?

1 dozen apples

MA.4.A.1.2 Multiply multi-digit whole numbers through four digits fluently, demonstrating understanding of the standard algorithm, and checking for reasonableness of results, including solving real-world problems.

Guided Practice*

Do you know HOW?

For **1** through **4**, estimate each product.

1. 24 × 18 rounds to ▢ × ▢ = ▢.

2. 33 × 31 is close to ▢ × ▢ = ▢.

3. 38 × 22   **4.** 45 × 48

Do you UNDERSTAND?

5. Writing to Explain Sue said that 870 is also a reasonable estimate for 87 × 12, and her teacher agreed. How could Sue get 870 as an estimate?

6. Howie used rounding to estimate the product of 35 × 42 and got 1,200. What did he do wrong?

Independent Practice

Leveled Practice For **7** through **24**, estimate each product.

7. 44 × 13 rounds to ▢ × ▢ = ▢.   **8.** 39 × 19 rounds to ▢ × ▢ = ▢.

9. 28 × 27 rounds to ▢ × ▢ = ▢.   **10.** 35 × 42 rounds to ▢ × ▢ = ▢.

11. 72 × 48 rounds to ▢ × ▢ = ▢.   **12.** 68 × 36 rounds to ▢ × ▢ = ▢.

13. 64 × 13   **14.** 24 × 28   **15.** 42 × 17   **16.** 82 × 36

17. 25 × 81   **18.** 15 × 38   **19.** 54 × 18   **20.** 66 × 41

21. 34 × 52   **22.** 74 × 34   **23.** 88 × 23   **24.** 57 × 49

Round both numbers in 87 × 12.

Round 87 to the nearest ten.
   7 > 5, so round 87 to 90.

Round 12 to the nearest ten.
   2 < 5, so round 12 to 10.

Estimate the product.

$$87 \times 12$$

$$90 \times 10 = 900$$

The workers picked about 900 apples.

Problem Solving

25. Julia worked about 18 hours last week making fruit baskets to sell as gifts. About how many minutes did she spend making fruit baskets?

Tip *There are 60 minutes in 1 hour.*

26. **Science** The world's smallest snake, the thread snake, can be 4 inches long. The world's largest snake, the anaconda, can be 60 times as long. How many inches long can an anaconda be?

27. **Reasonableness** Lenore uses rounding and estimates that the product of 52 × 38 is 1,500. Is this estimate reasonable? Why or why not?

28. **Number Sense** List the numbers from 50 to 60 that would make this number sentence true.

Critical THINKING

85 + 54 > ▨ + 85

Use the table at the right for **29** through **32**.

29. About how many Hamlin trees does Mr. Gonzalez have?

30. **Number Sense** Mr. Gonzalez has the same number of which two types of trees? Explain how you know.

Type of Orange Tree	Number of Rows	Number of Trees in Each Row
Hamlin	28	38
Temple	38	28
Valencia	31	46

31. **Writing to Explain** About how many more Valencia orange trees than Temple orange trees does Mr. Gonzalez have?

32. To the nearest hundred, about how many orange trees does Mr. Gonzalez have all together?

A 1,100   **C** 3,000

B 1,600   **D** 3,900

Lesson 6-4

MA.4.A.1.2 Multiply multi-digit whole numbers through four digits fluently, demonstrating understanding of the standard algorithm, and checking for reasonableness of results, including solving real-world problems.

Using Compatible Numbers to Estimate

How can you use compatible numbers to estimate?

Nolan set up an online blog for his friends to visit. Estimate the number of hits Nolan will have in 24 days.

Average number of hits per day: 41

Guided Practice*

Do you know HOW?

In **1** through **3**, estimate to find each product.

1. 24 × 18
   24 is close to 25.
   18 is close to ⬜ .
   Multiply 25 × ⬜ = ⬜

2. 24 × 37

3. 52 × 27

Do you UNDERSTAND?

4. In the example above, suppose the average number of hits per day were 61. If you estimate 24 × 61 as 25 × 60, what is the estimate?

5. Writing to Explain Rounding would give 20 × 60 as an estimate for 24 × 61. Why does 25 × 60 give a better estimate than 20 × 60?

Independent Practice

For **6** through **25**, estimate to find each product. When possible, use compatible numbers.

 Look for numbers near 25. Remember 2 × 25 = 50, 3 × 25 = 75, 4 × 25 = 100, 5 × 25 = 125, and so on.

6. 26 × 42

7. 31 × 46

8. 21 × 25

9. 58 × 12

10. 22 × 26

11. 78 × 21

12. 36 × 49

13. 66 × 31

14. 64 × 24

15. 21 × 19

16. 76 × 39

17. 32 × 24

18. 89 × 43

19. 79 × 79

20. 46 × 18

21. 86 × 37

22. 53 × 54

23. 68 × 39

24. 29 × 43

25. 48 × 16

Animated Glossary, eTools
www.pearsonsuccessnet.com

For another example, see Set D on page 131.

Estimate 24 × 41.

Rounding to the nearest ten gives 20 × 40 = 800 as an estimate.

However, you can get a closer estimate by using compatible numbers, which are <u>numbers that are easy to compute mentally</u>.

24 is close to 25
41 is close to 40.

It is easy to find 25 × 40, since 25 and 40 are compatible numbers. Remember that 25 × 4 = 100. So 25 × 40 = 1,000.

Nolan will have about 1,000 hits in 24 days.

Notice that 24 is closer to 25 than to 20. So, 25 × 40 gives a better estimate than 20 × 40. However, either method can be used to find an estimate.

Problem Solving

26. An electronics store sells about 45 computers a day. About how many computers could they sell in 4 weeks?

 There are 7 days in 1 week.

27. Geometry Maya has the poster below on her wall. What is the perimeter of the poster?

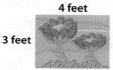

4 feet

3 feet   3 feet

4 feet

28. Writing to Explain Show how you would use estimation to decide which has the greater product, 39 × 21 or 32 × 32.

29. Mason swims about 55 minutes each day. Estimate the number of minutes he swims in 14 days.

30. A company ordered 28 cartons of tape. Each carton contained 24 rolls. What is the best estimate of the total number of rolls of tape ordered?

A 280   **C** 750

B 400   **D** 900

31. During her summer job at the local grocery store, Vivian earned $247 per week. If she worked for 6 weeks, how much money did she earn in all?

32. **Social Studies** In 1858, two ships connected a telegraph cable across the Atlantic Ocean for the first time. Using the diagram below, estimate the total distance of cable used.

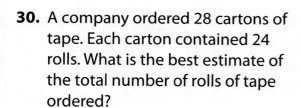

1,010 miles   1,016 miles

Lesson 6-5

MA.4.A.1.1 Use and describe various models for multiplication in problem-solving situations, and demonstrate recall of basic multiplication and related division facts with ease.

Problem Solving

Multiple-Step Problems

Paul and Libby sold some sock monkeys for a total of $72. Libby sold 5 monkeys from her collection. Paul sold 3 monkeys from his collection. If they sold each sock monkey for the same amount, how much did they sell each monkey for?

Paul sold 3 monkeys

Libby sold 5 monkeys

Guided Practice*

Do you know HOW?

Solve.

1. Adult admission to the town fair is $7. Child admission to the fair is $3. How much would it cost 2 adults and 4 children to enter the fair?

Do you UNDERSTAND?

2. What is the hidden question or questions from Problem 1?

3. **Write a Problem** Write a problem that contains a hidden question.

Independent Practice

Answer the hidden question or questions. Then solve the problem. Write your answer in a complete sentence.

4. Charlie and Lola like to walk around the perimeter of their town park. The perimeter is 2 miles long. Last week Charlie walked around the perimeter 4 times and Lola walked around it 5 times. How many more miles did Lola walk than Charlie last week?

5. Abby buys 15 sunflower plants and 12 petunia plants to plant in her garden. She plans to plant 3 flowers in each row. How many rows of flowers will Abby plant?

6. What is the hidden question in Problem 5?

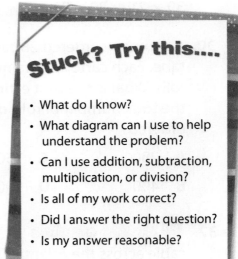

Stuck? Try this....

- What do I know?
- What diagram can I use to help understand the problem?
- Can I use addition, subtraction, multiplication, or division?
- Is all of my work correct?
- Did I answer the right question?
- Is my answer reasonable?

126   *For another example, see Set E on page 131.*

Find the hidden question. How many monkeys did Paul and Libby sell in all?

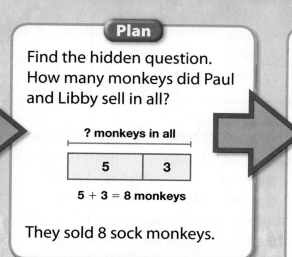

? monkeys in all

5	3

5 + 3 = 8 monkeys

They sold 8 sock monkeys.

Use the answer to the hidden question to solve the problem.

If they sold each sock monkey for the same amount, how much did they sell each sock monkey for?

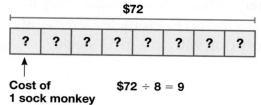

$72

?	?	?	?	?	?	?	?

Cost of 1 sock monkey $72 ÷ 8 = 9

Paul and Libby sold each sock monkey for $9.

Use the data at the right for **7** through **9**.

7. Carlos's family bought 3 hamburgers and 2 salads from Diner Delight. They paid with a $20 bill. How much change did they receive?

8. Amber and her family bought 3 chicken sandwiches, 2 salads, and 1 baked potato. They spent $4 on drinks. How much did they spend in all?

9. Gene spent exactly $11 on lunch, including tax. He bought a chicken sandwich, a salad, and a baked potato. How much did Gene spend on tax?

Diner Delight	
Hamburger	$4
Chicken Sandwich	$5
Baked Potato	$2
Salad	$3

Data

For **10** through **12**, use the table to the right.

10. Terrence and Jennifer went to Al's Discount Music Store. Terrence bought 4 CDs and two 3-packs of blank CDs. Jennifer bought 8 DVDs, 3 CDs, and one 3-pack of blank CDs. Together, how much did they spend?

11. Give an example of a hidden question in Problem 10.

12. In one hour, Al's Discount Music Store sold 22 DVDs, 36 CDs, and six 3-packs of blank CDs. How much money did the store earn from these sales?

Al's Discount Music Store		
	3-pack blank CDs	$7
	DVDs	$5
	CDs	$10

1 Don works <u>18</u> hours a week at the library. Which shows the best way to use rounding to estimate how many hours Don will work in 52 weeks? (6-3)

A. 10×50

B. 10×60

C. 20×50

D. 18×60

2 A Virginia opossum can have up to <u>21</u> babies at one time. Suppose 10 Virginia opossums had babies all at the same time. How many baby opossums could there be? (6-1)

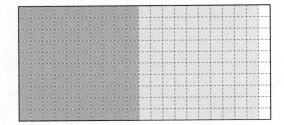

F. 320

G. 210

H. 110

I. 31

3 There are 24 rows in an auditorium. Each row has 42 seats. Which is the best estimate of the total number of seats? (6-4)

A. 70

B. 400

C. 500

D. 1,000

4 There are 24 schools competing in a cheerleading contest. There are 18 cheerleaders on each team. Which is the best way to use compatible numbers to estimate the number of cheerleaders that are competing? (6-4)

F. 20×10

G. 25×20

H. 30×10

I. 30×20

5 A movie theater sells 50 tickets for each showing of a movie. They showed the movie 40 times last week. How many tickets did they sell? (6-2)

A. 20,000

B. 2,000

C. 200

D. 20

6 Elaine is making 11 pinecone wreaths to sell at a fair. She needs 13 pinecones for each wreath. How many pinecones does she need in all? (6-1)

F. 24

G. 44

H. 143

I. 153

7 A tractor trailer has 18 wheels. How many more wheels are on 2 tractor trailers than on 5 cars? (6-5)

A. 14

B. 16

C. 20

D. 36

8 Mr. Hans bought 40 boxes of tiles for his kitchen floor. Each box of tiles cost $30. How much money did Mr. Hans pay for the tiles? (6-2)

F. $12,000

G. $1,200

H. $120

I. $70

9 Which is the best way to use rounding to estimate 31×82? (6-3)

A. 40×90

B. 40×80

C. 30×90

D. 30×80

10 A florist is making centerpieces for an event. He is putting 22 roses in each centerpiece. Using compatible numbers, about how many roses will he need for 26 centerpieces? (6-4)

F. 200

G. 300

H. 500

I. 800

11 Which pair of numbers best completes the number sentence? (6-2)

$$\blacksquare \times 20 = \blacksquare$$

A. 50 and 1,000

B. 50 and 100

C. 50 and 70

D. 5 and 1,000

12 Justine's plant stand has 6 shelves. Each shelf holds 4 plants. Justine has already placed 16 plants on her stand. How many more plants can fit on the plant stand? (6-5)

F. 8

G. 16

H. 24

I. 64

13 Felipe wants to keep his insect collection in display cases. Each case can hold 30 insects. How many insects can he put in the display case if he buys 20 display cases? (6-2)

14 Margo hikes 5 miles three times a week. Susan hikes 4 miles four times a week. Ralph hikes 2 miles seven times a week. How many miles do they hike in all? Explain your answer. (6-5)

THINK
SOLVE
EXPLAIN

Reteaching

Set A, pages 116–118

Use a model to multiply 20×14.

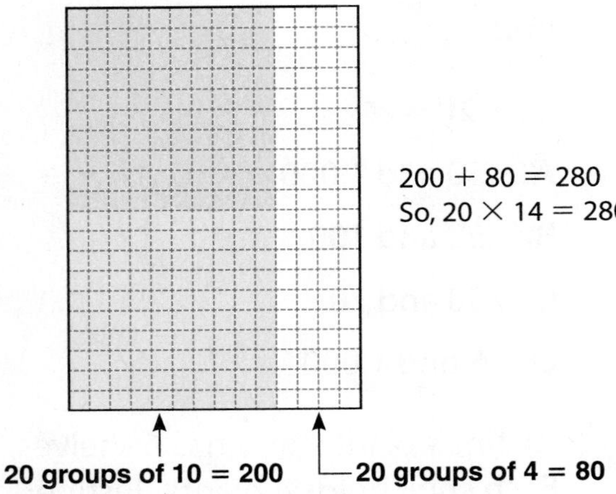
20 groups of 10 = 200
20 groups of 4 = 80

$200 + 80 = 280$
So, $20 \times 14 = 280$

Remember you can draw models to represent multiplication problems.

Draw a model to find each product.

1. 10×23 **2.** 20×34

3. 10×17 **5.** 30×15

4. 20×28 **6.** 40×33

7. 30×21 **8.** 20×16

9. 40×12 **10.** 30×18

Set B, pages 120–121

Use mental math to find 20×80.

Think about the pattern.

$2 \times 8 = 16$

$20 \times 8 = 160$

$20 \times 80 = 1{,}600$

Remember when the product of a basic fact has a zero, there is one more zero in the answer.

Use a pattern to find each product.

1. 40×10 **2.** 60×20

3. 80×50 **4.** 30×90

5. 70×40 **6.** 20×50

7. 60×40 **8.** 30×40

9. 80×70 **10.** 60×60

Set C, pages 122–123

Use rounding to estimate 24×16.

Round each number to the nearest ten.

24 rounds to 20.
16 rounds to 20.

20×20

$20 \times 20 = 400$
So, 24×16 is about 400.

Remember to check the digit to the right of the rounding place to decide how to round a number.

Estimate each product.

1. 27×21 **2.** 64×16

3. 53×32 **4.** 44×51

5. 35×42 **6.** 71×24

Set D, pages 124–125

Use compatible numbers to estimate 28×19.

28 is about 25.
19 is about 20.

Remember, if $25 \times 2 = 50$, then $25 \times 20 = 500$.

$25 \times 20 = 500$
So, 28×19 is about 500.

Remember compatible numbers are numbers that are easy to compute with mentally.

Estimate each product.

1. 26×32 **2.** 24×41

3. 29×31 **4.** 42×49

5. 73×18 **6.** 24×38

7. 19×31 **8.** 63×87

Set E, pages 126–127

When you solve multiple-step problems you need to answer the hidden question or questions before you can solve the problem.

Maggie bought 3 puzzles and 4 games at a garage sale. The puzzles cost $3 each and the games cost $2 each. Maggie paid for the items with a $20 bill. How much change should she get back?

Hidden questions:
How much did the puzzles cost? $3 \times \$3 = \$9$
How much did the games cost? $4 \times \$2 = \$8$
What was the total cost? $\$9 + \$8 = \$17$

Solve the problem:
$\$20 - \$17 = \$3$

Maggie should get $3 back.

Remember to answer the hidden questions first.

Use the hidden question to solve each problem.

1. Gwen bought 4 dozen apples at the store. The apples were equally divided into 6 bags. How many apples were in each bag? (Hint: 1 dozen = 12)

2. Cindy has 35 pennies, and her brother has 37 pennies. They put all of their pennies together and placed them into 8 equal stacks. How many pennies are in each stack?

3. Keith's dad spent $28 buying movie tickets for himself and his 3 children. An adult ticket cost $10. How much did one children's ticket cost?

Developing Fluency: Multi-Digit Multiplication

1 An ultralight plane tracks the trek of monarch butterflies from Canada, throughout the United States, and into Mexico. About how many miles do the butterflies travel each day? You will find out in Lesson 7-4.

2 Florida scrub jays can only survive in a very dry habitat called scrub. This type of habitat is disappearing. How many acres of scrub are needed for one family of scrub jays to survive? You will find out in Lesson 7-3.

Review What You Know!

3 The Queen Mary 2 is as tall as a 23-story building. How many feet high is this above the water? You will find out in Lesson 7-4.

4 How many people can the Florida Theatre in Jacksonville seat? You will find out in Lesson 7-1.

Vocabulary

Choose the best term from the box.

- rounding
- compatible
- Commutative Property
- Distributive Property

1. ? numbers are easy to compute mentally.

2. Breaking apart problems into two simpler problems is an example of the ? of Multiplication.

3. You can use ? when you do not need an exact answer.

Estimating Sums

Estimate each sum.

4. 16 + 13   **5.** 688 + 95

6. 1,511 + 269   **7.** 3,246 + 6,243

8. 283 + 178   **9.** 1,999 + 421

Multiplying by 1-Digit Numbers

Find each product.

10. 53×9 **11.** 172×7

12. 512×6 **13.** 711×4

14. 215×3 **15.** 914×5

Partial Products

16. **Writing to Explain** Explain why the array shown below represents 3×21.

Topic Essential Questions

- How can arrays be used to find greater products?
- What is a standard procedure for multiplying multi-digit numbers?

MA.4.A.1.2 Multiply multi-digit whole numbers through four digits fluently, demonstrating understanding of the standard algorithm, and checking for reasonableness of results, including solving real-world problems.

Arrays and Multiplying 2-Digit Numbers

Hands-On
grid paper

How can you multiply using an array?

There are 13 bobble-head dogs in each row of the carnival booth. There are 24 equal rows. How many dogs are there?

Choose an Operation
Multiply to join equal groups.

13 dogs per row

Another Example **What is another way to multiply 2-digit numbers?**

There are 37 rows with 26 seats set up at the ring at the dog show. How many seats are there?

Find 37 × 26.

Step 1 Draw a table. Separate each factor into tens and ones. (30 + 7) × (20 + 6)

	20	6
30		
7		

Step 2 Multiply to find each product.

	20	6
30	600	180
7	140	42

Step 3 Add to find the product.

```
      42
     140
     180
  +  600
     962
```

37 × 26 = 962
There are 962 seats at the dog show ring.

Explain It

1. How is breaking apart the problem 37 × 26 like solving four simpler problems?

2. **Reasonableness** Explain why the answer 962 is reasonable.

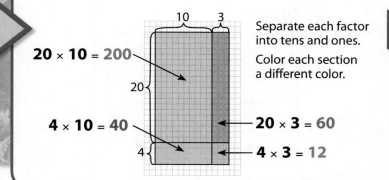

Step 1

Find 24 × 13.
Draw an array for 24 × 13.

Separate each factor into tens and ones.

Color each section a different color.

20 × 10 = 200

4 × 10 = 40

20 × 3 = 60

4 × 3 = 12

Step 2

Add the number of squares in each part of the array.

```
    1 2
    4 0
    6 0
+ 2 0 0
-------
  3 1 2
```

In the booth, there are 312 bobble-head dogs.

Guided Practice*

Do you know HOW?

In **1** and **2**, use the grid or table to find the product.

1. 17 × 13

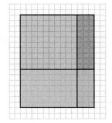

2. 24 × 16

	10	6
20		
4		

Do you UNDERSTAND?

3. In the example at the top, what four simpler multiplication problems were used to find 24 × 13?

4. At the dog show, the first 2 rows are reserved. How many people can sit in the remaining 35 rows?

 There are 26 seats per row.

Independent Practice

Leveled Practice For **5** and **6**, find the product. Use grid paper to help.

 You can solve the simpler problems in any order.

5. 14 × 21

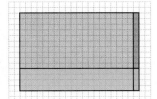

6. 14 × 12

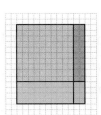

For **7** through **10**, find the product. Use grid paper to help.

7. 26 × 18

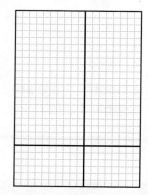

8. 19 × 27

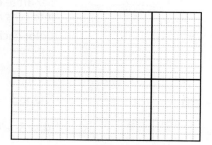

9. 11 × 16

10. 23 × 23

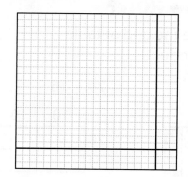

In **11** through **16**, copy and complete the table. Then find the total.

11. 18 × 25
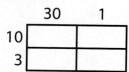

12. 12 × 28
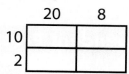

13. 17 × 68
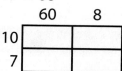

14. 13 × 31

15. 16 × 27
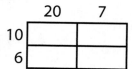

16. 22 × 88
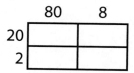

In **17** through **21**, find the product using either method.

17.   41
   × 12

18.   38
   × 27

19.   58
   × 19

20.   29
   × 15

21.   73
   × 47

22. Writing to Explain Why is the product of 15 × 32 equal to the sum of 10 × 32 and 5 × 32?

23. The flagpole in front of City Hall in Luis's town is 35 feet tall. How many inches tall is the flagpole?

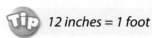 *12 inches = 1 foot*

24. The prices at Nolan's Novelties store are shown at the right. If 27 boxes of neon keychains and 35 boxes of glow-in-the-dark pens were purchased, what was the total cost?

Item	Price per box
Neon keychains	$15
Glow-in-the-dark pens	$10

25. The Florida Theatre in Jacksonville has 1,918 seats in all. Section 200 has 27 rows with 14 seats in each row. How many seats are in Section 200?

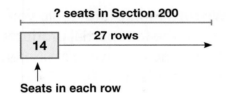

26. Algebra Elijah has *n* customers in his lawn-mowing business. He mows each lawn once a week. Which expression shows how many lawns he mows in 12 weeks?

A $n + 12$ **C** $12 - n$

B $n \times 12$ **D** $12 \div n$

For **27** and **28**, use the diagram to the right.

27. Maggie is making a balloon game for the school fair. Kids will throw darts to try to pop the balloons. How many balloons are needed to set up the game?

28. Think About the Process Maggie knows that she will have to completely refill the balloon board about 15 times a day. Which expression shows how to find the number of balloons she will need?

F 15×13 **H** $15 \times (13 \times 14)$

G 15×14 **I** $15 \times (13 + 14)$

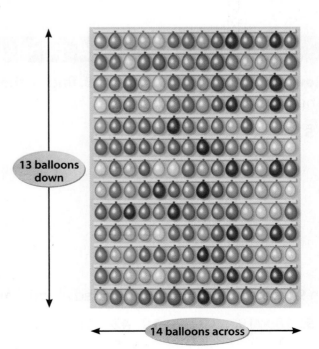

13 balloons down

14 balloons across

MA.4.A.1.2 Multiply multi-digit whole numbers through four digits fluently, demonstrating understanding of the standard algorithm, and checking for reasonableness of results, including solving real-world problems.

Arrays and an Expanded Algorithm

How can you record multiplication?

Marcia picked oranges and put them in 12 mesh bags. Each bag had the same number of oranges. What is the total number of oranges Marcia picked?

Choose an Operation
Multiply to join equal groups.

15 oranges in each bag

Guided Practice*

Do you know HOW?

In **1** and **2**, find all the partial products. Then add to find the product.

1.
```
   23
 × 14
```

2.
```
   41
 × 25
```

Do you UNDERSTAND?

3. In the example above, why do you find 2 × 10 rather than 2 × 1?

4. Writing to Explain Could you record the four partial products in the example above in a different order? Explain.

Independent Practice

Leveled Practice In **5** through **8**, find all the partial products. Then add to find the product.

5.
```
   34
 × 51
```

6.
```
   73
 × 81
```

7.
```
   64
 × 32
```

8.
```
   26
 × 53
```

In **9** through **16**, use the expanded algorithm to find each product.

9. 18 × 19

10. 42 × 16

11. 15 × 64

12. 27 × 51

For another example, see Set B on page 148.

Find 12 × 15.

Use an array to model 12 × 15.

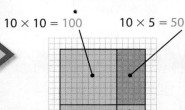

10 × 10 = 100   10 × 5 = 50

2 × 10 = 20   2 × 5 = 10

Step 1

Use the expanded algorithm to find 12 × 15.
Multiply the ones.

```
    15
  × 12
   10    2 × 5 = 10
   20    2 × 10 = 20
```

10 and 20 are partial products.

Step 2

Multiply the tens. Then add all the partial products.

```
      15
    × 12
      10
      20
      50    10 × 5 = 50
  +  100    10 × 10 = 100
     180
```

Marcia picked 180 oranges.

13. 17 × 38   **14.** 33 × 24   **15.** 43 × 19   **16.** 52 × 23

Problem Solving

17. A pair of one type of shoes weighs 15 ounces. The shoebox they come in weighs 2 ounces. Which is the total weight of 15 pairs of these shoes, including the boxes?

    A 147 ounces   **C** 225 ounces

    B 155 ounces   **D** 255 ounces

18. Runway 9 at the Miami Airport is 13,000 feet long, and Runway 12 is 9,354 feet long. How much shorter is Runway 12 than Runway 9?

19. Estimation Sara estimated 23 × 43 by using 20 × 40. Sam estimated 23 × 43 by using 25 × 40. Explain why Sam's method will give a closer estimate than Sara's method.

Critical THINKING

20. A school has two large patios. One is rectangular and is 24 feet long by 18 feet wide. The other is square and each side is 21 feet long. Which patio has a greater perimeter? Explain.

THINK
SOLVE
EXPLAIN

21. The Castillo de San Marcos is the Spanish fortress in old St. Augustine, Florida. It was built between 1672 and 1695. Rounded to the nearest ten thousand, how many pesos did it cost to build the fortress at that time?

It cost 138,375 pesos to build this fortress.

Lesson

7-3

MA.4.A.1.2 Multiply multi-digit whole numbers through four digits fluently, demonstrating understanding of the standard algorithm, and checking for reasonableness of results, including solving real-world problems.

Multiplying 2-Digit Numbers by Multiples of Ten

28 rocks per kit

How can you find the product?

Mr. Jeffrey buys 20 rock identification kits for his science classes. If each kit has 28 rocks, how many rocks are there in all?

Choose an Operation

Multiply to find the number of rocks.

Guided Practice*

Do you know HOW?

In **1** through **6**, multiply to find each product.

1. $\begin{array}{r} 12 \\ \times\ 20 \\ \hline \quad 0 \end{array}$

2. $\begin{array}{r} 21 \\ \times\ 30 \\ \hline \quad 0 \end{array}$

3. 35×20

4. 63×20

5. 27×60

6. 66×40

Do you UNDERSTAND?

7. **Writing to Explain** Why is there a zero in the ones place when you multiply by 20 in the example above?

8. What simpler multiplication problem can you solve to find 38×70?

9. Each year, Mr. Jeffrey's school orders 100 rock kits. How many rocks are in all of the kits?

Independent Practice

Leveled Practice In **10** through **30**, multiply to find each product.

10. $\begin{array}{r} 12 \\ \times\ 30 \\ \hline \quad 0 \end{array}$

11. $\begin{array}{r} 24 \\ \times\ 50 \\ \hline \quad ,\quad 0 \end{array}$

12. $\begin{array}{r} 33 \\ \times\ 20 \\ \hline \quad 0 \end{array}$

13. $\begin{array}{r} 71 \\ \times\ 30 \\ \hline \quad ,\quad 0 \end{array}$

14. $\begin{array}{r} 63 \\ \times\ 40 \\ \hline \quad ,\quad 0 \end{array}$

15. 18×30

16. 20×51

17. 32×30

18. 40×22

19. 24×40

20. 34×50

21. 40×73

22. 88×30

23. 75×40

24. 22×60

25. 13×50

26. 60×23

27. 32×20

28. 82×80

29. 62×60

30. 52×50

*For another example, see Set C on page 148.

One Way

Find 20 × 28.

Break 28 into tens and ones: **28 = 20 + 8.**

Use a grid to find the partial products.

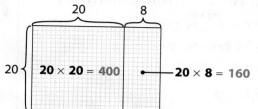

20 { **20 × 20 = 400** •————**20 × 8 = 160**

Add the partial products to find the total.
400 + 160 = 560

Another Way

Find 20 × 28.

Multiply 2 tens × 28.

```
  1
  28
× 20
─────
 560
```

Record a 0 in the ones place of the answer. This shows how many tens are in the answer.

There are 560 rocks in all.

Problem Solving

31. Number Sense Rex's class raised frogs from tadpoles. The class has 21 students, and each raised 6 tadpoles. All but 6 of the tadpoles grew to be frogs. Write a number sentence to show how many frogs the class has.

32. How many fossil kits with 12 samples each have the same number of fossils as 30 fossil kits with 8 samples each?

A 20   **C** 200

B 24   **D** 240

33. **Science** It took Davina 45 minutes to clean her room. How many seconds did it take her?

Tip *There are 60 seconds in one minute.*

34. One family of Florida scrub jays inhabits about 25 acres of land. No other scrub jay families live within this area. How many acres of land do 24 families of Florida scrub jays need?

35. A roller coaster runs rides 50 times an hour and reaches speeds of 70 miles per hour. Using the picture at the right, how many people ride each hour?

F   160

G   1,500

H   1,600

I   2,240

8 rows of 4 people

Lesson
7-4

MA.4.A.1.2 Multiply multi-digit whole numbers through four digits fluently, demonstrating understanding of the standard algorithm, and checking for reasonableness of results, including solving real-world problems.

Multiplying 2-Digit by 2-Digit Numbers

What is a common way to record multiplication?

A ferry carried an average of 37 cars per trip on Saturday. If the ferry made 24 one-way trips, how many cars did it carry?

Choose an Operation Multiply to join equal groups.

37 cars per trip

Guided Practice*

Do you know HOW?

In **1** through **6**, find the product. Estimate to check for reasonableness.

1.
```
   41
 × 23
   12▧
  ▧20
   9▧▧
```

2.
```
   63
 × 31
   ▧3
  18▧
 1,95▧
```

3. 27 × 12
4. 36 × 23
5. 18 × 42
6. 34 × 21

Do you UNDERSTAND?

Critical THINKING

7. In the example above, is 888 a reasonable answer for 37 × 24?

8. **Writing to Explain** The ferry made 36 one-way trips on Sunday and carried an average of 21 cars on each trip.

   a How many cars were ferried on Sunday?

   b On which day were more cars ferried, Saturday or Sunday? Explain.

Independent Practice

Leveled Practice For **9** through **13**, find the product. Estimate to check for reasonableness.

9.
```
   33
 × 18
   2▧▧
  ▧▧0
   5▧▧
```

10.
```
   46
 × 22
   ▧2
  ▧▧0
 ▧,▧▧▧
```

11.
```
   67
 × 57
   ▧▧9
  3▧▧▧
 3,▧▧▧
```

12.
```
   45
 × 16
   2▧▧
  ▧▧0
  ▧▧▧
```

13.
```
   35
 × 29
   ▧▧▧
  ▧▧▧
 ▧,▧▧▧
```

*For another example, see Set D on page 149.

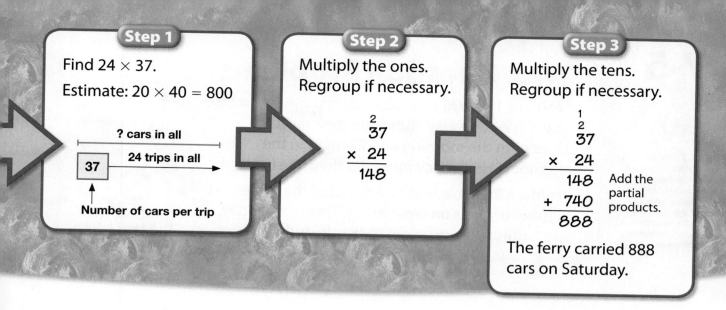

Step 1

Find 24 × 37.
Estimate: 20 × 40 = 800

? cars in all

37 | 24 trips in all →

Number of cars per trip

Step 2

Multiply the ones.
Regroup if necessary.

$$\begin{array}{r} \overset{2}{37} \\ \times\ 24 \\ \hline 148 \end{array}$$

Step 3

Multiply the tens.
Regroup if necessary.

$$\begin{array}{r} \overset{1}{\underset{}{\overset{2}{37}}} \\ \times\ 24 \\ \hline 148 \\ +\ 740 \\ \hline 888 \end{array}$$

Add the partial products.

The ferry carried 888 cars on Saturday.

In **14** through **23**, find the product. Estimate to check for reasonableness.

14. 37
× 21

15. 54
× 37

16. 63
× 22

17. 34
× 41

18. 81
× 17

19. 56 × 31   **20.** 53 × 17   **21.** 81 × 46   **22.** 15 × 16   **23.** 17 × 21

Problem Solving

24. Use the diagram to the right. The *Queen Mary 2*'s height above the water is the same as a 23-story building. If a single story is 11 feet tall, how high above the water is the *Queen Mary 2*?

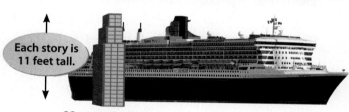

Each story is 11 feet tall.

23-story building   Queen Mary 2

25. Mr. Morris bought sketch pads for 24 of his students. Each pad contained 50 sheets. How many sheets of paper were there all together?

? sheets in all

50 | 24 students →

Sheets in each

26. There are 52 weeks in one year. How many weeks are in 10 years?

A   62 weeks   **C**   520 weeks

B   120 weeks   **D**   620 weeks

27. In 2005, an ultra light airplane tracked Monarch butterflies migrating to Mexico. Over 13 days, how many miles did the butterflies travel?

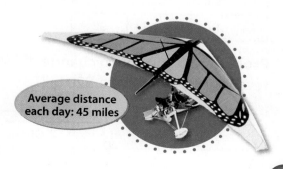

Average distance each day: 45 miles

MA.4.A.1.2 Multiply multi-digit whole numbers through four digits fluently, demonstrating understanding of the standard algorithm, and checking for reasonableness of results, including solving real-world problems.

Problem Solving

Two-Question Problems

Problem 1: Maya and Jose are preparing for a bike race. On Wednesday, they rode their bicycles 32 miles in the morning and 22 miles in the afternoon. How many miles did they ride in all?

Problem 2: Maya and Jose bicycled the same number of miles on Wednesday, Thursday, Friday, and Saturday. How far did they ride during the week?

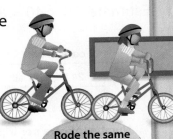

Rode the same distance 4 days in a row

Guided Practice*

Do you know HOW?

Solve.

1. **Problem 1:** Julia used 3 rolls of film to take pictures on her vacation. There were 24 pictures on each roll. How many pictures did Julia take?

   Problem 2: Julia had two copies made of each picture. How many copies were made?

Do you UNDERSTAND?

2. Why do you need to know how many pictures Julia took to solve Problem 2?

3. **Write a Problem** Write a problem that uses the answer from Problem 1 below.
   Problem 1: Cal puts one vase on each of 5 tables. There are 6 flowers in each vase. How many flowers does Cal use?

Independent Practice

Solve.

4. **Problem 1:** Martin buys a sandwich for $4, an apple for $1, and a drink for $2. How much did he pay in all?

   ? Cost of Martin's lunch

$4	$1	$2

   Problem 2: How much change did Martin receive if he paid with a $20 bill?

   $20

Lunch	Change

Stuck? Try this....

• What do I know?
• What diagram can I use to help understand the problem?
• Can I use addition, subtraction, multiplication, or division?
• Is all of my work correct?
• Did I answer the right question?
• Is my answer reasonable?

*For another example, see Set E on page 149.

Sometimes you have to answer one problem to solve another problem.

? miles bicycled on Wednesday

32	22

32 miles + 22 miles = 54 miles

Maya and Jose bicycled 54 miles on Wednesday.

Use the answer from Problem 1 to solve Problem 2.

? miles bicycled during the week

54	54	54	54

↑ Miles each day

4 × 54 miles = 216 miles

Maya and Jose rode 216 miles during the week.

---

5. Problem 1: Sally and Byron mow their neighbors' lawns in the summer. Sally mows 5 lawns each week. Byron mows three times as many lawns as Sally. How many lawns does Byron mow each week?

? lawns mowed each week

Byron	5	5	5	3 times as many
Sally	5			

Problem 2: Byron gets paid $20 for each lawn he mows. How much does Byron get paid each week?

? Amount Byron gets paid each week

20	15 lawns →

↑ amount paid for each lawn

6. Problem 1: June's mom brought 3 bags of plain popcorn and 2 bags of caramel popcorn to the park. How many bags of popcorn did June's mom bring to the park?

? bags in all

3	2

Problem 2: Each bag of popcorn that June's mom brought to the park contained 16 servings. How many servings of popcorn did June's mom bring to the park?

? servings in all

16	16	16	16	16

↑ Servings in each bag

7. 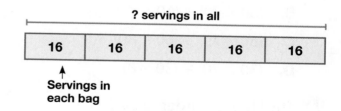 **Science** The Florida panther is known to sleep about 18 hours a day. About how many hours would a Florida panther sleep in 3 weeks?

A 478 hours   **C** 252 hours

B 378 hours   **D** 54 hours

8. **Critical THINKING** Dave plans to retile his porch floor. He wants to buy 25 black tiles and 23 white tiles. Each tile costs $2. How much money will it cost Dave to retile his porch floor?

1 Tess has 15 pages in her coin collector's album. Each page holds 32 coins. Tess is using the table below to find how many coins are in her album. Which number is missing from the table? (7-1)

A. 5

B. 150

C. 315

D. 480

	30	2
10	300	20
5		10

2 What is 35×64? (7-4)

F. 1,240

G. 2,140

H. 2,240

I. 2,340

3 Which shows one correct way to use partial products to find 60×78? (7-3)

A. $(60 \times 70) + (60 \times 8)$

B. $(60 \times 70) + (60 \times 780)$

C. $(60 \times 70) + (60 \times 80)$

D. $(30 \times 70) + (30 \times 8)$

4 The librarian ordered 24 sets of sturdy bookmarks. Each set contained 20 bookmarks with different designs. How many bookmarks did the librarian order? (7-3)

F. 4,800

G. 2,420

H. 480

I. 240

5 Jonah visited Key West, Florida. He bought 25 postcards that cost 17 cents each. He used partial products to find the total cost in cents. What is the missing partial product? (7-2)

A. 2

B. 20

C. 200

D. 425

$$\begin{array}{r} 17 \\ \times\ 25 \\ \hline 35 \\ 50 \\ 140 \\ +\ \blacksquare\blacksquare\blacksquare \\ \hline \end{array}$$

6 What is 15×29? (7-1)

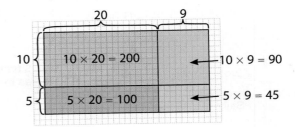

F. 335

G. 390

H. 435

I. 535

7 The Orlando Science Center bought 28 new microscopes for young visitors to use. The price for each microscope was $87. How much did the microscopes cost in all? (7-4)

A. $1,436

B. $1,756

C. $2,336

D. $2,436

8 Which partial products could be added to find 13 × 46? (7-2)

F. 9, 12, 60, and 40

G. 9, 120, 60, and 400

H. 18, 120, 60, and 400

I. 18, 12, 60, and 400

$$\begin{array}{r} 46 \\ \times\ 13 \\ \hline \end{array}$$

9 Tori's goal is to learn 15 new Spanish words each day. If Tori meets her goal, how many new Spanish words will she have learned after 40 days? (7-3)

A. 600

B. 590

C. 500

D. 55

10 Look at the table below. Which shows all of the parts to find the product of 78 and 49? (7-1)

	70	8
40		
9		

F. 280; 320; 630; 72

G. 30; 32; 61; 1

H. 110; 48; 79; 17

I. 2,800; 320; 630; 72

11 Sydney made 21 wooden penguins to sell at a fair. She used 5 pompoms and 4 beads to decorate each penguin. How many pompoms and beads did she use for the wooden penguins in all? (7-5)

A. 420

B. 189

C. 30

D. 20

12 A science museum in Fort Lauderdale, Florida, presented a live exhibit that showed different Florida butterflies. Each habitat area held 48 butterflies. There were 12 different habitat areas. How many butterflies were in the live exhibit in all? (7-4)

13 THINK SOLVE EXPLAIN

Problem 1: The longest book Toshi had read was 304 pages. She just finished *Kira-Kira* by Cynthia Kadohata, which is 256 pages. How much longer was the longest book Toshi read than *Kira-Kira*?

Problem 2: Toshi estimates that she needs 2 minutes to read one page. How many minutes longer did she spend reading the 304-page book than *Kira-Kira*? Explain how you found your answer. (7-5)

Set A, pages 134–137

Find 14 × 12. Draw a 14 × 12 array.

Separate each factor into tens and ones.
Color each section a different color.
Add each part to find the product.

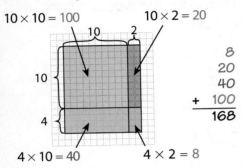

10 × 10 = 100   10 × 2 = 20

```
        8
       20
       40
   +  100
      168
```

4 × 10 = 40   4 × 2 = 8

Remember you can solve the simpler problems in any order and the answer will remain the same.

Find each product. Use grid paper to help.

1. 14 × 32   **2.** 64 × 12

3. 56 × 17   **4.** 72 × 15

5. 26 × 63   **6.** 47 × 27

Set B, pages 138–139

Find 16 × 35. List the partial products.

First multiply the ones:
```
    16
 ×  35
    30      5 × 6
    50      5 × 10
```

Now multiply the tens:
```
    16
 ×  35
    30
    50
   180      30 × 6
 + 300      30 × 10
```

Add: 30 + 50 + 180 + 300 = 560

Remember that to multiply two 2-digit factors, you must find four partial products. You can find them in any order. Be sure to use correct place value.

Multiply to find each product.

1. 18 × 34   **2.** 51 × 15

3. 53 × 17   **4.** 26 × 28

5. 22 × 66   **6.** 41 × 54

7. 64 × 86   **8.** 32 × 71

9. 93 × 44   **10.** 57 × 91

Set C, pages 140–141

Find 16 × 30.
Multiply 16 × 3 tens.

```
    1
    16
 ×  30
   480
```
The 0 in the ones places shows how many tens are in the answer.

Remember to record a 0 in the ones place of the answer.

Multiply to find each product.

1. 39 × 10   **2.** 56 × 30

3. 41 × 20   **4.** 60 × 13

Set D, pages 142–143

Use the standard algorithm to find 14×19.

Multiply the ones. Regroup if necessary.

$$\begin{array}{r} \overset{3}{1}9 \\ \times\ 14 \\ \hline 76 \end{array}$$

Multiply the tens. Regroup if necessary.

$$\begin{array}{r} 19 \\ \times\ 14 \\ \hline 76 \\ +\ 190 \\ \hline 266 \end{array}$$ Add the partial products.

Remember to regroup if necessary.

Find the product. Estimate to check for reasonableness.

1. $\begin{array}{r} 53 \\ \times\ 36 \end{array}$

2. $\begin{array}{r} 23 \\ \times\ 18 \end{array}$

3. $\begin{array}{r} 73 \\ \times\ 33 \end{array}$

4. $\begin{array}{r} 31 \\ \times\ 74 \end{array}$

5. 56×64

6. 39×82

Set E, pages 144–145

When you solve two-question problems, solve the first problem. Then use that answer to help you solve the second problem.

Problem 1: It costs $3 for a ticket to the pool and $7 for a ticket to the water park. How much does it cost for 4 people to go to the pool and the water park?

Cost of 4 pool tickets:
$4 \times \$3 = \$12$

Cost of 4 water park tickets:
$4 \times \$7 = \$28$

Add the totals:
$\$12 + \$28 = \$40$

It costs $40 for 4 people to go to the pool and the water park.

Problem 2: How much more does it cost the group of 4 to go to the water park than to the pool?

$28 - 12 = 16$

It costs $16 more.

Remember to use the information from Problem 1 to answer Problem 2.

Solve.

1. **Problem 1:** Rose visited 14 cities on her vacation. She bought 3 souvenirs in each city to send to her friends. How many souvenirs did Rose buy on her vacation?

   Problem 2: It costs Rose $2 to send each souvenir to her friends. How much did it cost Rose to send all of the souvenirs that she bought on vacation?

2. **Problem 1:** Mrs. Conrath bought 9 packages of lead pencils for her classroom. Each package has 8 lead pencils. How many lead pencils did she buy?

   Problem 2: Mrs. Conrath saved 25 lead pencils for the Math Club. How many lead pencils were used for her classroom?

Number Sense: Multiplying Greater Numbers

1 About how many baseballs are used in one professional baseball game? You will find out in Lesson 8-2.

2 The Pike's Peak Cog Railway is the highest cog railway in the world. How long is the train ride to the top? You will find out in Lesson 8-3.

3 About how many hours per year does a student in the United States spend in school? You will find out in Lesson 8-5.

4 Kilauea is the most active volcano in the world. About how many cubic meters of lava does it discharge in one hour? You will find out in Lesson 8-3.

Review What You Know!

Vocabulary

Choose the best term from the box.

- product
- factor
- array
- multiple

1. A(n) ? is the result of multiplication.

2. The number 9 is a(n) ? of 3.

3. You can use a(n) ? to display objects in equal rows.

Estimating Products

Estimate each product.

4. 19×32 5. 27×53

6. 41×83 7. 93×74

Multiplying by 2-Digit Numbers

Find each product.

8. 22×14 9. 35×47

10. 48×19 11. 75×27

Partial Products

12. **Writing to Explain** Explain how you could use the grid below to multiply 16×23.

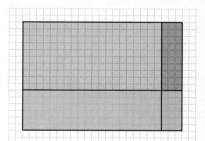

Topic Essential Questions
- How can greater products be estimated?
- How can greater numbers be multiplied by 10, 100, and 1,000?

Lesson

8-1

MA.4.A.1.2 Multiply multi-digit whole numbers through four digits fluently, demonstrating understanding of the standard algorithm, and checking for reasonableness of results, including solving real-world problems.

Multiplying Multiples of 10, 100, and 1,000

30 bottles in a case

How can you multiply with multiples of 10, 100, and 1,000?

The Blue Bottle Company produces water bottles. If it made 600 cases of water in one day, how many water bottles would it produce in all?

Choose an Operation Multiply to join equal groups.

Other Examples

When multiplying by multiples of 10, 100, and 1,000, the product is the basic fact followed by the number of zeros in both factors.

Find 400 × 800.
4 × 8 = 32
400 × 800 = 320,000

Find 2,000 × 700.
2 × 7 = 14
2,000 × 700 = 1,400,000

Find 6,000 × 5,000.
6 × 5 = 30
6,000 × 5,000 = 30,000,000

Guided Practice*

Do you know HOW?

In **1** through **4**, use basic facts and patterns to find each product.

1. 40 × 200

2. 60 × 2,000

3.   300
   × 500

4.   7,000
   × 3,000

Do you UNDERSTAND?

5. In the example above, suppose each case held 50 water bottles. How many bottles would there be in 600 cases?

6. The product of two multiples of 100 is 120,000. What are the possible factors?

Independent Practice

Leveled Practice In **7** through **18**, find each product.

7. 8 × 6 = ▢
80 × 600 = ▢

8. 4 × 9 = ▢
400 × 90 = ▢

9. 2 × 5 = ▢
20 × 500 = ▢

10. 5 × 7 = ▢
50 × 700 = ▢

11. 400 × 400

12. 500 × 600

13. 200 × 700

14. 800 × 500

15.   5,000
   ×   700

16.   8,000
   ×   300

17.   2,000
   ×   900

18.   6,000
   × 6,000

To find 600 × 30, use a pattern.

$$6 × 30 = 180$$
$$60 × 30 = 1,800$$
$$600 × 30 = 18,000$$

The Blue Bottle Company can produce 18,000 water bottles in one day.

The Blue Bottle Company received a special order for 500 cases of water bottles containing 40 water bottles each. How many water bottles did the company produce to fill this order?

Find 500 × 40.

When the product of a basic fact ends in zero, there will be an extra zero in the answer.

$$5 × 4 = 20$$
$$500 × 40 = 20,000$$

The Blue Bottle Company produced 20,000 water bottles to fill the special order.

Problem Solving

For **19** and **20**, use the table at the right.

19. **Science** The number of times that a heart beats each minute is called the heart rate. Smaller animals usually have higher heart rates than larger animals. Find the number of times each animal's heart beats in one hour.

TIP *There are 60 minutes in one hour.*

Average Animal Heart Rates	
Animal	**Beats per Minute**
Elephant	30
Pig	70
Small Dog	100
Rabbit	200
Mouse	600

20. How many more times would a mouse's heart beat in 1,000 minutes compared to an elephant's heart?

21. **Estimation** A hummingbird's heart can beat up to 1,260 times per minute. About how many times does it beat in 5 minutes?

22. In one year, a city recorded a total of 97 rainy days. How many days did it NOT rain during that year?

365 days in one year	
97	?

23. The goal of Beaumont School was to collect 15,000 soup labels. Did the school meet its goal if 20 classes collected 500 labels each? How many more or fewer labels than 15,000 did the school collect?

Critical THINKING

24. Kevin has saved $82. He wants to buy a skateboard that costs $63 and a helmet that costs $32. How much more does Kevin need to save?

   A $95   **C** $19

   B $31   **D** $13

25. **Writing to Explain** How many zeros will be in the product of 500 × 8,000? Explain how you know.

MA.4.A.1.2 Multiply multi-digit whole numbers through four digits fluently, demonstrating understanding of the standard algorithm, and checking for reasonableness of results, including solving real-world problems.

Estimating Products

What are some ways to estimate?

In 1991, NASA launched the Upper Atmosphere Research Satellite (UARS). It orbits Earth about 105 times each week. There are 52 weeks in one year.

About how many orbits does it make in one year?

Orbits Earth about 105 times each week

Another Example **How can you estimate the product of two 3-digit numbers?**

Northern Space Company has 415 employees. The company is ordering business cards for each of its employees. If each employee receives a set of 230 business cards, how many cards will the company order in all?

Estimate 230 × 415.

230 business cards

One Way

Use rounding to estimate.

230 × 415

Round 230 to 200.
Round 415 to 400.

200 × 400 = 80,000

The company will order about 80,000 business cards.

Another Way

Use compatible numbers to estimate.

230 × 415

Change 230 to 250.
Change 415 to 400.

250 × 400 = 100,000

The company will order about 100,000 business cards.

Explain It

1. Look at the estimate that was found using rounding. Is that estimate greater or less than the actual product? How do you know?

2. Which of the estimates above is the better estimate? Explain your thinking.

One Way

Use **rounding** to estimate the number of orbits in one year.

52×105

Round 105 to 100.

$52 \times 100 = 5,200$

UARS orbits Earth about 5,200 times each year.

Another Way

Use **compatible numbers** to estimate the number of orbits in one year.

Compatible numbers are easy to multiply.

52×105

Change 52 to 55.

Change 105 to 100.

$55 \times 100 = 5,500$

UARS orbits Earth about 5,500 times each year.

Guided Practice*

Do you know HOW?

In **1** through **4**, find the estimate for each product.

1. $\begin{array}{r} 203 \\ \times\ \ 37 \\ \hline \end{array}$

2. $\begin{array}{r} 716 \\ \times\ 106 \\ \hline \end{array}$

3. 425×62

4. 846×491

Do you UNDERSTAND?

5. **Writing to Explain** In the example above, why are the estimates not the same?

6. About how many times does UARS orbit Earth in 25 weeks?

Independent Practice

In **7** through **26**, find the estimate for each product.

 Tip You can round one number or both numbers to estimate the product.

7. $\begin{array}{r} 324 \\ \times\ \ 93 \\ \hline \end{array}$

8. $\begin{array}{r} 210 \\ \times\ 196 \\ \hline \end{array}$

9. $\begin{array}{r} 346 \\ \times\ \ 21 \\ \hline \end{array}$

10. $\begin{array}{r} 835 \\ \times\ 296 \\ \hline \end{array}$

11. $\begin{array}{r} 531 \\ \times\ 728 \\ \hline \end{array}$

12. $\begin{array}{r} 210 \\ \times\ \ 19 \\ \hline \end{array}$

13. $\begin{array}{r} 602 \\ \times\ 433 \\ \hline \end{array}$

14. $\begin{array}{r} 202 \\ \times\ \ 61 \\ \hline \end{array}$

15. 198×605

16. 153×28

17. 703×42

18. 387×24

19. 503×42

20. 885×526

21. 840×49

22. 922×396

23. 805×926

24. 47×530

25. 242×319

26. 785×668

27. In one mission, an American astronaut spent more than 236 hours in space. About how many minutes did he spend in space?

28. At a used book sale, Ms. Lane bought 3 novels for $5 each. She also bought 4 children's books for $3 each. She paid with a $50-bill. How much did Ms. Lane spend on books?

29. Estimate to decide which has a greater product, 396 × 321 or 324 × 325. Explain.

30. **Science** The Mars Orbiter circles the planet Mars every 25 hours. About how many hours does it take to make 125 orbits?

31. Describe how you would use compatible numbers to estimate 248 × 38.

THINK
SOLVE
EXPLAIN

32. A truck driver made 37 trips last year. Her average trip was 885 miles. About how far did she drive in all?

33. Elena and Carlos both took pictures while on vacation. Elena took 246 pictures. Carlos took 4 times as many. How many pictures did Carlos take?

? pictures

Carlos	246	246	246	246	4 times as many
Elena	246				

34. **Estimation** The Hubble Space Telescope (HST) orbits the Earth about 375 miles above Earth's surface. Earth's moon is located 637 times as far from Earth as the HST. About how many miles away is Earth's moon?

A 180,000   **C** 200,000

B 240,000   **D** 280,000

35. In a puzzle competition, 75 children each tried to complete a jigsaw puzzle with 385 pieces. About how many puzzle pieces were there in all?

36. A cat usually has 4 rows of 3 whiskers on each side of its face. How many whiskers are there on 18 cats?

37. **Think About the Process** What is the best way to estimate how many baseballs are used in a season of 162 games?

Critical THINKING

F 100 × 6   **H** 1,000 × 60

G 160 × 60   **I** 200 × 200

About 57 baseballs are used in one professional baseball game.

Find each product. Estimate to check
if the answer is reasonable.

1. 21
  × 4

2. 843
  × 6

3. 6,318
  × 5

4. 528
  × 9

5. 40
  × 3

6. 17
  × 8

7. 2,175
  × 2

8. 796
  × 7

9. 4,927
  × 6

10. 1,234
  × 9

11. 700
  × 5

12. 99
  × 9

13. 5,364
  × 4

Find each difference. Estimate to check
if the answer is reasonable.

14. 3,427 − 648

15. 7,005 − 6,496

16. 502 − 89

Error Search Find each product that is not correct.
Write it correctly and explain the error.

17. 6,829
  × 5
  34,145

18. 438
  × 9
  3,872

19. 2,365
  × 3
  7,098

20. 45
  × 4
  49

21. 777
  × 7
  5,439

Number Sense

Estimating and Reasoning Write whether each
statement is true or false. Explain your answer.

22. The product of 6 and 39 is less than 240.

23. The sum of 3,721 and 1,273 is greater than 4,000 but less than 6,000.

24. The product of 5 and 286 is greater than 1,500.

25. The product of 4 and 3,123 is closer to 12,000 than 16,000.

26. The sum of 4,637 and 2,878 is greater than 8,000.

27. The quotient of 4 divided by 1 is 1.

MA.4.A.1.2 Multiply multi-digit whole numbers through four digits fluently, demonstrating understanding of the standard algorithm, and checking for reasonableness of results, including solving real-world problems.

Multiplying by Multiples of 10, 100, and 1,000
How do you multiply greater numbers?

How much will the farm earn when 1,600 families take the one-hour tour and when 2,000 families take the two-hour tour?

Choose an Operation Multiply the cost per family by the number of families.

Barrington Farm Tours	
Tours	**Cost per Family**
1-hour	$20
2-hour	$25

Data

Guided Practice*

Do you know HOW?

In **1** through **6**, use mental math to find the product.

1. $\begin{array}{r} 100 \\ \times\ 25 \\ \hline \end{array}$

2. $\begin{array}{r} 200 \\ \times\ 54 \\ \hline \end{array}$

3. $\begin{array}{r} 3{,}000 \\ \times\quad 32 \\ \hline \end{array}$

4. $\begin{array}{r} 210 \\ \times\ 50 \\ \hline \end{array}$

5. $30 \times 3{,}230$

6. 20×150

Do you UNDERSTAND?

7. **Writing to Explain** Why does the product of $25 \times 2{,}000$ have 4 zeros when 2,000 only has 3 zeros?

8. A school gets a special family pass of $20 for each of its 134 families. How much will the school families be charged in all?

Independent Practice

In **9** through **23**, use mental math to find the product.

9. $\begin{array}{r} 240 \\ \times\ 20 \\ \hline \end{array}$

10. $\begin{array}{r} 440 \\ \times\ 20 \\ \hline \end{array}$

11. $\begin{array}{r} 9{,}000 \\ \times\quad 11 \\ \hline \end{array}$

12. $\begin{array}{r} 1{,}000 \\ \times\quad 25 \\ \hline \end{array}$

13. $\begin{array}{r} 170 \\ \times\ 30 \\ \hline \end{array}$

14. $\begin{array}{r} 1{,}500 \\ \times\quad 40 \\ \hline \end{array}$

15. $\begin{array}{r} 1{,}800 \\ \times\quad 20 \\ \hline \end{array}$

16. $\begin{array}{r} 200 \\ \times\ 32 \\ \hline \end{array}$

17. $\begin{array}{r} 290 \\ \times\ 20 \\ \hline \end{array}$

18. $\begin{array}{r} 4{,}200 \\ \times\quad 40 \\ \hline \end{array}$

19. $\begin{array}{r} 4{,}000 \\ \times\quad 24 \\ \hline \end{array}$

20. $\begin{array}{r} 660 \\ \times\ 40 \\ \hline \end{array}$

21. $\begin{array}{r} 2{,}000 \\ \times\quad 15 \\ \hline \end{array}$

22. $\begin{array}{r} 200 \\ \times\ 41 \\ \hline \end{array}$

23. $\begin{array}{r} 1{,}100 \\ \times\quad 30 \\ \hline \end{array}$

For another example, see Set C on page 168.

Find 1,600 × 20.

Use mental math.

$$16 \times 2 = 32$$
$$1,600 \times 20 = 32,000$$

The farm will earn $32,000 from the 1-hour tours.

Find 2,000 × 25.

Use mental math.

$$25 \times 2 = 50$$
$$25 \times 2,000 = 50,000$$

The farm will earn $50,000 from the 2-hour tours.

Problem Solving

For **24** and **25**, use the table at the right.

24. In 2010, how many DVDs were rented in 52 weeks? How many DVDs were purchased in this same time?

25. In 2011, how many more DVDs were purchased than rented in 52 weeks?

Critical THINKING

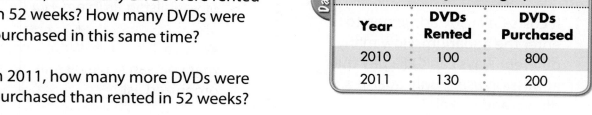

Videos-To-Go Sales Report (Weekly Averages)		
Year	DVDs Rented	DVDs Purchased
2010	100	800
2011	130	200

26. Think About the Process How could you break apart 9 × 25?

A (9 × 20) + (9 × 5)

B (9 × 20) + (9 × 25)

C (20 × 20) + (5 × 5)

D (3 × 20) + (3 × 5)

27. A ride on the Pike's Peak Cog Railway takes 75 minutes. If the train's average speed is 100 feet per minute, how long is the Pike's Peak Cog Railway?

28. Science Kilauea, a volcano on the island of Hawaii, has been active since 1983. About how many cubic meters of lava are discharged in one hour?

29. Mauna Kea is a dormant volcano on the island of Hawaii with an elevation of 13,796 feet. Kilauea rises 4,091 feet above sea level. How much taller is Mauna Kea than Kilauea?

Lava is discharged from the volcano at about 420 cubic meters per minute.

MA.4.A.6.1 Use and represent numbers through millions in various contexts, including estimation of relative sizes of amounts or distances.

Make an Organized List

Arthur is tiling a bathroom wall. He has 520 wall tiles. He wants to arrange them in patterns of hundreds and tens.

Using only hundreds and tens blocks, how many ways can he make 520?

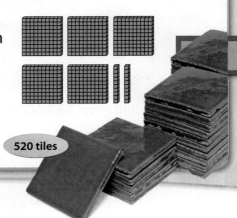

520 tiles

Guided Practice*

Do you know HOW?

Solve. Make an organized list to help you.

1. It costs Celia 50¢ admission to enter the aquarium. How many different ways can Celia pay the admission using only quarters, dimes, and nickels?

Do you UNDERSTAND?

2. What were the titles for the columns of your list in Problem 1?

3. **Write a Problem** Write a problem that you can solve by making an organized list.

Independent Practice

Solve.

4. List the ways to show 340 using patterns of hundreds and tens.

5. Simon asked Margaret to guess a number. He gave these hints.
   - The number has 3 digits.
   - The digit in the 100s place is less than 2.
   - The digit in the 10s place is greater than 8.
   - The number is even.

   What are the possible numbers?

6. Make a list showing the ways you can make a dollar using only quarters, dimes, and nickels and using no more than one nickel and no more than 9 dimes.

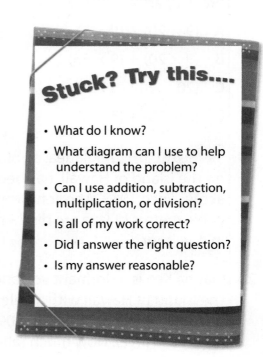

Stuck? Try this....

- What do I know?
- What diagram can I use to help understand the problem?
- Can I use addition, subtraction, multiplication, or division?
- Is all of my work correct?
- Did I answer the right question?
- Is my answer reasonable?

For another example, see Set D on page 169.

What do I know? I can use only hundreds blocks and tens blocks.

What am I asked to find? All of the combinations that show a total of 520

Record the combinations using an organized list.

Hundreds	5	4	3	2	1	0
Tens	2	12	22	32	42	52

There are 6 ways to make 520.

The answer is reasonable because the combinations have 5 or fewer hundreds blocks.

7. Lou's sandwiches are made with either wheat or white bread and have only one type of cheese—swiss, cheddar, provolone, or mozzarella. How many different kinds of sandwiches can Lou make?

8. A magazine stand sold 268 magazines in one week. If it sells the same number each week, how many magazines will the stand sell in 4 weeks?

9. Janie is making a bracelet. She has 1 red bead, 1 blue bead, and 1 white bead. How many possible ways can Janie arrange the beads?

10. Reasoning What two numbers have a sum of 12 and a difference of 4?

Critical THINKING

11. Alan has a cat, a goldfish, and a dog. He feeds them in a different order each day. How many different ways can he feed his pets?

12. Heather is writing a 3-digit number. She uses the digits 1, 5, and 9. What are the possible numbers she can write?

For **13** and **14**, use the picture at the right.

13. At the driving range, James wants to buy 200 golf balls. The golf balls are sold in buckets of 100, 50, and 10 golf balls. How many different ways can James buy 200 golf balls?

14. James hit 2 buckets of 100 golf balls, and his brother hit 1 bucket of 50. How many golf balls did they hit in all?

50 golf balls

100 golf balls

10 golf balls

MA.4.A.1.2 Multiply
multi-digit whole numbers
through four digits
fluently, demonstrating
understanding of the
standard algorithm, and
checking for reasonableness
of results, including solving
real-world problems.

Estimating Products with Greater Numbers

How can you estimate with greater numbers?

The average number of people that move to Florida each day is similar to the average number of people that move out. About how many people will move to Florida in one year?

In one day, 983 people moved to Florida.

Guided Practice*

Do you know HOW?

In **1** through **4**, estimate the product.

1.   175
       × 58

2.   495
       × 491

3. 8,125 × 62

4. 1,846 × 503

Do you UNDERSTAND?

5. Writing to Explain Is the rounding estimate in the example above greater or less than the actual product? How do you know?

6. If 212 people move to Kissimmee, Florida, each day, about how many people would move there in one year?

Independent Practice

In **7** through **22**, estimate the product.

7.   462
       × 75

8.   520
       × 778

9.   6,428
       ×   185

10.   1,748
        ×   846

11. 3,254
        × 755

12.   538
        × 29

13.   2,659
        ×   72

14.   631
        ×   408

15. 398 × 207

16. 2,916 × 78

17. 3,926 × 431

18. 218 × 639

19. 7,923 × 381

20. 673 × 415

21. 6,606 × 33

22. 9,121 × 137

For another example, see Set E on page 169.

One Way

Round each factor to the nearest hundred.

365 × 983

365 rounds to 400.
983 rounds to 1,000.

400 × 1,000 = 400,000

About 400,000 people will move to Florida in one year.

Another Way

Estimate by finding compatible numbers.

365 × 983

Change 983 to 1,000.

365 × 1,000 = 365,000

About 365,000 people will move to Florida in one year.

Problem Solving

23. 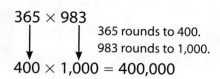 **Music** The Singing Tower is located in the Bok Tower Gardens in Lake Wales, Florida. It is known for housing one of the world's finest carillons, an instrument made up of bells. There are 211 steps from the ground to the bell chamber. Suppose the musician who plays the carillon walks up and down the steps every day. About how many steps in all does he walk up and down in 365 days?

THINK
SOLVE
EXPLAIN

24. **Geometry** What is the perimeter of the soccer field shown below?

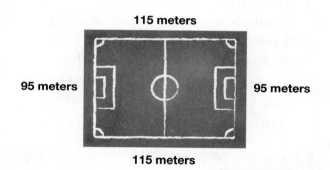

115 meters

95 meters   95 meters

115 meters

25. A movie theater sells large boxes of popcorn with about 280 pieces of popcorn in a box. If the theater sells 525 boxes in the month of July, about how many pieces of popcorn will it sell in all?

26. Which is a reasonable estimate for the product of 3,545 × 482?

Critical THINKING

A   20,000

B   200,000

C   2,000,000

D   20,000,000

27. In the United States, students spend about 900 hours each year in school. About how many hours would a student in the United States spend in school in 12 years?

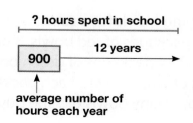

? hours spent in school

12 years

900

average number of hours each year

MA.4.A.1.2 Multiply multi-digit whole numbers through four digits fluently, demonstrating understanding of the standard algorithm, and checking for reasonableness of results, including solving real-world problems.

Problem Solving
Multiple-Step Problems

Justine and her father are going on a fishing trip. The prices for supplies, including tax, are shown in the table. Justine and her father have $41. They bought 2 box lunches, 4 bottles of water, 1 spinning reel, and 3 rolls of line. How many pounds of bait can they buy?

Captain Bob's Price List	
Bait	$3 per pound
Fishing Line	$3 each roll
Spinning reels	$10 each
Bottled water	$1 each
Box lunch	$6 each

Guided Practice*

Do you know HOW?

Solve.

1. Elsa babysits for the Smyth family. She earns $10 per hour on weekdays. She earns $15 per hour on the weekend. Last week, she worked 3 hours during the week and 4 hours on the weekend. How much did Elsa earn last week?

Do you UNDERSTAND?

2. What is the hidden question or questions in Problem 1?

3. **Write a Problem** Write a problem that contains a hidden question.

Independent Practice

For **4** through **7**, write and answer the hidden question or questions. Then solve the problem. Write your answer in a complete sentence.

4. Gabriella buys lunch for herself and her friend. She buys 2 sandwiches and 2 drinks. Each sandwich costs $4. The drinks cost a total of $3. How much did Gabriella spend on lunch?

5. Jamie is buying bowls for a school ice cream social. She buys 5 packages of red bowls, 3 packages of orange bowls, 4 packages of green bowls, and 7 packages of white bowls. Each package contains 8 bowls. How many bowls did she buy in all?

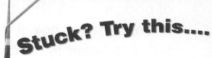

Stuck? Try this....

- What do I know?
- What diagram can I use to help understand the problem?
- Can I use addition, subtraction, multiplication, or division?
- Is all of my work correct?
- Did I answer the right question?
- Is my answer reasonable?

What do I know?

They bought:

2 lunches for $6 each
4 bottles of water for $1 each
1 spinning reel for $10
3 rolls of line for $3 each

What am I asked to find?

The number of pounds of bait they can buy with the money they have left

Plan

Find the hidden question. How much money do Justine and her father have left?

The cost of lunches is	2 × $6	= $12
The cost of water is	4 × $1	= $4
The cost of the reel is	1 × $10	= $10
The cost of the line is	3 × $3	= $9
	The total is	$35

$41 − $35 = $6   They have $6 left.

Divide to find how many pounds of bait they can buy.

6 ÷ 3 = 2   They can buy 2 pounds of bait.

---

6. Kelly used 6 cups of apples, 4 cups of oranges, and 2 cups of grapes to make a fruit salad. She put an equal amount in each of 6 bowls. How many cups of fruit salad were in each bowl?

7. Muriel used the same recipe as Kelly to make her fruit salad. Muriel also added 1 cup of cherries and 1 cup of bananas. She put 2 cups of fruit salad into each bowl. How many bowls did Muriel need?

Use the data at the right for **8** through **11**.

8. The band needs to purchase 48 T-shirts. How much would it cost to purchase them from Shirt Shack?

9. How much would it cost the band to purchase 48 T-shirts from Just Jerseys?

10. How much more would it cost to buy 24 T-shirts at Just Jerseys than at Shirt Shack?

11. Would it be less expensive to buy one shirt from Just Jerseys or Shirt Shack? Explain.

Critical THINKING

Data

Shirt Shack	
Number of shirts	**Price**
6	$42
12	$84
36	$252

Data

Just Jerseys	
Number of shirts	**Price**
8	$64
24	$192
40	$320

12. Each football practice is 45 minutes long. The team's next game is 6 practices away. How many minutes will they practice before the game?

A 135 minutes   **C** 243 minutes

B 270 minutes   **D** 2,430 minutes

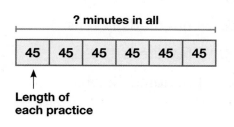

? minutes in all

| 45 | 45 | 45 | 45 | 45 | 45 |

Length of each practice

1 Frank owns an airplane. He flew it 104 times last year. Each flight was about 475 miles. About how far did Frank fly last year? (8-2)

A. 40,000 miles

B. 47,500 miles

C. 80,000 miles

D. 90,000 miles

2 How many zeros will be in the product of 600 × 500? (8-1)

F. 5

G. 4

H. 3

I. 2

3 Smith Elementary School purchased 1,250 new math textbooks. Each book cost $30. How much was spent on math textbooks? (8-3)

A. $3,650

B. $3,750

C. $36,500

D. $37,500

4 Which of the following is NOT a way to show 420, using patterns of hundreds and tens? (8-4)

F. 4 hundreds 2 tens

G. 3 hundreds 12 tens

H. 2 hundreds 12 tens

I. 1 hundred 32 tens

5 An amusement park sold 550 adult admission tickets. Each adult ticket cost $40. How much money was made on adult tickets? (8-3)

A. $22,000

B. $20,000

C. $2,200

D. $2,000

6 There are 16 ounces in one pound. A large St. Bernard dog can weigh up to 240 pounds. Which shows the best way to estimate the weight of the St. Bernard in ounces? (8-5)

F. 10 × 200

G. 10 × 240

H. 20 × 200

I. 20 × 300

7 Tia has 3 metamorphic, 8 igneous, and 7 sedimentary rocks. She stores her rocks equally in 2 cases. Which shows how she found the number of rocks to store in each case? (8-6)

A. 2 × 3

B. 10 ÷ 2

C. 2 × 18

D. 18 ÷ 2

8 There are 145 schools taking part in a band competition. Each school brings 38 band members. Which shows the best way to estimate how many band members are at the competition? (8-2)

  F. 200 × 40

  G. 150 × 40

  H. 100 × 40

  I. 100 × 30

9 Pat, Ron, and Sam are having their picture taken together. How many different ways can they stand in a row for the picture? (8-4)

  A. 6

  B. 5

  C. 4

  D. 3

10 The students in Arturo's school are collecting pennies to donate to a charity. If each student collects 200 pennies, how many pennies will 500 students collect? (8-1)

  F. 1,000

  G. 10,000

  H. 100,000

  I. 1,000,000

11 What is a reasonable estimate for the product of 4,256 and 380? (8-5)

  A. 1,000,000

  B. 1,200,000

  C. 1,600,000

  D. 2,000,000

12 Brendan takes violin and guitar lessons. Each day, he practices 40 minutes on the violin and 25 minutes on the guitar. How many minutes does he practice both instruments in 5 days? (8-6)

  F. 325 minutes

  G. 305 minutes

  H. 165 minutes

  I. 65 minutes

13 There are 30 flower beds in the park. There are 175 tulips in each flower bed. How many tulips are there in all? (8-3)

14 Harold is writing a 4-digit number. He is using the digits 0, 2, 5, and 6. Show all the possible numbers he could make that are less than 5,000. (8-4)

THINK
SOLVE
EXPLAIN

Set A, pages 152–153

Use basic facts and patterns to multiply multiples of 10, 100, and 1,000.

Find 600 × 2,000.

First find the product of the basic fact:
6 × 2 = 12

Then add zeros: 2 zeros + 3 zeros = 5 zeros

So 600 × 2,000 = 1,2**00,000**.

Remember if the product of a basic fact has a zero, the answer will have an extra zero.

Find the product.

1. 30 × 400   **2.** 50 × 3,000

3. 60 × 300   **4.** 200 × 500

5. 700 × 4,000   **6.** 5,000 × 400

7. 8,000 × 2,000 **8.** 6,000 × 3,000

Set B, pages 154–156

Round to estimate.

32 × 895

30 × 900 = 27,000

So, 32 × 895 is about 27,000.

Use compatible numbers to estimate.

463 × 106

463 × 100 = 46,300

So, 463 × 106 is about 46,300.

Remember to round one number or both numbers to estimate.

Estimate the product.

1.   486
     × 49

2.   386
     × 28

3.   759
     × 291

4.   882
     × 196

5. 389 × 26   **6.** 716 × 532

Set C, pages 158–159

Use mental math to multiply greater numbers.

Find 2,500 × 40.

First, use mental math: 25 × 4 = 100

Then add zeros: 2 zeros + 1 zero = 3 zeros

So, 2,500 × 40 = 100,**000**.

Remember to include any zero that is in the initial product in the final product.

Find the product.

1.   3,200
     × 30

2.   770
     × 20

3.   300
     × 120

4.   1,650
     × 30

5. 750 × 20   **6.** 2,500 × 30

Set D, pages 160–161

Using only hundreds and tens blocks, how many ways can you make 440?

What do I know? I can use only hundreds blocks and tens blocks.

What am I being asked to find? All of the combinations that make a total of 440

Record the combinations using an organized list.

Hundreds	4	3	2	1	0
Tens	4	14	24	34	44

Remember that the way you organize a list can help you find all the possibilities in a problem.

Solve. Make an organized list to help you.

1. Troy collects plastic banks. He has three different plastic banks: a pig, a cow, and a frog. How many ways can he arrange his banks on a shelf?

2. Jillene is writing a 3-digit number. She uses the digits 2, 7, and 8. What are the possible numbers she can write?

Set E, pages 162–163

Round to estimate.

42 × 6,895

40 × 7,000 = 280,000

So, 42 × 6,895 is about 280,000.

Remember you can round numbers or use compatible numbers to estimate products.

Estimate the product.

1. 256 × 38   2. 494 × 327

3. 3,496 × 29   4. 2,154 × 482

5. 675 × 492   6. 2,835 × 659

Set F, pages 164–165

Answer the hidden question first. Then solve the problem.

Brett bought 2 sandwiches for $6 each and 3 salads for $3 each. How much more did he spend on sandwiches than salads?

Hidden questions: What did the sandwiches cost in all? What did the salads cost in all?
Cost of sandwiches: 2 × $6 = $12
Cost of salads: 3 × $3 = $9

Subtract to solve the problem:
$12 − $9 = $3

Brett spent $3 more on sandwiches.

Remember to find the hidden questions before you try to solve the problem.

Solve.

1. Angelina works at a store at the mall. She earns $8 an hour during the week and $10 an hour on weekends. Last week, she worked 24 hours during the week. She worked 16 hours on the weekend. How much did Angelina earn last week?

Multiplying Greater Numbers

1 How many Earth days does it take Mars to revolve around the Sun? You will find out in Lesson 9-1.

2 On average, how long is the wingspan of a ruby-throated hummingbird? You will find out in Lesson 9-1.

3 On average, how much trash does each American produce in one year? You will find out in Lesson 9-4.

4 How many bones are there in an adult's body? You will find out in Lesson 9-2.

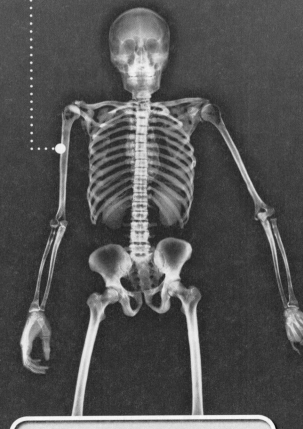

Review What You Know!

Vocabulary

Choose the best term from the box.

- multiple
- product
- factors
- round

1. One way to estimate with numbers is to ? each number.

2. A ? is the answer to a multiplication problem.

3. In the equation $9 \times 5 = 45$, 9 and 5 are both ? .

Rounding

Round each number to the place of the underlined digit.

4. <u>8</u>64   **5.** 6,5<u>1</u>8   **6.** <u>3</u>4,826

7. 9,<u>8</u>51   **8.** <u>4</u>,513,617   **9.** 749,<u>2</u>48

10. 5,3<u>7</u>6,457   **11.** 99,99<u>9</u>   **12.** 1<u>9</u>1,111,111

Multiplication

Find each product.

13. 13×9 **14.** 25×16 **15.** 43×86

16. 61×94 **17.** 57×4 **18.** 45×23

19. 12×12 **20.** 99×2 **21.** 55×55

22. Writing to Explain Explain how multiplying a 2-digit by 1-digit number is like multiplying a 2-digit by 2-digit number.

23. Betty went to a craft fair and bought 2 quilts for $45 each and 3 sun-catchers for $12 each. How much did Betty spend?

Topic Essential Question
- What is a standard procedure for multiplying multi-digit numbers?

MA.4.A.1.2 Multiply multi-digit whole numbers through four digits fluently, demonstrating understanding of the standard algorithm, and checking for reasonableness of results, including solving real-world problems.

Multiplying 3-Digit by 2-Digit Numbers

How do you multiply 3-digit numbers by 2-digit numbers?

Last month a bakery sold 389 trays of bagels. How many bagels did the store sell last month?

Choose an Operation
Multiply to join equal groups.

12 bagels per tray

Guided Practice*

Do you know HOW?

In **1** through **4**, find each product. Estimate to check that your answer is reasonable.

1.   236
     × 46

2.   425
     × 61

3. 23 × 827

4. 13 × 745

Do you UNDERSTAND?

5. In Step 2 of the example above, do you multiply 1 × 9 or 10 × 9?

6. **Writing to Explain** Is 300 × 10 a good estimate for the number of bagels sold at the bakery?

Independent Practice

Leveled Practice In **7** through **22**, find each product. Estimate to check that your answer is reasonable.

7.   612
       ×   32
       ■■24
     + 1■■■0
     ■■,■84

8.
        2 1
        132
      ×   47
        924
      + ■■■0
        ■,■4

9.
         ■ 1
         892
      ×   18
        ■■■6
      + 8920
       16,■■■

10.
          ■
          ■
         381
      ×   27
        2■■■
      + ■■■0
       ■■,■■■

11.   185
      × 55

12.   227
      × 87

13.   946
      × 33

14.   735
      × 41

15. 47 × 529

16. 19 × 763

17. 42 × 498

18. 72 × 116

19. 59 × 391

20. 35 × 515

21. 11 × 461

22. 58 × 785

For another example, see Set A on page 188.

Multiply by the ones, and regroup if necessary.

```
  1 1
  389
×  12
  778
```

2 × 9 ones = 18 ones or 1 ten and 8 ones

2 × 8 tens = 16 tens
16 tens + 1 ten = 17 tens
17 tens = 1 hundred 7 tens

2 × 3 hundreds = 6 hundreds
6 hundreds + 1 hundred = 7 hundreds

Multiply by the tens, and regroup if necessary.

```
  1 1
  389
×  12
  778
+ 3890
```

10 × 9 ones = 90 ones
10 × 8 tens = 80 tens or 8 hundreds
10 × 3 hundreds = 30 hundreds or 3 thousands

Add the partial products.

```
  389
×  12
  778
+ 3890
 4,668
```

The store sold 4,668 bagels last month.

Problem Solving

23. The wings of a ruby-throated hummingbird beat an average of 52 times per second. How many times do the wings beat in 3 minutes?

Tip *3 minutes is equal to 180 seconds.*

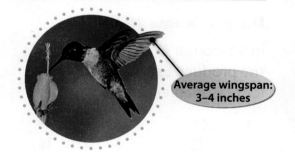

Average wingspan: 3–4 inches

24. The fourth-grade class at Monticello School sold more bags of popcorn than any other class. They ordered 17 cases of popcorn. Each case had 242 bags. How many bags of popcorn did the class sell?

25. A nursery sells plants in flats. There are 6 plants in each tray. Each flat has 6 trays. The nursery sold 16 flats on Saturday and 21 flats on Sunday. How many plants did the nursery sell in all?

26. A theater in Darling Harbour, Australia, can seat 540 people at one time. How many tickets can be sold if the theater sells out every seat for one 30-day month?

27. Writing to Explain Is 3,198 a reasonable product for 727 × 44? Why or why not?

Critical THINKING

28. It takes Mars 687 Earth days to revolve around the Sun. How many Earth days does it take Mars to revolve 24 times around the Sun?

 A 16,488 **C** 4,122

 B 15,068 **D** 1,374

29. The length of the Nile River in Africa is about 14 times the length of Lake Michigan. About how many miles long is the Nile River?

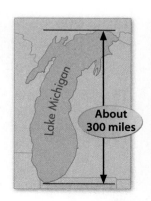

Lake Michigan

About 300 miles

MA.4.A.1.2 Multiply multi-digit whole numbers through four digits fluently, demonstrating understanding of the standard algorithm, and checking for reasonableness of results, including solving real-world problems.

Multiplying with Zeros

How can you multiply with zeros?

An antique steam train makes one sight-seeing tour each day. If every seat is filled for each trip, how many passengers can it carry for 31 tours?

Choose an Operation Multiply to find the number of passengers.

The train has a total of 208 seats.

Guided Practice*

Do you know HOW?

In **1** through **4**, multiply to find the product. Estimate to check for reasonableness.

1.   205
     × 23

2.   108
     × 34

3.   410
     × 44

4.   302
     × 30

Do you UNDERSTAND?

5. In the example above, is 6,448 a reasonable answer for 31 × 208?

6. Estimation Suppose an average of 103 seats are filled for each tour. What is a reasonable estimate for the number of passengers the train can carry in 28 tours?

Critical THINKING

Independent Practice

In **7** through **22**, multiply to find each product. Estimate to check for reasonableness.

7.   302
     × 17

8.   608
     × 23

9.   109
     × 47

10.   510
      × 72

11.   206
      × 34

12.   805
      × 80

13.   907
      × 52

14.   706
      × 30

15. 35 × 902

16. 61 × 207

17. 58 × 108

18. 77 × 505

19. 49 × 604

20. 80 × 401

21. 61 × 320

22. 93 × 703

For another example, see Set B on page 188.

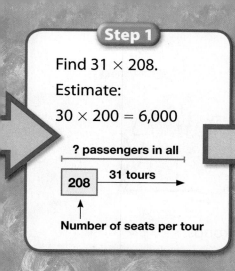

Step 1
Find 31 × 208.
Estimate:
30 × 200 = 6,000

? passengers in all

| 208 | 31 tours → |

↑
Number of seats per tour

Step 2

Multiply the ones.
Regroup if necessary.
Remember that multiplying with a zero gives a product of zero.

```
   208
×   31
   208
```

Step 3

Multiply the tens.
Regroup if necessary.

```
    2
   208
×   31
   208     Add the
+ 6240    partial
          products.
  6,448
```

The antique steam train can carry 6,448 passengers.

Problem Solving

23. Sal orders 108 loaves of sliced bread each day from the bakery for his deli. He gets a variety of white, wheat, and rye. Each loaf costs $2. How much does Sal spend each day on bread?

24. **Social Studies** Explorers from Spain first came to Florida in 1513. After 308 years, Spain gave up control of Florida to the United States. In what year did this change happen?

25. A flight departs at 8:45 A.M. It arrives 2 hours and 15 minutes later. Explain how to find the time that the flight arrives.

THINK
SOLVE
EXPLAIN

26. **Geometry** What figure has eight sides and eight angles?

A Hexagon   **C** Octagon

B Pentagon   **D** Parallelogram

For **27** and **28**, use the picture at the right.

27. There are 5 adult skeletons on display in an exhibit in a science museum. How many bones are there in all?

28. **Science** There are more bones in a child's body because some of a child's bones fuse together as they grow. How many more bones are in a child's body than in an adult's body?

300	
206	?

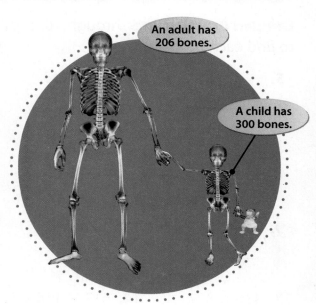

An adult has 206 bones.

A child has 300 bones.

MA.4.A.1.2 Multiply multi-digit whole numbers through four digits fluently, demonstrating understanding of the standard algorithm, and checking for reasonableness of results, including solving real-world problems.

Multiplying 3-Digit by 3-Digit Numbers

How can you extend multiplication to greater numbers?

A craft store received one gross of packages of foam shapes. One gross equals 12 dozen, or 144. How many shapes were delivered to the store?

Choose an Operation Multiply to join equal groups.

128 shapes per package

Guided Practice*

Do you know HOW?

In **1** and **2**, copy and complete the calculation to find each product.

1.
$$
\begin{array}{r}
324 \\
\times\ 132 \\
\hline
\blacksquare\blacksquare\blacksquare \\
\blacksquare\blacksquare\blacksquare\blacksquare \\
\blacksquare\blacksquare\blacksquare\blacksquare\blacksquare \\
\hline
\blacksquare\blacksquare,\blacksquare\blacksquare\blacksquare
\end{array}
$$

2.
$$
\begin{array}{r}
416 \\
\times\ 215 \\
\hline
\blacksquare\blacksquare\blacksquare\blacksquare \\
\blacksquare\blacksquare\blacksquare\blacksquare \\
\blacksquare\blacksquare\blacksquare\blacksquare\blacksquare \\
\hline
\blacksquare\blacksquare,\blacksquare\blacksquare\blacksquare
\end{array}
$$

Do you UNDERSTAND?

3. In the example above, how could you use estimation to check your answer for reasonableness?

4. Construction paper comes in packs of 275 sheets. How many sheets of construction paper are in 2 gross?

Independent Practice

Leveled Practice In **5** through **16**, copy and complete the calculation to find each product.

5.
$$
\begin{array}{r}
121 \\
\times\ \ 212 \\
\hline
\blacksquare\blacksquare\blacksquare \\
\blacksquare\blacksquare\blacksquare\blacksquare \\
+\ \blacksquare\blacksquare\blacksquare\blacksquare\blacksquare \\
\hline
\blacksquare\blacksquare,\blacksquare\blacksquare\blacksquare
\end{array}
$$

6.
$$
\begin{array}{r}
243 \\
\times\ \ 135 \\
\hline
\blacksquare\blacksquare\blacksquare\blacksquare \\
\blacksquare\blacksquare\blacksquare\blacksquare \\
+\ \blacksquare\blacksquare\blacksquare\blacksquare\blacksquare \\
\hline
\blacksquare\blacksquare,\blacksquare\blacksquare\blacksquare
\end{array}
$$

7.
$$
\begin{array}{r}
332 \\
\times\ \ 127 \\
\hline
\blacksquare\blacksquare\blacksquare\blacksquare \\
\blacksquare\blacksquare\blacksquare\blacksquare \\
+\ \blacksquare\blacksquare\blacksquare\blacksquare \\
\hline
\blacksquare\blacksquare,\blacksquare\blacksquare\blacksquare
\end{array}
$$

8.
$$
\begin{array}{r}
208 \\
\times\ \ 324 \\
\hline
\blacksquare\blacksquare\blacksquare \\
\blacksquare\blacksquare\blacksquare\blacksquare \\
+\ \blacksquare\blacksquare\blacksquare\blacksquare\blacksquare \\
\hline
\blacksquare\blacksquare,\blacksquare\blacksquare\blacksquare
\end{array}
$$

9.
$$
\begin{array}{r}
372 \\
\times\ 153
\end{array}
$$

10.
$$
\begin{array}{r}
414 \\
\times\ 126
\end{array}
$$

11.
$$
\begin{array}{r}
309 \\
\times\ 213
\end{array}
$$

12.
$$
\begin{array}{r}
425 \\
\times\ 231
\end{array}
$$

13. 436×327

14. 613×136

15. 707×218

16. 555×321

For another example, see Set C on page 188.

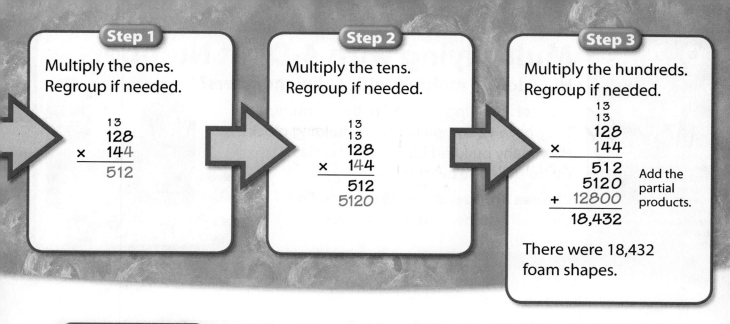

Step 1

Multiply the ones.
Regroup if needed.

```
  13
 128
×  144
 512
```

Step 2

Multiply the tens.
Regroup if needed.

```
   13
   13
  128
×  144
  512
 5120
```

Step 3

Multiply the hundreds.
Regroup if needed.

```
    13
    13
   128
×   144
   512
  5120
+ 12800
 18,432
```

Add the partial products.

There were 18,432 foam shapes.

Problem Solving

For **17** through **19**, use the table at the right.

17. Marika was captain of 168 full flights on the J-119 last fall. How many passengers did she have on her flights last fall?

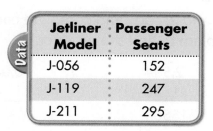

Jetliner Model	Passenger Seats
J-056	152
J-119	247
J-211	295

18. Reasoning Which jetliner could carry more passengers: 187 flights on a J-056 or 89 flights on a J-211? Explain.

19. Suppose there were 235 full flights of the J-211 last winter. What is a reasonable estimate of the number of passengers the flights carried?

20. Fido's dog food gives him 975 calories of energy a day. How many calories does he get from his food in 7 days?

21. Writing to Explain How is multiplying by a 3-digit number similar to multiplying by a 1-digit number? How is it different?

22. Renting a boat at a marina costs $189 a day. In one month, the marina rented boats 124 times. How much money did they earn from the rentals?

23. Gene and Eleanor each got new glasses. Gene's glasses cost $275. Eleanor's glasses cost $80 less. How much did Gene's and Eleanor's glasses cost together?

24. Which is NOT a partial product of the problem shown below?

```
   304
×  612
```

A   608

B   3,040

C   18,240

D   182,400

Multiplying with 4-Digit Numbers

How do you multiply with 4-digit numbers?

A class is building a model of their community. They have 12 complete sets of building blocks. How many building blocks can the class use to build the model?

Choose an Operation Multiply to find the total number of building blocks.

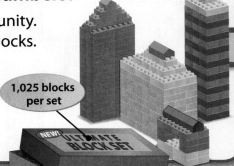

1,025 blocks per set

NEW! ULTIMATE BLOCK SET

MA.4.A.1.2 Multiply multi-digit whole numbers through four digits fluently, demonstrating understanding of the standard algorithm, and checking for reasonableness of results, including solving real-world problems.

Guided Practice*

Do you know HOW?

In **1** and **2**, copy and complete each problem to find the product.

1.
```
    2,594
  ×    36
   15564
 + ▦▦▦▦▦
```

2.
```
    6,085
  ×    47
   ▦▦▦▦▦
 + 243400
```

Do you UNDERSTAND?

3. In the example above, why are there only two partial products?

4. **Estimation** What is one way to estimate 12 × 1,025?

Independent Practice

Leveled Practice In **5** through **20**, copy and complete each problem to find the product.

5.
```
    1,956
  ×    27
   13692
 + ▦▦▦▦▦
```

6.
```
    4,152
  ×    83
   12456
 + ▦▦▦▦▦▦
```

7.
```
    3,207
  ×    67
   ▦▦▦▦▦
 + 192420
```

8.
```
    2,384
  ×    72
    ▦▦▦▦
 + 166880
```

9.
```
  3,124
 ×   12
```

10.
```
  1,627
 ×   41
```

11.
```
  1,789
 ×   35
```

12.
```
  6,153
 ×   24
```

13. 53 × 7,802

14. 66 × 5,403

15. 17 × 4,865

16. 64 × 2,327

17. 89 × 5,430

18. 39 × 2,706

19. 46 × 5,039

20. 37 × 2,811

Step 1

Find 12 × 1,025.

Multiply the ones. Regroup if needed.

$$\begin{array}{r} 1 \\ 1{,}025 \\ \times \quad 12 \\ \hline 2050 \end{array}$$

Step 2

Multiply the tens. Regroup if needed.

$$\begin{array}{r} 1 \\ 1{,}025 \\ \times \quad 12 \\ \hline 2050 \\ + \ 10250 \\ \hline 12{,}300 \end{array}$$ Add the partial products.

The class can use 12,300 building blocks.

Problem Solving

21. Social Studies The Seminole leader Osceola died in 1838. A Florida county was named in his honor 49 years later. In what year did Osceola County get its name?

22. Artie's school buys 1,275 pads of lined paper for students to use. Each pad has 80 sheets. How many sheets of paper is this in all?

23. There were 4,017 fans at the rodeo championship. Each fan paid $5 for admission. How much money was collected in all?

24. Geometry A rectangular flag has a length of 209 feet and a width of 110 feet. What is its perimeter?

25. On average, each American produces 1,657 pounds of trash in one year. About how much trash does each American produce in 10 years?

26. In 2007, Florida's population was estimated at 18,680,367. Which digit is in the ten millions place?

A 1 **C** 6

B 3 **D** 8

27. Think About the Process Jake walks dogs and delivers papers to Critical THINKING earn money. This month, he earned $54 delivering papers and $41 walking dogs. He spent $12 on a new watch. Which shows how much money Jake has left this month?

F $54 + $41 + $12   **H** $54 − $41 + $12

G $54 − $41 − $12   **I** $54 + $41 − $12

MA.4.A.1.2 Multiply multi-digit whole numbers through four digits fluently, demonstrating understanding of the standard algorithm, and checking for reasonableness of results, including solving real-world problems.

Multiplying Greater Numbers

How can you extend multiplication to greater numbers?

Each puzzle uses 144 letters.

An electronic word-search puzzle game is programmed with 1,225 word-search puzzles. How many letters were needed to create all of the puzzles for the game?

Find $144 \times 1,225$.

```
MATHBZQSLIJG
PRODUCTWICWM
YAFMHTIROGLA
FGJKVCELYSIZ
ARRAVBSBOMWE
CJEMULTIPLYF
TGDSUMIEYAJH
OVWJPBMFGKNE
RMBYSTANDARD
CQZMULTIPLEW
EWSGSVEHKJFS
MIDAQYBNORCG
```

SOUND   HI SCORE   ON/NEW

ENTER

Guided Practice*

Do you know HOW?

In **1** and **2**, estimate. Then find the product.

1. 65×623
$60 \times 600 = $ ▨
$70 \times 700 = $ ▨

2. $836 \times 7,294$
$800 \times 7,000 = $ ▨
$900 \times 8,000 = $ ▨

Do you UNDERSTAND?

3. In the example above, what is another way to find the estimate?

4. Each puzzle has 15 hidden words. If you complete 174 puzzles, how many words will you have found?

Independent Practice

Leveled Practice In **5** through **10**, estimate each product by finding a range.

5. 89×174
$80 \times 100 = $ ▨
$90 \times 200 = $ ▨
The answer is between ▨ and ▨.

6. 305×814
$300 \times 800 = $ ▨
$400 \times 900 = $ ▨
The answer is between ▨ and ▨.

7. $333 \times 2,222$
$300 \times 2,000 = $ ▨
$400 \times 3,000 = $ ▨
The answer is between ▨ and ▨.

8. 112×426
The answer is between ▨ and ▨.

9. 49×311
The answer is between ▨ and ▨.

10. $211 \times 4,391$
The answer is between ▨ and ▨.

In **11** through **18**, find each product. Estimate to check for reasonableness.

11.
$$\begin{array}{r} 253 \\ \times\ 76 \\ \hline \end{array}$$

12.
$$\begin{array}{r} 4,715 \\ \times\ 29 \\ \hline \end{array}$$

13.
$$\begin{array}{r} 541 \\ \times\ 809 \\ \hline \end{array}$$

14.
$$\begin{array}{r} 286 \\ \times\ 61 \\ \hline \end{array}$$

15. 386×216

16. $184 \times 9,876$

17. 716×428

18. $736 \times 3,122$

*For another example, see Set D on page 189.

You can use compatible numbers and find a range before you multiply.

Change each factor to a smaller number:
$100 \times 1,000 = 100,000$

Change each factor to a larger number:
$200 \times 1,500 = 300,000$

The exact answer must be between 100,000 and 300,000.

Multiply the ones, tens, and hundreds. Regroup if needed.

$$
\begin{array}{r}
\overset{1\ 2}{\underset{}{}}\\
\overset{1\ 2}{1,225} \\
\times \quad 144 \\
\hline
4900 \\
49000 \\
+\ 122500 \\
\hline
176,400
\end{array}
$$

Add the partial products.

There were 176,400 letters needed to create the game. The answer is reasonable because it is between 100,000 and 300,000.

Problem Solving

19. **Critical THINKING** Estimates show that an average family in America uses about 350 gallons of water per day. At this rate, how much water would a family use in 365 days?

20. THINK SOLVE EXPLAIN The official distance of a modern marathon is 26 miles, plus 1,155 feet. There are 5,280 feet in one mile. How many feet are in a marathon? Explain.

21. Which is NOT a partial product of the problem below?

$$
\begin{array}{r}
706 \\
\times\ 413 \\
\end{array}
$$

A 282,400   **C** 7,060

B 28,240   **D** 2,118

22. Lake Okeechobee is Florida's largest lake. A 110-mile trail loops around its shore. Andre has biked 73 miles of the trail so far. How many miles does he have left to complete the whole trail?

23. 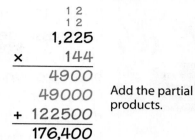 **Science** The Earth is always rotating even though you cannot feel it. A point on the equator travels about 1,038 miles every hour. How far would the point travel over 12 hours?

24. On average, it takes about 2,500 pearls to decorate a gown. If a dress shop expects to sell 200 beaded gowns, about how many pearls would be used?

25. A recycling center recycles about 1,250 aluminum cans each day. At that rate, how many cans would be recycled in 31 days?

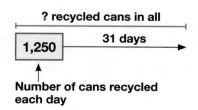

? recycled cans in all

1,250   31 days

Number of cans recycled each day

MA.4.A.6.6 Estimate and describe reasonableness of estimates; determine the appropriateness of an estimate versus an exact answer.

Exact Answer or Estimate

Flight 719 carries 39 passengers. Each passenger brings 2 suitcases. The airplane can safely carry 5,000 pounds of luggage. Is an exact answer needed or is an estimate enough to decide if the luggage for this flight is under the weight limit?

Average weight: 36 pounds per suitcase

Another Example There are 44 adults who want to take a group tour of Mexico City. The cost of each ticket is $12. Is an exact answer needed or is an estimate enough to find the total cost of the tickets?

Read & Understand

What do I know?   There are 44 adults who want to take a tour. The cost of each ticket is $12.

What am I asked to find?   Is an exact answer needed or is an estimate enough to find the total cost of the tickets?

Plan & Solve

The problem asks for the total cost of the tickets, so an exact answer is needed.

Find the total cost of the tickets.

$$44 \times 12 = 528$$

The total cost is $528.

Explain It

1. Why would finding the estimate NOT give enough information to solve the problem correctly?

I do not need to know the exact weight of all the luggage. I just need to know if the total weight is less than 5,000 pounds.

I only need an estimate.

Estimate the number of suitcases.
$40 \times 2 = 80$ suitcases

Then estimate the weight of all the suitcases.
80×40 pounds $= 3,200$ pounds

Compare the estimated weight to the limit.
$3,200$ pounds $< 5,000$ pounds

The luggage for this flight is under the weight limit.

Guided Practice*

Do you know HOW?

For **1**, tell whether an exact answer is needed or if an estimate is enough. Then solve.

1. Dario bought two T-shirts for $12 each and a pair of shorts for $18. He paid with a 50-dollar bill. How much change did he get back?

Do you UNDERSTAND?

2. In the example above, why was an estimate enough to solve the problem?

3. **Write a Problem** Write a problem where an estimate is enough to find the answer. Then solve it.

Independent Practice

In **4** through **6**, tell whether an exact answer is needed or if an estimate is enough. Then solve. Use the tables at the right.

4. At the craft fair, Colleen sold 13 bracelets, 24 pairs of earrings, and 7 necklaces. How much did she make in all?

Colleen's Collection	
Earrings	$18
Bracelets	$15
Necklaces	$23

5. At the same fair, Alenna wanted to make at least $2,000 in sales. She sold 18 necklaces, 28 pairs of earrings, and 16 bracelets. Did she sell enough pieces of jewelry to meet her goal?

6. How much more did Alenna earn by selling bracelets than Colleen earned by selling bracelets?

Alenna's Collection	
Earrings	$19
Bracelets	$17
Necklaces	$28

7. Eli's highest score on a video game is 398,540 points. Amy has a high score of 407,735 points. How much greater is Amy's score than Eli's? Tell whether an exact answer is needed or an estimate is enough.

THINK
SOLVE
EXPLAIN

8. Writing to Explain Terry needed to buy supplies to paint his garage. He set aside $100 for paint. He bought 4 gallons of paint that cost $23 each. Did he stay within his budget? Explain your answer.

9. A sports store sold 536 baseball caps during a clearance sale. The goal was to sell at least 700 caps. How many more caps did the store need to sell to reach the goal?

10. Number Sense A sports reporter said that 50,000 fans were at a soccer game. Explain how this number could be both an exact answer and an estimate.

Critical
THINKING

For **11** through **13**, use the data at the right.

11. Estimation A 10-pound bag of puppy food has about 8,130 pieces of food. How many pieces of food are in 20 bags of puppy food?

Kitty Litter
Each 50-pound bag: ONLY $14

Sale!

Puppy Food
Each 10-pound bag: ONLY $19

12. The pet store sold 28 bags of kitty litter during the first day of the sale. How much money did the store earn on these bags?

13. At a sale, the pet store sold 47 bags of kitty litter and 63 bags of puppy food. How much money did the pet store make from the sale?

Think About the Process

14. Many bands compete in the Florida Marching Band Championship each year. Band members at one school plan to practice 6 hours a week for 21 weeks. Which equation shows how to find how much time the band members will practice?

A $20 \times 10 = 200$ hours

B $21 \times 7 = 147$ hours

C $21 \times 6 = 126$ hours

D $20 \times 5 = 100$ hours

15. A one-month city bus pass costs $39. Which of the following expressions could you use to find the cost of the bus pass in dollars for one year?

F $12 + 39$

G 12×39

H $52 + 39$

I 52×39

Mixed Problem Solving

Juan Ponce de León landed on the peninsula we now call Florida on April 2, 1513. On March 3, 1845, Florida became the 27th state of the United States of America. The table below gives facts about some of Florida's state symbols.

Florida State Symbol	Fact
Flag	The current design was adopted in 1900.
Flower: Orange Blossom	This sweet-smelling flower became the official state flower in 1909.
Reptile: Alligator	It takes about 2 months for an egg to hatch into a baby alligator.
Song: "The Old Folks at Home" (The Swanee River)	Stephen C. Foster wrote this song in 1851. It became the official state song in 1935.
Tree: Sabal Palm	The sabal palm grows all over the state. Its average height is 50 feet.
Water Mammal: Bottlenose Dolphin	This dolphin lives in groups called pods. Each pod consists of as many as 12 dolphins.

1. How many years passed between the year Stephen Foster wrote "The Swanee River" and the year it became the state song of Florida?

2. If a large group of 18 pods joined together, how many dolphins could there be?

3. Britton Hill, Florida, is the location of the highest point in the state. It is 345 feet above sea level. About how many sabal palms on top of each other would equal the height of the highest point?

   Tip ☐ × 50 is about 350.

The largemouth bass is the state freshwater fish of Florida.

4. What is the difference between the greatest and least number of eggs that a female largemouth bass may lay?

5. If a female largemouth bass lays an average of 4,000 eggs each year, how many eggs might she lay in her lifetime?

Life Span: Up to 16 years

Florida Largemouth Bass	
Number of Eggs	From 2,000 to 145,000

1 In one day Mr. Fein got 187 e-mails at his job. If he got 187 e-mails each day for 22 days, how many e-mails would he get? (9-1)

A. 3,004

B. 3,014

C. 3,114

D. 4,114

2 Tickets to an ice show cost $28. If 2,692 tickets were sold, how much money was collected? (9-4)

F. $65,366

G. $74,376

H. $75,376

I. $75,476

3 A new edition of a Zora Neale Hurston book costs $35. The table below shows the sales of her book to libraries in one month. What is the total amount of money collected from the books sold to middle and high school libraries? (9-1)

Libraries	Number of Books Sold
Middle School	108
High School	240
Public	375

Data

A. $13,125

B. $12,580

C. $12,180

D. $12,050

4 A year has 365 days. Each day, a rancher puts out 430 pounds of grain for his herd of cattle to eat. How many pounds of grain does the rancher use in one year? (9-3)

F. 156,950

G. 154,950

H. 142,050

I. 136,950

5 Union County is the smallest county in Florida. It covers 245 square miles. On average, 57 people live in each square mile of this county. What is the average population of Union County? (9-1)

A. 13,965

B. 13,955

C. 13,795

D. 11,965

6 There are 36 large fish tanks at a zoo. Each tank holds 205 gallons of water. How many gallons of water would it take to fill all of the tanks? (9-2)

F. 7,380

G. 7,210

H. 6,380

I. 6,361

7 Ryan has docked his boat in the same small marina for the past 13 years. He pays $1,044 each year to reserve his spot. How much has Ryan spent docking his boat in this marina? (9-4)

A. $13,672

B. $13,582

C. $13,572

D. $13,562

8 A new apartment tower is going up near Fort Lauderdale Beach. It will have 225 apartments. Each apartment needs 222 tiles for its kitchen floor. How many tiles are needed for all the kitchen floors in the new apartment tower? (9-3)

F. 1,350

G. 9,450

H. 48,840

I. 49,950

9 A weekly magazine prints 3,450 copies every week. How many copies will the magazine print in 52 weeks? Estimate to check for reasonableness. (9-5)

A. 179,400

B. 179,310

C. 177,900

D. 168,200

10 A candy maker ships candy bars in boxes that hold 125 bars. How many candy bars are in 250 boxes? (9-3)

F. 3,550

G. 4,250

H. 26,050

I. 31,250

11 Find the product of 384 and 3,256. Estimate to check for reasonableness. (9-5)

A. 1,239,204

B. 1,250,304

C. 1,223,684

D. 3,640

12 A shipment of 23 refrigerators is being loaded onto a truck. Each refrigerator weighs 306 pounds. How much weight in pounds is being loaded onto the truck? (9-2)

13 THINK SOLVE EXPLAIN A theater has 1,024 seats. There will be at least 92 events at the theater this season. If each seat is filled for each event, about how many people will attend in all? Tell if an exact answer is needed or if an estimate is enough. Then solve. (9-6)

Set A, pages 172–173

Find 38 × 425.

| Step 1 | Step 2 | Step 3 |

Multiply the ones.

$$\begin{array}{r} \scriptstyle 24 \\ 425 \\ \times\ \ 38 \\ \hline 3400 \end{array}$$

Multiply the tens.

$$\begin{array}{r} \scriptstyle 1 \\ 425 \\ \times\ \ 38 \\ \hline 3400 \\ 12750 \end{array}$$

Add the partial products.

$$\begin{array}{r} 425 \\ \times\ \ 38 \\ \hline 3400 \\ +\ 12750 \\ \hline 16,150 \end{array}$$

Remember to regroup if needed. Estimate to check that your answer is reasonable.

Find each product.

1. 54 × 119
2. 16 × 923
3. 13 × 189
4. 55 × 125
5. 67 × 482
6. 81 × 199
7. 51 × 625
8. 32 × 871

Set B, pages 174–175

Find 53 × 406.
Estimate: 50 × 400 = 20,000

Multiply the ones. Then multiply the tens.

$$\begin{array}{r} \scriptstyle 3 \\ \scriptstyle 1 \\ 406 \\ \times\ \ \ 53 \\ \hline 1218 \\ +\ 20300 \\ \hline 21,518 \end{array}$$

← 3 × 406
← 50 × 406

Remember to add any regrouped numbers after multiplying by zero.

Find each product.

1. 34 × 108
2. 76 × 504
3. 47 × 302
4. 83 × 206
5. 604 × 55
6. 708 × 94

Set C, pages 176–177

Find 317 × 246.

$$\begin{array}{r} \scriptstyle 11 \\ \scriptstyle 34 \\ 246 \\ \times\ \ \ 317 \\ \hline 1722 \\ 2460 \\ +\ 73800 \\ \hline 77,982 \end{array}$$

← Multiply the ones.
← Multiply the tens.
← Multiply the hundreds.

Remember to find as many partial products as the number of digits in the multiplier.

Find each product.

1. 642 × 485
2. 174 × 521
3. 406 × 323
4. 558 × 876

Set D, pages 178–179; 180–181

Use the standard algorithm to multiply greater numbers.

Find $345 \times 4,123$.

Estimate:
$300 \times 4,000 = 1,200,000$
$400 \times 5,000 = 2,000,000$

```
        1
      1 1
      4123
  ×    345
     20615
    164920
 + 1236900
  1,422,435
```

1,422,435 is between 1,200,000 and 2,000,000. So, the answer is reasonable.

Remember to regroup when needed.

Find each product. Estimate to check for reasonableness.

1. $67 \times 4,152$ **2.** $21 \times 3,946$

3. 365×407 **4.** 614×842

5. $\begin{array}{r} 2,056 \\ \times\ 638 \end{array}$ **6.** $\begin{array}{r} 9,345 \\ \times\ 871 \end{array}$

7. $\begin{array}{r} 7,777 \\ \times\ 888 \end{array}$ **8.** $\begin{array}{r} 2,948 \\ \times\ 502 \end{array}$

Set E, pages 182–184

Tell whether an exact answer is needed or an estimate is enough. Then solve.

Bill drew 36 frames for his comic book. If he wants to put only 4 frames on each page, how many pages long will his comic book be?

What do I know?   Bill drew 36 frames. Each page will have 4 frames.

What am I asked to find?   The number of pages long the comic book will be

The problem gives a limit of 4 frames on each page, so an exact answer is needed.

$36 \div 4 = 9$

Bill's comic book will be 9 pages long.

Remember that an estimate may be all you need to solve a problem when the words "about" and "almost" are used in the question.

Tell whether an exact answer is needed or an estimate is enough. Then solve.

1. Joy is making name tags for the members of the Sunshine Club. She must make tags for 18 girls and 12 boys. How many name tags must she make?

2. On Tuesday, a snack bar sold 309 big pretzels, 286 boxes of popcorn, and 78 bags of peanuts. About how many snacks did the snack bar sell?

Patterns and Expressions

1 How many flowers can decorate one float for the Tournament of Roses Parade? You will find out in Lesson 10-1.

2 How can an algebraic expression be used to show the number of minutes you spend exercising each day? You will find out in Lesson 10-5.

3 How many members does Florida have in Congress? You will find out in Lesson 10-2.

4 Kudzu is the world's fastest growing plant. How fast can this weed grow? You will find out in Lesson 10-3.

Review What You Know!

1. A _?_ is the product of two whole numbers.

2. _?_ are the result of breaking one factor in a multiplication problem into expanded form and then multiplying each value by the other factor.

3. $3,000 + 400 + 70 + 6$ shows the number 3,476 written in _?_.

4. _?_ are numbers multiplied together to find a product.

Patterns

For each set of numbers, find the missing number.

5. 2, ▨, 4, 5, 6

6. ▨, 10, 15, 20

7. 3, 6, 9, ▨

8. 4, 8, ▨, 16

9. 17, ▨, 35, 44

10. 50, 39, ▨, 17

Multiplication

Solve.

11. 500×60

12. 120×4

13. 35×200

14. 29×8

15. 14×30

16. 132×5

17. **Writing to Explain** How would you describe the pattern for multiples of 2? multiples of 5?

Topic Essential Question
- How can math quantities be described and written using variables?

Lesson 10-1

Variables and Expressions

How can you use expressions with variables?

A variable is a symbol or letter that stands for a number.

A Tae Kwon Do class has 23 people. If *n* more people sign up, how many people will be taking the class?

n	23 + n
3	▨
5	▨
7	▨

MA.4.A.4.1 Generate algebraic rules and use all four operations to describe patterns, including nonnumeric growing or repeating patterns. Also MA.4.A.4.2

Other Examples

An algebraic expression is a mathematical phrase involving a variable or variables, a number or numbers, and at least one operation.

Word form	Expression
a number plus 5	$n + 5$
2 times a number	$2 \times n$

Guided Practice*

Do you know HOW?

In **1** through **3**, copy and complete the table.

	c	c + 8
1.	4	▨
2.	9	▨
3.	13	▨

Do you UNDERSTAND?

4. **Writing to Explain** Could you use the variable *k* instead of *n* to represent more students signing up for the Tae Kwon Do class?

5. If *n* is 12, how many people will be taking the Tae Kwon Do class?

Independent Practice

For **6** through **8**, copy and complete the table for each problem.

6.

d	d + 30
3	▨
7	▨
12	▨

7.

g	5 × g
6	▨
9	▨
15	▨

8.

m	m ÷ 9
63	▨
45	▨
18	▨

DIGITAL Animated Glossary
www.pearsonsuccessnet.com

For another example, see Set A on page 212.

Use the expression, $23 + n$, to find the missing numbers.

$23 + n$

n	$23 + n$
3	26
5	28
7	30

$23 + 3 = 26$

If 3 more people sign up, there will be 26 people in the class.

If 5 more people sign up, there will be 28 people in the class.

If 7 more people sign up, there will be 30 people in the class.

For **9** through **12**, fill in the missing numbers.

9.

z	24	56	64	72
$z \div 8$	3		8	9

10.

t	43	134	245	339
$t + 47$	90	181		386

11.

y	387	201	65	26
$y - 13$	374	188		

12.

x	5	7	10	20
$x \times 12$	60	84		

Problem Solving

13. One float for the Tournament of Roses Parade uses as many flowers as a florist usually uses in 5 years. If f is the number of flowers a florist uses in 1 year, write an algebraic expression for the number of flowers used to make a float.

14. If s represents the number of seconds in one minute, which expression represents how many seconds are in 5 minutes?

A $5 + s$

B $5 \div s$

C $5 \times s$

D $5 - s$

15. A Ferris wheel has 12 cars. The operator needs to keep 2, 4, or 6 cars empty. Make a table to show how many people can ride if each car holds 4 people.

16. Write an expression to represent the cost of parking a car for n hours in a lot that charges $7 per hour. Find the cost of parking the car for 3 hours.

17. Reasonableness Edgar used $10 \times d$ to represent the number of pennies in d dollars. Is this reasonable?

18. Writing to Explain If you multiply 392×6 and get 2,452, how does estimation help you know your answer is wrong?

MA.4.A.4.1 Generate algebraic rules and use all four operations to describe patterns, including nonnumeric growing or repeating patterns. Also MA.4.A.4.2

Addition and Subtraction Expressions

How can you find a rule and write an expression?

What is a rule for the table?
How can you use a rule to write an expression and find the sale price when the regular price is $18?

Let *p* stand for the regular price.

Regular price (p)	$21	$20	$19	$18
Sale price	$16	$15	$14	

Guided Practice*

Do you know HOW?

For **1** and **2**, use the table below.

Total number of test questions (q)	20	30	40	50
Number of multiple-choice questions	10	20	30	

1. What is a rule for the table in words? in symbols?

2. How many multiple-choice questions would be on a 50-question test?

Do you UNDERSTAND?

3. **Writing to Explain** How could you use place-value blocks to find a rule in the table to the left?

4. Tony earns $7 and saves $2. When he earns $10, he saves $5. When he earns $49, he saves $44. Write an expression for the amount he saves.

   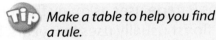 *Make a table to help you find a rule.*

5. In the example at the top, what is the sale price when the regular price is $30?

Independent Practice

For **6** through **11**, find a rule.

6.

n	3	4	5
n + ▢	7	8	9

7.

b	31	42	55
b − ▢	23	34	47

8.

q	0	2	8
q + ▢	15	17	23

9.

p	3	4	5
p + ▢	68	69	70

10.

x	18	21	26
x − ▢	5	8	13

11.

r	112	96	62
r − ▢	73	57	23

For another example, see Set B on page 212.

Subtract to find the sale price.

For a regular price of $21:

$21 - 5 = 16$

For a regular price of $20:

$20 - 5 = 15$

For a regular price of $19:

$19 - 5 = 14$

A rule is subtract 5.
So, the expression is $p - 5$.

Use the expression $p - 5$ to find the missing value when $p = 18$.

$p - 5 = 18 - 5$

Regular price (p)	$21	$20	$19	$18
Sale price	$16	$15	$14	$18 - 5

When the regular price is $18, the sale price is $13.

For **12** through **15**, copy and complete each table, and find a rule.

12.

n	15	18	20	27
n + ▨	58	61	63	▨

13.

u	212	199	190	188
u − ▨	177	164	155	▨

14.

c	31	54	60	64
c − ▨	5	28	34	▨

15.

a	589	485	400	362
a − ▨	575	471	386	▨

Problem Solving

For **16** and **17**, use the table at the right.

16. **Social Studies** The United States Congress includes 2 senators from each state plus members of the House of Representatives. If r represents the number of representatives from each state, which rule represents the total number of members each state has in Congress?

A $r \times 2$ **C** $r - 2$

B $r \div 2$ **D** $r + 2$

Data

Number of Members in the United States Congress		
State	House	Senate
Florida	25	2
Missouri	9	2
Hawaii	2	2
New York	29	2

17. How many members in Congress does each state in the table have?

18. What is the value of n if $1,000 \times n = 0$?

Critical THINKING

19. Chang has driven 1,372 miles. If the total mileage for his trip is 2,800 miles, how many miles does Chang have left to drive? Explain.

THINK
SOLVE
EXPLAIN

MA.4.A.4.1 Generate algebraic rules and use all four operations to describe patterns, including nonnumeric growing or repeating patterns. Also MA.4.A.4.2

Multiplication and Division Expressions

How can you find a rule and write an expression?

What is a rule for the table? How can Josie use a rule to write an expression and find the number of cards in 4 boxes? Let b equal the number of boxes.

Number of boxes (b)	1	2	3	4
Number of note cards	15	30	45	

Guided Practice*

Do you know HOW?

For **1** and **2**, use the table below.

Number of tickets (t)	2	4	6	8
Total price	$60	$120	$180	

1. What is a rule for the table in words? in symbols?

2. How much would 8 tickets cost?

Do you UNDERSTAND?

3. **Writing to Explain** How could you use place-value blocks to describe a rule in the table to the left?

4. How could you find the price of 1 ticket using the information from Problems 1 and 2?

5. In the example above, how many note cards are in 13 boxes?

Independent Practice

For **6** through **8**, find a rule.

6.

n	3	8	10
n × ▢	18	48	60

7.

p	2	4	8
p ÷ ▢	1	2	4

8.

t	2	3	4
▢ × t	16	24	32

For **9** through **12**, copy and complete each table, and find a rule.

9.

e	4	8	12	16
e ÷ ▢	1	2	3	▢

10.

j	4	9	10	16
▢ × j	28	63	70	▢

11.

w	5	7	8	10
▢ × w	35	49	56	▢

12.

s	20	35	40	45
s ÷ ▢	4	7	8	▢

 *For another example, see Set B on page 212.

Multiply to find the number of cards.

For 1 box:
$1 \times 15 = 15$

For 2 boxes:
$2 \times 15 = 30$

For 3 boxes:
$3 \times 15 = 45$

A rule is multiply by 15. So, the expression is $b \times 15$.

Use the expression $b \times 15$ to find the missing value when $b = 4$.

$b \times 15 = 4 \times 15$

Number of boxes (b)	1	2	3	4
Number of note cards	15	30	45	4×15

There are 60 note cards in 4 boxes.

Problem Solving

For **13** and **14**, use the table at the right.

The Baker family is deciding which type of television to purchase for the family room.

13. How much more does a 50-inch Plasma cost than a 34-inch Flat Screen?

Type of Television	Cost
50-inch Plasma	$2,800
34-inch Flat Screen	$900
26-inch LCD	$500

Data

14. How much less does a 26-inch LCD cost than a 50-inch Plasma?

15. There are 60 minutes in one hour and 7 days in one week. About how many minutes are in one week?

Critical THINKING

   A About 1,500 minutes

   B About 6,000 minutes

   C About 10,000 minutes

   D About 42,000 minutes

16. Cami bought two books for $12 each and two journals for $4 each. How much change would she get if she paid with two $20 bills?

   F $2

   G $8

   H $32

   I $40

For **17**, use the table at the right.

17. Kudzu is the world's fastest growing weed. Copy and complete the table to the right to find a rule for the growth rate of kudzu. What is a rule for the table?

THINK SOLVE EXPLAIN

Day (d)	1	2	3	4	5	6
Inches	12	24	▢	▢	▢	72

Lesson 10-4

MA.4.A.4.1 Generate algebraic rules and use all four operations to describe patterns, including nonnumeric growing or repeating patterns. Also MA.4.A.4.2

Problem Solving

Look for a Pattern

Ella is learning how to play a waltz on the piano. Her teacher gives her a beginner's exercise for her left hand.

The music shows 4 measures. If this pattern continues, how many notes will she play in 8 measures?

3, 6, 9, 12, ▨, ▨, ▨, ▨

Guided Practice*

Do you know HOW?

Solve. Find a pattern.

1. Julia is printing files. The first file is 2 pages, the second file is 4 pages, the third file is 6 pages, and the fourth file is 8 pages. If this pattern continues, how many pages will be in the eighth file?

Do you UNDERSTAND?

2. What multiplication facts can you use to help find the answer to Problem 1? Why?

3. **Write a Problem** Write a problem that uses the music measures above.

Independent Practice

Look for a pattern. Draw the next two shapes.

4.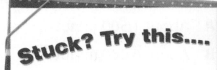

5.

6.

7.

Stuck? Try this....

- What do I know?
- What diagram can I use to help understand the problem?
- Can I use addition, subtraction, multiplication, or division?
- Is all of my work correct?
- Did I answer the right question?
- Is my answer reasonable?

For another example, see Set C on page 213.

Read and Understand

What do I know? The pattern for the first 4 measures is: 3, 6, 9, and 12.

What am I asked to find? The number of notes she will play in 8 measures.

Plan and Solve

Find a pattern.
Skip count by 3s.

3, 6, 9, 12,...

What are the next four numbers?

3, 6, 9, 12, 15, 18, 21, 24

Ella plays 24 notes in 8 measures.

Look Back and Check

Is the answer reasonable?

There are 12 notes in 4 measures.

The number of notes in 8 measures is double the number in 4 measures.

The answer is reasonable.

For **8** through **10**, look for a pattern. Copy and complete each number sentence.

8. $30 + 5 = 35$
$300 + 5 = 305$
$3{,}000 + 5 = \blacksquare$
$30{,}000 + 5 = \blacksquare$

9. $55 + 0 = 55$
$505 + 50 = 555$
$5{,}005 + 550 = \blacksquare$
$50{,}005 + 5{,}550 = \blacksquare$

10. $68 + 0 = 68$
$608 + 60 = 668$
$6{,}008 + 660 = \blacksquare$
$60{,}008 + 6{,}660 = \blacksquare$

11. Kaylee delivers invitations to everyone on her floor of her apartment building. There are 10 apartments on her floor. The numbers of the first four apartments are 2, 4, 6, and 8. If the pattern continues, what are the rest of the apartment numbers?

12. Look for a pattern in the table below to find the missing numbers.

300	320	340	■	380
400	■	440	460	■
500	520	■	560	580

13. Kerry has a newspaper route. The first four houses she delivers to are numbered 322, 326, 330, and 334. If this pattern continues, what will be the next four numbers?

14. Marvin is looking for a radio station on the AM dial. He tries these three stations: 1040, 1080, and 1120. If this pattern continues, what will be the next three station numbers?

15. Critical Thinking Jonas saves coins in his piggy bank. He drops in these two groups of coins: 1 penny, 2 nickels, 3 dimes, 4 quarters and 5 pennies, 6 nickels, 7 dimes, 8 quarters. If this pattern continues, what is the next group of coins?

16. THINK SOLVE EXPLAIN Suppose there are 18 bowls arranged in this pattern: big bowl, little bowl, big bowl, little bowl, and so on. Is the last bowl a big bowl or a little bowl? Explain.

MA.4.A.4.3 Recognize and write algebraic expressions for functions with two operations. Also MA.4.A.4.2

Expressions with 2 Operations

How can you write and evaluate expressions with variables?

Write an expression for finding the total cost of a service call from Matteo's Electrical Repair. Evaluate the expression for a service call that lasts 2 hours.

MATTEO'S ELECTRICAL REPAIR

SERVICE CALL CHARGES
$55 Fee Plus $65 Per Hour

Another Example **How can you write a word phrase as an algebraic expression?**

Let *n* represent the number.

Word Phrase	Algebraic Expression
Five times a number, plus two	$(5 \times n) + 2$
Two less than five times a number	$(5 \times n) - 2$
Two more than five times a number	$(5 \times n) + 2$

Sometimes a word phrase can be interpreted in different ways.

Word phrase: Ten minus two times a number

One person might find $10 - 2$, and then multiply the difference by *n*. Another person might find $2 \times n$, and then subtract the product from 10.

By using parentheses, you can make it clear which operation is done first.

$(10 - 2) \times n$ means that subtraction is done first.
$10 - (2 \times n)$ means that multiplication is done first.

Explain It

1. Why is the comma in the first word phrase above important?

2. How do the parentheses make the expressions $(5 \times n) + 2$ and $5 \times (n + 2)$ different?

Write an expression for the total cost. Let h represent the number of hours.

The expression for the total cost in dollars is

$$55 + (65 \times h).$$

↑ ↑ ↑
service fee   charge per hour   hours

Evaluate the expression for a 2-hour service call. Do the operation inside the parentheses first.

$$55 + (65 \times h)$$
$$55 + (65 \times 2)$$
$$55 + 130$$
$$185$$

The total cost for a 2-hour service call is $185.

Guided Practice*

Do you know HOW?

Write an algebraic expression for each word phrase. Let n represent the number.

1. Three times a number, plus 10

2. Four less than a number times 2

3. Eight plus a number times 5

4. Forty minus two times a number

Do you UNDERSTAND?

5. How much does Matteo Electrical Repair charge for 3 hours of work?

6. Evaluate $(3 \times n) + 18$ for $n = 2$.

7. Evaluate $(3 \times n) + 18$ for $n = 3$.

8. Can the word phrase "3 times a number plus 18" be interpreted in two different ways?

Independent Practice

For **9** through **12**, write an algebraic expression for each phrase. Let n represent the number.

9. Nine times a number, minus six

10. Seven less than a number times three

11. Four more than a number, times twelve

12. Eight plus a number times sixteen

For **13** through **16**, evaluate the expressions for $p = 21$.

13. $(3 \times p) + 52$

14. $(20 \times p) - 29$

15. $432 - (2 \times p)$

16. $(3 \times p) + (4 \times 64)$

For **17** through **20**, evaluate the expressions for $r = 13$.

17. $(8 + r) \times 3$

18. $196 - (4 \times r)$

19. $(5 \times r) + 97$

20. $(9 \times r) - (2 \times 52)$

You walk for 30 minutes each day on a treadmill. You also do a number of weight-lifting exercises. You do each weight-lifting exercise for 5 minutes.

21. Write an algebraic expression for the number of minutes you spend exercising each day. Let e represent the number of weight-lifting exercises.

22. How many minutes do you exercise on a day when you do 3 weight-lifting exercises? 6 weight-lifting exercises?

Sasha works in a clothing store. He earns $20 per day, plus a $2 commission for each sale.

23. Write an algebraic expression for the amount of money Sasha earns each day. Let s represent the number of sales he makes.

24. How much does Sasha earn per day if he has 12 sales? 19 sales? 32 sales?

For **25** and **26**, use the table at the right.

25. A plane travels 425 miles every hour. Use the expression $425 \times t$, where t represents hours, to find how many miles it is from Los Angeles to Tampa.

26. How much farther is it to fly from Los Angeles to Tampa than it is to fly from Los Angeles to Dallas?

Travel Times	
From Los Angeles, CA	Time
To Dallas, TX	3 hrs
To Tampa, FL	5 hrs

27. A plane traveled 200 miles before arriving in Cleveland. It then departed Cleveland and traveled at a speed of 395 miles per hour. Write an algebraic expression for the total distance it will have traveled when it reaches the next stop.

28. Josephine fixes cars at the rate of $50 an hour. She also charges a cleanup fee of $30. Which expression represents her total charges?

A $\$50 + (\$30 \times h)$

B $(\$50 \times h) - \$30$

C $(\$30 \times h) - \$50$

D $(\$50 \times h) + \$30$

29. All DVDs at the See These video store cost $12. You have a coupon for $2 off the total purchase. Which expression represents the total cost in dollars of d videos?

F $2 - (12 \times d)$ **H** $(12 \times d) - 2$

G $(12 \times d) - 2d$ **I** $12 - (2 \times d)$

Algebra Connections

What's the Conversion Rule?

How can you use tables to find out how two units are related?

The rules for converting one unit into another are not always given. Sometimes it is necessary to compare two different units.

A dram is a small customary unit of weight.

How many drams are there in an ounce?

Ounces	Drams
2	32
4	64
5	

Think *How are these units related?*

2×16 drams per ounce = 32 drams
4×16 drams per ounce = 64 drams
So, there are 16 drams in 1 ounce.

How many drams are there in 5 ounces?
$5 \times 16 = 80$ drams

In **1** through **4**, complete the tables and find a rule of conversion.

1.

Dash	Teaspoon
8	1
16	2
24	
32	

8 dashes per teaspoon

2.

Hogshead	Gallon
1	63
2	
4	252
5	

63 gallons per hogshead

3.

Quart	Peck
16	2
24	3
40	5
56	

8 quarts per peck

4.

Bushel	Peck
	8
4	16
6	
7	28

4 pecks per bushel

5. A "stone" is an old unit of weight used in Ireland and England to measure potatoes. A stone is 14 pounds, and 160 stones make up a "long ton." How many pounds is a long ton?

6. A furlong is a unit of length still used today in racing and agriculture. A race that is 8 furlongs is 1 mile. A furlong is 660 feet. How many feet are in 1 mile?

7. A famous novel by Jules Verne is titled *20,000 Leagues Under the Sea*. A league is a nautical measurement equal to 3 miles. The deepest point in the ocean is about 6.84 miles. About how many leagues deep can you actually go?

8. Neil is reading a sign of old measures of volume from England. He sees that there are 2 pecks in 1 kenning. There are 2 kennings in 1 bushel. There are 2 bushels in 1 strike. There are 4 strikes in 1 quarter. There are 4 quarters in 1 chaldron. Write a number sentence to show the number of pecks in a chaldron.

Lesson

10-6

MA.4.A.4.3 Recognize and write algebraic expressions for functions with two operations.

More Expressions with 2 Operations

How can you use algebraic expressions to describe patterns?

Mary needs to buy cereal. If she uses a coupon with her purchase, how much will 3 boxes of cereal cost?

$5 $5

Save $5

when you buy 3 boxes

$5 $5

Redeem at your Grocer

Guided Practice*

Do you know HOW?

1. Jack pays $4 each hour to skate and $8 to rent roller skates. Write an algebraic expression to describe how much money Jack spends roller skating.

2. Copy and complete the table using your algebraic expression from Problem 1.

Number of Hours	Amount Spent
2	
4	
5	

Data

Do you UNDERSTAND?

3. **Writing to Explain** In the example above, could you write $3 + c$ instead of $3c$ to represent the total cost of the cereal? Why or why not?

4. Write an algebraic expression to describe how much Mary spends for cereal each week if she buys 2 boxes of cereal and has a coupon for $3 off any purchase.

Independent Practice

For **5** through **8**, write an algebraic expression for each phrase.
Let n represent the number.

5. Two times a number, plus three

6. Two less than four times a number

7. Nineteen less than five times a number

8. Eleven plus a number times eight

For **9** through **12**, evaluate the expressions for $p = 6$, $q = 7$, $r = 8$, and $s = 9$.

9. $8p + 11$
10. $18 - 2q$
11. $9r - 15$
12. $5s + 9$

For another example, see Set D on page 213.

Step 1

Let *c* be the price of one box of cereal. → *c*

Mary buys 3 boxes. → $3 \times c$ or $3c$ is the total cost of 3 boxes.

She has a $5 off coupon. → $3c - 5$ is what she pays in dollars.

Tip $3c - 5$ is the same as $(3 \times c) - 5$.

Step 2

A box of cereal costs $4. Use the algebraic expression to find the total.

$$(3 \times c) - 5$$
$$(3 \times 4) - 5$$
$$12 - 5$$
$$7$$

Mary spends $7 on three boxes of cereal.

Problem Solving

Use the information below for **13** and **14**.

Passes for the Go-Cart track cost $9 per person.
Mrs. Santanna has a coupon for $3 off her total purchase.

13. Write an algebraic expression to describe how much Mrs. Santanna spends in dollars for Go-Cart passes.

14. How much will Mrs. Santanna spend if she pays for 7 Go-Cart passes?

Use the picture at the right for **15** and **16**. Jennifer looked at some fossils from the Hall of Fossils at the Florida Museum of Natural History in Gainesville.

15. Write an expression to describe how many fossils Jennifer has left to look at if she wants to see them all. Let *f* be the number of fossils Jennifer has already looked at.

16. Jennifer has looked at 147 fossils so far. How many fossils does she have left to look at?

The Hall of Fossils has 500 fossils on display.

17. A large pizza with cheese costs $12. Each additional topping costs $2. How much would two large pizzas with sausage and one large pizza with mushrooms and green peppers cost?

Critical THINKING

    A $50   **C** $44

    B $48   **D** $42

18. **Social Studies** Florida adopted the nickname "Sunshine State" in 1970. Write an expression to describe how long ago "Sunshine State" became Florida's official nickname. Use *y* to represent the current year.

MA.4.A.4.2 Describe
mathematics relationships
using expressions, equations,
and visual representations.

Problem Solving

Solve a Simpler Problem and Make a Table

Each side of a triangle cracker below is one inch long. If there are 12 triangle crackers in a row, what is the perimeter of the figure?

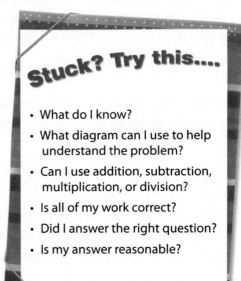

1 inch

Guided Practice*

Do you know HOW?

1. Cora is cutting a piece of paper to get equal-sized pieces. After the first cut, she stacks the two pieces and makes another cut. After she makes the second cut, she stacks the pieces again. If this pattern continues, how many pieces will she have after the fourth cut?

Do you UNDERSTAND?

2. How was the problem above broken into simpler problems?

3. **Write a Problem** Write a problem that you can solve by making a table.

Independent Practice

Solve.

4. Troy is helping his father build a fence. Each section of the fence has a post at each end. Make a table showing how many posts will be needed if there are 1, 3, 5, 10, 15, or 20 sections of the fence. Look for a pattern.

5. How many posts will be needed if the fence has 47 sections?

Stuck? Try this....

- What do I know?
- What diagram can I use to help understand the problem?
- Can I use addition, subtraction, multiplication, or division?
- Is all of my work correct?
- Did I answer the right question?
- Is my answer reasonable?

For another example, see Set E on page 213.

Change the problem into problems that are simpler to solve.

Look at 1 triangle, then 2 triangles, then 3 triangles.

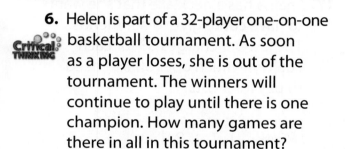

perimeter = 3 inches

perimeter = 4 inches

perimeter = 5 inches

The perimeter is 2 more than the number of triangles.

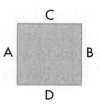

Number of triangles	1	2	3
Perimeter (inches)	3	4	5

So, for 12 triangles the perimeter is 14 inches.

Problem Solving

6. Helen is part of a 32-player one-on-one basketball tournament. As soon as a player loses, she is out of the tournament. The winners will continue to play until there is one champion. How many games are there in all in this tournament?

7. The figure below is a square. If sides A and B are doubled, will this figure still be a square?

C

A   B

D

For **8** through **10**, use the table at the right.

8. The missing classes in the schedule to the right are Math, Science, Reading, Spelling, and Social Studies. Math is after morning break. Spelling is at 9:40. Reading and Science are the two afternoon classes. At what time is Math class?

9. What class is at 8:45?

10. Science class is before Reading. What time is Science class?

Data

Class Schedule	
Morning	**Afternoon**
8:30: Opening	12:15:
8:45:	1:00: Break
9:30: Break	1:30:
9:40:	1:55: Recess
10:25: Recess	2:05: Art, Music or P.E.
10:55:	2:40: Pack Up
11:30: Lunch	2:45: School's Out

11. THINK SOLVE EXPLAIN Six friends are playing checkers. If each friend plays against every other friend once, how many games of checkers will they play all together? Explain how you found your answer.

12. Mr. McNulty's classroom library has 286 books. If he buys 12 books each month for five months, how many books will he have in all?

13. Jolene, Timmy, Nicholas, Paul, and Kathryn are all planting in a community garden. If each of their plots holds 7 rows with 13 plants each, how many plants will they be able to grow all together?

14. Thomas is training for a marathon. He runs for 2 miles and then he walks for a half a mile. If he trains by running 22 miles every day, how many miles will he walk?

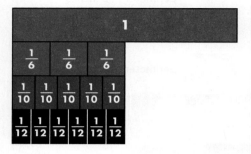

15. Every day, James spends $\frac{5}{10}$ of an hour on the phone, $\frac{6}{12}$ of an hour reading, and $\frac{3}{6}$ of an hour on the computer. Use the fraction strips to the right to tell which activity James spends the most time doing.

16. Maya is putting 3 ice cubes in each red cup and 4 ice cubes in each blue cup. The cups alternate colors starting with red. How many ice cubes will she use if she has 15 cups?

17. Shaina has a necklace that she wants to have cut to give to her friends. The jeweler charges $3 for each cut. How much does Shaina need to pay for 5 cuts?

18. Danielle can type 15 words per minute. How many words can she type in 7 minutes?

Minutes	1	2	3
Words Typed	15	30	45

Think About the Process

19. It takes a plumber 4 minutes to cut a pipe. Which expression would you use to find how long it would take the plumber to cut 7 pipes?

 A $4 + 7$

 B 4×4

 C 7×4

 D 7×7

20. On every train car there are two connectors, one at the front and one at the back. These connectors are there so each car can be linked with another car. If a train has 30 cars, how would you find out the number of connections made?

 F The number of cars minus 1

 G The number of connectors on all the cars minus 1

 H Same as the number of cars

 I The number of cars plus 1

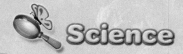
Plants make seeds in order to reproduce. The seeds of a sunflower are arranged in a spiral pattern. Some scientists believe this arrangement of seeds in a pattern keeps the seeds at the best distance apart for growing well. The number of seed spirals is always the same on the kind of sunflower shown.

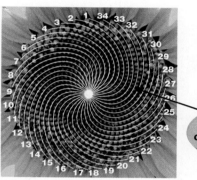

34 counter-clockwise spirals

1. A scientist is studying the seed spirals on 12 sunflowers. How many counter-clockwise spirals are on 12 sunflowers in all?

2. Suppose the scientist studies the spirals on 100 sunflowers. How many counter-clockwise spirals are on 100 sunflowers in all?

3. If there are about 22 seeds in each spiral, estimate the total number of seeds in 34 spirals.

4. Write an expression to find the total number of counter-clockwise spirals if *n* stands for the number of sunflowers.

55 clockwise spirals

Notice that spirals also go in the opposite direction. The number of spirals going in the opposite direction is always the same for the kind of sunflower shown.

5. Suppose a scientist studies the spirals in the opposite direction on 12 sunflowers. What is the total number of clockwise spirals on 12 sunflowers like the one shown to the right?

1 There are 24 dancers in Joy's recital. If *n* represents the number of jazz dancers, which expression represents the number of other types of dancers? (10-1)

A. $24 + n$

B. $24 - n$

C. $24 \times n$

D. $24 \div n$

2 Shanna and Riley have the same birthday, but Riley is 7 years older. In the table, *s* is Shanna's age and $s + 7$ is Riley's age. What is Riley's age when Shanna is 11 years old? (10-1)

s	3	6	11
$s + 7$	10	13	▧

F. 18

G. 17

H. 14

I. 12

3 Every year a dog lives is like 7 years a human lives. Which is a way to find the number of human years that are equal to 9 dog years? (10-3)

Dog Years	1	2	3	4
Human Years	7	14	21	28

A. Subtract 7 from 9

B. Add 7 and 9

C. Divide 9 by 7

D. Multiply 9 by 7

4 What is a rule for the table? (10-2)

Regular Price (p)	$157	$145	$133	$121
Price with the Coupon	$145	$133	$121	$109

F. $p + 13$

G. $p - 13$

H. $p + 12$

I. $p - 12$

5 Mr. Robinson used the table below to calculate how many adults are needed to help on the fourth-grade trip to the observatory.

Number of Students (s)	8	16	24	32
Number of Adults	1	2	3	4

Which rule shows how many adults are needed for *s* students? (10-3)

A. $s - 7$

B. $8 \times s$

C. $s \div 8$

D. $8 + s$

6 The cost in dollars for *n* students to attend a workshop is $(7 \times n) + 12$. What is the cost for 6 students to attend the workshop? (10-5)

F. $25

G. $54

H. $126

I. $156

7 Tad had numbers printed on the back of football jerseys. Below are the first five numbers he had printed. If the pattern continues, what are the next three numbers he will have printed on the jerseys? (10-4)

9, 18, 27, 36, 45, ▪, ▪, ▪

A. 54, 63, 72

B. 54, 63, 71

C. 63, 64, 72

D. 63, 72, 81

8 There are 3 chaperones on the field trip and 7 students in each group. Let g equal the number of groups. Which algebraic expression can be used to find the total number of people on the field trip? (10-6)

F. $7g - 3$

G. $g + 3$

H. $3g + 7$

I. $7g + 3$

9 Which number completes a rule for the table? (10-2)

x	5	9	14
$x +$ ▪	27	31	36

A. 20

B. 21

C. 22

D. 23

10 What is the value of the expression $9b - 2$ for $b = 5$? (10-6)

F. 40

G. 43

H. 45

I. 93

11 Each cube has 6 faces. If Tandra connects 2 cubes, she can see 10 faces. If Tandra connects 7 cubes, how many faces of the cubes will she be able to see? (10-7)

Cubes	2	3	4	5	6	7
Faces	10	14	18	22	26	▪

12 Draw the next two shapes in the pattern. Explain how you decided what shapes to draw. (10-4)

THINK
SOLVE
EXPLAIN

Set A, pages 192–193

Each car on a ride holds 8 children. For c children, $c \div 8$ cars will be full on the ride. How many cars will be full if there are 16, 24, or 40 children?

Find the value of $c \div 8$ for each value of c.

c	$c \div 8$
16	2
24	3
40	5

If there are 16 children, 2 cars will be full.

If there are 24 children, 3 cars will be full.

If there are 40 children, 5 cars will be full.

Remember that to find unknown values, you replace the variable with known values.

Complete each table.

1.
e	16	25	36
$20 + e$	▨	▨	▨

2.
h	14	16	18
$h \times 4$	▨	▨	▨

3.
n	112	56	28
$n - 14$	▨	▨	▨

4.
f	18	36	42
$f \div 6$	▨	▨	▨

Set B, pages 194–197

Look at the table below. Start with the number in the first column. What rule tells you how to find the number in the second column?

Regular price (p)	Sale price	
$43	$41	$43 - 2 = 41$
$45	$43	$45 - 2 = 43$
$46	$44	$46 - 2 = 44$
$47	▨	

A rule is subtract 2, or $p - 2$.

Use a rule to find the missing number in the table.

$47 - 2 = 45$

When the regular price is $47, the sale price is $45.

Remember to ask "What is a rule?"

Copy and complete each table and find a rule.

1.
n	$n -$ ▨
18	3
20	5
25	10
37	▨

2.
x	$x +$ ▨
34	100
0	66
8	74
13	▨

3.
n	2	6	8	9
▨ $\times n$	6	18	24	▨

4.
s	45	40	35	15
$s \div$ ▨	9	8	▨	3

Set C, pages 198–199

Look for a pattern. Find the missing numbers.

1, 5, 9, 13, ▨ , ▨

Find the pattern.	Finish the pattern.
1 + 4 = 5	**13 + 4 = 17**
5 + 4 = 9	**17 + 4 = 21**
9 + 4 = 13	

The missing numbers are 17 and 21.

Remember that in some patterns, you do not add the same number each time.

Complete the pattern.

1. 2, 10, 18, 26, ▨ , ▨ , ▨

2. 3, 6, 9, 12, ▨ , ▨ , ▨

3. ▲, ▲▲▲, ▲▲▲▲▲, ▨ ▨

Set D, pages 200–202, 204–205

Write an algebraic expression for the following word phrase. Let *m* represent the number.

Word Phrase
Five less than three times a number

Algebraic Expression
$(3 \times m) - 5$
or $3m - 5$

m	$(3 \times m) - 5$ Think:	Solve
4	$(3 \times 4) - 5$	7
7	$(3 \times 7) - 5$	16
8	$(3 \times 8) - 5$	19

Remember that when a number is next to a variable you multiply.

Write an algebraic expression.

1. Four times a number, plus 8

2. Six less than three times a number

Evaluate each expression for $n = 3$ and $n = 6$.

3. $6n + 2$

4. $3n - 5$

Set E, pages 206–208

Each side of each triangle is two inches. What is the perimeter of the figure with 5 triangles?

2 in.
2 in.

The perimeter increases by 2.

Number of Triangles	1	2	3	4	5
Perimeter (inches)	6	8	10	12	14

The perimeter of 5 triangles is 14 inches.

Remember you can break the problem apart and solve.

Solve.

1. Each side of a square in the figure is one inch. If there are 14 squares in a row, what is the perimeter of the figure?

Equations

1 The United States produces about 17.2 million bales of cotton each year. In the fields, cotton is compressed into modules that can weigh more than 6 tons. How many bales are in a module? You will find out in Lesson 11-2.

2 The Thrust SSC was the first land vehicle to go faster than the speed of sound. How fast did this supersonic car go? You will find out in Lesson 11-4.

Review What You Know!

Vocabulary

Choose the best term from the box.

- difference
- quotient
- expression
- variable

1. A(n) ? is a symbol or letter that stands for a number.

2. When you divide you find the ? .

3. A(n) ? may include numbers and at least one operation.

Comparing Numbers

Copy and complete. Write $>$, $<$, or $=$ in the ◯.

4. $15 - 3$ ◯ 2×6

5. $5 + 3$ ◯ $9 - 2$

6. 7×4 ◯ 6×5

7. $20 \div 5$ ◯ $1 + 3$

Mixed Practice

Find each answer.

8. $42 \div 6$ 9. $73 - 19$

10. 9×8 11. $36 \div 4$

12. $16 + 45$ 13. 3×7

14. 1×0 15. $49 - 7$

Writing to Explain Write an answer to the question.

16. What number should go in the box to make the statement true? Explain.

$9 \times \boxed{} = 18$

3

Launched from the Kennedy Space Center in 1969, *Apollo 11* became the first space mission to land people on the Moon. How long did the trip to the Moon take? You will find out in Lesson 11-3.

4

These tiles form an interesting design. How can you use an equation to express a pattern in a row of tiles? You will find out in Lesson 11-2.

Topic Essential Questions

- What does it mean for two math quantities to be equal?
- How can equations involving addition, subtraction, multiplication, or division be solved?

11-1

MA.4.A.4.2 Describe mathematics relationships using expressions, equations, and visual representations.

Equal or Not Equal

How can you change both sides of an equation so that it stays true?

An equation is a number sentence stating that two expressions are equal.

Decide if these equations are true. Use the balance scale to the right.

Does $5 + 3 - 3 = 8 - 3$?

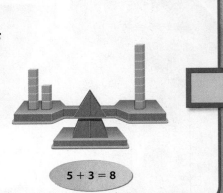

$5 + 3 = 8$

Guided Practice*

Do you know HOW?

For **1** through **4**, tell if the equation is true or false.

1. $8 + 6 + 2 = 14 + 2$

2. $30 \div 5 \div 2 = 8 \div 2$

3. $12 \times 2 = 24 \times 2$

4. $15 - 5 = 10 - 5$

Do you UNDERSTAND?

5. In the first example above, how can you tell that the equation is true using a pan balance?

6. Writing to Explain If 5 is being subtracted from different numbers on both sides of an equation, is the equation true?

Independent Practice

For **7** through **12**, tell if the equation is true or false.

7. $5 \times 3 - 8 = 12 - 8$

8. $2 + 2 + 4 = 4 + 4$

9. $4 + 7 - 2 = 11 - 9$

10. $5 + 13 + 10 = 18 + 10$

11. $6 + 4 - 3 = 10 - 3$

12. $12 \div 4 = 16 \div 4$

For **13** through **18**, write the missing number that makes each equation true.

Tip *Complete the operations inside the parentheses first.*

13. $4 \times 6 = (2 \times 2) \times \boxed{}$

14. $(14 - 2) \div 2 = \boxed{} \div 2$

15. $6 + \boxed{} = (3 \times 2) + 9$

16. $(6 + 8) \div \boxed{} = 14 \div 2$

17. $(4 + 5) \div 3 = \boxed{} \div 3$

18. $\boxed{} + (9 - 5) = 8 + (9 - 5)$

DIGITAL

Animated Glossary
www.pearsonsuccessnet.com

For another example, see Set A on page 228.

Is this true?

$5 + 3 - 3 = 8 - 3$

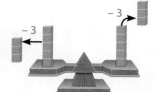

You can add or subtract the same number from both sides of an equation and the sides remain equal.

Check by finding the value of each side.

$5 + 3 - 3 = 8 - 3$
$8 - 3 = 5$
$5 = 5$

The equation is true.

Is this true?

$10 \div 2 = 5 \times 2 \div 5$

You can multiply both sides of an equation by the same number or divide both sides of an equation by the same number except 0 and the sides remain equal.

Check by finding the value of each side.

$10 \div 2 = 5 \times 2 \div 5$
$5 = 10 \div 5$
$5 \neq 2$

The symbol $\neq$ means "is not equal to."

The equation is false.

Problem Solving

19. The equation $8 + 4 = 7 + 5$ shows that Hope and Cole have the same number of bookmarks. What equation would show how many bookmarks each has after giving away 3 bookmarks?

20. Rich delivers newspapers in his neighborhood. He started with 27 customers. Then 9 customers canceled their orders, and he gained 9 new customers. How many customers does Rich have now?

21. Harry had 8 autographed baseballs. He gave 2 to his sister and half of what he had left to his brother. How many autographed baseballs does Harry have now?

22. Writing to Explain Becky says $8 \times 3 - 6$ is equal to 2×9. Is Becky correct? Why or why not?

For **23** and **24**, use the table at the right.

A class was asked how many siblings each student had. The results are listed in the table.

23. How many students have more than 1 sibling?

24. How many students have fewer than 2 siblings?

Students' Siblings	
Number of Siblings	Number of Students
Zero	20
One	1
Two	6
Three or more	3

25. If $\star + 25 = \triangle + 25$ which statement is true?

  A $\star = \triangle$
  B $\star = \triangle - 25$
  C $\star > \triangle$
  D $\star > \triangle + 25$

26. There are 7 days in one week. Which expression represents the number of days in n weeks?

  F $n + 7$
  G $n - 7$
  H $n \times 7$
  I $n \div 7$

Lesson
11-2

MA.4.A.4.2 Describe mathematics relationships using expressions, equations, and visual representations.

Solving Addition and Subtraction Equations

How can you use addition and subtraction to solve equations?

Addition and subtraction have an inverse relationship. How many blocks should be removed from each side to get b by itself? Solve for b.

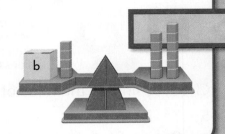

Guided Practice*

Do you know HOW?

Solve for each ▢.

1. $r + 3 = 12$

$r + 3 - ▢ = 12 - ▢$

$r = ▢$

2. $s - 5 = 9$

$s - 5 + ▢ = 9 + ▢$

$s = ▢$

Do you UNDERSTAND?

3. In the second example above, why do you add 10 to both sides?

4. Henry balanced box n and 12 blocks on one side of a pan balance and 16 blocks on the other side. How many blocks should he remove from both sides to find the mass of n?

Independent Practice

Leveled Practice For **5** through **18**, solve each equation.

5. $c - 4 = 16$

$c - 4 + ▢ = 16 + ▢$

$c = ▢$

6. $e + 7 = 19$

$e + 7 - ▢ = 19 - ▢$

$e = ▢$

7. $z - 6 = 21$

$z - 6 + ▢ = 21 + ▢$

$z = ▢$

8. $p + 8 = 18$

$p + 8 - ▢ = 18 - ▢$

$p = ▢$

9. $q - 5 = 17$

$q - 5 + ▢ = 17 + ▢$

$q = ▢$

10. $m + 1 = 8$

$m + 1 - ▢ = 8 - ▢$

$m = ▢$

11. $c - 4 = 23$

12. $e + 7 = 53$

13. $d - 6 = 3$

14. $4 + s = 17$

15. $x + 200 = 400$

16. $z - 8 = 3$

17. $y + 37 = 42$

18. $m - 51 = 29$

Animated Glossary
www.pearsonsuccessnet.com

DIGITAL

For another example, see Set B on page 228.

A **solution** is <u>the value of the variable that makes the equation true</u>.

Solve $b + 4 = 11$.

Undo adding 4 by subtracting 4 from each side.

$b + 4 - 4 = 11 - 4$

Simplify each side.

$b = 7$

The solution to $b + 4 = 11$ is 7.

Solve $n - 10 = 30$.

Undo subtracting 10 by adding 10 to each side.

$n - 10 + 10 = 30 + 10$

Simplify each side.

$n = 40$

The solution to $n - 10 = 30$ is 40.

Problem Solving

19. There are 3 bones in each finger and 2 bones in each thumb. How many bones are in the fingers and thumbs of two hands?

20. THINK SOLVE EXPLAIN Debra solved the equation $f - 17 = 40$ and got 50. Is this solution reasonable? Explain.

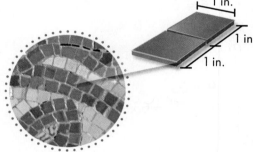

21. Elizabeth is using 1-inch-square tiles to decorate a wall. Use the equation $p = 2t + 2$ to find the perimeter, p, of t tiles in a single row when t is 1, 2, 3, and 6.

22. Estimation Grace bought 9 chairs at $52 each. Did she spend more or less than $500?

23. A factory produces 3,500 pairs of sneakers each day. How many pairs does it produce in 14 days?

24. Think About the Process A school is selling magazine subscriptions to raise money. The first week they sold 435 subscriptions. If their goal is to sell 640 subscriptions in two weeks, which equation would you use to find how many subscriptions need to be sold in the second week?

A $s - 435 = 640$

B $s - 640 = 435$

C $s + 435 = 640$

D $640 + 435 = s$

25. Reasoning At harvest time, most of the cotton in the fields is compressed into modules. A large module weighs 7 tons. How many bales of cotton are in a large module?

Tons of Cotton	1	3	5	7
Bales of Cotton	4	12	20	

MA.4.A.4.2 Describe mathematics relationships using expressions, equations, and visual representations.

Solving Multiplication and Division Equations

n books in 7 groups

How can you use multiplication and division to solve equations?

Jolene organized *n* books into 7 groups. Each group had 6 books. How many books did Jolene have? She wrote the equation $n \div 7 = 6$ to show the result. What is the value of *n*?

Guided Practice*

Do you know HOW?

Solve for each ▢.

1. $m \div 6 = 6$
$m \div 6 \times \boxed{} = 6 \times \boxed{}$
$m = \boxed{}$

2. $t \times 9 = 63$
$t \times 9 \div \boxed{} = 63 \div \boxed{}$
$t = \boxed{}$

3. $n \div 7 = 4$
$n \div 7 \times \boxed{} = 4 \times \boxed{}$
$n = \boxed{}$

Do you UNDERSTAND?

4. In the first example above, what is another way to describe the problem?

5. In the second example above, why must the solution to $w \times 4 = 32$ be less than 32?

6. Write an equation to show the following: Jolene put 16 books into *g* groups. Each group had 4 books. Find the value of *g*.

Independent Practice

Leveled Practice For **7** through **12**, solve for each ▢.

7. $p \div 3 = 6$
$p \div 3 \times \boxed{} = 6 \times \boxed{}$
$p = \boxed{}$

8. $r \times 7 = 49$
$r \times 7 \div \boxed{} = 49 \div \boxed{}$
$r = \boxed{}$

9. $t \div 6 = 1$
$t \div 6 \times \boxed{} = 1 \times \boxed{}$
$t = \boxed{}$

10. $n \times 9 = 45$
$n \times 9 \div \boxed{} = 45 \div \boxed{}$
$n = \boxed{}$

11. $q \div 5 = 4$
$q \div 5 \times \boxed{} = 4 \times \boxed{}$
$q = \boxed{}$

12. $s \times 3 = 15$
$s \times 3 \div \boxed{} = 15 \div \boxed{}$
$s = \boxed{}$

For another example, see Set C on page 229.

Solve $n \div 7 = 6$ to find the number of books, n.

$n \div 7 = 6$

The inverse of dividing by 7 is multiplying by 7.

$n \div 7 \times 7 = 6 \times 7$

Simplify each side.

$n = 42$

The solution to $n \div 7 = 6$ is 42.

Jolene has 42 books.

Solve $w \times 4 = 32$.

The inverse of multiplying by 4 is dividing by 4.

$w \times 4 \div 4 = 32 \div 4$

Simplify each side.

$w = 8$

The solution to $w \times 4 = 32$ is 8.

For **13** through **22**, solve each equation.

13. $t \div 5 = 7$ **14.** $3 \times e = 18$ **15.** $j \div 4 = 8$ **16.** $d \div 3 = 3$ **17.** $c \div 5 = 5$

18. $2 \times r = 18$ **19.** $s \div 7 = 3$ **20.** $m \times 7 = 63$ **21.** $p \div 3 = 2$ **22.** $7 \times a = 56$

Problem Solving

23. Howard did homework from 5:05 P.M. until 6:25 P.M. Half of that time was spent studying for a science exam. How long did Howard study for the science exam?

24. Ms. Porter ran a total of 63 miles last week training for a race. She ran the same distance each day. Write and solve an equation using multiplication to find out how many miles Ms. Porter ran for each of 7 days.

25. Algebra If the pattern below continues, what will the next three numbers be?

22 23 25 28 32 ▨ ▨ ▨

26. Writing to Explain Why must the solution to $6 \times k = 12$ be less than 12?

Critical THINKING

27. Science *Apollo 11* was the first mission to land people on the Moon. Launched in 1969, the flight to the Moon took about 75 hours. The average speed of the spacecraft was 5,200 kilometers per hour. Multiply the rate by the total time to find the distance from Earth to the Moon.

Tip *The rate is 5,200 kilometers per hour.*

28. A baseball team is selling T-shirts. If their goal is to sell 72 T-shirts in all, and they sell an average of 8 T-shirts a week, which equation would you NOT use to find out how many weeks they will be selling T-shirts?

A $8 \times w = 72$ **C** $72 \div w = 8$

B $w \times 8 = 72$ **D** $w \div 72 = 8$

MA.4.A.4.1 Generate algebraic rules and use all four operations to describe patterns, including nonnumeric growing or repeating patterns. Also MA.4.A.4.2

Solving Equations

Which operation do you choose to solve an equation?

Sally is putting *n* roses in each of 4 vases.
Solve the equation $n \times 4 = 20$ to find *n*.

Think Is *n* greater or less than 20? Since *n* is multiplied by 4 and the product is 20, I know *n* is less than 20.

Undo multiplying by 4 by dividing each side by 4.

$n \times 4 \div 4 = 20 \div 4$
$n = 5$

20 roses

Guided Practice*

Do you know HOW?

Without solving, decide if *n* is less than 48 or greater than 48.

1. $n - 6 = 48$ **2.** $n \times 6 = 48$

Solve each equation. Name the operation you used.

3. $g \div 5 = 4$ **4.** $17 + h = 52$

5. $p \times 5 = 30$ **6.** $q - 14 = 23$

Do you UNDERSTAND?

7. Number Sense In $n - 24 = 63$, is *n* greater than 63 or less than 63? Explain without solving the equation.

8. Gretchen reads 21 hours each week. The equation $7 \times n = 21$ can be used to find how many hours she reads each day. Explain how you would use inverse operations to solve the equation.

Independent Practice

In **9** through **11**, decide if *n* is less than 32 or greater than 32. Do not solve the equation.

9. $n \times 4 = 32$ **10.** $n - 4 = 32$ **11.** $n \div 4 = 32$

In **12** through **23**, solve each equation. Name the operation you used.

12. $7 \times n = 28$ **13.** $n \div 3 = 4$ **14.** $n + 33 = 47$

15. $n - 25 = 25$ **16.** $n \times 6 = 36$ **17.** $n \div 5 = 8$

18. $s - 12 = 15$ **19.** $t + 55 = 80$ **20.** $p \div 8 = 7$

21. $r - 27 = 35$ **22.** $k \times 9 = 45$ **23.** $m + 12 = 12$

For another example, see Set D on page 229.

Start with x roses and take away 4 roses. 20 are left. Solve $x - 4 = 20$.	Divide y roses into 4 equal groups, with 20 in each group. Solve $y \div 4 = 20$.	Add 4 roses to z roses. The total is 20. Solve $z + 4 = 20$.

Think Is x greater or less than 20?

Undo subtracting 4 by adding 4 to each side.

$x - 4 = 20$
$x - 4 + 4 = 20 + 4$
$x = 24$

Think Is y greater or less than 20?

Undo dividing by 4 by multiplying each side by 4.

$y \div 4 = 20$
$y \div 4 \times 4 = 20 \times 4$
$y = 80$

Think Is z greater or less than 20?

Undo adding 4 by subtracting 4 from each side.

$z + 4 = 20$
$z + 4 - 4 = 20 - 4$
$z = 16$

Problem Solving

24. **Science** The Thrust SSC jet-car set a land speed record of 766 miles per hour. Starting at 0 miles per hour, the Thrust SSC's speed increased by about 40 miles per hour each second, on average. Copy and complete the table to find the speed at 10 seconds and at 15 seconds.

Time (seconds)	5	7	9	10	15
Speed (miles per hour)	200	280	360	▨	▨

25. **Number Sense** If $n + 18 = 100$, how do you know if n is more than 100 or less than 100 before you solve? Explain.

Critical THINKING

26. **Geometry** Each side of a hexagon is 9 centimeters in length. What is the perimeter of the hexagon?

9 cm
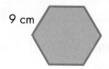

27. Ty has 10 reading questions for homework. He did 4 before soccer practice and half of the remaining questions before dinner. How many reading questions does Ty have left to do after dinner?

28. There are 67 students in the school chorus, and 34 of the students are girls. Write and solve an equation to find how many boys are in the chorus.

THINK SOLVE EXPLAIN

29. Jeremiah needs to solve the equation $9 \times p = 45$ to find how many volunteers are needed for the booths at the school fair. Which operation should Jeremiah use to solve the equation?

   A Division   **B** Multiplication   **C** Subtraction   **D** Addition

MA.4.A.4.2 Describe
mathematics relationships
using expressions, equations,
and visual representations.

Work Backward

You can use operation trains to build numbers.
Here is one example:

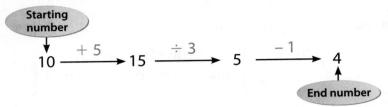

Guided Practice*

Do you know HOW?

Solve by working backward. Use an
operation train to find your answer.

1. Charlie picked some peppers from
   his garden. He gave 14 peppers to
   his brother and 7 peppers to his
   neighbor. He has 24 peppers left.
   How many peppers did Charlie
   pick from his garden?

Do you UNDERSTAND?

2. In the example above, how can
   you check the answer?

3. **Write a Problem** Write a problem
   that uses an operation train. Then
   work backward to answer your
   question.

Independent Practice

Solve each problem. Write the answer in a
complete sentence.

4. Kenny wants to get to the pool 25 minutes
   before the pool opens. It takes him 20 minutes
   to drive and 15 minutes to pack up. At what
   time should he start packing up if the pool
   opens at 5:30 P.M.?

5. Drew drove to Karen's house. He drove 2 miles
   west, then 4 miles south, and 1 mile east.
   How can Drew drive home from Karen's
   house using the same path?

Stuck? Try this....

- What do I know?
- What diagram can I use to help
  understand the problem?
- Can I use addition, subtraction,
  multiplication, or division?
- Is all of my work correct?
- Did I answer the right question?
- Is my answer reasonable?

Use the operation train below. Find the starting number, *x*.

If you know the end number and how the number was built, you can work backward to find the starting number.

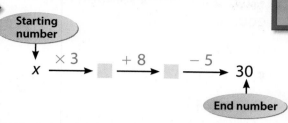

Do the inverse of the given operations and work backward.

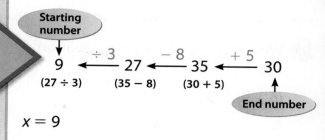

x = 9

The starting number is 9.

6. Alice shredded cheese to top 6 pizzas. She spread 4 ounces of cheese on each of 5 pizzas. On the sixth pizza, she added twice as many ounces. She had 2 ounces of shredded cheese left. How many ounces of cheese did Alice shred?

Critical Thinking

7. Andy bought a 78-piece puzzle. He put some of the pieces together by himself. He and his brother put 24 more pieces together. Andy's sister then put 33 more pieces together to finish the puzzle. How many pieces did Andy put together himself?

8. Tara is 6 years older than Karen. Karen is 5 years younger than Dave. Dave is 3 years older than Luz. If Luz is 10 years old, how old is Tara?

9. Jason is thinking of a number. He adds 5, multiplies by 5, subtracts 4, and then divides by 6. The result is 6. What number is Jason thinking of?

10. Wendy took the bus to get to the mall. At the first stop, 8 people got off and 5 got on. At the next stop, 4 people got off and 3 more got on. There were 26 people left on the bus. How many people were on the bus when Wendy got on?

    A   5 people   **C** 22 people

    B 20 people   **D** 30 people

11. Kristy has band practice at 10:40 A.M. It takes her 15 minutes to get from home to practice. She spends 5 minutes before practice warming up. What time should she leave home to get to practice on time?

    F 10:15 A.M.   **H** 10:45 A.M.

    G 10:20 A.M.   **I** 11:00 A.M.

12. Joel took home a list of words to practice for a spelling bee. He already knew 12 of the words on the list. His mom tested him on 23 words. His dad asked him to spell 18 words. Joel had 22 more words left to practice on his own. How many words were on Joel's list? Explain how you know.

THINK
SOLVE
EXPLAIN

? Spelling words in all			
12	23	18	22

1 What number makes the equation true? (11-1)

$(6 + 9) \div 3 = \boxed{} \div 3$

A. 54

B. 15

C. 5

D. 3

2 How many counters equal the mass of box s? (11-2)

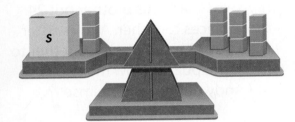

F. 3

G. 6

H. 9

I. 12

3 Mrs. Iverson bought 8 identical packages of pencils. She bought a total of 48 pencils. How many pencils did each package have? Let p equal the number of pencils in each package. Use the equation $8 \times p = 48$ to solve the problem. (11-3)

A. 384 pencils

B. 40 pencils

C. 6 pencils

D. 4 pencils

4 What number is a solution to the equation below? (11-2)

$w - 28 = 59$

F. $w = 89$

G. $w = 87$

H. $w = 32$

I. $w = 31$

5 Which number makes the equation true? (11-1)

$12 \div \boxed{} = (6 + 6) \div 2$

A. 2

B. 3

C. 4

D. 6

6 Which equation is true? (11-1)

F. $(45 \div 9) \times 9 = 5 + 9$

G. $(45 \div 9) - 9 = 5 + 9$

H. $(45 \div 9) + 9 = 5 + 9$

I. $(45 \div 9) \div 5 = 5 - 5$

7 Liya needs to solve the equation $7 \times p = 56$ for her homework. Which operation should Liya use to solve the equation? (11-4)

A. Addition

B. Subtraction

C. Multiplication

D. Division

8 Gentry has won a number of trophies. He put the trophies on 4 different shelves. Each shelf had 5 trophies. Gentry used the equation $t \div 4 = 5$ to find the number of trophies he had. What should Gentry do to find the value of t? (11-3)

   F. Divide each side by 5.

   G. Divide each side by 4.

   H. Multiply each side by 5.

   I. Multiply each side by 4.

9 The equation below shows that Joseph and Dillon both had some money, spent some of the money, and then earned more money.

      Joseph   Dillon

$(17 - 8) + 5 = (12 - \blacksquare) + 5$

How much money did Dillon spend? (11-1)

   A. 8

   B. 5

   C. 4

   D. 3

10 What is the value of n? (11-2)

$n - 15 = 8$

   F. $n = 38$

   G. $n = 33$

   H. $n = 23$

   I. $n = 7$

11 Veronica bought a bouquet of 14 flowers for her mother. The bouquet had 8 daisies and some roses. Which equation would Veronica use to find how many roses, r, were in the bouquet? (11-2)

   A. $8 + r = 14$

   B. $8 \times r = 14$

   C. $r - 8 = 14$

   D. $8 + 14 = r$

12 What is the value of x in the diagram below? (11-5)

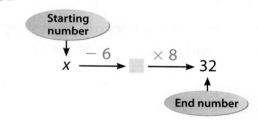

13 In $n + 22 = 86$, is n more than 86 or less than 86? Explain without solving the equation. (11-4)

THINK
SOLVE
EXPLAIN

Set A, pages 216–217

Is this equation true?

$6 + 4 - 4 = 10 - 4$

When you make the same change to both sides of an equation that is true, the equation remains true.

$6 + 4 - 4 = 10 - 4$ Subtract 4 from both sides.

$10 - 4 = 6$ Find the value of each side.

$6 = 6$

The equation is true.

Is this equation true?

$12 \div 2 = 6 \times 2 \div 4$

The equation is false because both sides were not divided by the same number.

Remember that both sides of an equation must have the same value for the equation to be true.

Tell whether each equation is true or false.

1. $7 + 7 - 4 = 14 - 4$

2. $3 + 5 + 8 = 8 + 4$

3. $3 + 9 - 2 = 12 - 2$

4. $6 \times 8 + 12 = 48 + 12$

Write the number that makes each equation true.

5. $11 + 4 = 5 + \boxed{} + 4$

6. $18 - 9 - 2 = 9 - \boxed{}$

7. $2 \times 2 \times 2 = \boxed{} \times 2$

Set B, pages 218–219

Solve $x + 7 = 41$.

Use subtraction to undo addition.

$x + 7 - 7 = 41 - 7$ Subtract 7 from each side.

$x = 34$ Simplify each side.

The solution to $x + 7 = 41$ is 34.

Solve $y - 14 = 50$.

Use addition to undo subtraction.

$y - 14 + 14 = 50 + 14$ Add 14 to each side.

$y = 64$ Simplify each side.

The solution to $y - 14 = 50$ is 64.

Remember to add or subtract the same number from both sides of the equation.

Solve each equation.

1. $y + 20 = 31$ **2.** $n - 10 = 36$

3. $r + 16 = 40$ **4.** $v - 25 = 25$

5. $l + 5 = 20$ **6.** $n - 8 = 17$

7. $x + 32 = 42$ **8.** $y - 18 = 13$

9. $p + 15 = 30$ **10.** $q - 11 = 19$

11. $s + 16 = 95$ **12.** $m - 15 = 0$

Set C, pages 220–221

Solve $n \div 6 = 5$.

Use multiplication to undo division.

$n \div 6 \times 6 = 5 \times 6$ Multiply each side by 6.

$n = 30$ Simplify each side.

The solution to $n \div 6 = 5$ is 30.

Remember to use division to undo multiplication.

Solve each equation.

1. $n \times 2 = 18$ **2.** $y \div 6 = 6$

3. $m \times 9 = 36$ **4.** $y \div 6 = 5$

5. $z \times 5 = 25$ **6.** $t \div 7 = 4$

Set D, pages 222–223

Solve $n + 29 = 42$.

Decide what operation was applied to the unknown. Then use the inverse operation to solve.

$n + 29 = 42$ Think: 29 was added to n, and the result is 42. So, n must be less than 42.

Subtracting 29 undoes adding 29.
Subtract 29 from each side to solve.

$n + 29 - 29 = 42 - 29$

The solution is $n = 13$.

Remember to choose the operation that "undoes" the operation that was applied to the unknown.

Solve each equation. Name the operation you used.

1. $a + 4 = 17$ **2.** $b \div 5 = 8$

3. $c - 18 = 46$ **4.** $g \times 8 = 56$

5. $r \times 3 = 27$ **6.** $13 + f = 27$

7. $p \div 9 = 4$ **8.** $s - 11 = 15$

Set E, pages 224–225

What is the value of x?

Start with the end number. Use inverse operations to work backward to find x.

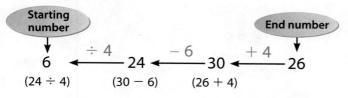

The value of x is 6.

Remember to identify all the steps in the process before solving.

Work backward to solve.

1. For a school play, Juan sold 18 tickets, Teri sold 14 tickets, and Al sold 22 tickets. If they ended up with 45 unsold tickets, how many tickets did they start with?

2. Jen writes down a number. She subtracts 2, divides by 3, and adds 1. The result is 5. What number did Jen write?

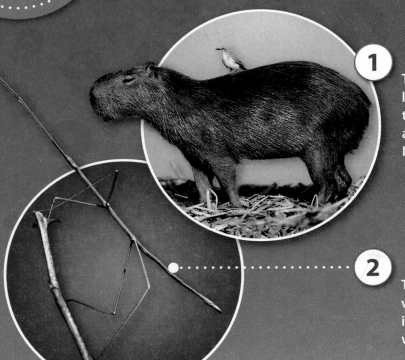

Topic 12

Decimals and Numeration

1 The capybara is the world's largest rodent. It is related to the guinea pig. How long is a capybara? You will find out in Lesson 12-1.

2 The longest stick insect in the world lives in Borneo. How long is the Borneo stick insect? You will find out in Lesson 12-2.

3 What is the size of a grain of sand? You will find out in Lesson 12-6.

Vocabulary

Choose the best term from the box.

> • ones • one hundred
> • tens • number line

1. The number 438,572 has a 7 in the ? place.

2. Ten tens are equal to ?.

3. A ? can be used to show numbers in order using a scale.

Comparing Numbers

Compare. Write >, <, or = for each ◯.

4. 1,909 ◯ 1,990

5. 43,627 ◯ 43,167

6. 629,348 ◯ 629,348

7. 455,311 ◯ 455,331

8. 101,101 ◯ 101,011

9. 95,559 ◯ 95,555

Ordering Numbers

Order the numbers from greatest to least.

10.	3,687	3,867	3,678	3,768
11.	41,101	41,011	41,110	41,001
12.	4,593	4,395	4,595	4,359

13. **Writing to Explain** How would you order the numbers below from least to greatest? Explain.

15,420   154,200   1,542

④ This Green Darner dragonfly has a wingspan of about 4 inches. How much does it weigh? You will find out in Lesson 12-1.

⑤ How much does the sea level at Key West rise each year? You will find out in Lesson 12-4.

Topic Essential Questions

• How is decimal numeration related to whole number numeration?

• How can decimals be compared and ordered?

Lesson 12-1

MA.4.A.2.1 Use decimals through the thousandths place to name numbers between whole numbers.

Tenths and Hundredths

How are decimal models used to represent decimals?

A squirrel can weigh 1.6 pounds. Use a decimal model to show 1.6.

1.6 pounds

Other Example

A decimal model can also show hundredths, <u>one of one hundred equal parts of a whole</u>.

Show 1.64.

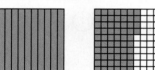

Expanded form: 1 + 0.6 + 0.04

Standard form: 1.64

Word form: one and sixty-four hundredths

Guided Practice*

Do you know HOW?

In **1** through **4**, write the expanded form and word form for each number.

1. 3.91   **2.** 6.8

3. 1.06   **4.** 2.3

Do you UNDERSTAND?

5. In Exercise 1, what digit is in the tenths place? in the hundredths place?

6. If there are 3.29 seconds left in a ballgame, how would you say this number?

Independent Practice

In **7** through **10**, write the decimal for each shaded part.

7.   **8.**   **9.**   **10.**

*For another example, see Set A on page 252.

A decimal model can show **tenths**, <u>one of ten equal parts of a whole</u>.

Write the decimal in expanded form, standard form, and word form.

1.6

decimal point: <u>a dot used to separate ones from tenths in a number.</u> A decimal point is read as "and."

Expanded form: 1 + 0.6

Standard form: 1.6

Word form: one and six tenths

In **11** through **15**, write the number in word form and give the value of the red digit for each number.

11. 2.47   **12.** 23.79   **13.** 1.8   **14.** 14.1   **15.** 9.05

In **16** through **20**, write each number in expanded form.

16. 3.19   **17.** 13.6   **18.** 0.78   **19.** 8.07   **20.** 17.2

Problem Solving

21. Reasoning Write a number that has a 4 in the tens place and a 6 in the hundredths place.

22. The Green Darner is one of the largest dragonflies. It weighs about four hundredths of an ounce. Write four hundredths in standard form.

23. Writing to Explain Use the decimal model below to explain why 0.08 is less than 0.1.

24. What is the value of the 5 in 43.51?

   A Five hundredths

   B Five tenths

   C Fifty-one hundredths

   D Five

25. **Science** The capybara can grow to be 1.3 meters long. Write 1.3 in expanded form and in word form.

1.3 meters

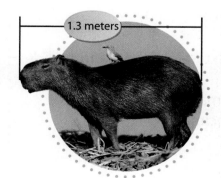

Animated Glossary
www.pearsonsuccessnet.com

DIGITAL

MA.4.A.2.1 Use decimals through the thousandths place to name numbers between whole numbers.

Thousandths

How are place-value charts used to represent decimals?

Jessie bought 2.568 pounds of horned melons. What are some different ways to show 2.568?

4 melons weigh 2.568 pounds.

Other Example

An **equivalent decimal** names the same amount as another decimal. Name two other decimals equivalent to 1.4.

One and four tenths names the same amount as 1 and 40 hundredths.

So, 1.4 = 1.40.

One and four tenths names the same amount as 1 and 400 thousandths.

So, 1.4 = 1.400.

So, 1.4 = 1.40 = 1.400.

1 whole

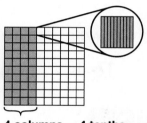

4 columns = 4 tenths
40 small squares = 40 hundredths
= 400 thousandths

Guided Practice*

Do you know HOW?

Write the word form for each number.

1. 4.737   **2.** 9.806

Write each number in standard form.

3. 6 + 0.6 + 0.03 + 0.007

4. four and sixty-eight thousandths

Write two decimals that are equivalent to the given decimal.

5. 3.700   **6.** 5.60

Do you UNDERSTAND?

7. Writing to Explain The number 3.453 has two 3s. Why does each 3 have a different value?

8. How do you read the decimal point in word form?

9. José finished a race in 2.6 hours, and Pavel finished the same race in 2.600 hours. Which runner finished the race first?

For another example, see Set A on page 252.

A place-value chart can show **thousandths**, <u>one of one thousand equal parts of a whole</u>.

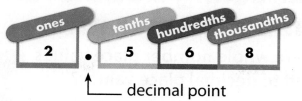

ones	.	tenths	hundredths	thousandths
2	.	5	6	8

decimal point

Expanded form: 2 + 0.5 + 0.06 + 0.008
Standard form: 2.568
Word form: two and five hundred sixty-eight thousandths

Independent Practice

In **10** through **13**, write the word form for each number and tell the value of the underlined digit.

10. 2.<u>3</u>00   **11.** 9.0<u>2</u>7   **12.** 1.9<u>8</u>2   **13.** 6.<u>1</u>7

In **14** through **18**, write each number in standard form.

14. two and sixteen thousandths   **15.** five and one hundred four thousandths

16. 3 + 0.3 + 0.009   **17.** 9 + 0.2 + 0.04   **18.** 7 + 0.6 + 0.05 + 0.007

In **19** through **21**, write two decimals that are equivalent to the given decimal.

19. 2.200   **20.** 8.1   **21.** 9.50

Problem Solving

22. Kay is buying juice at the market. She has $9, and each bottle of juice costs $2. Does she have enough money to buy 5 bottles of juice? Explain.

THINK SOLVE EXPLAIN

23. The Borneo stick insect has a total length, including its legs, of 21.5 inches. Name two decimals that are equivalent to 21.5.

24. Why are 7.63 and 7.630 equivalent? Use a place-value chart to help you.

Critical THINKING

25. Worker leafcutter ants can measure 0.5 inch. Write 0.5 in word form.

26. Mr. Yu made 19 pancakes. He took 7 and gave an equal number to his two sons. How many pancakes did each son get?

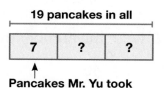

19 pancakes in all

7	?	?

Pancakes Mr. Yu took

Lesson
12-3

MA.4.A.2.2 Describe decimals as an extension of the base-ten number system.

Connecting Decimal and Whole Number Numeration

5,342.435 feet

How are whole number place values related to decimal place values?

A telephone company has large spools of cable that they use to install phone lines. Suppose each spool is 5,342.435 feet long.

Show this number in a place-value chart.

Guided Practice*

Do you know HOW?

In **1** through **4**, write the place value for the red digit.

1. 34.67

2. 856.472

3. 486.359

4. 6,095.375

For **5** through **8**, write the number that is ten times as many.

5. 1

6. 0.01

7. 100

8. 0.001

Do you UNDERSTAND?

9. A telephone worker used 340.75 feet of cable. What is the place value of the 5 in 340.75?

10. The grid below shows one hundred equal parts. Each part is equal to one hundredth. How many hundredths are in one tenth?

1 whole

Independent Practice

In **11** through **22**, write the place value for the red digit.

11. 572.67

12. 2,368.795

13. 1,435.889

14. 9,654.328

15. 601.65

16. 1,754.709

17. 4,597.624

18. 6,332.470

19. 2,867.435

20. 9,555.392

21. 1,843.2

22. 5,642.437

For **23** through **26**, write the number that is ten times as many.

23. 0.07

24. 40

25. 0.008

26. 0.9

For another example, see Set B on page 252.

Each place-value position is ten times as much as the place value to its right.

thousands	hundreds	tens	ones		tenths	hundredths	thousandths
1,000	100	10	1		$0.1 = \frac{1}{10}$	$0.01 = \frac{1}{100}$	$0.001 = \frac{1}{1,000}$
5	3	4	2	.	4	3	5

Problem Solving

27. Number Sense There are 100 fiction books in Ms. Clark's classroom library. The school library has ten times as many fiction books. What is the number of fiction books in the school library?

28. Number Sense Jake found two shells that are the same shape but are different sizes. One weighs 0.01 pound. The other weighs ten times as much. How much does the heavier shell weigh?

29. Jennifer and Linda collected aluminum cans for one month. Look at the table at the right to see how many aluminum cans each student collected.

Data		
Jennifer	:	1,353 cans
Linda	:	1,328 cans

  a Who collected more cans?

  b Find the difference between the number of cans collected.

30. Angela baked 3 times as many muffins as Jasmine for the bake sale. If Jasmine baked 36 muffins, how many did Angela bake?

? muffins

Angela	36	36	36	3 times as many
Jasmine	36			

31. Name the place-value position that is ten times as much as the thousandths position.

  A Ones

  B Tenths

  C Hundredths

  D Thousands

32. THINK SOLVE EXPLAIN Mr. Cooper has 6 gallons of gas in his car. His tank can hold 15 gallons of gas. Will Mr. Cooper need more or less than 10 gallons to fill his tank?

33. Critical THINKING Bob says the value of the first 1 is greater than the value of the second 1 in 4.115. Is he correct? Explain.

MA.4.A.2.1 Use decimals through the thousandths place to name numbers between whole numbers.

Decimals on the Number Line

How can you locate decimals on a number line?

The thickness of a nickel is 1.95 millimeters. How can you use a number line to show this length?

Thickness is 1.95 millimeters

Guided Practice*

Do you know HOW?

For **1** through **3**, use the number line below to name the decimal for each point.

1. A   **2.** B   **3.** C

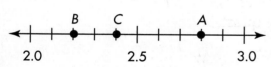

For **4** through **6**, use the number line below to name the point for each decimal.

4. 1.59   **5.** 1.57   **6.** 1.53

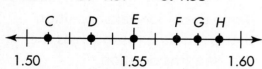

Do you UNDERSTAND?

7. Look at the number line in the example above. Is 1.09 closer to 1 or closer to 2? Explain.

8. What is the value of the decimal 1.428?

9. Look at the second number line on the left. What are other decimal names for 1.50 and 1.60?

10. The thickness of a penny is 1.55 millimeters. Using the second number line on the left, find which point shows 1.55.

Independent Practice

For **11** through **15**, name the point on the number line below for each decimal.

11. 9.6   **12.** 10.2   **13.** 9.3   **14.** 10.8   **15.** 10.9

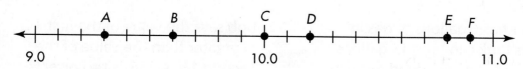

For another example, see Set C on page 252.

On a number line, 1.95 is between 1 and 2. These whole numbers can also be written as 1.0 and 2.0. The distance between 1.0 and 2.0 can be divided into tenths.

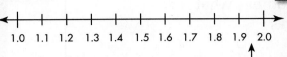

1.95 is between 1.9 and 2.0

The distance between 1.9 and 2.0 can be divided into hundredths.

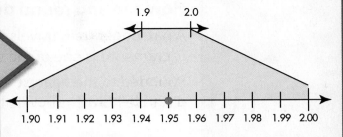

Since decimals represent numbers, decimals can be shown on a number line.

For **16** through **20**, use the number line below to name the decimal.

16. *J*   **17.** *K*   **18.** *L*   **19.** *M*   **20.** *N*

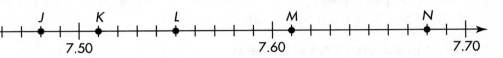

Problem Solving

In **21** through **23**, copy and complete the number lines shown at the right. Then use the number lines to answer the questions.

21. Which points on the two number lines represent the same decimal? How do you know?

THINK
SOLVE
EXPLAIN

22. Name three decimals between 8.4 and 8.6.

23. Name two decimals that 8.72 comes between.

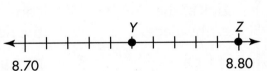

24. How many tenths are between 0 and 1? Write two greater numbers that have the same number of tenths between them as 0 and 1 do.

Critical
THINKING

25. **Social Studies** Sea level at Key West is rising about 1.8 millimeters per year. What is the place value of the digit 8 in this number?

26. Which does NOT describe Point *M* on the number line below?

A 2 wholes and 5 tenths

B 2 wholes and 50 hundredths

C 2.5

D 2.55

MA.4.A.2.1 Use decimals through the thousandths place to name numbers between whole numbers.

Rounding Decimals

How can you round decimals?

A passenger train travels from Emeryville to Sparks. Sacramento is one of the stops along the route.

Rounded to the nearest whole number, what is the distance from Emeryville to Sparks?

Emeryville to Sacramento: 77.86 miles	Sacramento to Sparks: 134.12 miles

211.98 miles

Another Example **How do you round to the nearest tenth?**

You have learned how to round whole numbers.
Now you will learn how to round decimals.

What is 211.98 rounded to the nearest tenth?

A 211.0

B 211.9

C 211.99

D 212.0

Step 1

Look at the tenths place.

211.9̲8

Step 2

Look at the digit to the right.

211.98̲

If the digit to the right is less than 5, round to 211.9. If the digit is 5 or greater than 5, round to 212.0.

Step 3

211.98 rounds to **212.0**.

Since this digit is 8, the digit in the tenths place increases by 1.

So, 211.98 rounded to the nearest tenth is 212.0.
The correct choice is **D**.

Explain It

1. **Reasonableness** Why does the ones place change when you round 211.98 to the nearest tenth?

Look at the ones place.

211.98

Look at the digit to the right.

211.98

Since 9 > 5, round to the next whole number.

The distance from Emeryville to Sparks is about 212 miles.

A number line shows that the rounded answer is reasonable.

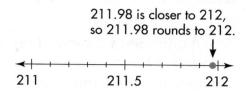

211.98 is closer to 212, so 211.98 rounds to 212.

211   211.5   212

Other Example

Round 68.142 to the nearest hundredth.

Step 1

Look at the hundredths place.

68.142

Step 2

Look at the digit to the right.

68.142

Step 3

Since 2 < 5, the hundredths digit stays the same.

68.142 rounds to **68.14**.

Guided Practice*

Do you know HOW?

For **1** through **4**, round each decimal to the place of the underlined digit.

1. 17.23   **2.** 19.805

3. 49.562   **4.** 67.591

Do you UNDERSTAND?

5. Writing to Explain In the example at the top, explain why the number line shows that 212 is a reasonable answer.

6. Round 134.129 to the nearest tenth.

Independent Practice

For **7** through **21**, round each decimal to the place of the underlined digit. You may use a number line to help you.

7. 60.82   **8.** 88.3   **9.** 2.283   **10.** 0.695   **11.** 72.564

12. 41.483   **13.** 0.819   **14.** 147.61   **15.** 857.95   **16.** 63.667

17. 78.61   **18.** 4.108   **19.** 312.12   **20.** 591.95   **21.** 7.452

---

22. Number Sense Name 3 decimals that, when rounded to the nearest tenth, round to 7.8.

23. Ed filled his car with 8.53 gallons of gasoline. To the nearest tenth of a gallon, how much gasoline did Ed buy?

24. Which of these decimals, when rounded to the nearest whole number, does NOT round to 6?

A 5.713   **C** 6.249

B 5.91   **D** 6.82

25. What is 17.638 rounded to the nearest hundredth?

F 17   **H** 17.64

G 17.6   **I** 18

26. THINK SOLVE EXPLAIN Use a number line to explain why 0.28 rounded to the nearest whole number is 0.

27. Barbara's dog weighs 35.5 pounds. To the nearest whole number, how much does Barbara's dog weigh?

28. Reasonableness Danny wanted to know the total mass of two pieces of volcanic rock. The first piece had a mass of 4.99 grams and the second had a mass of 2.85 grams. Danny needs to record the combined masses of the two pieces of volcanic rock to the nearest gram. Is 4.0 + 2.9 a reasonable estimate of the masses to the nearest gram?

29. Dawn jogs 12 miles a week. How many miles does Dawn jog in 1 year?

Tip *1 year = 52 weeks*

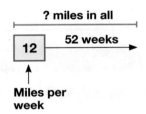

30. Reasoning Round 4.97 to the nearest tenth. Did the ones place change? Explain.

31. Writing to Explain What do the decimal numbers below have in common?

3.6, 4.2, 4.1

32. Number Sense THINK SOLVE EXPLAIN Marissa was asked to round 89.367 to the nearest hundredth. She answered 89.36. Is she correct? Explain.

33. Joel has 10 bagels. Three-tenths of the bagels are plain. The rest of the bagels are wheat bagels. How many wheat bagels are there?

34. According to Mica's rain gauge, it had rained 2.28 inches in 24 hours. What is 2.28 rounded to the nearest tenth? To the nearest whole number?

35. The distance between Happy Valley and Rolling Meadow is 53.19 miles. What is this distance rounded to the nearest mile?

Mixed Problem Solving

Graphic organizers are often used in reading to show how different pieces of information are related. Graphic organizers can also be very helpful in math.

Copy and complete the graphic organizers below to show how the math terms are related.

dividend	divisor	factor	product	quotient

1.

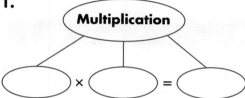

2.

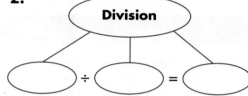

3. Make your own graphic organizer to show how the math terms are related.
terms *sum, addend,* and *addition* are related to each other.

· ·

Venn diagrams are another kind of graphic organizer that is very useful in math. Venn diagrams show how data belong to groups. If shapes overlap, the data belong in more than one group.

Use the Venn diagram below for **4** through **7**.

4. Which numbers in the Venn diagram are multiples of 2?

5. Which numbers in the Venn diagram are multiples of 3?

6. Which numbers in the Venn diagram are multiples of both 2 and 3? How can you tell?

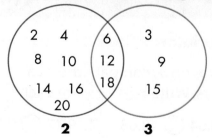

Multiples of 2 and 3 through 20

7. Number Sense Suppose you want to put the numbers 21, 22, and 24 in the Venn diagram. Where would you put each of the numbers?

MA.4.A.2.4 Compare and order decimals, and estimate fraction and decimal amounts in real-world problems.

Comparing Decimals

How can you compare decimals?

Scientists collected and measured the lengths of different cockroach species. Which cockroach had the greater length, the American or the Oriental cockroach?

Oriental
3.432 centimeters

American
3.576 centimeters

Australian
3.582 centimeters

Other Example

Use a number line to help you compare 0.159 and 0.152.

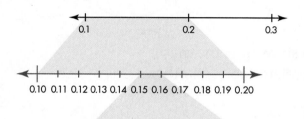

There are 10 equal parts between 0.1 and 0.2. Each part is 0.01.

There are 10 equal parts between 0.15 and 0.16. Each part is 0.001.

0.159 is to the right of 0.152. So, 0.159 > 0.152.

Guided Practice*

Do you know HOW?

In **1** through **5**, compare the two numbers. Write >, <, or = for each ◯.

1. 48.64 ◯ 48.68   **2.** 9.27 ◯ 9.2

3. 3.692 ◯ 3.697   **4.** 7.21 ◯ 7.203

5. Use the number line to help you compare 2.453 and 2.458.

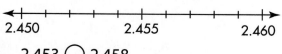

2.453 ◯ 2.458

Do you UNDERSTAND?

6. In Exercise 2, which place did you use to compare 9.27 and 9.2?

7. Write a number that is greater than 4.508 but less than 4.512.

8. Scientists measured a Madeira cockroach and found it to be 3.438 cm long. Which cockroach shown above is shorter in length than the Madeira cockroach?

Step 1	Step 2	Step 3

Step 1

Line up the decimal points.

Start at the left.

Compare digits of the same place value.

3.576
3.432

Step 2

Find the first place where the digits are different.

3.576
3.432

Step 3

Compare.

5 > 4

Think 0.5 > 0.4

So, 3.576 > 3.432.

The American cockroach is longer than the Oriental cockroach.

Independent Practice

In **9** through **20**, copy and complete. Write >, <, or = for each ◯.
Draw a number line to help you.

9. 0.890 ◯ 0.89

10. 5.733 ◯ 5.693

11. 9.70 ◯ 9.71

12. 4.953 ◯ 4.951

13. 1.403 ◯ 1.4

14. 3.074 ◯ 3.740

15. 0.7 ◯ 0.57

16. 0.23 ◯ 0.32

17. 6.562 ◯ 6.559

18. 1.1 ◯ 1.10

19. 3.406 ◯ 3.4

20. 6.57 ◯ 6.571

Problem Solving

21. Writing to Explain Why do you need to line up the decimal points before comparing numbers with decimals?

22. Judith earns $4 a week doing chores. If one flower costs $2, how many flowers can Judith buy if she saves for three weeks?

Critical THINKING

A grain of fine sand can have a width of 0.125 millimeter.

23. There are five types of grains of sand: coarse, very coarse, medium, fine, and very fine.

Which number is less than 0.125?

A   0.5

B   0.2

C   0.13

D   0.12

MA.4.A.2.4 Compare and order decimals, and estimate fraction and decimal amounts in real-world problems.

Ordering Decimals

How do you order decimals?

Patrick has a 1982 penny, a 2006 penny, and a dime in his pocket. Order the weights of the coins from least to greatest.

1982 penny
0.11 ounce

2006 penny
0.088 ounce

Dime
0.1 ounce

Other Example

Use a number line to order 4.826, 4.816, and 4.861 from least to greatest.

Plot the numbers on a number line.

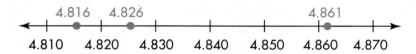

4.816   4.826   4.861

4.810   4.820   4.830   4.840   4.850   4.860   4.870

Order the numbers. Remember, on a number line, numbers to the right are greater.

From least to greatest: 4.816, 4.826, 4.861

Guided Practice*

Do you know HOW?

In **1** and **2**, order the numbers from least to greatest.

1. 0.65, 0.6, 0.71   **2.** 1.218, 1.01, 1.21

In **3** through **5**, order the numbers from greatest to least.

3. 5.541, 5.631, 5.625

4. 0.693, 1.35, 0.675

5. 3.7, 3.07, 3.707

Do you UNDERSTAND?

6. Order the weights of the coins from greatest to least.

7. Use the number line above. Order 4.84, 4.826, and 4.855 from least to greatest.

8. Kate said the numbers 3.04, 0.43, and 2.4 are in order from greatest to least. Is she correct? If not, what mistake did she make?

Critical THINKING

Step 1	Step 2	Step 3

Step 1

Use place value to order numbers.

Write the numbers, lining up the decimal points. Include any extra zeros to line up each place value. First compare the tenths.

0.110
0.088
0.100

0.088 is the least because it has a 0 in the tenths place.

Step 2

Write the remaining numbers. Compare the hundredths place.

0.110
0.100

1 > 0, so 0.110 is the greatest decimal.

Step 3

Write the numbers from least to greatest.

0.088, 0.100, 0.110

In order of the weights from least to greatest, the coins are the 2006 penny, the dime, and the 1982 penny.

Independent Practice

For **9** through **14**, order the numbers from least to greatest.

9. 1.2, 1.23, 1.1

10. 0.56, 4.56, 0.659

11. 0.218, 0.12, 0.215

12. 3.85, 0.851, 3.085

13. 0.71, 0.07, 1.7

14. 6.5, 6.525, 6.05

In **15** and **16**, copy and complete the number lines. Then use the number lines to order the numbers from greatest to least.

15. 2.911, 2.919, 2.914

2.910 ←———————————————————→ 2.920

16. 5.13, 5.132, 5.1

5.10 ←———————————————————→ 5.14

Problem Solving

17. Number Sense A bag of 500 nickels weighs 5.5 pounds. A bag of 200 half dollars weighs 5 pounds. Which bag weighs more?

18. Evan said the numbers 7.37, 7.36, 2.59, and 2.95 were in order from greatest to least. Is he correct?

THINK SOLVE EXPLAIN

19. Which number is NOT greater than 0.643?

A 6.43

B 4.63

C 0.436

D 0.663

20. Which numbers are NOT in order from least to greatest?

F 0.352, 0.7, 0.9

G 0.04, 0.091, 0.12

H 0.15, 0.19, 0.234

I 0.24, 0.09, 0.186

MA.4.A.2.4 Compare and order decimals, and estimate fraction and decimal amounts in real-world problems.

Draw a Picture

A hiking path is being planned for the local park. The planner started marking the drawing of the path with distances, but stopped. Where should the 1-mile mark be placed?

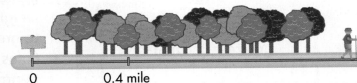

0   0.4 mile

Guided Practice*

Do you know HOW?

Solve.

1. Look at the hiking path below. Carla begins at the starting point and walks 0.8 mile. Where on the drawing would Carla end her walk?

   +---------+------------------
   0   0.4

Do you UNDERSTAND?

2. How are the numbers 0.4 and 0.8 related? How can this help you to find where 0.8 is located on the drawing?

3. **Write a Problem** Write a problem that uses the drawing below to solve.

   +------+--------------------
   0   0.3

Independent Practice

Solve.

4. Look at the drawing below. How can you use the mark on the line to find where 1.0 should be located?

   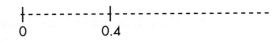

   +--+------------------------
   0 0.1

5. Copy the drawing from Problem 4. Find 1.0.

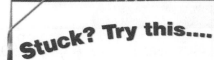

Stuck? Try this....

- What do I know?
- What diagram can I use to help understand the problem?
- Can I use addition, subtraction, multiplication, or division?
- Is all of my work correct?
- Did I answer the right question?
- Is my answer reasonable?

What do I know?	The hiking path must be 1 mile long. The marker for 0.4 mile is located on the drawing.
What am I asked to find?	Where the 1-mile mark should be located on the drawing

Plan

Double the distance from 0 to 0.4 to get 0.8.

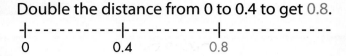

0.2 is halfway from 0 to 0.4

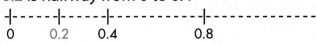

Move 0.2 to the right of 0.8 and get to 1.

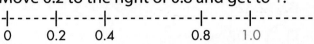

6. Allie needed to design a banner for field day. She wanted her banner to be 2 feet long. Allie marked 0.5 foot on her drawing. How can she use this distance to find 2 feet?

Allie's drawing |---|------------
                0   0.5

7. Dawn has 45 customers on her paper route. She delivers newspapers every day. How many newspapers does she deliver in five days?

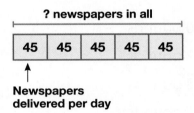

8. Writing to Explain Blake jogged 1.7 miles one morning. His sister jogged 1.75 miles that same day. Who jogged farther? Explain your answer.

THINK SOLVE EXPLAIN

9. What would be a good estimate for Point *G* on the drawing below?

|-----------+---------+--------|
0   0.4   G   1.0

A 0.3 **B** 0. 5 **C** 0.7 **D** 0.8

10. Shawn marked 0.8 foot on the board. How can Shawn use this distance to find 2 feet?

Critical THINKING

Shawn's drawing |------+----------
                0   0.8

11. Algebra John has twice as many brothers as Bob. If Bob has *b* brothers, how many brothers does John have?

12. Nick wrote a four-digit number. He used the digits 2, 4, 6, and 8. How many four-digit numbers could Nick have written?

13. Mary has 3 coin purses with 58 coins in each. How many coins does Mary have?

1 Which of the following is equal to two and forty-two thousandths? (12-2)

A. 2.420

B. 2.42

C. 2.402

D. 2.042

2 Mr. Molina is cooking 2.587 pounds of ground beef. To the nearest hundredth, how many pounds of ground beef is Mr. Molina cooking? (12-5)

F. 2.60 pounds

G. 2.59 pounds

H. 2.58 pounds

I. 2.57 pounds

3 Which decimal is shown in the model below? (12-1)

A. 1.26

B. 1.62

C. 2.61

D. 6.12

4 Which of the following has a 9 in the thousandths place? (12-2)

F. 9,265.794

G. 709.898

H. 165.91

I. 128.759

5 What is ten times as many as 0.01? (12-3)

A. 0.001

B. 0.01

C. 0.1

D. 1.0

6 Which number is best represented by Point *B* on the number line below? (12-4)

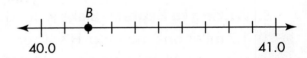

F. 40.5

G. 40.2

H. 40.0

I. 39.9

7 The numbers below are the scores Jake got in a diving competition. Which show the scores in order from least to greatest? (12-7)

A. 9.8, 9.78, 9.87

B. 9.87, 9.8, 9.78

C. 9.78, 9.87, 9.8

D. 9.78, 9.8, 9.87

8 Louise is creating a 1-foot long comic strip. She has marked 0.5 on a piece of paper. What should she do next to find 1 foot? (12-8)

   F. Find the distance halfway to 1.

   G. Move 5 to the right of 0.5.

   H. Double the distance from 0.5.

   I. Move 0.5 to the left of 0.5.

9 Which of the following is less than 5.004? (12-6)

   A. 5.001

   B. 5.100

   C. 5.010

   D. 5.040

10 Which of the following statements is true? Use the number line to help you. (12-6)

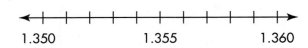

   F. 1.352 < 1.350

   G. 1.350 = 1.360

   H. 1.353 < 1.360

   I. 1.358 > 1.360

11 Which of the following is equal to 20 + 7 + 0.9 + 0.03? (12-1)

   A. 20.79

   B. 20.93

   C. 27.39

   D. 27.93

12 Which number is best represented by Point X on the number line below? (12-4)

   F. 5.96

   G. 5.97

   H. 5.98

   I. 5.99

13 What is the place value of the 8 in 2,351.784 (12-3)

   A. Ones

   B. Tenths

   C. Hundredths

   D. Thousands

14 Cynthia is mailing a package that weighs 12.395 pounds. To the nearest tenth, how many pounds does the package weigh? (12-5)

15 Describe how you could use place value to order the decimals below from least to greatest. (12-7)

THINK
SOLVE
EXPLAIN

   80.25   80.2   8.195

Set A, pages 232–233, 234–235

Write the decimal shown in expanded, standard, and word form.

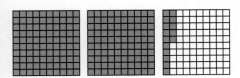

Expanded form: 2 + 0.1 + 0.05
Standard form: 2.15
Word form: Two and fifteen hundredths

Remember to use the word *and* for the decimal point when you write a decimal in word form.

Write the number in expanded form and word form.

1. 14.2   **2.** 3.902

3. 12.13   **4.** 88.05

5. 1.09   **6.** 6.582

Set B, pages 236–237

Decimal place values are related to whole-number place values.

tens	ones		tenths	hundredths	thousandths
10	1		$0.1 = \frac{1}{10}$	$0.01 = \frac{1}{100}$	$0.001 = \frac{1}{1,000}$
4	2	•	4	3	5

Each place value to the left is ten times as much as the place value to its right.

Remember, tenths, hundredths, and thousandths can be written as decimals or fractions.

Write the place value for the red digit.

1. 1,432.86   **2.** 6,940.048

3. 8,602.541   **4.** 3,582.053

Set C, pages 238–239

There are 10 tenths between 4.0 and 5.0. There are 10 hundredths between 4.70 and 4.80.

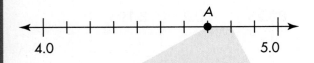

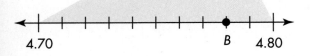

Point *A* is 4.7.
Point *B* is 4.78.

Remember, numbers increase as you move to the right on a number line.

Use the number lines below to name the decimal for each point.

1. C   **2.** B   **3.** A

4. D   **5.** F   **6.** E

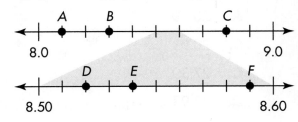

Set D, pages 240–242

Round 35.448 to the nearest hundredth.

Look at the hundredths place.　35.4<u>4</u>8

Look at the digit to the right.　35.44<u>8</u>

If the digit to the right is less than 5, round to 35.44. If the digit is 5 or greater, round to 35.45.

8 > 5

So, 35.448 rounds to 35.45.

Remember you round decimals the same way you round whole numbers.

Round each decimal to the place of the underlined digit.

1. <u>3</u>.78 　　　　**2.** 54.6<u>7</u>4

3. 50.<u>0</u>5 　　　　**4.** 82.1<u>6</u>8

5. <u>9</u>.763 　　　　**6.** 23.<u>9</u>7

Set E, pages 244–245, 246–247

Compare 1.359 and 1.265.

Write the numbers, lining up the decimal points. Then compare digits by place value.

1.359
1.265　　3 tenths > 2 tenths

So, 1.359 > 1.265.

Order these decimals from greatest to least: 0.198, 0.248, 0.235.

0.198　　0.1< 0.2, so this is the least decimal.
0.248　　0.04 > 0.03, so this is the greatest decimal.
0.235

From greatest to least the numbers are: 0.248, 0.235, 0.198.

Remember to line up the decimal points before comparing.

Write >, <, or = for each ◯. Compare.

1. 1.82 ◯ 1.91

2. 1.1 ◯ 1.10

3. 2.912 ◯ 2.902

4. 32.380 ◯ 32.38

Order from greatest to least.

5. 0.475, 0.52, 1.2

6. 6.25, 6.254, 6.399

Set F, pages 248–249

A biking trail is being planned for a town. Where should the 2-mile marker be placed?

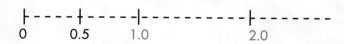

0　　0.5　　1.0　　　　2.0

Think: 1.0 is double 0.5, and 1.0 is half of 2.0.

Double the distance and mark 1.0.
Now double this distance and mark 2.0.

Remember that drawing a picture can help you solve a problem.

Draw a picture to solve the problem.

1. Look at the walking path below. Bill begins at the starting point and walks 0.6 mile. Where on the path would Bill end his walk?

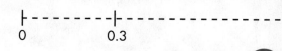

0　　　　0.3

Fractions

1 Asia is the largest continent, covering about $\frac{3}{10}$ of Earth's total land area. About what fraction of the people on Earth live in Asia? You will find out in Lesson 13-1.

2 Pandas eat up to 60 pounds of food a day. For what fraction of their time awake are pandas eating? You will find out in Lesson 13-6.

Vocabulary

Choose the best term from the box.

- fraction
- denominator
- thirds
- numerator

1. Three equal parts of a shape are called ? .

2. A ? can name a part of a whole.

3. The number below the fraction bar in a fraction is the ? .

3 The world's largest pumpkin pie was made in 2005. How much did the pie weigh? You will find out in Lesson 13-4.

4 In the world, 1,500 volcanoes could possibly be active. About how many of these erupt every year? You will find out in Lesson 13-2.

Division Facts

Divide.

4. $45 \div 5$ **5.** $6 \div 3$ **6.** $36 \div 4$

7. $25 \div 5$ **8.** $27 \div 3$ **9.** $49 \div 7$

10. $24 \div 8$ **11.** $16 \div 2$ **12.** $28 \div 4$

13. $36 \div 6$ **14.** $12 \div 3$ **15.** $72 \div 9$

Fraction Concepts

Name the number of equal parts in each figure.

16.   **17.**   **18.**

19.   **20.**   **21.**

22. Writing to Explain Is $\frac{1}{4}$ of the figure below red? Why or why not?

Topic Essential Question

- How can the same fractional amount be named using symbols in different ways?

MA.4.A.2.4 Compare and order decimals, and estimate fraction and decimal amounts in real-world problems.

Estimating Fractional Amounts

How can you estimate parts?

Emma helped her mom begin to paint a mural downtown. About what fraction of the wall has been painted?

Emma's mural

Guided Practice*

Do you know HOW?

For **1** and **2**, estimate the fractional part that is orange.

1.

2.

Do you UNDERSTAND?

3. **Writing to Explain** How can you estimate whether a part of a region is about $\frac{1}{2}$ of the whole?

4. About what fraction of the wall is NOT painted at all?

Independent Practice

In **5** through **7**, estimate the fractional part of each that is green.

 Tip *The numerator tells how many equal parts are shaded. The denominator tells how many equal parts in all.*

5.

6.

7.

In **8** through **10**, estimate the fractional part of each that is flowers.

8.

9.

10.

For another example, see Set A on page 274.

Step 1

Think about benchmark fractions. A **benchmark fraction** is a simple fraction that is easy to visualize, such as $\frac{1}{4}$, $\frac{1}{3}$, $\frac{1}{2}$, $\frac{2}{3}$, and $\frac{3}{4}$.

You can use benchmark fractions to estimate fractional parts.

Step 2

Compare the benchmark fractions to the part of the wall that has been painted.

The painted part is more than $\frac{1}{4}$, but less than $\frac{1}{2}$. About $\frac{1}{3}$ of the wall is painted.

Problem Solving

11. Asia has more people than any other continent. About what fraction of the people on Earth live in Asia?

Populations of 6 Continents

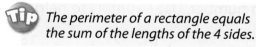

12. At the bowling alley, there are 32 bowling balls. Of these, 8 are blue, 5 are pink, 6 are red, and the rest are black. How many of the bowling balls are black?

13. THINK SOLVE EXPLAIN If less than half of a garden is planted with corn, is it reasonable to estimate that $\frac{2}{3}$ of the garden is planted with corn? Explain.

14. Number Sense Compare the bars in the graph below. Decide which farmer has about $\frac{1}{3}$ as many cows as Mr. Harris.

Critical THINKING

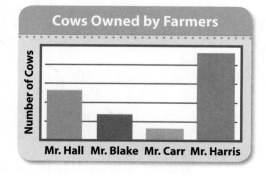

15. Geometry What is the perimeter of the figure shown below?

Tip *The perimeter of a rectangle equals the sum of the lengths of the 4 sides.*

A   6 units

B   8 units

C   12 units

D   16 units

MA.4.A.6.4 Determine factors
and multiples for specified
whole numbers.

Factors

counters

Hands-On

How can you use multiplication to find all the factors of a number?

Jean has 16 action figures. She wants to arrange them in equal sized groupings around her room. What are the ways that Jean can arrange the action figures? Jean needs to think of all the factors of 16.

16 action
figures

Guided Practice*

Do you know HOW?

In **1** through **4**, write each number as a product of two factors in two ways.

1. 36   **2.** 42

3. 10   **4.** 64

In **5** through **8**, find all the factors of each number. Use counters to help.

5. 12   **6.** 20

7. 28   **8.** 8

Do you UNDERSTAND?

9. What factor besides 1 does every even number have?

10. Writing to Explain Is 5 a factor of 16?

11. Jean got 2 more action figures. What are all the different equal groupings she can make now?

12. Jean's brother has 29 action figures. What are all of the factors for 29?

Independent Practice

In **13** through **32**, find all the factors of each number. Use counters to help.

Tip *For each number, find each way you can arrange counters into arrays.*

13. 6   **14.** 32   **15.** 17   **16.** 11   **17.** 9

18. 25   **19.** 13   **20.** 22   **21.** 15   **22.** 30

23. 14   **24.** 18   **25.** 27   **26.** 21   **27.** 40

28. 4   **29.** 10   **30.** 35   **31.** 7   **32.** 19

DIGITAL

eTools
www.pearsonsuccessnet.com

16 = 1 × 16

Jean can arrange
16 figures in 1 group
or
16 groups of 1 figure.

So, 1 and 16 are
factors of 16.

16 = 2 × 8

Jean can arrange
2 figures in 8 groups
or
2 groups of 8 figures.

So, 2 and 8 are
factors of 16.

16 = 4 × 4

Jean can arrange
4 figures in 4 groups.

4 is a factor of 16.

The factors of 16 are
1, 2, 4, 8, and 16.

Problem Solving

33. As part of her science project, Shay is making a model of a wind farm. She wants to put 24 turbines in her model. What are all the ways she can make arrays using 24 turbines?

4 is a factor of 24.

34. Anita wants to include an array of 15 photos on her web site. Describe the arrays that she can make.

THINK
SOLVE
EXPLAIN

35. Which lists all the factors of 38?

A 1, 38 **C** 1, 2, 38

B 1, 2, 14, 38 **D** 1, 2, 19, 38

36. Number Sense Any number that has 9 as a factor also has 3 as a factor. Why is this?

Critical
THINKING

37. What factors do 12 and 16 have in common?

38. About 50 of the 1,500 possibly active volcanoes on Earth erupt every year. What are the factors of 50?

39. On a large wind farm, there are 6 rows of 15 wind turbines each and 4 rows of 11 wind turbines each. How many wind turbines are there on the wind farm in all?

40. The largest volcano on Earth is Mauna Loa, located in Hawaii. It is 30,080 feet tall from the sea floor to its highest point. If 13,680 feet of the volcano is above sea level, how many feet are below sea level?

41. A manatee is 12 feet long. If 1 foot equals 12 inches, how many inches long is the manatee?

F 12 inches **H** 120 inches

G 24 inches **I** 144 inches

Lesson
13-3

MA.4.A.6.4 Determine factors and multiples for specified whole numbers.

Multiples

How can you find multiples of a number?

It takes 8 minutes for Car A to make one full turn on the Ferris wheel. If the Ferris wheel continues to turn at the same speed for the next hour, at what times during the hour will Car A return to the starting point?

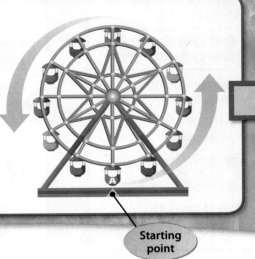

Starting point

Guided Practice*

Do you know HOW?

In **1** through **4**, write five multiples of each number.

1. 2

2. 9

3. 3

4. 10

In **5** through **8**, tell whether the first number is a multiple of the second number.

5. 14, 2

6. 19, 3

7. 56, 9

8. 42, 7

Do you UNDERSTAND?

9. If the Ferris wheel in the example above continues to turn at the same speed, will Car A return to the starting point after 75 minutes? Explain.

10. Suppose the Ferris wheel speeds up so it makes one full turn in 6 minutes. When will Car A return to the starting point if the Ferris wheel continues to turn for one half hour?

11. Writing to Explain Is 9 a multiple of 3 or a factor of 3? Explain.

Independent Practice

In **12** through **15**, write five multiples of each number.

12. 7

13. 4

14. 6

15. 5

In **16** through **23**, tell whether the first number is a multiple of the second number.

16. 44, 6

17. 27, 3

18. 30, 6

19. 54, 9

20. 28, 3

21. 45, 5

22. 64, 7

23. 48, 8

For another example, see Set B on page 274.

Step 1	Step 2	Step 3

Step 1

You can use multiples of 8 to find when Car A reaches the starting point.

One full turn takes 8 minutes.

$$1 \times 8 = 8$$

Car A is back at the starting point after 8 minutes.

Step 2

Car A is at the starting point after another 8 minutes.

Second full turn:

$$2 \times 8 = 16$$

Two full turns take 16 minutes.

Car A is back to the starting point after 16 minutes.

Step 3

Car A is at the starting point every 8 minutes after that:

$$3 \times 8 = 24$$
$$4 \times 8 = 32$$
$$5 \times 8 = 40$$
$$6 \times 8 = 48$$
$$7 \times 8 = 56$$

During the hour, Car A returns to the starting point after 8, 16, 24, 32, 40, 48, and 56 minutes.

Problem Solving

For **24** and **25**, use the table at the right.

24. Which activities are scheduled to last more than 1 hour and 30 minutes?

25. Paulo's family arrived at the reunion at 8:30 A.M. How long do they have before the trip to Scenic Lake Park?

Data

Suarez Family Reunion Schedule	
Trip to Scenic Lake Park	10:15 A.M. to 2:30 P.M.
Slide show	4:15 P.M. to 5:10 P.M.
Dinner	5:30 P.M. to 7:00 P.M.
Campfire	7:55 P.M. to 9:30 P.M.

26. Which is NOT a multiple of 7?

   A 20   **C** 35

   B 21   **D** 42

27. Jason's family went apple picking. They picked 5 bags of red apples and 1 bag of green apples. Write a fraction to represent the part of the bags containing green apples.

28. Lisa made a Venn diagram showing five multiples of 3 and five multiples of 4. What does the shaded section in her diagram show?

Lisa's Venn Diagram

Multiples of 3 | Multiples of 4

3   6   12   4   8

9   15   16   20

29. Number Sense Name at least one number that is a multiple of 2 and a multiple of 5.

Critical THINKING

30. Lindsay says that all numbers that are multiples of 4 have a factor of 2. Is Lindsay correct? Explain.

THINK SOLVE EXPLAIN

MA.4.A.6.3 Generate
equivalent fractions
and simplify fractions.
Also MA.4.A.6.4

Equivalent Fractions

Hands-On
fraction strips $\frac{1}{8}$

How can you find two fractions that name the same part of a whole?

Lee ate $\frac{1}{4}$ of a pizza. Write another fraction that is equivalent to $\frac{1}{4}$.

Equivalent fractions name the same part of a whole.

Lee ate $\frac{1}{4}$ of a pizza.

Another Example ## How can you divide to find an equivalent fraction?

Sara ate $\frac{6}{8}$ of a small mushroom pizza. Which fraction is equivalent to $\frac{6}{8}$?

Divide the numerator and denominator by the same number to find an equivalent fraction.

$$\frac{6}{8} = \frac{3}{4}$$ ÷ 2   So, $\frac{3}{4}$ is equivalent to $\frac{6}{8}$.
÷ 2

Check your answer using fractions strips.

Find $\frac{6}{8}$ by counting 6 of the $\frac{1}{8}$ strips.

Find $\frac{3}{4}$ by counting 3 of the $\frac{1}{4}$ strips.

Both $\frac{6}{8}$ and $\frac{3}{4}$ name the same part of a whole.

1											
$\frac{1}{2}$						$\frac{1}{2}$					
$\frac{1}{3}$				$\frac{1}{3}$				$\frac{1}{3}$			
$\frac{1}{4}$			$\frac{1}{4}$			$\frac{1}{4}$			$\frac{1}{4}$		
$\frac{1}{5}$		$\frac{1}{5}$		$\frac{1}{5}$		$\frac{1}{5}$		$\frac{1}{5}$			
$\frac{1}{6}$	$\frac{1}{6}$	$\frac{1}{6}$	$\frac{1}{6}$	$\frac{1}{6}$	$\frac{1}{6}$						
$\frac{1}{8}$	$\frac{1}{8}$	$\frac{1}{8}$	$\frac{1}{8}$	$\frac{1}{8}$	$\frac{1}{8}$	$\frac{1}{8}$	$\frac{1}{8}$				
$\frac{1}{10}$	$\frac{1}{10}$	$\frac{1}{10}$	$\frac{1}{10}$	$\frac{1}{10}$	$\frac{1}{10}$	$\frac{1}{10}$	$\frac{1}{10}$	$\frac{1}{10}$	$\frac{1}{10}$		
$\frac{1}{12}$	$\frac{1}{12}$	$\frac{1}{12}$	$\frac{1}{12}$	$\frac{1}{12}$	$\frac{1}{12}$	$\frac{1}{12}$	$\frac{1}{12}$	$\frac{1}{12}$	$\frac{1}{12}$	$\frac{1}{12}$	$\frac{1}{12}$

Explain It

1. Can you divide 6 and 8 by any number to find an equivalent fraction? Explain.

2. Using fraction strips, find two fractions that are equivalent to $\frac{9}{12}$.

One Way

You can multiply the numerator and the denominator by the same number to find an equivalent fraction.

$$\overset{\times\,2}{\frac{1}{4} = \frac{2}{8}}$$
$$\underset{\times\,2}{}$$

$$\frac{1}{4} = \frac{2}{8}$$

Another Way

Use fraction strips to find equivalent fractions.

Both $\frac{1}{4}$ and $\frac{2}{8}$ name the same part of a whole.

So, $\frac{1}{4}$ and $\frac{2}{8}$ are equivalent fractions.

Guided Practice*

Do you know HOW?

In **1** through **6**, multiply or divide to find an equivalent fraction.

1.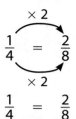
$$\overset{\times\,3}{\frac{2}{3} = \frac{\blacksquare}{\blacksquare}}$$
$$\underset{\times\,3}{}$$

2.
$$\overset{\div\,5}{\frac{10}{15} = \frac{\blacksquare}{\blacksquare}}$$
$$\underset{\div\,5}{}$$

3. $\dfrac{1}{4} = \dfrac{\blacksquare}{16}$

4. $\dfrac{10}{12} = \dfrac{5}{\blacksquare}$

5. $\dfrac{15}{20} = \dfrac{\blacksquare}{4}$

6. $\dfrac{3}{8} = \dfrac{9}{\blacksquare}$

Do you UNDERSTAND?

7. Suppose Lee's pizza had 12 equal slices instead of 4. How many slices are gone if he ate $\frac{1}{4}$ of the pizza? Explain.

8. **Reasoning** Josh, Lisa, and Vicki each ate $\frac{1}{2}$ of a pizza. The pizzas were the same size, but Josh ate 1 slice, Lisa ate 3 slices, and Vicki ate 4 slices. How is this possible?

Independent Practice

Leveled Practice For **9** through **16**, multiply or divide to find equivalent fractions.

 You can check your answers using fraction strips.

9.
$$\overset{\times\,5}{\frac{4}{9} = \frac{\blacksquare}{\blacksquare}}$$
$$\underset{\times\,5}{}$$

10.
$$\overset{\div\,3}{\frac{9}{15} = \frac{\blacksquare}{\blacksquare}}$$
$$\underset{\div\,3}{}$$

11.
$$\overset{\times\,2}{\frac{5}{7} = \frac{\blacksquare}{\blacksquare}}$$
$$\underset{\times\,2}{}$$

12.
$$\overset{\div\,2}{\frac{2}{4} = \frac{\blacksquare}{\blacksquare}}$$
$$\underset{\div\,2}{}$$

13. $\dfrac{10}{10} = \dfrac{1}{\blacksquare}$

14. $\dfrac{3}{4} = \dfrac{12}{\blacksquare}$

15. $\dfrac{10}{20} = \dfrac{\blacksquare}{4}$

16. $\dfrac{30}{40} = \dfrac{6}{\blacksquare}$

In **17** through **26**, find an equivalent fraction for each.

17. $\frac{8}{18}$ **18.** $\frac{2}{10}$ **19.** $\frac{1}{3}$ **20.** $\frac{3}{5}$ **21.** $\frac{24}{30}$

22. $\frac{25}{30}$ **23.** $\frac{2}{15}$ **24.** $\frac{21}{28}$ **25.** $\frac{12}{15}$ **26.** $\frac{12}{20}$

Problem Solving

For **27** and **28**, use the fraction strips at the right.

27. Name 10 pairs of equivalent fractions.

28. Reasoning How can you show
 that $\frac{6}{8}$ and $\frac{9}{12}$ are equivalent by multiplying and dividing?

> **Tip** *First, divide the numerator and denominator of $\frac{9}{12}$ by 3. Then multiply.*

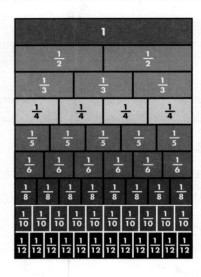

29. The world's largest pumpkin pie weighed 2,020 pounds. The pie was $12\frac{1}{3}$ feet across and $\frac{1}{3}$ foot thick. Write a fraction equivalent to $\frac{1}{3}$.

30. In a school poetry contest, 15 out of the 25 students who entered will win a small prize. Half of the remaining students receive a certificate. How many students get a certificate?

31. Algebra James has 18 mystery books and 12 sports books. Rich has twice as many mystery books and three times as many sports books. How many books does Rich have?

32. Writing to Explain In the United States, $\frac{2}{5}$ of all states start with the letters M, A, or N. How can you use equivalent fractions to find out how many states this is?

33. Look at the model. Name three equivalent fractions for the part of the circle that is red.

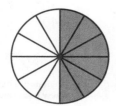

34. Which shows $\frac{1}{2}$ and $\frac{1}{5}$ as fractions with the same denominator?

A $\frac{5}{10}$ and $\frac{2}{10}$

B $\frac{1}{10}$ and $\frac{5}{10}$

C $\frac{5}{10}$ and $\frac{1}{10}$

D $\frac{5}{10}$ and $\frac{3}{10}$

Going Digital

Equivalent Fractions

Use 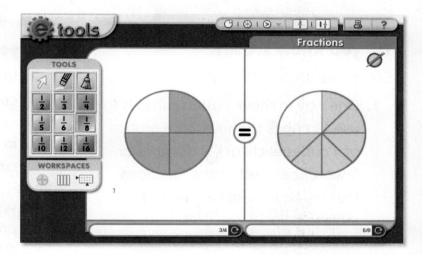 **e tools** Fractions.

Find the numerator that makes the fractions equivalent. $\frac{3}{4} = \frac{\Box}{8}$

Step 1 Go to the Fractions eTool. Select the equivalence workspace mode.

$\bigodot$ Select $\frac{1}{4}$ three times, to show $\frac{3}{4}$ in the first circle.

Step 2 Select the second circle by clicking on it. Select $\frac{1}{8}$ until the symbol changes from > to =. Read the fractions at the bottom of the workspace. $\frac{3}{4} = \frac{6}{8}$

Step 3 Use the Broom tool to clear the workspace before doing another problem.

Practice

Use the Fractions eTool to find the numerator that makes the fractions equivalent.

1. $\frac{1}{4} = \frac{\Box}{8}$

2. $\frac{2}{5} = \frac{\Box}{10}$

3. $\frac{4}{6} = \frac{\Box}{3}$

4. $\frac{6}{16} = \frac{\Box}{8}$

5. $\frac{1}{2} = \frac{\Box}{16}$

6. $\frac{1}{3} = \frac{\Box}{12}$

7. $\frac{8}{10} = \frac{\Box}{5}$

8. $\frac{3}{12} = \frac{\Box}{4}$

9. $\frac{3}{4} = \frac{\Box}{12}$

10. $\frac{5}{8} = \frac{\Box}{16}$

11. $\frac{3}{4} = \frac{\Box}{16}$

12. $\frac{4}{8} = \frac{\Box}{2}$

13. $\frac{1}{2} = \frac{\Box}{12}$

14. $\frac{1}{2} = \frac{\Box}{10}$

15. $\frac{5}{6} = \frac{\Box}{12}$

16. $\frac{4}{5} = \frac{\Box}{15}$

Lesson
13-5

MA.4.A.6.3 Generate
equivalent fractions and
simplify fractions.

Problem Solving

Use Objects and Make a Table

Hands-On
Cubes

Al has 12 containers of sand. One way to show $\frac{1}{2}$ is two groups of 6.

Using 12 or fewer cubes, how many other fractions can Al find that are equivalent to $\frac{1}{2}$?

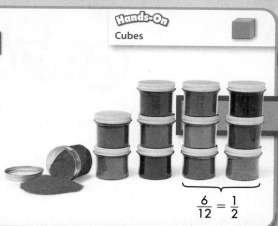

$$\frac{6}{12} = \frac{1}{2}$$

Guided Practice*

Do you know HOW?

Solve. Use objects to help.

1. One way to show $\frac{1}{3}$ using cubes is to use 12 cubes to show three groups of 4 cubes each, or $\frac{4}{12}$. Using 12 or fewer cubes, find 2 other fractions that are equivalent to $\frac{1}{3}$. Make a table to help.

Do you UNDERSTAND?

2. In the example above, how many cubes are in each group to show $\frac{3}{6}$?

3. In the example above, how many cubes are in each group to show $\frac{2}{4}$?

4. **Write a Problem** Write a word problem that uses the table you created in Problem 1 as an answer.

Independent Practice

Solve. Use objects and make a table or list to help.

5. Marianne has 12 cubes. She uses all 12 cubes and separates them into 4 groups. Then she uses 8 cubes and separates them into 4 groups. What fraction is Marianne trying to make?

6. Using 12 or fewer cubes, how many fractions can you find that are equivalent to $\frac{1}{5}$?

7. At a car wash, Jim washed 8 cars per hour, and David washed 6 cars per hour. How many cars did Jim wash if David washed 24 cars?

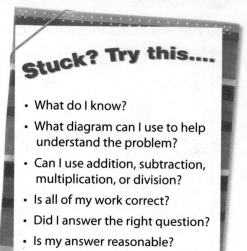

Stuck? Try this....

- What do I know?
- What diagram can I use to help understand the problem?
- Can I use addition, subtraction, multiplication, or division?
- Is all of my work correct?
- Did I answer the right question?
- Is my answer reasonable?

For another example, see Set D on page 275.

Al can use cubes to solve this problem.

Using two groups of 7 gives $\frac{7}{14} = \frac{1}{2}$.

This uses more than 12 cubes.

Using two groups of 5 gives $\frac{5}{10} = \frac{1}{2}$.

This works. Al only used 10 cubes.

Make a table to show the other fractions equivalent to $\frac{1}{2}$.

First group	Second group	Fraction equivalent to $\frac{1}{2}$
4	4	$\frac{4}{8}$
3	3	$\frac{3}{6}$
2	2	$\frac{2}{4}$

Count all of the different ways to make $\frac{1}{2}$.

There are 4 other fractions that are equivalent to $\frac{1}{2}$ using 12 cubes or less.

8. Charlie had 12 cubes. He showed $\frac{8}{12}$ is equivalent to $\frac{2}{3}$ by making three groups of 4 and drawing a circle around two of the groups. Using 12 or fewer cubes, what is another fraction that is equivalent to $\frac{2}{3}$?

9. At Tara's Video Outlet, you can buy any 6 used DVDs for 48 dollars. At Sam's DVD Palace, you can buy any 4 used DVDs for 28 dollars. In which store do DVDs cost less? How much less?

Critical THINKING

10. Tyrone runs 4 miles each week. Francis runs 4 times as many miles each week. How many miles does Francis run each week?

? Miles each week

| Francis | 4 | 4 | 4 | 4 | 4 times as many |
| Tyrone | 4 |

11. **Writing to Explain** If you know a person runs a certain number of miles every week, then how would you find out how many miles that person runs in one year?

Tip Remember 1 year is 52 weeks.

12. Jane has 24 pennies. She separated the pennies equally into 4 cups with 6 pennies in each cup. Copy and complete the table at the right to show some ways Jane can separate the pennies into equal groups.

Number of cups	Number of pennies in each cup	Total number of pennies
4	▢	24
▢	12	24
3	▢	24

13. A store sells school-supply packs that contain 6 pencils and 4 pens. A customer bought enough packs to get 36 pencils. How many pens did the customer get?

eTools
www.pearsonsuccessnet.com

DIGITAL

MA.4.A.6.3 Generate equivalent fractions and simplify fractions.

Fractions in Simplest Form

How do you write a fraction in simplest form?

Jason ran $\frac{4}{12}$ of the way around the track. Write $\frac{4}{12}$ in simplest form.

Since 4 is a factor of 12, it is a common factor of 4 and 12.

A fraction is in simplest form when the numerator and denominator have no common factor other than 1.

$\frac{4}{12}$ of the way around the track

Guided Practice*

Do you know HOW?

For **1** through **6**, write each fraction in simplest form.

1. $\frac{6}{8}$ 2. $\frac{15}{27}$

3. $\frac{10}{20}$ 4. $\frac{16}{18}$

5. $\frac{21}{24}$ 6. $\frac{12}{14}$

Do you UNDERSTAND?

7. **Writing to Explain** Explain how you can tell $\frac{4}{9}$ is in simplest form.

8. Jamal ran $\frac{8}{12}$ of the way around a track. Write this fraction in simplest form.

 If the numerator and denominator are even numbers, they have 2 as a common factor.

Independent Practice

In **9** through **33**, write each fraction in simplest form.
If it is in simplest form, write "simplest form."

9. $\frac{3}{12}$ 10. $\frac{2}{10}$ 11. $\frac{4}{8}$ 12. $\frac{12}{16}$ 13. $\frac{4}{6}$

14. $\frac{2}{5}$ 15. $\frac{2}{6}$ 16. $\frac{3}{16}$ 17. $\frac{8}{10}$ 18. $\frac{5}{12}$

19. $\frac{3}{7}$ 20. $\frac{8}{20}$ 21. $\frac{9}{10}$ 22. $\frac{9}{15}$ 23. $\frac{12}{20}$

24. $\frac{5}{6}$ 25. $\frac{3}{9}$ 26. $\frac{15}{18}$ 27. $\frac{3}{4}$ 28. $\frac{30}{35}$

29. $\frac{2}{3}$ 30. $\frac{7}{14}$ 31. $\frac{9}{16}$ 32. $\frac{4}{12}$ 33. $\frac{5}{15}$

Animated Glossary
www.pearsonsuccessnet.com

For another example, see Set E on page 275.

Write $\frac{4}{12}$ in simplest form by dividing twice.

$$\frac{4}{12} \overset{\div 2}{\underset{\div 2}{=}} \frac{2}{6}$$

4 and 12 are both even. Two is a common factor.

$$\frac{2}{6} \overset{\div 2}{\underset{\div 2}{=}} \frac{1}{3}$$

2 and 6 are both even. Two is a common factor.

Write $\frac{4}{12}$ in simplest form by dividing by 4.

$$\frac{4}{12} \overset{\div 4}{\underset{\div 4}{=}} \frac{1}{3}$$

In simplest form, $\frac{4}{12} = \frac{1}{3}$.

Problem Solving

34. Reasoning If the numerator and the denominator of a fraction are both odd numbers and not equal to each other, can the fraction be simplified?

35. Estimation About what fraction of this model is red?

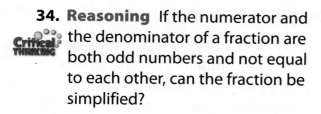

Use the table at the right for **36** and **37**.

36. What fraction of the band members practice for more than 2 hours a week? Write your answer in simplest form.

37. What fraction of the band members spend more time on lessons than on practice? Write your answer in simplest form.

Weekly Band Log		
Band Member	**Lessons (Hours)**	**Practice (Hours)**
Will	1.5	1
Kaitlyn	1	3.5
Madison	0.75	1.75
Ryan	1.5	1.25
Kirk	1.25	4
Gina	1	0.75

38. Science Each day, pandas are awake for about 12 hours. They eat for about 10 hours. What fraction of their time awake are pandas eating? Write your answer in simplest form.

Eats about 10 hours a day, and is awake about 12 hours a day

39. What fraction of the day are pandas awake?

A $\frac{1}{12}$

B $\frac{1}{4}$

C $\frac{2}{4}$

D $\frac{1}{2}$

Lesson 13-6   **269**

MA.4.A.6.4 Determine factors and multiples for specified whole numbers.

Problem Solving

Make and Test Generalizations

A **generalization** is a <u>general statement that you think is true.</u>

You use observations to make a generalization.

You can test your generalization to see if it appears to be true.

Make a generalization about multiples of 5.

Guided Practice*

Do you know HOW?

1. Write the factors for 8, 16, and 20. What generalization can you make about all multiples of 4?

2. Write the factors for 9. What generalization can you make about all factors of 9?

Do you UNDERSTAND?

3. **Writing to Explain** Is the generalization that all the factors of 15 are odd numbers correct? Explain why or why not.

4. **Write a Problem** Write a generalization about factors or multiples that you can test to see if it appears to be true.

Independent Practice

Solve.

5. Look at each number sentence below. Compare the size of the factor to each product. What generalization can you make about factors and products of whole numbers greater than 0?

   $8 \times 7 = 56$ $5 \times 46 = 230$ $1 \times 873 = 873$

6. **Geometry** Steve said that all squares are parallelograms. Is Steve's generalization correct? Explain.

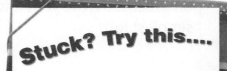

Stuck? Try this....

- What do I know?
- What am I asked to find?
- What diagram can I use to understand the problem?
- Can I use addition, subtraction, multiplication, or division?
- Is all of my work correct?
- Did I answer the right question?
- Is my answer reasonable?

Plan

Make a generalization:

The multiples of 5 have either a 0 or a 5 in the ones place.

Solve

Test your generalization for several cases:

$5 \times 1 = 5$
$5 \times 2 = 10$
$5 \times 3 = 15$
$5 \times 4 = 20$
$5 \times 5 = 25$
$5 \times 6 = 30$
$5 \times 7 = 35$

Each of the multiples tested has a 0 or a 5 in the ones place.

Based on these results, the generalization appears to be true.

7. Look at the pattern below. Draw the shape that would come next.

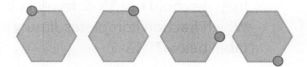

8. Look at each group of three letters below. Make a generalization for each group of letters that does not apply to the other group of three letters.

E F T	C O S

9. Write five multiples of 10. What generalization can you make about all multiples of 10?

THINK
SOLVE
EXPLAIN

10. Lisa's puppy weighs 5 pounds more than Coby's puppy. Together, the puppies weigh 21 pounds. How much does each puppy weigh?

11. What generalization can you make about all multiples of 2?

A They are all odd numbers.

B They are all multiples of 4.

C They are all factors of 10.

D They are all even numbers.

12. Michael lives on the twenty-second floor of a 25-story building. If each floor is 12 feet in height, how many feet above ground level is the floor of Michael's apartment?

13. **Reasoning** The factors for 3 and 6 are shown

Critical THINKING

in the table at the right. James concluded that if you double a number, then you double the number of factors. Is James's generalization correct? Why or why not?

Number	3	6
Factors	1, 3	1, 2, 3, 6

1 Jase completed 8 of 10 laps needed to pass his swimming test. What fraction, in simplest form, of the laps did he complete? (13-6)

   A. $\frac{8}{10}$

   B. $\frac{4}{5}$

   C. $\frac{3}{4}$

   D. $\frac{2}{3}$

2 What number should go in the box to make the fractions equivalent? (13-4)

$$\frac{3}{5} = \frac{9}{\boxed{}}$$

   F. 10

   G. 11

   H. 15

   I. 20

3 Elmer is painting one wall in his room. About what fraction of the wall has he painted blue? (13-1)

   A. About $\frac{3}{4}$

   B. About $\frac{2}{3}$

   C. About $\frac{1}{2}$

   D. About $\frac{1}{4}$

4 Tabitha's teacher asked her to write all the factors of 18. Which list shows all the factors of 18? (13-2)

   F. 1, 2, 3, 6, 9, 10, 12, 18

   G. 1, 2, 9, 18

   H. 2, 3, 6, 9

   I. 1, 2, 3, 6, 9, 18

5 Jimmy used cubes and made a table to model fractions equivalent to $\frac{1}{3}$. He could use 15 or fewer cubes. Which fraction completes Jimmy's table below? (13-5)

Data	Cubes in Group 1	Cubes in Group 2	Cubes in Group 3	Fraction Equivalent to $\frac{1}{3}$
	2	2	2	$\frac{2}{6}$
	3	3	3	$\frac{3}{9}$
	4	4	4	$\frac{4}{12}$
	5	5	5	

   A. $\frac{10}{15}$

   B. $\frac{3}{5}$

   C. $\frac{5}{10}$

   D. $\frac{5}{15}$

6 Which list shows only multiples of 6? (13-3)

   F. 6, 12, 18, 24

   G. 6, 16, 26, 36

   H. 1, 2, 3, 6

   I. 6, 16, 60, 66

7 Which statement is a correct generalization about all multiples of 8? (13-7)

   A. All multiples of 8 are odd numbers.

   B. All multiples of 8 have 6 as a factor.

   C. All multiples of 8 have 4 as a factor.

   D. All multiples of 8 have a 4 or 6 in the ones place.

8 About how much of this circle is shaded? (13-1)

   F. About $\frac{1}{8}$

   G. About $\frac{1}{3}$

   H. About $\frac{1}{2}$

   I. About $\frac{3}{4}$

9 Which of the following helps you find the simplest form of $\frac{6}{8}$? (13-6)

   A. Subtract 6 from 8.

   B. Multiply 6 and 8.

   C. Compare fraction strips for fourths and eighths.

   D. Compare fraction strips for eighths and twelfths.

10 What generalization is true about all multiples of 9? (13-7)

   F. They are all odd numbers.

   G. They are all even numbers.

   H. They are all factors of 3.

   I. They are all multiples of 3.

11 What is the missing number that makes the fractions equivalent? (13-4)

$$\frac{2}{7} = \frac{6}{\boxed{}}$$

12 THINK SOLVE EXPLAIN

Explain the difference between a factor and a multiple using the number 6 as an example. (13-2, 13-3)

Set A, pages 256–257

Estimate the fractional part of the rectangle that is blue.

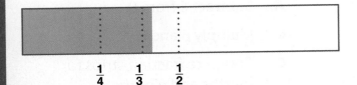

$$\frac{1}{4} \qquad \frac{1}{3} \qquad \frac{1}{2}$$

Compare the part that is blue. The blue part is more than $\frac{1}{3}$ but less than $\frac{1}{2}$ of the whole rectangle. About $\frac{1}{3}$ of the rectangle is blue.

Remember the benchmark fractions are basic fractions such as $\frac{1}{4}, \frac{1}{3}, \frac{1}{2}, \frac{2}{3}$, and $\frac{3}{4}$.

Estimate the fractional part of each that is green.

1. 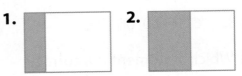 **2.**

Set B, pages 258–261

Find the factors of 8. Use multiplication.

$$1 \times 8 = 8 \qquad 2 \times 4 = 8$$

So the factors are 1, 2, 4, and 8.

Find three multiples of 8.

$$8 \times 1 = 8 \qquad 8 \times 2 = 16 \qquad 8 \times 3 = 24$$

Three multiples of 8 are 8, 16, and 24.

Remember you can use counters to help you find factors of a number.

Find all the factors of each number.

1. 18   **2.** 15

3. 9   **4.** 19

Find five multiples of each number.

5. 3   **6.** 7

7. 4   **8.** 9

Set C, pages 262–264

Find an equivalent fraction for $\frac{2}{6}$ using multiplication.

Multiply the numerator and the denominator by the same number to find an equivalent fraction.

$$\overset{\times 2}{\underset{\times 2}{\frac{2}{6} = \frac{4}{12}}}$$

So, $\frac{2}{6}$ is equivalent to $\frac{4}{12}$.

Remember to find an equivalent fraction you must multiply or divide the numerator and denominator by the same number.

Multiply or divide to find an equivalent fraction.

1. $\frac{8}{16} = \frac{\square}{8}$ **2.** $\frac{5}{6} = \frac{20}{\square}$

3. $\frac{12}{15} = \frac{4}{\square}$ **4.** $\frac{2}{9} = \frac{\square}{72}$

Set D, pages 266–267

You have 10 cubes. One way to show $\frac{1}{2}$ is two groups of 5. Using 10 or fewer cubes, how many other fractions can you make that are equivalent to $\frac{1}{2}$?

Make a table and count the ways to make $\frac{1}{2}$.

Group 1	Group 2	Fraction
4	4	$\frac{4}{8} = \frac{1}{2}$
3	3	$\frac{3}{6} = \frac{1}{2}$
2	2	$\frac{2}{4} = \frac{1}{2}$
1	1	$\frac{1}{2} = \frac{1}{2}$

Remember you can use objects and make a table.

Solve.

1. You have 16 cubes. One way to show $\frac{1}{4}$ is four groups of 4. Using 16 or fewer cubes, what other fractions can you find that are equivalent to $\frac{1}{4}$?

2. You have 12 cubes. One way to show $\frac{1}{3}$ is three groups of 2. Using 12 or fewer cubes, what other fractions can you make that are equivalent to $\frac{1}{3}$?

Set E, pages 268–269

Write $\frac{4}{10}$ in simplest form.

The numerator, 4, and denominator, 10, have 2 as a common factor.

$$\frac{4}{10} \overset{\div\, 2}{\underset{\div\, 2}{=}} \frac{2}{5}$$

The only common factor for 2 and 5 is 1. So, $\frac{2}{5}$ is the simplest form of $\frac{4}{10}$.

Remember that a fraction is in simplest form if the numerator and the denominator have no common factor other than 1.

Write each fraction in simplest form.

1. $\frac{3}{6}$ 2. $\frac{2}{10}$ 3. $\frac{4}{6}$

4. $\frac{10}{12}$ 5. $\frac{9}{12}$ 6. $\frac{8}{16}$

Set F, pages 270–271

What is true about all multiples of 6?

Make a generalization: All multiples of 6 have 2 and 3 as factors.

Test your generalization:

Factors of 6: 1, **2**, **3**, 6
Factors of 12: 1, **2**, **3**, 4, 6, 12
Factors of 18: 1, **2**, **3**, 6, 9, 18

The generalization seems to be true because these multiples of 6 all have 2 and 3 as factors.

Remember to test your generalizations.

Solve.

1. Look at each group of numbers below. Make a generalization for each group of numbers that does not apply to the other group of numbers.

2 3   4
  7   6 9

Topic 14

Fractions and Decimals

1 According to the Greek mathematician Zeno, who lived in the fourth century B.C., this ball will never stop bouncing. You will find out why in Lesson 14-3.

2 How many gallons of milk does an average milk cow produce each day? You will find out in Lesson 14-4.

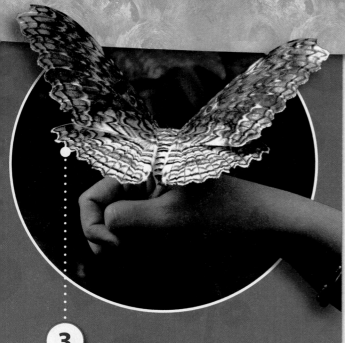

3 The Great Owlet Moth of Brazil has one of the largest wingspans of all insects. How many inches long is its wingspan? You will find out in Lesson 14-4.

4 The Roman Colosseum is one of the best examples of Roman architecture. The arena is what fractional part of the Colosseum? You will find out in Lesson 14-1.

Review What You Know!

Vocabulary

Choose the best term from the box.

> • greater   • tenth
> • hundredth   • decimal point

1. One of ten equal parts of a whole is one _?_.

2. A dot used to separate dollars from cents or ones from tenths in a number is a _?_.

3. One part of 100 equal parts of a whole is one _?_.

4. The number 3,704 is _?_ than the number 3,407.

Decimal Numbers

Write the decimal for each shaded part.

5.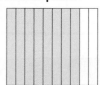

6.

Write the number in word form.

7. 1.02   **8.** 5.3

9. 0.067   **10.** 12.8

Equivalent Fractions

Write each fraction in simplest form.

11. $\frac{2}{4}$ **12.** $\frac{4}{10}$

13. **Writing to Explain** How do you know that $\frac{3}{8}$ is in simplest form?

Topic Essential Questions

• How are fractions and decimals related?

• How are fractions, decimals, and percents related?

Lesson
14-1

MA.4.A.2.3 Relate equivalent fractions and decimals with and without models, including locations on a number line.

Fractions and Decimals

How can you write a fraction as a decimal and a decimal as a fraction?

On Kelsey Street, six out of 10 homes have swing sets in their backyards.

Write $\frac{6}{10}$ as a decimal.

6 of 10 houses have swing sets.

Other Example

Use a decimal model showing thousandths to write $\frac{317}{1,000}$ as a decimal.

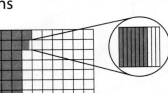

7 thousandths are shaded.

$$\frac{317}{1,000} = 0.317$$

Guided Practice*

Do you know HOW?

For **1** through **5**, write a decimal and a fraction for the part of each grid that is shaded.

1.

2.

3.

4.

5.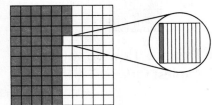

Do you UNDERSTAND?

6. **Writing to Explain** Why is the fraction $\frac{6}{10}$ not written 0.06?

7. When the decimals 0.7 and 0.70 are each written as a fraction, are the fractions equivalent? Explain your answer.

8. On Kelsey Street, what fraction of homes do NOT have swings? Write your answer as a fraction and a decimal.

9. Look back at Other Example. Write 0.317 in word form.

*For another example, see Set A on page 300.

Write $\frac{6}{10}$ as a decimal.

$\frac{6}{10}$ is six tenths, or 0.6.

$$\frac{6}{10} = 0.6$$

So, 0.6 of the houses have swing sets.

In Rolling Hills, 0.75 of the houses are two-story homes.

Write 0.75 as a fraction.

0.75 is seventy-five hundredths, or $\frac{75}{100}$.

$$0.75 = \frac{75}{100}$$

So, $\frac{75}{100}$ of the houses are two-story homes.

Independent Practice

For **10** through **24**, write an equivalent decimal or fraction.

10. $\frac{4}{10}$ **11.** $\frac{21}{100}$ **12.** 0.428   **13.** $\frac{81}{100}$ **14.** 0.651

15. $\frac{50}{100}$ **16.** 0.48   **17.** $\frac{7}{10}$ **18.** 0.3   **19.** $\frac{456}{1,000}$

20. 0.082   **21.** $\frac{73}{100}$ **22.** $\frac{926}{1,000}$ **23.** 0.741   **24.** 0.69

Problem Solving

25. Estimation About what fraction of the rectangle to the right is shaded green?

26. **Social Studies** The arena of the Colosseum in Rome was about $\frac{3}{20}$ of the entire Colosseum. Write this amount as a decimal.

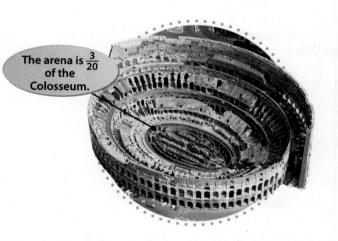

The arena is $\frac{3}{20}$ of the Colosseum.

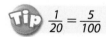 $\frac{1}{20} = \frac{5}{100}$

27. Which fraction is the same as 0.85?

A $\frac{85}{1,000}$ **C** $\frac{85}{1}$

B $\frac{85}{100}$ **D** $\frac{85}{10}$

28. **Science** The table at the right shows the average monthly rainfall in inches for Vero Beach, Florida. For which month(s) shown is the rainfall greater than 2.5 inches but less than 3 inches?

Average Rainfall in Inches			
Jan.	**Feb.**	**March**	**April**
2.89	2.45	4.20	2.88

MA.4.A.2.3 Relate equivalent fractions and decimals with and without models, including locations on a number line.

Equivalent Fractions and Decimals

How can you use equivalent fractions to change a fraction to a decimal?

A pan of cornbread was divided into 15 equal pieces, and 3 out of 15 pieces or $\frac{3}{15}$ of the cornbread remains. Write a fraction equivalent to $\frac{3}{15}$, and then change the fraction to a decimal.

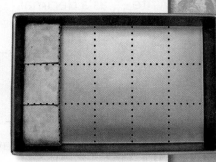

Other Examples

Write $\frac{9}{36}$ as a decimal.

In simplest form $\frac{9}{36}$ is $\frac{1}{4}$.

Find an equivalent fraction with a denominator of 100.

Think 4 times what number equals 100?

$$\overset{\times\,25}{\frac{1}{4} = \frac{25}{100}}$$
$$\times\,25$$

$\frac{25}{100}$ is twenty-five hundredths, or 0.25.

So, $\frac{9}{36} = 0.25$.

Write $\frac{1}{500}$ as a decimal.

Multiply to find an equivalent fraction with a denominator of 1,000.

Think 500 times what number equals 1,000?

$$\overset{\times\,2}{\frac{1}{500} = \frac{2}{1,000}}$$
$$\times\,2$$

$\frac{2}{1,000}$ is two thousandths, or 0.002.

So, $\frac{1}{500} = 0.002$.

Explain It

1. **Reasoning** Why is the fraction $\frac{1}{2}$ not written as 0.12?

2. What steps would you take to rename $\frac{3}{25}$ as an equivalent fraction with a denominator of 100?

In simplest form $\frac{3}{15}$ is $\frac{1}{5}$. Find an equivalent fraction with a denominator of 10.

Think 5 times what number equals 10?

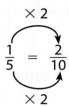

$$\frac{1}{5} = \frac{2}{10}$$

$\frac{2}{10}$ is two tenths, or 0.2.

So, 0.2 of the cornbread remains.

Write $\frac{11}{20}$ as a decimal.

Multiply to find an equivalent fraction with a denominator of 100.

Think 20 times what number equals 100?

$$\frac{11}{20} = \frac{55}{100}$$

$\frac{11}{20} = \frac{55}{100}$

$\frac{55}{100}$ is fifty-five hundredths, or 0.55.

Guided Practice*

Do you know HOW?

For **1** through **6**, write each fraction as a decimal.

1. $\frac{3}{5} = \frac{\blacksquare}{10}$ **2.** $\frac{2}{4} = \frac{50}{\blacksquare}$

3. $\frac{6}{15}$ **4.** $\frac{3}{20}$

5. $\frac{2}{8}$ **6.** $\frac{9}{50}$

Do you UNDERSTAND?

7. Write a fraction and an equivalent decimal to show the part of the cornbread that has been eaten.

8. Writing to Explain When you write a fraction as a decimal, why do you need to rename the fraction as an equivalent fraction with a denominator of 10, 100, or 1,000?

Independent Practice

Leveled Practice In **9** through **18**, write each fraction as a decimal.

9. $\frac{2}{5} = \frac{\blacksquare}{10}$ **10.** $\frac{9}{20} = \frac{\blacksquare}{100}$ **11.** $\frac{1}{25} = \frac{4}{\blacksquare}$ **12.** $\frac{4}{20} = \frac{\blacksquare}{10}$ **13.** $\frac{7}{500} = \frac{\blacksquare}{1,000}$

14. $\frac{3}{12}$ **15.** $\frac{9}{18}$ **16.** $\frac{3}{200}$ **17.** $\frac{5}{25}$ **18.** $\frac{7}{20}$

In **19** through **30**, tell whether each pair shows equivalent numbers.

19. $\frac{4}{8}$, 0.5   **20.** $\frac{1}{5}$, 0.15   **21.** $\frac{13}{20}$, 0.65   **22.** $\frac{10}{25}$, 0.35

23. $\frac{16}{20}$, 0.08   **24.** $\frac{12}{16}$, 0.6   **25.** $\frac{15}{50}$, 0.3   **26.** $\frac{7}{250}$, 0.028

27. $\frac{13}{50}$, 0.26   **28.** $\frac{3}{10}$, 0.03   **29.** $\frac{24}{30}$, 0.8   **30.** $\frac{1}{2}$, 0.005

31. Roger got 24 hits out of 40 times at bat. What is his batting average as a fraction in simplest form? Then write an equivalent decimal.

$$\text{Batting Average} = \frac{\text{Number of hits}}{\text{Number of times at bat}}$$

32. The model below represents 1 whole. Maura says that the shaded part of the model shows that $\frac{70}{100} = 0.07$. Is Maura correct? Explain why or why not.

33. THINK SOLVE EXPLAIN A band has 20 instruments. Tyler says that $\frac{2}{5}$ of the instruments are string instruments and 0.5 of the instruments are wind instruments. Does the band have the same number of wind instruments and string instruments? Explain.

34. Gina wrote a 4-digit number. She used each of the digits 1, 3, 5, and 7 once. How many different 4-digit numbers can Gina write?

35. Writing to Explain Which is greater, $\frac{3}{4}$ or 0.75? Explain your answer.

36. The cell phone was invented in Sweden in 1979. How many years ago was the cell phone invented?

37. Number Sense Write a fraction in simplest form and an equivalent decimal to show what part of a dollar 5 cents represents. (Hint: 1 dollar = 100 cents.)

For **38**, use the diagram at the right.

38. Kwan has 37 customers on his paper route. He delivers newspapers every day. How many newspapers does he deliver in one week?

Newspapers delivered
each day

39. Betty's score on a 5-point quiz was 4 out of 5, or $\frac{4}{5}$. What is $\frac{4}{5}$ written as a decimal?

  A   0.4

  B   0.45

  C   0.6

  D   0.8

40. Nine of the 12 students in the school play are fourth graders. Which decimal represents the part of the students that are fourth graders?

  F   0.25

  G   0.6

  H   0.75

  I   0.9

Solve each equation for z.

1. $z + 22 = 24$ **2.** $z - 19 = 24$ **3.** $z \times 4 = 32$

4. $z \div 9 = 4$ **5.** $15 + z = 24$ **6.** $z - 22 = 22$

7. $6 \times z = 6$ **8.** $z \div 5 = 1$ **9.** $3 \times z = 18$

Round each decimal to the nearest tenth.

10. 9.64   **11.** 1.05   **12.** 3.52   **13.** 16.67   **14.** 87.24

Find the sum. Estimate to check if the answer is reasonable.

15. $9 + 3{,}529 + 27 + 621$ **16.** $17{,}868 + 913 + 2{,}781$

17. $475 + 25 + 5{,}350 + 25{,}275$ **18.** $2 + 129 + 56 + 374$

Error Search Find each value of w that is not correct.
Write it correctly, and explain the error.

19. $20 + w = 68$ **20.** $w - 12 = 50$ **21.** $w \div 2 = 9$ **22.** $w \times 6 = 42$
        $w = 88$ $w = 62$ $w = 11$ $w = 8$

Number Sense

Estimating and Reasoning Write whether each
statement is true or false. Explain your answer.

23. The expression $101 - 25$ equals 76.

24. The product of 4 and 682 is closer to 2,400 than 2,800.

25. The sum of 251 and 173 is less than 400.

26. The quotient of 0 divided by 1 is 1.

27. The product of 5 and 45 is 25 more than 200.

28. The difference of 844 and 172 is greater than 600.

Fractions and Decimals on the Number Line

How can you locate points on a number line?

MA.4.A.2.3 Relate equivalent fractions and decimals with and without models, including locations on a number line.

In long-track speed skating, each lap is 0.4 kilometer.
In short-track speed skating, each lap is 0.11 kilometer.
How can you use a number line to show these distances?

One lap = 0.4 km

One lap = 0.11 km

Another Example **How can you name points on a number line?**

Naming fractions on a number line

What fraction is at Point *P*?

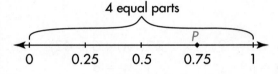

4 equal parts

| P |

0   0.25   0.5   0.75   1

There are 4 equal parts between 0 and 1. There are 3 equal
parts between 0 and Point *P*. So, Point *P* is at $\frac{3}{4}$.

Naming decimals on a number line

What number is at Point *Q*?

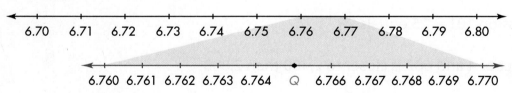

6.70 6.71 6.72 6.73 6.74 6.75 6.76 6.77 6.78 6.79 6.80

6.760 6.761 6.762 6.763 6.764   *Q*   6.766 6.767 6.768 6.769 6.770

There are 5 equal parts between 6.760 and Point *Q*.
Each of these parts is 0.001, so Point *Q* is at 6.765.

Explain It

1. Describe where you would place Point *Q* on a number
   line that shows only hundredths.

2. What number is at Point *R*?

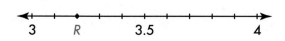

3   *R*   3.5   4

Locate 0.4 on a number line. You know that $0.4 = \frac{4}{10}$.

Draw a number line, and divide the distance from 0 to 1 into 10 equal parts to show tenths.

Draw a point at $\frac{4}{10}$.

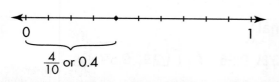

$\frac{4}{10}$ or 0.4

Locate 0.11 on a number line.

Draw another number line, and divide the distance from 0.10 to 0.20 into 10 equal parts to show hundredths.

Draw a point at 0.11.

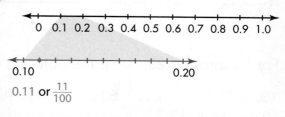

0.11 or $\frac{11}{100}$

Guided Practice*

Do you know HOW?

For **1** and **2**, use the number line below to name the fraction at each point.

1. A

2. B

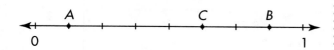

For **3** and **4**, name the point on the number line for each decimal.

3. 1.33

4. 1.39

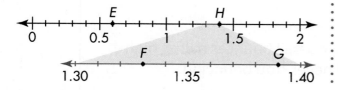

Do you UNDERSTAND?

5. Where would you locate 0.15 on the bottom number line above?

6. Use the number line for Exercises 1 and 2. What fraction is located at Point *C*?

7. A speed skater would race 13.5 laps around the short track in a 1,500-meter race. Show 13.5 on a number line.

8. Use the number line for Exercises 3 and 4. What point is at $\frac{6}{10}$?

Independent Practice

For **9** through **13**, use the number line below to name the decimal.

9. J

10. K

11. L

12. M

13. N

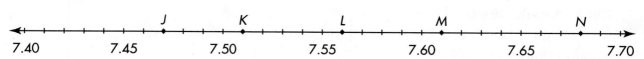

For another example, see Set C on page 300.

For **14** through **18**, name the fraction that should be written at each point.

14. V   **15.** Z   **16.** X   **17.** W   **18.** Y

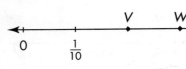   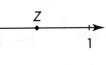

For **19** through **23**, name the point for each decimal.

19. 9.61   **20.** 9.628   **21.** 9.625   **22.** 9.56   **23.** 9.59

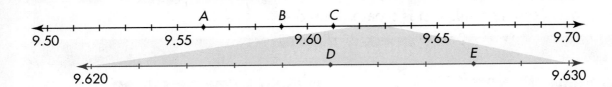

24. Writing to Explain Which point on the number line to the right represents the same point as Point Z?

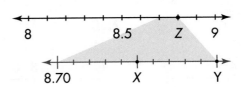

25. Jack walked $\frac{4}{5}$ mile to the library. What is this distance as a decimal?

  A 0.4   **C** 0.54

  B 0.45   **D** 0.8

26. Write an expression that tells how to find the perimeter of a triangle with each side 2 inches long.

Use the diagram below for **27** and **28**.

According to the Greek mathematician Zeno, if a ball bounces half as high each bounce as the one before it, then it will never stop bouncing.

27. Name the fractions that should be written at points D and E.

28. Writing to Explain Do you think it would be possible for the ball to reach zero by moving halfway closer at every step? Why or why not?

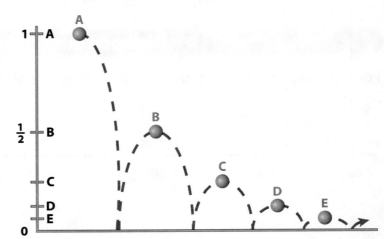

Algebra Connections

Missing Numbers and Operations

Often there is more than one way to connect two numbers when a number and the operation are missing.

Here are some rules:

- If the number that appears first is less than the second number, try using addition and multiplication.

- If the number that appears first is greater than the second number, try using subtraction and division.

Example: 2 ☐ ▯ = 6

Use addition:

Think *2 plus what number equals 6?*

$2 + 4 = 6$

Use multiplication:

Think *2 times what number equals 6?*

$2 \times 3 = 6$

Find the missing operation for each ☐ and the missing number for each ▯.

1. 4 ☐ ▯ = 8

4 ☐ ▯ = 8

2. 45 ☐ ▯ = 9

45 ☐ ▯ = 9

3. 72 ☐ ▯ = 8

72 ☐ ▯ = 8

4. 6 ☐ ▯ = 30

6 ☐ ▯ = 30

5. 8 ☐ ▯ = 56

8 ☐ ▯ = 56

6. 54 ☐ ▯ = 6

54 ☐ ▯ = 6

7. 3 ☐ ▯ = 21

3 ☐ ▯ = 21

8. 64 ☐ ▯ = 8

64 ☐ ▯ = 8

9. 28 ☐ ▯ = 4

28 ☐ ▯ = 4

10. 6 ☐ ▯ = 36

6 ☐ ▯ = 36

11. 5 ☐ ▯ = 40

5 ☐ ▯ = 40

12. 49 ☐ ▯ = 7

49 ☐ ▯ = 7

For **13** through **16**, find the missing operation and number. Then find the answer.

13. Cassie has $4. She wants to buy a blouse that costs $16. How much more money does Cassie need?

$4 ☐ $▯ = $16

14. Doug had 42 patio blocks. He stacked them in equal groups of 7 blocks. How many stacks were there?

42 ☐ ▯ = 7

15. Lesley had 37 postcards. She mailed some to her friends. If 25 postcards were left, how many stamps did she use?

37 ☐ ▯ = 25

16. There were 4 rabbits in each litter. Gerta's pet rabbit was mother to 20 rabbits. How many litters of rabbits were there?

4 ☐ ▯ = 20

MA.4.A.2.3 Relate equivalent
fractions and decimals
with and without models,
including locations on a
number line.

Mixed Numbers and Decimals

**How can you write a mixed number
as a decimal?**

Kai has $2\frac{3}{4}$ yards of cloth to make a costume
for the school play. Remember that a number
such as $2\frac{3}{4}$ that has a whole-number part and
a fraction part is called a mixed number.

Write $2\frac{3}{4}$ as a decimal.

$2\frac{3}{4}$ yards of cloth

Another Example **How can you write a decimal greater
than 1 as a mixed number?**

Write 1.32 as a mixed number.

The word form for 1.32 is one and thirty-two hundredths. So, $1.32 = 1\frac{32}{100}$.

1. Why is the mixed number for 1.032 different from the mixed
number for 1.32?

Guided Practice*

Do you know HOW?

Write a decimal and mixed number for
the shaded part of the grids.

1.

Do you UNDERSTAND?

2. **Writing to Explain** How do you
decide what denominator to use
when writing a decimal as a mixed
number?

3. For scenery, Kai needs 1.5 yards of
cloth. Write 1.5 as a mixed number
in simplest form.

Independent Practice

For **4** and **5**, write a decimal and mixed number for the shaded
part of the grids.

4.

5.

For another example, see Set D on page 301.

One Way

Use grids to show a model for $2\frac{3}{4}$.

The model shows that $\frac{3}{4}$ is the same as $\frac{75}{100}$. So, $2\frac{3}{4} = 2.75$.

Another Way

Change $\frac{3}{4}$ to a decimal.

Think 4 times what number equals 100?

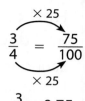

$$\frac{3}{4} = 0.75$$

Replace the fraction part of $2\frac{3}{4}$ with the decimal. Since $\frac{3}{4} = 0.75$, $2\frac{3}{4} = 2.75$.

For **6** through **15**, write an equivalent decimal for each mixed number or a mixed number for each decimal.

6. $2\frac{3}{100}$

7. $1\frac{499}{1,000}$

8. 3.2

9. $5\frac{17}{100}$

10. 3.289

11. $9\frac{3}{10}$

12. 2.117

13. 1.6

14. $1\frac{81}{100}$

15. 1.23

Problem Solving

---

16. 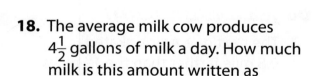 **Science** It takes Neptune 164.8 years to revolve once around the Sun. Write this decimal as a mixed number.

17. Algebra A medium pizza with **Critical THINKING** cheese costs $9. Each additional topping, t, costs $2. Write an algebraic expression to represent the cost of a pizza with t toppings in dollars.

18. The average milk cow produces $4\frac{1}{2}$ gallons of milk a day. How much milk is this amount written as a decimal?

    A 45 gallons   **C** 4.5 gallons

    B 5 gallons   **D** 0.45 gallons

19. The tiny harvest mouse weighs about $\frac{1}{4}$ ounce. What is $\frac{1}{4}$ in decimal form?

20. The Great Owlet Moth has a wingspan of 12.13 inches. Write this number as a mixed number.

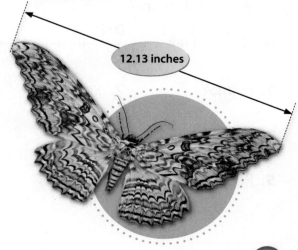

12.13 inches

MA.4.A.2.3 Relate equivalent fractions and decimals with and without models, including locations on a number line.

Mixed Numbers and Decimals on the Number Line

How can you locate mixed numbers and decimals on a number line?

Laurie and Aaron went rollerblading. Laurie skated 1.6 miles, and Aaron skated $1\frac{3}{5}$ miles.

Who skated farther?

Aaron skated $1\frac{3}{5}$ miles.

Laurie skated 1.6 miles.

Other Examples

What mixed number should be written at Point *A*?

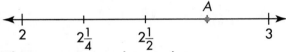

There are 4 equal parts between 2 and 3. Each part is $\frac{1}{4}$.

So, $2\frac{3}{4}$ should be written at Point *A*.

What decimal should be written at Point *B*?

There are 10 equal parts between 1.40 and 1.50. There are 8 equal parts between 1.40 and Point *B*.

So, 1.48 should be written at Point *B*.

Guided Practice*

Do you know HOW?

For **1** through **6**, what decimal and fraction or mixed number should be written at each point?

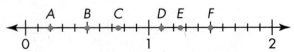

1. Point *A*
2. Point *B*
3. Point *C*
4. Point *D*
5. Point *E*
6. Point *F*

Do you UNDERSTAND?

7. The next day, Aaron skated 0.8 mile farther than the $1\frac{3}{5}$ miles he had skated the day before. Use a number line to show this total distance as a decimal and as a mixed number.

   Tip *Convert 0.8 to a fraction.*

8. If Laurie skated between 3.5 and 4.0 miles, what distances, in tenths, could she have skated?

Show $1\frac{3}{5}$ and 1.6 on the same number line.

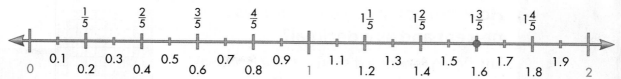

Draw a number line and label 0, 1, and 2.

Divide the distance between 0 and 1 and 1 and 2 into 5 equal lengths. Label the points $\frac{1}{5}$, $\frac{2}{5}$, and so on.

Then divide the distance between 0 and 1 and 1 and 2 into 10 equal lengths. Label 0.1, 0.2, and so on.

Draw a point at $1\frac{3}{5}$ and 1.6.

Laurie and Aaron skated the same distance.

Independent Practice

For **9** through **13**, name the decimal for each point.

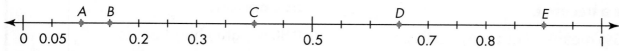

9. Point *A*   **10.** Point *B*   **11.** Point *C*   **12.** Point *D*   **13.** Point *E*

For **14** through **18**, name the mixed number for each point.

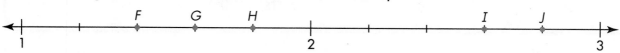

14. Point *F*   **15.** Point *G*   **16.** Point *H*   **17.** Point *I*   **18.** Point *J*

Problem Solving

19. The table at the right shows what you might have paid to buy different foreign currencies in a recent year. Write each decimal as a fraction or mixed number.

Currency	Cost in U.S. Dollars
1 British pound	$1.758
1 Canadian dollar	$0.932
1 Euro	$1.381
1 Mexican peso	$0.089

20. From one day to the next, the cost of 1 British pound changed from $1.79 to 1\frac{794}{1,000}$. Did the cost increase or decrease? Explain.

THINK
SOLVE
EXPLAIN

21. Jen lives $2\frac{1}{2}$ miles from school. Dot lives 2.45 miles from school. Who lives closer to the school? Use a number line to compare the two distances.

Critical
THINKING

22. Renee and George ate $\frac{4}{10}$ of a pie. Which is equal to $\frac{4}{10}$?

A $\frac{4}{15}$ **C** $\frac{2}{5}$

B $\frac{1}{3}$ **D** $\frac{1}{2}$

MA.4.A.6.5 Relate halves, fourths, tenths, and hundredths to decimals and percents.

Fractions, Decimals, and Percents

How can you write a fraction as a percent and as a decimal?

The floor plan for a discount store is shown at the right. It is divided into 100 equal parts.

Write the amount of space each department occupies as a fraction, a decimal, and a percent.

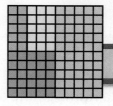

☐ Checkout
☐ Women's Clothing
☐ Men's Clothing
☐ Children's Clothing

Other Examples

Write 55% as a fraction and as a decimal.

55% means 55 out of 100 parts.

Written as a fraction: $\frac{55}{100}$

Written as a decimal: $\frac{55}{100} = 0.55$

Write 0.80 as a fraction and as a percent.

0.80 is eighty hundredths.

Written as a fraction: $\frac{80}{100}$

Written as a percent: 80 out of 100 parts, or 80%

Guided Practice*

Do you know HOW?

In **1** through **3**, write the fraction, decimal, and percent for the shaded part of each grid.

1.   2.   3.

In **4** through **6**, write the missing fraction, decimal, or percent.

4. $\frac{98}{100} = 0.98 = $ ▢

5. ▢ $= 0.13 = 13\%$

6. $\frac{51}{100} = $ ▢ $= 51\%$

Do you UNDERSTAND?

7. **Number Sense** If all 100 squares in a 100-grid are shaded, what percent represents the shaded part?

8. **Writing to Explain** Could the floor space in the store be divided this way: Women's clothing 45%, Children's clothing 25%, Men's clothing 30%, and Checkout 15%? Explain your answer.

9. Chloe said that the fraction of floor space occupied by men's clothing is $\frac{1}{4}$. Is Chloe correct? Why or why not?

For another example, see Set E on page 301.

Percent means <u>per hundred</u>.
The percent symbol is %.

Women's clothing occupies 50 out of 100 parts, or 50%.

50% is read "fifty percent."

Written as a fraction: $\frac{50}{100}$

Written as a decimal: 0.50

Floor space occupied by the other departments:

Men's clothing: 25 out of 100 parts
$\frac{25}{100} = 0.25 = 25\%$

Children's clothing: 15 out of 100 parts
$\frac{15}{100} = 0.15 = 15\%$

Checkout: 10 out of 100 parts
$\frac{10}{100} = 0.10 = 10\%$

Independent Practice

In **10** through **14**, write the fraction, decimal, and percent for the shaded part of each grid.

10. **11.** **12.** **13.** **14.**

In **15** through **22**, write the missing fraction, decimal, or percent.

15. $\frac{38}{100} = $ ▢ $= 38\%$ **16.** ▢ $= 0.17 = 17\%$ **17.** $\frac{5}{100} = $ ▢ $= 5\%$ **18.** $\frac{88}{100} = 0.88 = $ ▢

19. $\frac{74}{100} = $ ▢ $= 74\%$ **20.** $\frac{2}{100} = 0.02 = $ ▢ **21.** ▢ $= 0.07 = 7\%$ **22.** ▢ $= 0.69 = 69\%$

In **23** through **32**, write each fraction or decimal as a percent.

23. 0.47 **24.** $\frac{50}{100}$ **25.** 0.76 **26.** $\frac{9}{100}$ **27.** $\frac{35}{100}$

28. 0.92 **29.** 0.41 **30.** $\frac{11}{100}$ **31.** 0.73 **32.** $\frac{67}{100}$

In **33** through **42**, write each percent as a fraction and decimal.

33. 4% **34.** 81% **35.** 49% **36.** 97% **37.** 22%

38. 54% **39.** 39% **40.** 18% **41.** 6% **42.** 99%

43. Writing to Explain Is 75% the same as the fraction $\frac{3}{4}$? Why or why not?

44. In a group of 100 people, 37 people wear glasses. What percent of the people in the group wear glasses?

45. A florist is preparing 10 vases of flowers. Each vase will contain 3 roses and 8 carnations. How many of each type of flower will be needed?

46. 🌐 **Social Studies** The deepest lake in the United States is Crater Lake in Oregon. It is one thousand, nine hundred thirty-two feet deep! Write this depth in standard form.

47. The Glenview Orchestra has 100 members. The conductor shaded the grid below to represent the members in each section. What percent of the members are in each section?

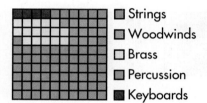

☐ Strings
☐ Woodwinds
☐ Brass
☐ Percussion
■ Keyboards

   a Strings

   b Woodwinds

   c Brass

   d Percussion

   e Keyboards

48. Algebra What is the value of n in the equation $n \times 4 = 36$?

   A $n = 9$

   B $n = 12$

   C $n = 32$

   D $n = 40$

49. Copy the table below. Fill in the missing values.

Percent		45%	19%
Fraction	$\frac{30}{100}$		$\frac{19}{100}$
Decimal	0.30	0.45	

50. Jill colors $\frac{38}{100}$ of a 100-grid purple. She colors the rest of the grid green. What percent of the grid is shaded green?

51. A merry-go-round takes 2 minutes to make a complete turn. Mary gets on and rides without stopping for the next 12 minutes. How many times will Mary have returned to the starting point when the ride stops?

52. Connor surveys 100 students in his school. He finds that $\frac{60}{100}$ of the students plan to go to the soccer game after school. What percent of the students plan to go to the game?

   F 6%   **G** 16%   **H** 40%   **I** 60%

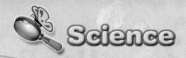

Mixed Problem Solving

The Fish and Wildlife Research Institute in Florida is helping with the recovery of Kemp's Ridley Sea Turtles.

1. How many more Kemp's Ridley Sea Turtles were there in 1947 than in 1968?

2. Did the population of Kemp's Ridley Sea Turtles increase or decrease between 1991 and 2000? What was the amount of increase or decrease?

3. Were there more or fewer sea turtles in 1968 than in 1991? How many more or fewer sea turtles were there?

Data

Kemp's Ridley Sea Turtles	
Year	Female Kemp's Ridley Sea Turtles Found Nesting
1947	40,000
1968	5,000
1991	200
2000	6,000

Use the table for Exercises **4** through **7**.

4. Which is taller: the trumpetweed or the giant ironweed?

5. Which is shorter: the lizard's tail or the lady lupine?

6. Order the giant ironweed, the lady lupine, and the Turk's cap lily from tallest to shortest.

7. Write the height of the lady lupine as a mixed number.

Data

Heights of Native Wildflowers in Florida	
Giant ironweed	7 feet
Lizard's tail	1 foot
Trumpetweed	6 feet
Lady lupine	1.5 feet
Turk's cap lily	9 feet

8. **Strategy Focus** Solve the problem by using the strategy Make a Table.

   Mr. Thomas was planting 5 rows of flowers. He planted 10 flowers in the first row, 8 flowers in the second row, and 6 flowers in the third row. If he continues this pattern, how many flowers will be in the fifth row?

Lesson 14-7

MA.4.A.4.2 Describe
mathematics relationships
using expressions, equations,
and visual representations.

Problem Solving

Use Reasoning

Mary, Kristen, Deborah, and
Amy met on vacation. They
are from New York, Georgia,
Nevada, and Maine. Amy is
from New York, and Kristen is
not from Georgia. If Deborah is
from Nevada, where is Mary from?

Amy is from
New York.

Deborah is
from Nevada.

Guided Practice*

Do you know HOW?

Make a table and use reasoning to
solve. Write the answer in a complete
sentence.

1. Tony has 4 rabbits named Lenny,
   Emma, Beau, and Blossom. One is
   orange, one is gray, one is black, and
   one is spotted. Emma is orange.
   Beau is not gray. Blossom is spotted.
   What color is Lenny?

Do you UNDERSTAND?

2. In the example above, when a "Y" is
   placed in a cell, why does an "N" get
   placed in the other cells in the same
   row and column?

3. **Write a Problem** Write a problem
   using the reasoning strategy.

Independent Practice

Solve each problem. Write the answer in
a complete sentence.

4. There are 5 people in the Robinson family: Harry,
   Barb, Roger, Laurie, and Carrie. Their ages are
   37, 36, 13, 10, and 5. Barb is the oldest and Carrie
   is the youngest. Laurie is 13. Harry is not 10. He is
   older than Roger. How old is Roger?

5. Six dancers want to form a triangle so that the
   same number of dancers is on each side. How
   should they stand? Draw a picture to solve.

Stuck? Try this....

- What do I know?
- What diagram can I use to help
  understand the problem?
- Can I use addition, subtraction,
  multiplication, or division?
- Is all of my work correct?
- Did I answer the right question?
- Is my answer reasonable?

296 *For another example, see Set F on page 301.

Make and fill in the table with the information you know.

	NY	GA	NV	ME
Mary	▦	▦	▦	▦
Kristen	▦	N	▦	▦
Deborah	▦	▦	Y	▦
Amy	Y	▦	▦	▦

Each row and each column can have only one Yes because each girl can be from only one of the four states.

Fill in the row and column with No's (N) where there is one Yes (Y).

	NY	GA	NV	ME
Mary	N	**Y**	N	N
Kristen	N	N	N	**Y**
Deborah	N	N	Y	N
Amy	Y	N	N	N

Use reasoning to draw conclusions. There are 3 No's in Kristen's row. She must live in Maine. Put a Y in the Maine column. Complete the chart.

Mary is from Georgia.

---

6. What comes next in the pattern to the right? Explain.

THINK
SOLVE
EXPLAIN

7. Wendy, Chris, Lauren, and Santiago live on four different streets: Highland, East, Brook, and Elm. Wendy lives on Highland. Lauren lives on Elm. Chris does not live on East. What street does Santiago live on?

	Brook	East	Elm	Highland
Chris	▦	No	▦	▦
Lauren	▦	▦	Yes	▦
Santiago	▦	▦	▦	▦
Wendy	▦	▦	▦	Yes

8. Eric and his friends are playing volleyball. They made a total of 6 teams. If there are 4 players on each team, how many people are playing volleyball?

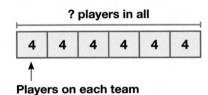

? players in all

| 4 | 4 | 4 | 4 | 4 | 4 |

↑
Players on each team

9. Vicki has a bag with 6 blue marbles, 4 red marbles, 7 green marbles, and 8 yellow marbles. What fraction in simplest form represents the marbles that are blue or red?

A $\frac{4}{25}$ **C** $\frac{2}{5}$

B $\frac{6}{25}$ **D** $\frac{2}{3}$

Critical THINKING

10. Weddell, von Bellingshausen, Cook, Palmer, and Wilkes each explored Antarctica. Two were British, and one was Russian. The other two were from the United States. Palmer and Wilkes were from the same country. Cook was British. Weddell was from the same country as Cook. Which country was von Bellingshausen from?

1 Quinton's frog leaped $2\frac{3}{4}$ feet on its first leap. Which point on the number line best represents the point where the frog landed? (14-5)

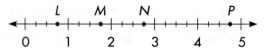

A. L

B. M

C. N

D. P

2 What is $\frac{205}{1,000}$ written as a decimal? (14-1)

F. 205.0

G. 2.05

H. 0.250

I. 0.205

3 Which of the following does NOT represent the shaded area? (14-6)

A. 0.42

B. $\frac{42}{100}$

C. 42%

D. 4.2

4 Robert has 15 sports movies. Six out of 15, or $\frac{6}{15}$, of his movies are about baseball. What decimal represents $\frac{6}{15}$? (14-2)

F. 0.15

G. 0.4

H. 0.6

I. 6.0

5 What is another way to write 1.47? (14-4)

A. $\frac{1}{147}$

B. $\frac{47}{100}$

C. $1\frac{47}{100}$

D. $1\frac{47}{10}$

6 Which number is best represented by Point R on the number line? (14-3)

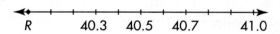

F. 40.1

G. 40.0

H. 39.9

I. 39.0

7 Which is 60% written as a decimal and as a fraction? (14-6)

A. 0.06, $\frac{60}{100}$

B. 0.60, $\frac{60}{100}$

C. 0.60, $\frac{6}{100}$

D. 0.06, $\frac{6}{100}$

8 Which fraction and decimal represent the part that is green? (14-1)

F. $\frac{63}{100}$ and 0.63

G. $\frac{63}{100}$ and 0.063

H. $\frac{63}{100}$ and 6.3

I. $\frac{63}{10}$ and 0.63

9 What fraction and decimal are best represented by Point *B* on the number line? (14-5)

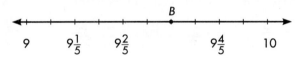

A. $9\frac{3}{5}$ and 9.3

B. $9\frac{3}{5}$ and 9.6

C. $9\frac{3}{10}$ and 9.3

D. $9\frac{3}{10}$ and 9.6

10 What fraction is best represented by Point *D* on the number line? (14-3)

F. $\frac{2}{5}$

G. $\frac{3}{5}$

H. $\frac{1}{2}$

I. $\frac{3}{10}$

11 Ben, Gracie, Josh, and Avery all attend Glenn Oaks School. They each get to school in a different way. They come by bus, walking, riding a bike, or in a car. Ben walks to school. Gracie does not come in a car. If Josh rides the bus, how does Avery get to school? (14-7)

A. Bus

B. Walking

C. Riding a bike

D. Car

12 What decimal is shown in the grids below? (14-4)

13 Of the 28 students in Emma's class, 7 have cats. So $\frac{7}{28}$ of the students have cats. What decimal represents $\frac{7}{28}$? Explain. (14-2)

Set A, pages 278–279

Write $\frac{37}{100}$ as a decimal.

 $\frac{37}{100}$ is thirty-seven hundredths, or 0.37.

Remember the denominator shows the total number of equal parts in the whole.

Write a decimal and a fraction for the shaded part of the grid.

1.   **2.**

Write an equivalent decimal or fraction.

3. $\frac{4}{10}$ **4.** 0.57   **5.** 0.103

Set B, pages 280–282

Write $\frac{6}{15}$ as a decimal.

Write $\frac{6}{15}$ in simplest form: $\frac{6}{15} = \frac{2}{5}$

Find an equivalent fraction with a denominator of 10.

$\frac{4}{10}$ is four tenths, or 0.4

Remember you can multiply or divide to find an equivalent fraction.

Write each fraction as a decimal.

1. $\frac{3}{6}$ **2.** $\frac{1}{25}$ **3.** $\frac{3}{50}$

4. $\frac{15}{20}$ **5.** $\frac{8}{40}$ **6.** $\frac{19}{200}$

Set C, pages 284–286, 290–291

Show $6\frac{1}{4}$ on a number line.

Divide the distance from 6 to 7 into 4 equal parts. Draw a point at $6\frac{1}{4}$.

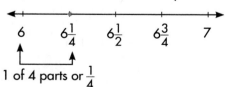

Show 7.7 on a number line. Divide the distance from 7 to 8 into 10 equal parts. Draw a point at 7.7.

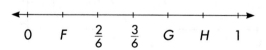

7 of 10 parts or 0.7

Remember tick marks are evenly spaced.

Name the fraction at each point.

0 F $\frac{2}{6}$ $\frac{3}{6}$ G H 1

1. G   **2.** F   **3.** H

Name the point for each decimal or mixed number.

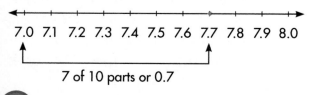

4. 5.47   **5.** $5\frac{3}{5}$ **6.** 5.42

Set D, pages 288–289

Write 1.7 as a mixed number.

Think: 1.7 is one and seven tenths

Since $0.7 = \frac{7}{10}$

$1.7 = 1\frac{7}{10}$.

Remember you can use a model and the word form of the number to help.

Write an equivalent decimal or mixed number.

1. $2\frac{3}{10}$ **2.** 5.41   **3.** $1\frac{18}{100}$

4. 4.375   **5.** $3\frac{8}{100}$ **6.** 25.6

Set E, pages 292–294

You can write a fraction, decimal, or percent to represent the part of the grid that is shaded.

33 out of 100 parts are shaded.

Fraction: $\frac{33}{100}$

Decimal: 0.33

Percent: 33 out of 100 parts, or 33%

Remember that a percent compares a number to 100.

Write each fraction or decimal as a percent. Draw a grid to help.

1. 0.22   **2.** $\frac{64}{100}$ **3.** 0.48

Write each percent as a fraction and a decimal.

4. 4%   **5.** 59%   **6.** 91%

Set F, pages 296–297

Margaret put blue, green, and orange book covers on her math, science, and spelling books. She did not put green on her math book. She put blue on her science book. What color cover did she put on her spelling book? Use reasoning to solve.

	Math	Science	Spelling
Blue	No	Yes	No
Green	No	No	Yes
Orange	Yes	No	No

Margaret put a green cover on her spelling book.

Remember you can use information from the problem to draw conclusions.

Use reasoning to solve.

1. One person gets off on the 5th, 6th, 8th, or 10th floor. When Larry gets off, he says good-bye to Terri, the only person still in the elevator. Evelyn is the first person off the elevator. Vivian gets off after Evelyn. If the elevator is going up, on what floor does each person get off?

Understanding and Finding Area

1 Al Lopez Park is one of the most visited city parks in Tampa, Florida. What polygon does the park look like? You will find out in Lesson 15-1.

2 The Pyramids at Giza were built by the Egyptians. What is the length of one of the sides of the Great Pyramid of Khufu? You will find out in Lesson 15-7.

Review What You Know!

Choose the best term from the box.

- rectangle
- square
- height
- perimeter

1. The ? is the distance around a shape.

2. A shape that has 4 right angles and 4 equal sides is called a ? .

3. A shape that has 4 right angles and 2 pairs of parallel sides is called a ? .

Multiplication Facts

Find each product.

4. 6×5 **5.** 7×9 **6.** 8×8

7. 7×4 **8.** 3×6 **9.** 5×4

10. 4×9 **11.** 8×5 **12.** 9×6

13. 8×4 **14.** 3×9 **15.** 8×7

Shapes

Identify each shape.

16.   **17.**   **18.**

19.   **20.**   **21.**

22.   **23.**   **24.**

25. Writing to Explain Explain how the shapes in Exercises 16–18 are alike and how they are different.

3 Where was the world's largest leather boot made? You will find out in Lesson 15-5.

4 Forty-two colorful murals are painted along the sides of buildings in Lake Placid, Florida. What is the area of this mural? You will find out in Lesson 15-3.

Topic Essential Questions

- What does area mean?
- What are different ways to find the area of a shape?

15-1

MA.4.G.3.1 Describe and determine area as the number of same-sized units that cover a region in the plane, recognizing that a unit square is the standard unit for measuring area.

Covering Regions
How do you measure area?

Emily made a collage in art class. She cut shapes to make her design.

What is the area of one of the shapes?

Area is <u>the number of square units needed to cover a region</u>.

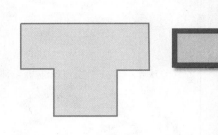

Guided Practice*

Do you know HOW?

For **1** and **2**, count to find the area. Tell if the area is exact or an estimate.

1.   2.

Do you UNDERSTAND?

3. If the first shape above had two more rows of 4 squares, what would the new area be?

4. Make two different shapes that each have an area of 16 square units.

Independent Practice

For **5** through **12**, count to find the area. Tell if the area is exact or an estimate.

5.   6. 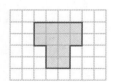   7. 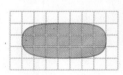   8.

9.   10.   11.   12.

Animated Glossary
www.pearsonsuccessnet.com

For another example, see Set A on page 324.

Count the square units inside the shape. The exact count is the area of the shape.

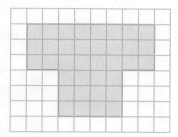

There are 36 squares inside the shape. The area of the shape is 36 square units.

Sometimes you can estimate the area.

Count the squares inside the shape.

There are about 27 squares inside the shape.

The area of the shape is about 27 square units.

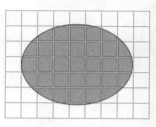

Problem Solving

13. Maggie bought 4 sketch pads and 2 boxes of art pencils. How much money did Maggie spend on her supplies?

$7 each

$4 per box

14. What would be a good estimate (in square units) of the green shaded area shown below?

A About 13

B About 10

C About 4

D About 2

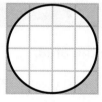

15. A bookstore is having a sale. When customers buy 2 books, they get another book free. If Pat buys 8 books, how many books will he get for free?

Critical THINKING

For **16** and **17**, use the map at the right.

16. Which is the best estimate for the area of Al Lopez Park?

F About 160 square units

G About 125 square units

H About 27 square units

I About 6 square units

17. Which polygon best describes the shape of Al Lopez Park?

THINK SOLVE EXPLAIN

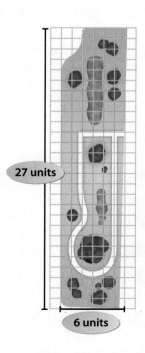

27 units

6 units

MA.4.G.3.1 Describe and determine area as the number of same-sized units that cover a region in the plane, recognizing that a unit square is the standard unit for measuring area.

Standard Units

How can you measure area using standard units of length?

Meg bought a poster to hang in her bedroom. What is the area of the poster?

2 ft

3 ft

Guided Practice*

Do you know HOW?

For **1** and **2**, count the square units. Then write the area.

1.
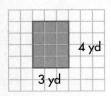
4 yd
3 yd

2.
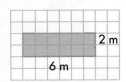
2 m
6 m

Do you UNDERSTAND?

3. If the poster above measured 2 yards by 3 yards, what would its area be?

4. Zoey has a picture on her wall that measures 8 inches by 10 inches. Use grid paper to find the area of the picture.

Independent Practice

For **5** through **10**, count the square units. Then write the area.

5.
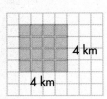
4 km
4 km

6.

3 ft
3 ft

7.
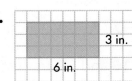
3 in.
6 in.

8.
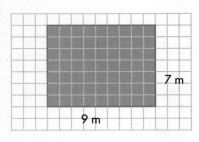
7 m
9 m

9.
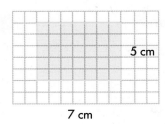
5 cm
7 cm

10.
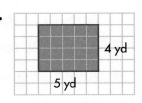
4 yd
5 yd

eTools
www.pearsonsuccessnet.com

For another example, see Set A on page 324.

Count the square units.

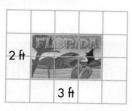

1 square unit = 1 square foot

The poster covers 6 of the square units.
The poster is measured in feet.

So, the area of the poster is 6 square feet.

Standard Units of Length and Area

Unit	Square Unit
inch (in.)	square inch
foot (ft)	square foot
yard (yd)	square yard
mile (mi)	square mile
centimeter (cm)	square centimeter
meter (m)	square meter
kilometer (km)	square kilometer

Problem Solving

For **11** through **13**, use the picture at the right.

11. Mr. Sanchez grows three types of vegetables in his garden. What is the area of the section he uses to grow cucumbers?

12. Mr. Sanchez leaves one section unused each growing season. What is the area of the garden that is being left unused this season?

13. What is the area in square feet of the garden that is being used to grow crops?

Mr. Sanchez's Garden

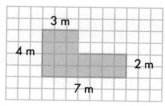

1 ☐ = 1 square foot

14. Erica drew the shape shown at the right. What is the area of the shape?

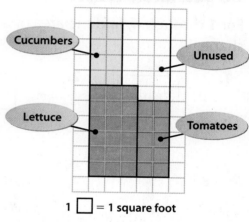

3 m
4 m
2 m
7 m

15. Brad says a square that has a length of 9 feet will have an area of 18 square feet. Why is Brad incorrect?

16. Amy bought 0.6 pound of green grapes and 0.42 pound of red grapes. Did she buy more green grapes or red grapes? Explain.

17. What is the area of the rectangle at the right?

    A 12 feet   **C** 12 square feet

    B 32 feet   **D** 32 square feet

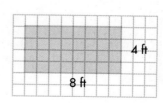

4 ft
8 ft

MA.4.G.3.2 Justify the
formula for the area of the
rectangle "area = base ×
height."

Area of Squares and Rectangles

How can you find the area of a figure?

A small can of chalkboard paint covers 40 square feet. Does Mike need more than one small can to paint one wall of his room?

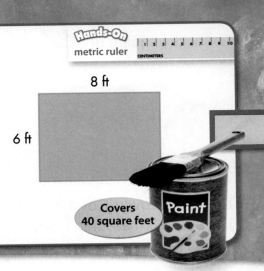

Hands-On
metric ruler

8 ft

6 ft

Covers
40 square feet

Paint

Guided Practice*

Do you know HOW?

For **1** through **4**, find the area of each shape.

1.
3 in.
7 in.

2.
4 m
5 m

3.
8 ft
14 ft

4.
9 cm

Do you UNDERSTAND?

5. Find the formula for the area of a rectangle using the terms *length* and *width*. Explain how you know.

6. Mike plans to paint another wall in his room blue. That wall measures 12 feet by 8 feet. How much area does Mike need to paint?

Independent Practice

Leveled Practice In **7** and **8**, measure the sides and find the area of each shape.

7.
cm
cm

8.
cm
cm

In **9** through **12**, find the area of each shape.

9.
9 ft
4 ft

10.
9 m
13 m

11.
7 in.
5 in.

12.
4 yd

*For another example, see Set B on page 324.

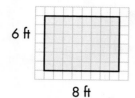
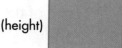
You can count the square units to find area.

6 ft

8 ft

There are 48 square units.

The area of Mike's wall is 48 square feet.

You can measure to find the base and height of the rectangle and use a formula to find area.

Area = base × height

$A = b \times h$
$A = 8 \times 6$
$A = 48$

(height)

(base)

Sometimes the terms *length* and *width* are used for *base* and *height*.

The area of Mike's wall is 48 square feet. He will need more than one small can of paint.

Problem Solving

13. Reasoning Jen's garden is 4 feet wide and has an area of 28 square feet. What is the length of the garden?

Critical THINKING

14. Diane drew a polygon with 4 sides. The polygon has 1 set of parallel sides. What type of polygon did Diane draw?

For **15** and **16**, use the mural shown at the right.

15. The mural at the right is called *Serene*. What is the area of the mural in square feet?

16. What is the perimeter of the mural?

A 22 feet

B 28 feet

C 44 feet

D 54 feet

Height = 8 feet
Base = 14 feet

17. Mr. Chen is putting tile down in his kitchen. The kitchen is 16 feet long and 8 feet wide. The tile costs $5 per square foot. How much will it cost Mr. Chen to tile his kitchen?

18. A store received 2 boxes of caps to sell. Each box contained the same number of caps. Four caps from one box were put on display. Twelve caps were still in the box. How many caps did the store receive?

eTools
www.pearsonsuccessnet.com

DIGITAL

Lesson
15-4

MA.4.G.3.2 Justify the formula for the area of the rectangle "area = base × height."

Solve a Simpler Problem

Janet wants to paint the door to her room. The shaded part of the figure shows the part of the door that needs paint.

What is the area of the part of the door that needs paint?

☐ = 1 square foot

Guided Practice*

Do you know HOW?

Solve. Use simpler problems.

1. Lil glued square beads on the shaded part of the frame. What is the area of the part she decorated?

☐ = 1 square inch

Do you UNDERSTAND?

2. What simpler problems did you use to solve Problem 1?

3. **Write a Problem** Write a problem that you can answer by solving a simpler problem. You may draw a picture to help.

Independent Practice

For **4** through **8**, solve. Use simpler problems.

4. Reg wants to put tiles on a wall. The shaded part of the figure shows the part that needs tiles. What is the area of the shaded part?

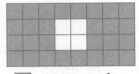

☐ = 1 square foot

Stuck? Try this....

- What do I know?
- What am I asked to find?
- What diagram can I use to help understand the problem?
- Can I use addition, subtraction, multiplication, or division?
- Is all of my work correct?
- Did I answer the right question?
- Is my answer reasonable?

For another example, see Set C on page 324.

I can solve simpler problems.

I can find the area of the whole rectangle and then the area of the square.

Then I can subtract to find the area of the shaded part.

<u>Area of the whole rectangle</u>
7 rows with 5 squares in each row
$7 \times 5 = 35$

<u>Area of the square</u>
3 rows with 3 squares in each row
$3 \times 3 = 9$

<u>Subtract</u>
$35 - 9 = 26$

The area of the part of the door that needs paint is 26 square feet.

5. Jim wants to tile the floor. The shaded part of the figure shows the part of the floor that needs tiles. What is the area of the shaded part?

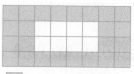

☐ = 1 square meter

6. Dan wants to paint the bottom of a pool. The shaded part of the figure shows the part that needs paint. What is the area of the shaded part?

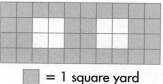

☐ = 1 square yard

7. Macy drew two designs. How much greater is the area of the yellow figure than the area of the green figure?

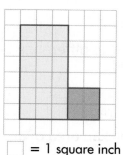

☐ = 1 square inch

8. Mr. Eli grows vegetables in different fields on his farm. What is the total area of the corn and bean fields?

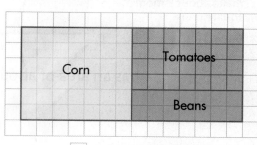

Corn
Tomatoes
Beans

☐ = 1 square meter

9. Neva built these figures using toothpicks. If she continues the pattern, how many toothpicks in all will she use for the 4th figure? the 5th figure?

Critical THINKING

1st figure

2nd figure

3rd figure

MA.4.G.3.3 Select and use appropriate units, both customary and metric, strategies, and measuring tools to estimate and solve real-world area problems.

Area of Irregular Shapes

Hands-On
metric ruler

How can you find the area of an irregular figure?

Mr. Fox is covering a miniature golf course hole with artificial grass. How many 1-foot squares of carpet will Mr. Fox need to cover the miniature golf course hole?

1-foot square of carpet

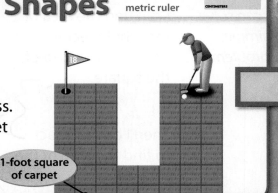

Another Example **How can you estimate area?**

Some shapes contain partial square units.

Estimate the area of the trapezoid to the right.

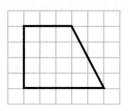

One Way

Count the whole square units. Then estimate the number of units made from combining partial squares.

There are 14 whole square units. The partial square units make about 2 more square units.

14 + 2 = 16

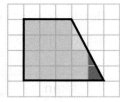

The trapezoid has an area of about 16 square units.

Another Way

Draw a rectangle around the trapezoid and find the rectangle's area.
$A = 4 \times 5 = 20$

Find the area outside the trapezoid but inside the rectangle.

There are about 4 square units not in the trapezoid.

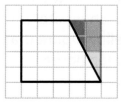

Subtract to find the difference between the two areas.

20 − 4 = 16

The trapezoid has an area of about 16 square units.

Explain It

1. Why is the answer of 16 square units considered an estimate?

2. Can the trapezoid be divided into rectangles to find the area?

DIGITAL
eTools
www.pearsonsuccessnet.com

Count the square units to find the area.

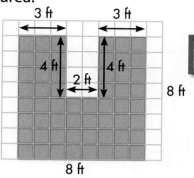

3 ft   3 ft
4 ft 2 ft 4 ft
8 ft
8 ft

The area of the golf course hole is 56 square feet.

Divide the hole into rectangles. Find the area of each rectangle and add.

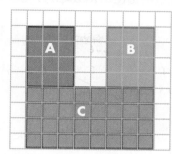

A   B

C

Rectangle A
$A = 4 \times 3 = 12$

Rectangle B
$A = 4 \times 3 = 12$

Rectangle C
$A = 4 \times 8 = 32$

Add the areas: $12 + 12 + 32 = 56$
The area of the golf course hole is 56 square feet.

Guided Practice*

Do you know HOW?

For **1** and **2**, find the area of each figure.

1.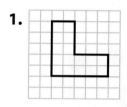

2.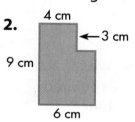

4 cm
3 cm
9 cm
6 cm

For **3** and **4**, estimate the area of each shape.

3.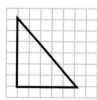

4.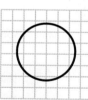

Do you UNDERSTAND?

5. Writing to Explain Could the golf course hole be divided into any other set of rectangles?

6. Suppose Mr. Fox bought 75 square feet of artificial grass. How much artificial grass will be left over?

7. Mr. Fox decided the area of the hole was too large. What would the new area of the hole be if he uses only rectangles A and C in the example above?

Independent Practice

For **8** and **9**, measure and find the area of each figure.

8.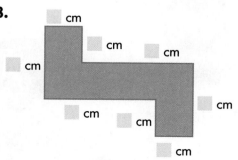

cm
cm
cm
cm
cm
cm
cm
cm

9.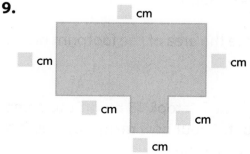

cm
cm
cm
cm
cm
cm

For **10** through **13**, estimate the area of each shape.

10.

11.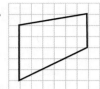

12.

13.

Problem Solving

14. Jared drew the figure to the right on grid paper. Which is NOT a way in which the figure could be divided to find the total area?

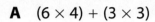

A $(6 \times 4) + (3 \times 3)$

B $(3 \times 7) + (2 \times 4) + (1 \times 4)$

C $(4 \times 6) + (3 \times 7)$

D $(2 \times 4) + (3 \times 3) + (4 \times 1) + (3 \times 4)$

15. Algebra Write an algebraic equation to represent the phrase "six times a number is 24." Solve the equation.

16. What fraction is colored blue?

F $\frac{2}{8}$ **G** $\frac{4}{8}$ **H** $\frac{8}{8}$ **I** $\frac{8}{4}$

For **17** through **20**, use the pictures at the right.

17. The world's largest leather boot was made in Red Wing, Minnesota. How tall is the work boot in inches?

 There are 12 inches in one foot.

Footprint of Work Boot

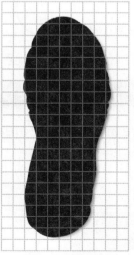

1 ☐ = 1 square foot

18. The sole of the boot weighs 1,150 pounds. How many pounds does the top part of the boot weigh?

19. Estimate the area of the footprint of the boot.

20. Estimation It took 13 months to complete the boot. About how many days did it take to complete the boot?

The world's largest leather work boot is 16 feet tall and weighs 2,300 pounds.

Finding Area with a Calculator

One Way Find the area of the figure shown at the right:

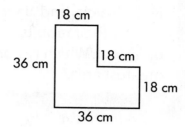

18 cm

36 cm

18 cm

18 cm

36 cm

Divide the figure into two rectangles.
Rectangle A is 18 cm by 18 cm.
Rectangle B is 18 cm by 36 cm.

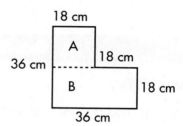

18 cm

36 cm

A

18 cm

B

18 cm

36 cm

Find the area of each rectangle and add.

Press: 18 ⊗ × 18 ⊗ ENTER =   18 ⊗ × 36 ⊗ ENTER =   324 ⊗ + 648 ⊗ ENTER =

Display: *324*   *648*   *972*

Another Way Find the area of the figure in one step.

Press: 18 ⊗ × 18 ⊗ + 18 ⊗ × 36 ⊗ ENTER =

Display: *972*

The area of the figure is 972 square centimeters.

Practice

Use a calculator to find the area of each figure.

1.

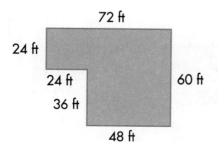

72 ft

24 ft

24 ft

36 ft

60 ft

48 ft

2.

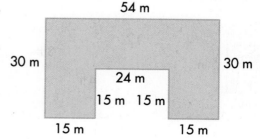

54 m

30 m

30 m

24 m

15 m 15 m

15 m

15 m

MA.4.G.3.2 Justify the formula for the area of the rectangle "area = base × height."

Different Area, Same Perimeter

Can rectangles have different areas but the same perimeter?

Beth, Marcia, and Nancy built a rectangular pen for their rabbits. Each pen has a perimeter of 12 feet. Which rectangular pen has the greatest area?

Hands-On
grid paper

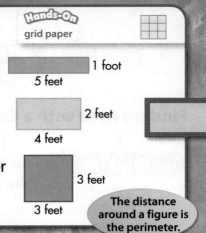

The distance around a figure is the perimeter.

Guided Practice*

Do you know HOW?

For **1** through **4**, use grid paper to draw two different rectangles with the given perimeter. Tell the dimensions and area of each rectangle. Circle the one that has the greater area.

1. 16 feet

2. 20 centimeters

3. 24 inches

4. 40 meters

Do you UNDERSTAND?

5. In the example above, what do you notice about the area of the rectangles as the shape becomes more like a square?

6. Alex is building a rabbit pen with 25 feet of fence. What rectangle can he build that has the greatest possible area?

Independent Practice

For **7** through **10**, use grid paper to draw two different rectangles with the given perimeter. Tell the dimensions and area of each rectangle. Circle the one that has the greater area.

7. 10 inches   **8.** 22 centimeters   **9.** 26 yards   **10.** 32 feet

For **11** through **14**, describe a different rectangle with the same perimeter as the one shown. Then tell which rectangle has the greater area.

11.
5 in.
4 in.

12.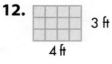
3 ft
4 ft

13.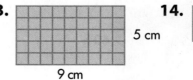
5 cm
9 cm

14.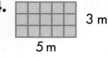
3 m
5 m

DIGITAL
eTools
www.pearsonsuccessnet.com

Beth's Pen

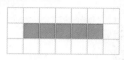

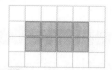

$P = 5 + 1 + 5 + 1$
$= 12$ feet

$A = b \times h$
$= 5 \times 1$
$= 5$ square feet

The pen has an area of 5 square feet.

Nancy's Pen

$P = 4 + 2 + 4 + 2$
$= 12$ feet

$A = b \times h$
$= 4 \times 2$
$= 8$ square feet

The pen has an area of 8 square feet.

Marcia's Pen

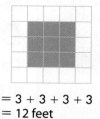

$P = 3 + 3 + 3 + 3$
$= 12$ feet

$A = s \times s$
$= 3 \times 3$
$= 9$ square feet

The pen has an area of 9 square feet.

The 3×3 rectangular pen has the greatest area.

Problem Solving

15. Reasoning Rectangles X and Y have the same perimeter. Without measuring or multiplying, how can you tell which rectangle has the greater area?

16. Suppose you arrange 48 counters into groups. The first group has 3 counters. Each group after that has 2 more counters than the group before. How many groups do you need to make to use all 48 counters?

17. Writing to Explain Karen drew a rectangle with a perimeter of 20 inches. The smaller side measured 3 inches. Karen said the longer side of the rectangle had to be 7 inches. Is she correct?

18. Marcus made the same number of free throws in each of 4 basketball games. If he made a total of 24 free throws, how many did he make in each game?

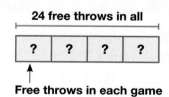

19. Which statement about the rectangles at the right is true?

  A They both have the same height.

  B They both have the same base.

  C They both have the same perimeter.

  D They both have the same area.

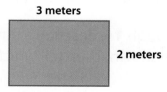

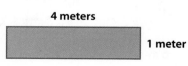

MA.4.G.3.2 Justify the formula for the area of the rectangle "area = base × height."

Same Area, Different Perimeter

Can rectangles have the same area but different perimeters?

In a video puzzle game, you have 16 castle tiles to make a rectangular castle and 16 water tiles for a moat. How can you completely surround the castle with water?

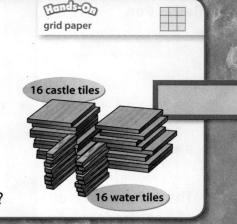

Hands-On
grid paper

16 castle tiles

16 water tiles

Guided Practice*

Do you know HOW?

For **1** through **4**, use grid paper to draw two different rectangles with the given area. Tell the dimensions and perimeter of each rectangle. Circle the one that has the smaller perimeter.

1. 6 square feet   **2.** 36 square yards

3. 64 square meters   **4.** 80 square inches

Do you UNDERSTAND?

5. In the example above, what do you notice about the perimeter of the rectangles as the shape becomes more like a square?

6. In Round 2 of the video puzzle game, you have 24 castle tiles. What is the least number of water tiles you will need to surround your castle?

Independent Practice

For **7** through **10**, use grid paper to draw two different rectangles with the given area. Tell the dimensions and perimeter of each rectangle. Circle the one that has the smaller perimeter.

7. 9 square inches   **8.** 18 square feet   **9.** 30 square meters   **10.** 32 square centimeters

For **11** through **14**, describe a different rectangle with the same area as the one shown. Then tell which rectangle has a smaller perimeter.

11.
4 m
6 m

12.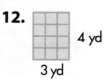
4 yd
3 yd

13.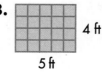
4 ft
5 ft

14.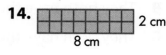
2 cm
8 cm

DIGITAL
eTools
www.pearsonsuccessnet.com

*For another example, see Set E on page 325.

Make rectangles that have an area of 16 square units. Find the perimeter of each rectangle.

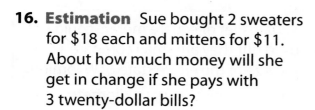

$A = b \times h$
$= 16 \times 1$
$= 16$ square units

$P = 16 + 1 + 16 + 1$
$= 34$ units

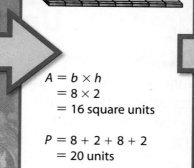

$A = b \times h$
$= 8 \times 2$
$= 16$ square units

$P = 8 + 2 + 8 + 2$
$= 20$ units

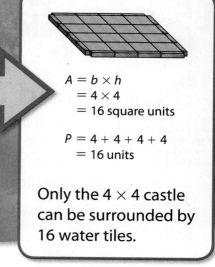

$A = b \times h$
$= 4 \times 4$
$= 16$ square units

$P = 4 + 4 + 4 + 4$
$= 16$ units

Only the 4×4 castle can be surrounded by 16 water tiles.

Problem Solving

15. Park School and North School cover the same area. In physical education classes, each student runs one lap around the school. At which school do the students have to run farther?

THINK SOLVE EXPLAIN

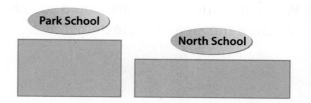

16. Estimation Sue bought 2 sweaters for $18 each and mittens for $11. About how much money will she get in change if she pays with 3 twenty-dollar bills?

17. Number Sense The perimeter of rectangle P is 12 feet. The perimeter of rectangle Q is 18 feet. Both rectangles have the same area. Find the area of each rectangle.

Critical THINKING

18. Geometry Which shape cannot be congruent to a rectangle?

A Square

B Rhombus

C Circle

D Quadrilateral

19. Ms. Fisher is using 64 carpet tiles to make a reading area in her classroom. Each tile is a square that measures 1 foot by 1 foot. What is the length and width of the rectangular area she can make with the smallest possible perimeter?

20. The length of the base of each side of the the Great Pyramid of Khufu is about 756 feet. If the Great Pyramid of Khufu is a square pyramid, what is the distance around the base of the pyramid?

MA.4.G.3.3 Select and use appropriate units, both customary and metric, strategies, and measuring tools to estimate and solve real-world area problems.

Selecting Appropriate Measurement Units and Tools

Which measurement unit and tool are the best choice for measuring the sides of a basketball court in order to find its area?

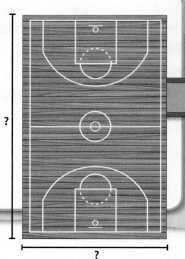

Other Examples

Which measurement units would you choose to measure the area of these items?

notebook

The state of Wyoming

WYOMING

Cheyenne

- Square feet or square meters are much larger than the notebook.
- Square inches or square centimeters are smaller than the notebook and would be better to measure the area of something small.

- Square feet or square meters could be used but they are small compared to the size of the entire state of Wyoming.
- Square miles or square kilometers are larger and would be better to measure the area of something large.

Guided Practice*

Do you know HOW?

For **1** and **2**, name the measurement unit you would use to measure the area of each item.

1. state of Florida   **2.** envelope

For **3** and **4**, name the measurement tool you would use to measure the area of each item.

3. classroom floor   **4.** textbook cover

Do you UNDERSTAND?

5. Give an example of an area that you would measure in square feet.

6. Give an example of an area that you would measure in square meters.

7. Give an example of a length that you would measure in inches or feet.

Independent Practice

For **8** through **11**, name the measurement unit you would use to measure the area of each item.

8. soccer field   **9.** large lake   **10.** cell phone   **11.** bedroom wall

For **12** through **15**, name the measurement tool you would use to measure the area of each item.

12. garage door   **13.** calculator   **14.** white board   **15.** postage stamp

Problem Solving

16. What unit of measurement would you use to measure the area of a national park?

17. Which measurement tool would you use to measure the length of a row boat? Explain your thinking.

THINK
SOLVE
EXPLAIN

18. Alexander is thinking of two whole numbers. The product of the two numbers is 28. Their difference is 3. What are the numbers?

19. Mary has 3 hats, 4 scarves, and 2 pairs of gloves. How many different choices of 1 hat, 1 scarf, and 1 pair of gloves does she have?

Critical
THINKING

20. Anna displayed 8 paintings in each of 4 rows. Which equation could NOT be used to find how many paintings she displayed in all?

A $4 \times 8 = x$ **C** $8 \div x = 4$

B $x \div 4 = 8$ **D** $8 + 8 + 8 + 8 = x$

21. There are 250 horses entered in a show. All but 95 are jumpers. How many jumpers are entered?

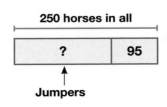

250 horses in all

?	95

Jumpers

1 A drawing of the floor in Curt's fort is shown below. What is the area of the fort's floor? (15-1)

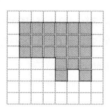

A. 23 square units

B. 30 square units

C. 41 square units

D. 64 square units

2 Howie used 20 feet of edging to design four different gardens. He wants the garden with the greatest area. Which design should Howie use? (15-6)

F.

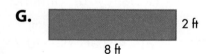

4 ft

6 ft

G.

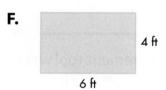

2 ft

8 ft

H.

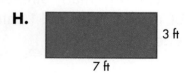

3 ft

7 ft

I.

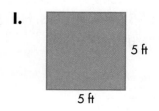

5 ft

5 ft

3 A diagram of Izzi's bedroom is shown below. What is the area of her room? (15-5)

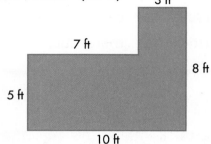

3 ft

7 ft

8 ft

5 ft

10 ft

A. 80 square feet

B. 59 square feet

C. 36 square feet

D. 33 square feet

4 A picnic table is 9 feet long and 3 feet wide. What is the area of the rectangular surface of the table? (15-3)

F. 12 square feet

G. 24 square feet

H. 27 square feet

I. 36 square feet

5 Pepper's dog pen is shown below. What is the area of the dog pen? (15-2)

5 m

4 m

A. 20 square meters

B. 18 square meters

C. 14 square meters

D. 9 square meters

6 Which measurement tool is the best choice for measuring the area of a football field? (15-8)

   F.   Inch ruler

   G.   Balance scale

   H.   Yardstick

   I.   Centimeter ruler

7 Jabari drew the shape shown below. What is the best estimate of its area in square units? (15-5)

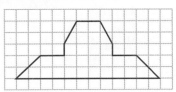

   A.   26 square units

   B.   30 square units

   C.   34 square units

   D.   50 square units

8 Ms. Walton wants to tile part of her kitchen wall. The shaded part of the shape below shows the part that she wants to tile. What is the area of the shaded part? (15-4)

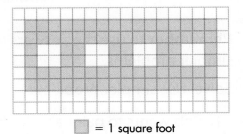

= 1 square foot

   F.   96 square feet

   G.   80 square feet

   H.   70 square feet

   I.   16 square feet

9 Which unit of measurement is best to use to measure the area of a large city? (15-8)

   A.   Square centimeters

   B.   Square meters

   C.   Square yards

   D.   Square miles

10 Ryan made a wooden frame for a rectanglar picture with side lengths of 4 inches and 10 inches. He wants to use the same amount of wood to make a frame for another rectangular picture frame with a different area. What could be the lengths of the sides of the picture? (15-6)

   F.   5 inches and 8 inches

   G.   7 inches and 4 inches

   H.   9 inches and 5 inches

   I.   6 inches and 4 inches

11 Sandra is covering a square-bulletin board with felt. The height of the bulletin board is 4 feet. What is the area of the bulletin board in square feet? (15-3)

12 Mrs. Gee has 24 carpet squares. Each square measures 1 foot by 1 foot. How many different rectangles could Mrs. Gee make with the carpet squares? Which of the rectangles would have the smallest perimeter? (15-7)

THINK
SOLVE
EXPLAIN

Set A, pages 304–307

Count to find the area.

The shape fully covers 9 squares and partially covers 7 squares. Each partial cover is about one half of a square.

So, the shape has an area of about 13 square units.

Remember you can count partial squares to estimate an area.

Count to find the area. Tell if the area is exact or an estimate.

1.   **2.**

Count the square units. Then write the area.

3. 4 in. 6 in. **4.** 5 m 5 m

Set B, pages 308–309

Use a formula to find the area of the rectangle.

Area = base × height

$A = b \times h$
$A = 5 \times 4$
$A = 20$ square feet

4 ft
5 ft

The area of the rectangle is 20 square feet.

Remember the terms *length* and *width* are sometimes used for *base* and *height*.

Find the area of each shape.

1. 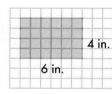 6 cm **2.** 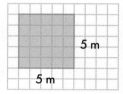 7 km 4 km

Set C, pages 310–311

Use simpler problems to find the area of the shaded part of the rectangle

Find the area of the whole rectangle.
$5 \times 7 = 35$

Find the area of the square.
$3 \times 3 = 9$

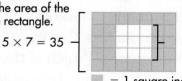
= 1 square inch

Subtract: $35 - 9 = 26$

The area of the shaded part of the rectangle is 26 square inches.

Remember to use the answers to the simpler problems.

Solve. Use simpler problems.

1. Rob wants to paint a wall. The shaded part of the wall is the part that needs to be painted. What is the area of the shaded part?

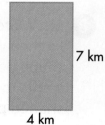
= 1 square foot

Set D, pages 312–314

You can divide a figure into rectangles to find the area.

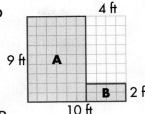

Find the area of each rectangle.

Rectangle A   Rectangle B
$A = 9 \times 6$ $A = 2 \times 4$
$A = 54$ $A = 8$

Add the partial areas: $54 + 8 = 62$ square feet

Remember you can count the square units to find the area.

Find each area.

1.
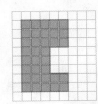

2.
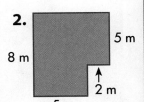

Set E, pages 316–319

Draw a different rectangle with the same perimeter as the one shown. Then find its area.

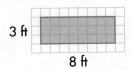

$P = 8 + 3 + 8 + 3$ $A = 8 \times 3$
$P = 22$ feet $A = 24$ square feet

A 7-foot-by-4-foot rectangle has the same perimeter.

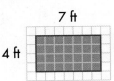

$P = 7 + 4 + 7 + 4$ $A = 7 \times 4$
$P = 22$ feet $A = 28$ square feet

Remember two rectangles can have the same area but different perimeters.

Draw two different rectangles each with the perimeter listed. Find the area of each rectangle, and tell which has the greater area.

1. $P = 24$ feet

2. $P = 40$ centimeters

Draw two different rectangles each with the area listed. Find the perimeter of each, and tell which one has the smaller perimeter.

3. $A = 64$ square feet

4. $A = 80$ square yards

Set F, pages 320–321

Choose an appropriate measurement unit and tool to measure the area of a napkin.

- Square feet or square meters are too large compared to the size of a napkin.

- Square inches or square centimeters are smaller and easier to use.

The best tool would be an inch ruler or a centimeter ruler.

Remember a good measurement unit is smaller than the amount to be measured but large enough to make it easy to measure.

Name the measurement unit and tool you would use to measure the area of each item.

1. door   **2.** index card

Topic 16

Two-Dimensional and Three-Dimensional Shapes

1 Eartha is the world's largest rotating scale model of Earth. Where is this model located? You will find out in Lesson 16-9.

2 How many lines of symmetry does Florida's Historic Capitol in Tallahassee have? You will find out in Lesson 16-5.

3

The Hall of Mirrors in Versailles, France, contains 357 mirrors. How long is the room? You will find out in Lesson 16-4.

4

In this M.C. Escher drawing, what are some of the ways these horses have been moved? You will find out in Lesson 16-3.

Topic Essential Questions

- How can angles be classified and drawn?
- What are ways to describe motions of shapes in the plane?
- How can 3-dimensional figures be shown and analyzed?

Review What You Know!

Vocabulary

Choose the best term from the box.

- line
- ray
- quadrilateral
- line segment
- rhombus
- triangle

1. A polygon with three sides is known as a ?.

2. A part of a line that has one endpoint is a ?.

3. A four-sided polygon in which opposite sides are parallel, and all sides are the same length is a ?.

4. A ? is a straight path of points that goes on without end in two directions.

Area

Find the area of each polygon.

5.

2 ft
8 ft

6.
6 m

Perimeter

Find the perimeter of each polygon.

7.
2 in.   2 in.
2 in.

8.
2 ft
1 ft   1 ft
2 ft

9.
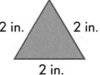
1 m
3 m
2 m
4 m

10.
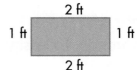
1 cm   1 cm
1 cm   1 cm
1 cm

11. **Writing to Explain** Describe when you might need to know the perimeter of something at home.

MA.4.G.5.1 Classify angles of two-dimensional shapes using benchmark angles (i.e. 45°, 90°, 180°, and 360°).

Classifying Angles

How do you classify angles using benchmark angles?

An angle is <u>a figure formed by two rays that have the same endpoint.</u> <u>That endpoint</u> is also known as the vertex of the angle. What is the angle measure of this section of the roller coaster?

vertex

Other Example

You can use the benchmark angles to estimate angle measures.

Tell which of the statements below best describes the angle shown.

A Less than 45 degrees

C Less than 90 degrees but greater than 45 degrees

B 45 degrees

D 90 degrees

The angle is less than 90 degrees but more than 45 degrees. The correct answer choice is **C**.

Guided Practice*

Do you know HOW?

For **1** through **4**, classify each angle as 45°, 90°, or 180°.

1.

2.

3.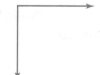

4.

Do you UNDERSTAND?

5. Writing to Explain How can you describe the angle below using benchmarks?

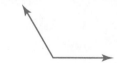

6. The roller coaster has a brace that forms a square corner. What is the angle measure of the angle formed by the brace?

*For another example, see Set A on page 360.

Angles are usually measured in units called **degrees**. The symbol ° indicates degrees. You can use benchmark angles to classify angles.

A 90° angle makes a square corner.

A 45° angle is an angle that is open half as much as a 90° angle.

A 180° angle is an angle that forms a straight line.

The roller coaster rises at an angle of 45 degrees.

This angle has a measure of 45 degrees, or 45°.

Independent Practice

For **7** through **9**, classify each angle as 45°, 90°, or 180°.

7.

8.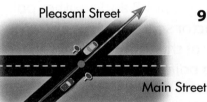
Pleasant Street
Main Street

9.

For **10** through **12**, describe the angle shown using benchmarks.

10.

11.

12.

Problem Solving

13. Amy drew a rectangle that has a length of 6 inches and a width of 4 inches. Describe a different rectangle with the same perimeter as Amy's rectangle. Then tell which rectangle has the greater area.
Critical Thinking

14. Algebra Write an equation to represent the phrase "three times a number is 15." Then solve the equation.

15. The hands of a clock show that the time is 6:00. How can you classify the angle formed by the hands on the clock?

16. Kim drew an angle that is less than 45 degrees. Which of the following could NOT be its measure?

   A 12°   **C** 41°

   B 35°   **D** 86°

MA.4.G.5.1 Classify angles
of two-dimensional shapes
using benchmark angles
(i.e. 45°, 90°, 180°, and 360°).

Drawing Angles
How do you draw angles?

A <mark>protractor</mark> is a <u>tool that is used to measure and draw angles</u>.

Use the protractor to draw an angle that measures 90°.

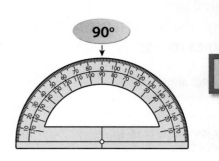

Other Example

Draw an angle with a measure of 360 degrees.

Draw a ray and label the endpoint B and another point on the ray A. Place the protractor so the middle of the bottom edge is over the endpoint of the ray. Find the 0° mark on the protractor and place a point. Label it C. Draw ray BC.

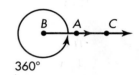

360°

Think The 0° and the 360° mark are the same because 360° is one full revolution around a circle. A 360° angle begins and ends with the same ray.

The measure of angle ABC is 360°.

Guided Practice*

Do you know HOW?

1. Draw an angle that is 45°.

2. Draw an angle that is less than 90°.

3. Draw an angle that is 180°.

Do you UNDERSTAND?

4. Trevor draws an angle that is a straight line. What is the measure of his angle?

5. **Writing to Explain** How can you use a protractor to draw a 180° angle?

Independent Practice

For **6** through **9**, draw each angle.

6. 180°   7. 90°   8. 360°   9. 75°

Animated Glossary
www.pearsonsuccessnet.com

*For another example, see Set A on page 360.

Draw a ray.

T   U

Label the endpoint T
and another point U.

Place the protractor so the middle of the bottom
edge is over the endpoint of the ray. Find the 90°
mark on the protractor and place a point. Label
it W. Draw ray TW.

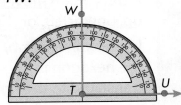

The measure of angle WTU is 90°. The angle could
also be named angle UTW or just angle T.

For **10** through **13**, draw each angle as described.

10. Draw an angle that is greater than
45° but less than 90°.

11. Draw an angle that is greater than
90° but less than 180°.

12. Draw an angle that is greater than
180° but less than 360°.

13. Draw an angle that is less than 45°.

Problem Solving

14. Jorge is reading a book containing
3 chapters. The first chapter is 20
pages long. The second chapter is 36
pages long. There are 83 pages in the
book. How many pages are in the
third chapter?

15. Mariah made 5 three-point shots in
her first game and 3 in her second
game. She also made 4 two-point
shots in each game and no one-point
free throws in either game. How
many total points did she score?

16. Look at the angle shown on the home plate used in
baseball. Which of the following best describes the angle?

A more than 90° but
less than 180°

C exactly 180°

B exactly 90°

D less than 90° but
more than 45°

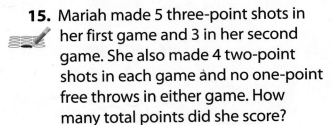

17. Draw a Picture The point where
two streets cross each other forms
four square corners. Draw a picture
of the streets crossing each other
and label each angle with the
number of degrees.

18. Draw an angle that is greater than
90° but less than 180°. Explain how
you used a protractor to draw the
angle.

THINK
SOLVE
EXPLAIN

MA.4.G.5.2 Identify and describe the results of translations, reflections, and rotations of 45, 90, 180, 270, and 360 degrees, including figures with line and rotational symmetry.

Translations

What is one way to move a figure?

A translation moves a figure up, down, left, or right.

In this honeycomb, the hexagon is translated to the right.

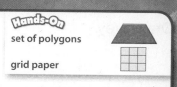

set of polygons

grid paper

Guided Practice*

Do you know HOW?

For **1** through **4**, tell if the figures are related by a translation.

1.
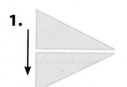

2.
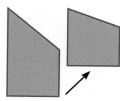

3.

4.
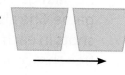

Do you UNDERSTAND?

5. Does a translation change a figure's shape or size?

6. Is moving a figure horizontally a translation?

7. Does moving a ruler across your desk affect its shape?

8. **Writing to Explain** Can a translation of a figure be done in many different directions?

Independent Practice

For **9** through **17**, tell if the figures are related by a translation. You may use grid paper or pattern blocks to decide.

Tip *Another name for translation is slide.*

9.
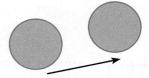

10.
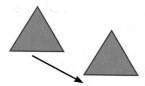

11.
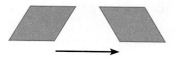

12.
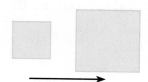

13.
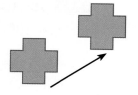

14.

Animated Glossary, eTools
www.pearsonsuccessnet.com

For another example, see Set B on page 360.

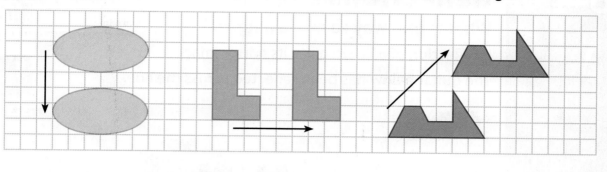

When a figure is translated, the size and shape of the figure do not change.

15.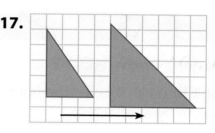

16.

17.

Problem Solving

For **18** and **19**, use the table at the right.

18. How many sticks would you need to make 10 kites?

19. If Scott made 2 kites and Jess made 5 kites, how many sticks did they use in all?

Critical
THINKING

Number of Kites	Number of Sticks
1	2
2	4
3	6

Data

20. Draw an angle that is 360°.

21. Which of the following best represents a translation?

    A An ice cube melting   **C** A windmill spinning

    B A plant growing   **D** A hockey puck sliding

22. In the M.C. Escher drawing at the right, which horse(s) are a translation of the horse labeled X?

    F Horse A   **H** Horses A and C

    G Horse B   **I** Horses A, B, and C

Symmetry Drawing 78 By M.C. Escher

23. On grid paper, draw a rectangle that moves to the right and then down. Is this a translation (slide)? Explain.

MA.4.G.5.2 Identify and describe the results of translations, reflections, and rotations of 45, 90, 180, 270, and 360 degrees, including figures with line and rotational symmetry.

Reflections

What is one way to move a figure?

A **reflection** of a figure gives its mirror image.

The guitar below has been reflected across the line.

Hands-On

set of polygons

grid paper

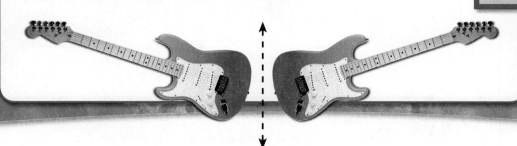

Guided Practice*

Do you know HOW?

For **1** through **4**, tell if the figures are related by a reflection.

1.   **2.**

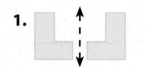 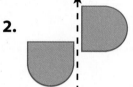

3.   **4.**

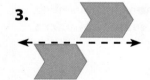 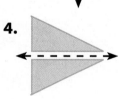

Do you UNDERSTAND?

5. Does a reflection change a figure's size or shape?

6. **Writing to Explain** Is the second triangle a reflection of the first triangle?

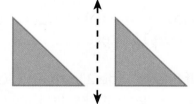

Independent Practice

For **7** through **12**, tell if the figures are related by a reflection. You may use grid paper or pattern blocks to decide.

Tip *Another name for reflection is flip.*

7.   **8.**   **9.**

 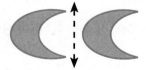 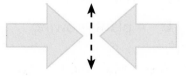

10.   **11.**   **12.**

 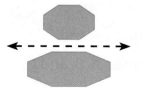

When a figure is reflected, the size and shape of the figure do not change.

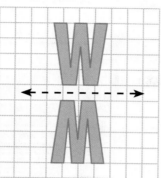 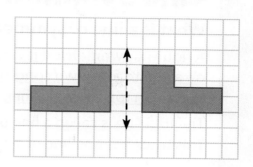

For **13** through **15**, draw the reflection (flip) of the given figure.

13.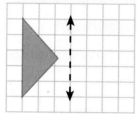

14.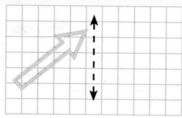

15.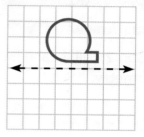

Problem Solving

16. In the drawing below, explain why the figure on the right is not a reflection of the figure on the left.

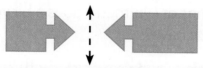

17. Draw an example of two figures that look the same when they are translated and when they are reflected.

18. Vanessa can run five miles in fifty minutes. If she keeps this pace, how many miles can she run in sixty minutes?

Critical THINKING

19. Number Sense How can you tell that you have made a mistake if you find that $418 \times 7 = 1,236$?

20. Which shows a pair of figures related by a reflection (flip)?

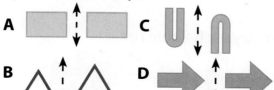

21. The Hall of Mirrors in the Palace of Versailles in France is 73 meters long. A guide posted at one end of the room walks in a straight line to the mirror at the other end, and then back to his post. How far in all did he walk?

? meters total

73	73

MA.4.G.5.2 Identify and
describe the results of
translations, reflections, and
rotations of 45, 90, 180, 270,
and 360 degrees, including
figures with line and
rotational symmetry.

Line Symmetry

Hands-On
grid paper

What is a line of symmetry?

A figure is symmetric if it can be folded
on a line to form two congruent halves
that fit on top of each other.

The fold line is called a line of symmetry.
This truck has one line of symmetry.

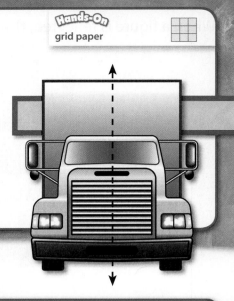

Guided Practice*

Do you know HOW?

For **1** and **2**, tell if each line is a line
of symmetry.

1. **2.**

For **3** and **4**, tell how many lines of
symmetry each figure has.

3. **4.**

Do you UNDERSTAND?

5. Do some figures have no lines
of symmetry?

6. How many lines of symmetry does
the figure below have?

7. Writing to Explain How many
lines of symmetry does a bicycle
tire have?

Independent Practice

For **8** through **11**, tell if each line is a line of symmetry.

8.  **9.**   **10.** **11.**

For **12** through **15**, tell how many lines of symmetry each figure has.

12. 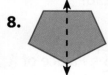 **13.** 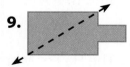 **14.**   **15.**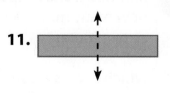

DIGITAL
Animated Glossary, eTools
www.pearsonsuccessnet.com

For another example, see Set C on page 361.

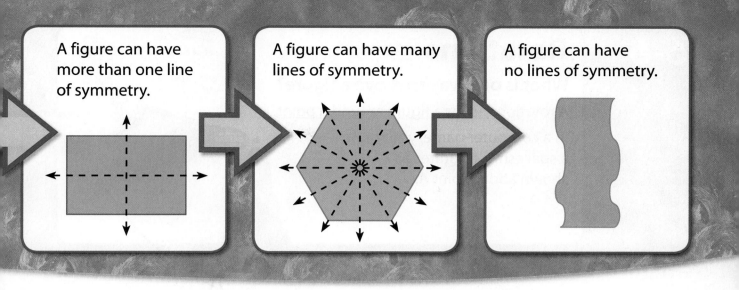

A figure can have more than one line of symmetry.

A figure can have many lines of symmetry.

A figure can have no lines of symmetry.

For **16** through **23**, trace each figure on grid paper, and draw lines of symmetry if you can.

16.

17.

18.

19.

20.

21.

22.

23.

Problem Solving

24. How many lines of symmetry does a scalene triangle have?

25. How many lines of symmetry does an isosceles triangle have?

26. Reasoning Vanessa drew a figure and said that it had an infinite number of lines of symmetry. What figure did she draw?

27. Draw a quadrilateral that does not have a line of symmetry.

28. Florida's Historic Capitol in Tallahassee has one line of symmetry. Use the picture at the right to describe where the line of symmetry is.

29. Write 5 capital letters that have at least one line of symmetry.

Critical THINKING

30. Exactly how many lines of symmetry does a square have?

    A None   **C** 4 lines

    B 2 lines   **D** 6 lines

MA.4.G.5.2 Identify and
describe the results of
translations, reflections, and
rotations of 45, 90, 180, 270,
and 360 degrees, including
figures with line and
rotational symmetry.

Rotations

What is one way to move a figure?

A rotation <u>moves a figure around a point</u>.

In a computer game, you rotate
a spaceship. It rotates as
shown about Point *A*.

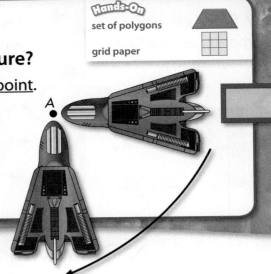

Hands-On

set of polygons

grid paper

Guided Practice*

Do you know HOW?

For **1** through **4**, tell if the figures are
related by a rotation.

1.

2.

3.

4.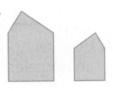

Do you UNDERSTAND?

5. Does a rotation change a figure's
size or shape?

6. Can every figure be rotated so that
it lands on top of itself?

7. If you rotate the arrow below
180 degrees about Point *X*,
in which direction
will the arrow
be pointing?

X

Independent Practice

For **8** through **13**, tell if the figures are related by a rotation.
You may use grid paper or pattern blocks to decide.

Tip *Another name for
rotation is turn.*

8.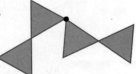

9.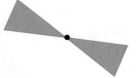

10.

11.

12.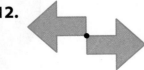

13.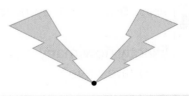

DIGITAL Animated Glossary, eTools
www.pearsonsuccessnet.com

For another example, see Set B on page 360.

When a figure is rotated, the size and shape of the figure do not change.

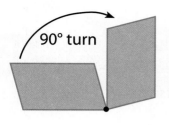
90° turn

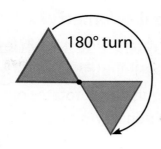
180° turn

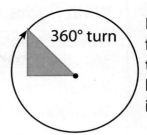
360° turn

In one full turn, the figure lands on itself.

For **14** through **16**, copy each figure on grid paper. Draw the figure rotated 90° to the right about the given point.

14.

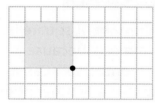

15.

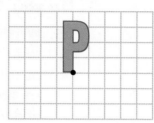

16.

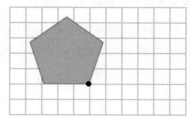

Problem Solving

17. Draw a Picture Jim says that a 180° turn of any figure is the same as a reflection of that figure. Do you agree with Jim's statement? Draw a picture to explain your reasoning.

Critical THINKING

18. What figure is formed when a triangle has rotated 90°?

  A Circle   **C** Rectangle

  B Square   **D** Triangle

19. The shape to the right shows a pattern of translations, reflections, and rotations. Describe each step.

For **20** through **22**, use the table at the right.

20. How much does one turtle cost?

21. Cal bought 1 chameleon and 2 hamsters. How much did he pay?

22. How much would it cost to buy 1 of each animal?

Animals	Price
Hamsters	3 for $27
Turtles	4 for $8
Chameleons	2 for $14

Lesson 16-7

MA.4.G.5.2 Identify and describe the results of translations, reflections, and rotations of 45, 90, 180, 270, and 360 degrees, including figures with line and rotational symmetry.

Rotational Symmetry

Hands-On
set of polygons

What is rotational symmetry?

When a figure can rotate onto itself in less than 360°, the figure has rotational symmetry.

If you rotate this figure 90°, it rotates onto itself. This figure has rotational symmetry.

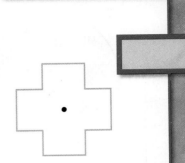

Guided Practice*

Do you know HOW?

For **1** through **4**, tell if the figure has rotational symmetry. Write yes or no.

1. 2.

3. 4.

Do you UNDERSTAND?

5. **Writing to Explain** A square has rotational symmetry because it can be rotated 90° onto itself. Can a square be rotated any other number of degrees onto itself? Explain.

6. Which figure can be rotated any number of degrees onto itself?

Independent Practice

In **7** through **14**, does the figure have rotational symmetry? Write yes or no. Give the least angle measure that will rotate the figure onto itself. You may use pattern blocks to help.

7.  8. 9. 10.

11. 12. 13. 14.

DIGITAL Animated Glossary, eTools
www.pearsonsuccessnet.com

340 *For another example, see Set D on page 361.*

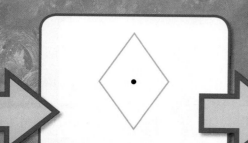

This figure has rotational symmetry. It must be rotated 180° to land on itself.

This figure has rotational symmetry. It can be rotated 45° to land on itself.

This figure does not have rotational symmetry. It must be rotated 360° to land on itself.

Problem Solving

For **15** and **16**, use the table to the right.

15. Valerie has 16 yards of fencing material to build a dog run. She wants to put the fence around a rectangular area. Complete the table to the right to find the possible ways Valerie can build the dog run.

Critical THINKING

Side A Length	Side B Length	Area
1 yd		7 sq. yd
2 yd		
3 yd		
4 yd		

16. Which area is the largest? What is another name for this shape?

17. There are 48 boxes in a warehouse. If there are 22 packages of paper in each box, how many packages of paper are there in the warehouse?

? packages of paper

22   48 boxes →

↑
Packages of paper in each box

18. Which capital letter below has rotational symmetry?

A   N   C   T

B   Y   D   E

19. Determine if the following statement is true or false. Explain your reasoning.

A figure with no lines of symmetry will not have rotational symmetry.

20. The Megaray Kite has an area of almost 1,500 square meters. Suppose the wind suddenly changes and the kite moves 25 meters east. Has the shape or size of the kite changed? Explain.

MA.4.G.5.2 Identify and describe the results of translations, reflections, and rotations of 45, 90, 180, 270, and 360 degrees, including figures with line and rotational symmetry.

Tessellations

What is a tessellation?

A tessellation is a <u>repeating pattern of shapes without any gaps or overlaps</u>. There are many shapes you can use to make a tessellation.

Can all shapes be used to make a tessellation?

Another Example **How can shapes be combined to make a tessellation?**

Start with a square and an equilateral triangle.

Use reflection to get adjacent figures.

Rotate 180°.

Finally, use a translation to continue the pattern.

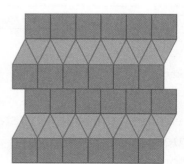

Explain It

1. How can you tell if two shapes can be used together to make a tessellation?

Squares can make a tessellation. There are no gaps or overlaps.

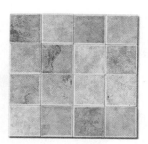

There are gaps in the pattern below.

Not all shapes make a tessellation.

Guided Practice*

Do you know HOW?

For **1** and **2**, use each polygon to draw a tessellation.

1.
hexagon

2.
rectangle

For **3** and **4**, tell if each shape tessellates. Write yes or no. If yes, trace the shape and draw the tessellation.

3.

4.

Do you UNDERSTAND?

5. Can the trapezoid shown below be used alone to make a tessellation? Explain why or why not.

6. Reasoning Were translations, reflections, or rotations used to make the square tessellation shown above? Explain your answer.

Independent Practice

For **7** through **10**, use each polygon to draw a tessellation.

7.
square

8.
right triangle

9.
parallelogram

10.
equilateral triangle

For **11** through **14**, tell if each shape tessellates. Write yes or no. If yes, trace the shape and draw the tessellation.

11.

12.

13.

14.

*For another example, see Set E on page 362.

For **15** through **17**, describe the transformation(s) used to tessellate the shapes.

15.

16.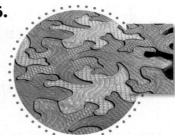

17.

18. **Science** The diagram below shows the percent of Earth's atmosphere that is made up of oxygen. Write a fraction, decimal, and percent to represent this.

19. **Reasoning** Julio drew two **Critical Thinking** pentagons. Which one tessellates?

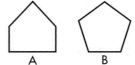

A   B

20. **Draw a Picture** Start with a square. Draw a pattern that will tessellate using at least two shapes.

21. If a website that sells sports equipment gets 675 visitors a day, how many visitors will the website get in one week?

Tip *There are 7 days in one week.*

22. Describe how the two tessellations at the right are alike and how they are different.

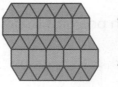
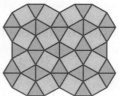

23. Which shape has fewer than two lines of symmetry?

    A Circle

    B Square

    C Rectangle

    D Trapezoid

24. Which shape tessellates?

F   H

G   I

Algebra Connections

Numerical Patterns

Remember that a numerical pattern is a sequence of numbers that occurs in some predictable way. Numerical patterns can be based on one or more operations.

For **1** through **6**, find a pattern and the next three numbers in each sequence, using that pattern.

> **Example:** Find a pattern and the next three numbers in the sequence 2, 3, 6, 7, 14, 15, 30, …
>
> **Think** $2 + 1 = 3, 3 \times 2 = 6, 6 + 1 = 7,$
> $7 \times 2 = 14, 14 + 1 = 15, 15 \times 2 = 30.$
>
> The pattern is add 1, multiply by 2. The next three numbers are 31, 62, 63.

1. 7, 15, 23, 31, 39, …

2. 50, 44, 38, 32, 26, …

3. 12, 22, 20, 30, 28, 38, 36, …

4. 65, 60, 63, 58, 61, 56, 59, …

5. 2, 4, 8, 16, 32, …

6. 3, 7, 15, 31, …

7. 1, 3, 6, 10, …
What is the 8th number in this pattern?

8. 75, 72, 69, 66, …
What is the 7th number in this pattern?

9. 1, 4, 9, 16, …
What is the nth number in this pattern?

- -

10. The table shows Jamie's savings account balances. If he continues his pattern of spending and saving, how much money will Jamie have in his bank on March 15?

March	Day 1	Day 2	Day 3	Day 4	Day 5
Amount	$15	$13	$18	$16	$21

11. Justyne sets her alarm clock for 5:45 A.M. on school days. Hitting "snooze" lets her sleep 3 more minutes before the alarm rings again. Today, Justyne hit "snooze" 4 times. What time did she finally wake up?

12. A train starts with 35 passengers on board. It makes 7 stops before it arrives in the city. At the first stop, 10 new passengers get on board. At the next stop, 6 passengers get off. This pattern continues all the way into the city. How many passengers are on the train when it arrives in the city?

MA.4.G.5.3 Identify and build a three-dimensional object from a two-dimensional representation of that object and vice versa.

3-Dimensional Shapes

How can you describe and classify solids?

A solid figure has three dimensions: length, width, and height.

Solids can have curved surfaces.

Sphere   Cylinder   Cone

Other Examples

Flat surfaces of solids that have some curved surfaces are called bases.

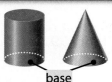

base

Guided Practice*

Do you know HOW?

For **1** and **2**, identify each solid.

1.

2.

Do you UNDERSTAND?

3. Which solid is composed of four triangular faces and one square face?

4. How many bases does a cone have?

Independent Practice

Leveled Practice For **5** through **7**, copy and complete the table.

	Solid	Faces	Edges	Vertices	Shape(s) of Faces
5.	Rectangular prism	■	■	■	6 rectangles
6.	Cube	6	■	■	■
7.	Rectangular pyramid	■	8	■	■

Animated Glossary
www.pearsonsuccessnet.com

*For another example, see Set F on page 362.

Some solids have all flat surfaces. They are named by referring to their faces.

face-flat surface of a solid

vertex-point where 3 or more edges meet (plural: vertices)

edge-line segment where 2 faces meet

rectangular prism
6 rectangular faces

cube
6 square faces

triangular prism
2 triangular faces
3 rectangular faces

rectangular pyramid
1 rectangular face
4 triangular faces

square pyramid
1 square face
4 triangular faces

Problem Solving

For **8** through **11**, tell what solid figure best represents each object.

8.

9.

10.

11.

12. Todd's father offered to drive some members of the soccer team to a game. His car can hold 4 players. He drives 10 players from his home to the game. How many one-way trips must he make if he stays to watch the game?

Critical THINKING

TIP *Draw a picture to show each one-way trip.*

13. A square pyramid has 1 square face and 5 vertices. How many triangular faces does a square pyramid have?

14. Which number is NOT between 0.5 and $\frac{3}{4}$ on a number line?

A $\frac{65}{100}$ **B** 0.6 **C** $\frac{4}{5}$ **D** 0.7

15. Eartha is located in Yarmouth, Maine. Identify the solid that best describes Eartha.

16. In one soccer season, the Cougars scored six times as many goals as Jason made all season. Jason scored 12 goals. How many goals did the Cougars score throughout the season?

? goals

| Cougars | 12 | 12 | 12 | 12 | 12 | 12 | 6 times as many |

| Jason | 12 |

Lesson
16-10

MA.4.G.5.3 Identify and build a three-dimensional object from a two-dimensional representation of that object and vice versa.

Nets

How can you use a two-dimensional shape to represent a three-dimensional solid?

A **net** <u>is a pattern that can be used to make a solid</u>. You can open up a three-dimensional object to show the net.

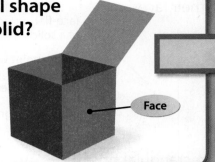

Face

Guided Practice*

Do you know HOW?

For **1** and **2**, name the solid that can be made.

1.
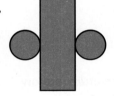

2.
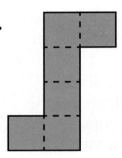

Do you UNDERSTAND?

3. Explain why the net for a cube has six squares.

4. Why does the net for a triangular prism have two triangles and three rectangles?

5. Draw a different net for the cube in the example above.

Independent Practice

For **6** through **9**, name the solid that can be made.

6.
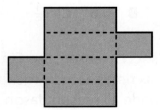

7.
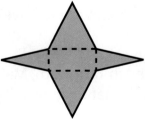

8.
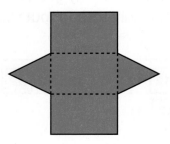

9.
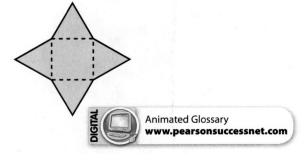

Animated Glossary
www.pearsonsuccessnet.com

DIGITAL

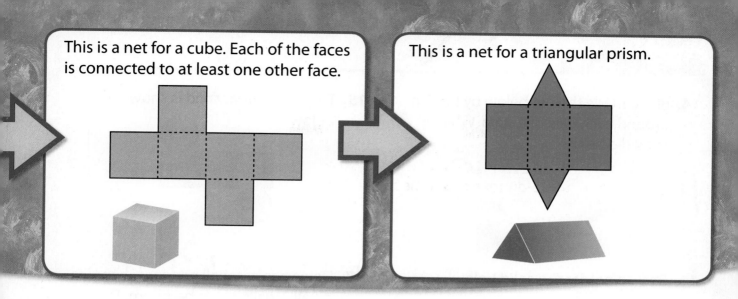

This is a net for a cube. Each of the faces is connected to at least one other face.

This is a net for a triangular prism.

For **10** through **13**, trace each net and cut it out. Fold and tape it together to make a solid. The dotted lines shown are the fold lines. Name the solid.

10.

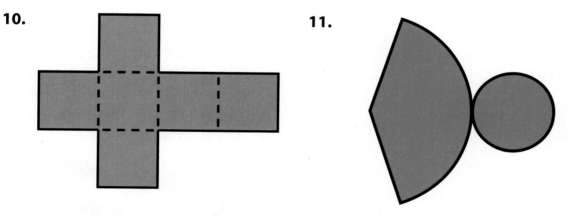

11.

12.

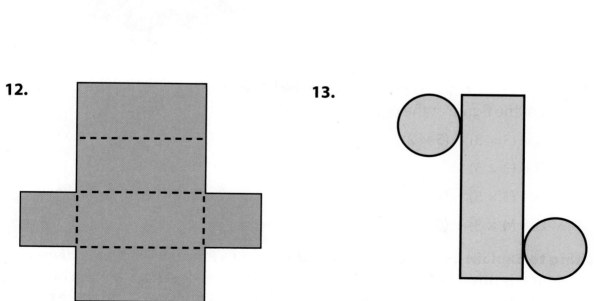

13.

14. Bruce made the net below by tracing around each face of a solid. What solid did he use?

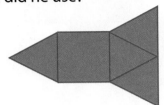

15. The net of what solid is shown below?

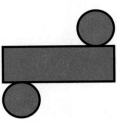

16. Draw a net for the solid below.

17. Helga has baseball pennants hanging on all 4 walls of her bedroom. There are 7 pennants on each wall. How many pennants are there?

18. What is the name of the quadrilateral shown below?

  A Parallelogram   **C** Rhombus

  B Rectangle   **D** All of the above

19. Florida's state insect is the zebra longwing butterfly, shown below. How many lines of symmetry does the butterfly have? Does it have rotational symmetry?

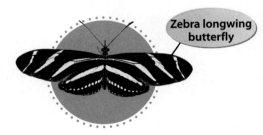

Zebra longwing butterfly

20. **Think About the Process** Which is NOT a way in which the total area of the figure at the right can be found?

  F $(1 \times 7) + (3 \times 3) + (5 \times 2)$

  G $(2 \times 6) + (3 \times 5)$

  H $(1 \times 7) + (3 \times 5) + (2 \times 2)$

  I $(1 \times 2) + (4 \times 3) + (6 \times 2)$

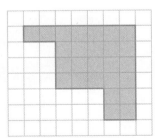

21. **Writing to Explain** Peg says that the net for any prism will always include rectangles. Is she correct? Explain why or why not.

22. **Draw a Picture** Find two different rectangles that have an area of 24 square centimeters. Then give the dimensions and perimeter of each rectangle. Use grid paper or draw a picture to help you solve.

♪♪ Music

Different musical instruments make different sounds. The shape of an instrument can affect how it sounds. Use the table at the right to answer **1–4**.

1. Which instrument is made up of a long, narrow rectangular prism and a short cylinder?

2. Which of the percussion instruments has a cylinder shape?

3. Which instrument has the shape of a 3-sided figure?

4. What solid does the recorder look like?

5. The instrument that makes the sound with the greatest number of decibels is the loudest. Which instrument in the table below can make the loudest sound?

Musical Instruments	
Name of Instrument	**Group of Instruments**
Banjo	String
Drum	Percussion
Recorder	Woodwind
Triangle	Percussion

Data

Instrument	Maximum Loudness (in decibels)
Trumpet	95
Cymbal	110
Bass drum	115
Piano	100

6. **Strategy Focus** Solve. Use the strategy Work Backward.

Elian plays three instruments. The drum weighs 5 pounds more than the guitar. The trumpet weighs 5 pounds less than the guitar. The trumpet weighs 3 pounds. How many pounds does the drum weigh?

MA.4.G.5.3 Identify and build a three-dimensional object from a two-dimensional representation of that object and vice versa.

Perspectives

How can you get information about a solid from different perspectives?

You can think about solids from different perspectives. What would this solid look like from the front? From the side? From the top?

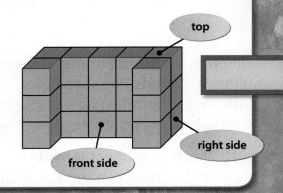

top

right side

front side

Guided Practice*

Do you know HOW?

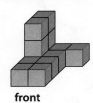

front

1. Draw the top view of the solid above.

2. Draw a side view of the solid above.

3. Draw a front view of the solid above.

Do you UNDERSTAND?

4. How many blocks make up the 3-dimensional shape above?

5. How many blocks are not visible from the top view of the 3-dimensional shape above?

6. How many blocks are not visible in the front view of the 3-dimensional shape to the left?

Independent Practice

For **7** through **12**, draw front, right, and top views of each stack of unit blocks.

7.

front

8.
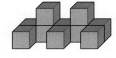

front

9.

front

10.
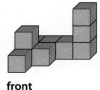

front

11.
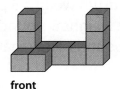

front

12.
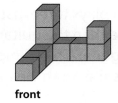

front

*For another example, see Set H on page 363.

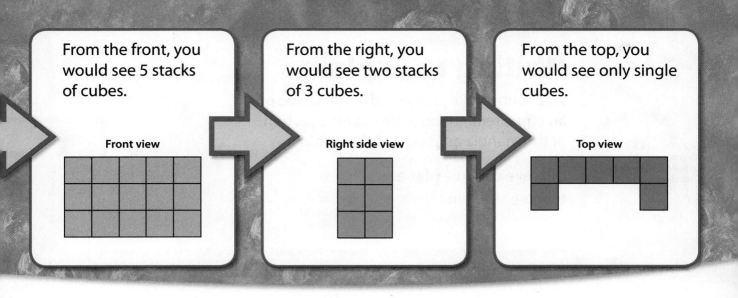

From the front, you would see 5 stacks of cubes.

Front view

From the right, you would see two stacks of 3 cubes.

Right side view

From the top, you would see only single cubes.

Top view

Problem Solving

13. How many edges does this rectangular prism have?

   A 4 edges   **C** 8 edges

   B 6 edges   **D** 12 edges

14. The net of what solid is shown below?

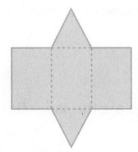

15. Which choice below gives the number of faces, edges, and vertices of a cube?

   F 6, 12, 8   **H** 4, 5, 6

   G 6, 8, 12   **I** None of the above

16. Writing to Explain What would the top view of the cylinder shown below look like? Explain how you know.

THINK
SOLVE
EXPLAIN

Front

For **17** through **19**, use the solid at the right.

17. Draw the front, right, and top views of the solid.

18 Yamir said that the front and top views are identical. Do you agree? Explain why or why not.

Critical THINKING

19. How many blocks are not visible in the top view of the solid?

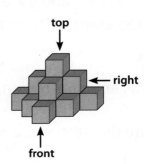

top

right

front

MA.4.A.2.4 Compare and order decimals, and estimate fraction and decimal amounts in real-world problems.

Writing to Explain

Jake found a piece of wood in the shape of an equilateral triangle. He cut off a section of the triangle as shown to the right.

Did Jake cut off $\frac{1}{3}$ of the triangle? Explain.

Section of wood cut off

Another Example

Erin says that $\frac{1}{2}$ is always the same amount as $\frac{2}{4}$. Matthew says that $\frac{1}{2}$ and $\frac{2}{4}$ are equivalent fractions, but they could be different amounts. Which student is correct? Explain.

The circles are the same size.

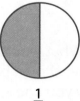 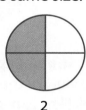

$\frac{1}{2}$ $\frac{2}{4}$

The amounts are the same.

The circles are not the same size.

$\frac{1}{2}$ $\frac{2}{4}$

The amounts are different.

Matthew is correct. $\frac{1}{2}$ and $\frac{2}{4}$ are equivalent fractions, but they could represent different amounts.

Explain It

1. When will amounts of $\frac{1}{2}$ and $\frac{2}{4}$ be equal?

2. When are the fractional amounts $\frac{3}{6}$ and $\frac{2}{4}$ not equal?

Read & Understand

What do I know?

The triangle is an equilateral triangle. One piece is cut off.

What am I asked to find?

Is the section that is cut off $\frac{1}{3}$ of the triangle?

Plan

Use words, pictures, numbers, or symbols to write a math explanation.

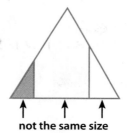

not the same size

$\frac{1}{3}$ means that the whole has to be divided into 3 equal parts. The parts have to be the same size.

The shaded section is not $\frac{1}{3}$ of the triangle.

Guided Practice*

Do you know HOW?

1. A board is cut into 12 equal pieces. How many pieces together represent $\frac{3}{4}$ of the board? Explain how you arrived at your answer.

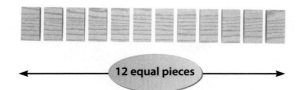

12 equal pieces

Do you UNDERSTAND?

2. Copy and draw the triangle above. Shade in $\frac{1}{3}$ of the triangle.

3. **Write a Problem** Write a problem that would use the figure below as part of its explanation.

Independent Practice

Write to explain.

4. Devon and Amanda knit the same size scarf. Devon's scarf is $\frac{3}{5}$ yellow. Amanda's scarf is $\frac{3}{4}$ yellow. How can you use a picture to show whose scarf is more yellow?

5. The school newspaper has a total of 18 articles and ads. There are 6 more articles than ads. How many articles and ads are there? Explain how you found your answer.

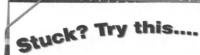

Stuck? Try this....

- What do I know?
- What diagram can I use to help understand the problem?
- Can I use addition, subtraction, multiplication, or division?
- Is all of my work correct?
- Did I answer the right question?
- Is my answer reasonable?

---

6. **Science** Look at the cell pattern below. Explain how the number of cells changes as the number of divisions changes.

1 cell   1st division   2nd division   3rd division

7. **Algebra** Look at the number sentences below. What numbers replace ⬤, ▲, and ⬛? Explain your answer.

▲ + ⬛ = 18

⬤ + ▲ = 20

⬛ + ⬛ = 14

8. **Geometry** Three streets intersect with one another. East Street runs horizontally, North Street runs vertically and Fourth Street runs diagonally and intersects both East Street and North Street. What geometric figure do the three streets form?

Use the data at the right for problems **9** and **10**.

9. How can you find the number of cards Linda has in her collection?

10. **Critical THINKING** George has 100 rookie cards in his collection. How can you find the number of pictures in the pictograph that represent George's rookie cards?

Baseball Card Collections

George	🂠🂠🂠🂠🂠🂠🂠🂠🂠🂠
Becky	🂠🂠🂠🂠🂠🂠🂠🂠🂠🂠🂠
Trent	🂠🂠🂠🂠🂠🂠🂠🂠🂠🂠🂠🂠🂠
Linda	🂠🂠🂠🂠🂠🂠🂠🂠🂠🂠🂠

Each 🂠 = 25 cards

Think About the Process

11. Janet gets $25 a week to buy lunch at school. She spends $4 each day and saves the rest. Which expression can be used to find how much money Janet will save at the end of the 5 days?

A (4 × 5) + 25   **C** (25 − 5) + 4

B 25 + (5 − 4)   **D** 25 − (5 × 4)

12. During recess, Rachel played on the bars and swings. She spent 10 minutes on the bars and twice as long on the swings. Which expression can be used to find how much time she spent on the equipment?

F 10 − (2 + 10)   **H** (10 + 2) − 10

G 10 + (2 × 10)   **I** (10 ÷ 2) + 10

Find each product. Estimate to check
if the answer is reasonable.

1.	923 × 7	2.	222 × 168	3.	6,204 × 18	4.	32 × 17

5.	606 × 28	6.	451 × 23	7.	4,972 × 18	8.	5,126 × 132

Find each difference. Estimate to check
if the answer is reasonable.

9.	9,000 − 258	10.	6,932 − 2,784	11.	485 − 396	12.	4,001 − 3,873	13.	6,249 − 123

14. 2,060 − 793   **15.** 401 − 96   **16.** 6,920 − 760

17. 3,750 − 2,950   **18.** 888 − 599   **19.** 8,898 − 7,361

Error Search Find each answer that is not correct.
Write it correctly and explain the error.

20.	4,859 + 745 5,604	21.	262 × 15 1,572	22.	206 × 4 832	23.	7,502 − 2,823 10,325	24.	2,222 × 5 11,110

Number Sense

Estimating and Reasoning Write whether each
statement is true or false. Explain your answer.

25. The sum of 595 + 268 is 5 less than 868.

26. The product of 82 and 209 is less than 16,000.

27. The product of 3 and 206 is 18 more than 600.

28. The difference of 500 − 198 is more than 300.

29. The sum of 1,819 + 2,245 will NOT be more than 4,000.

1 Dan drew the figure below. Exactly how many lines of symmetry does the figure have? (16-5)

A. 1

B. 2

C. 3

D. 4

2 Which figure below has rotational symmetry? (16-7)

F.

G.

H.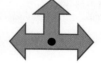

I.

3 Which shape cannot be used to make a tessellation? (16-8)

A. Equilateral triangle

B. Circle

C. Rectangle

D. Square

4 Which of the following represents a translation? (16-3)

F. Turning over a pancake

G. Seeing yourself in a mirror

H. Moving a checker diagonally on a checker board

I. A dog rolling over

5 Which of the following angles can be classified as 45°? (16-1)

A.

B.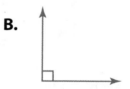

C.

D.

6 Lily is using a protractor to draw angle *ABC*. If angle *ABC* is 45°, which is NOT a step she should follow to draw the angle? (16-2)

F. Draw a ray and label the endpoint *B* and another point *C*.

G. Place the middle of the protractor at endpoint *B*.

H. Place a point at the 45° mark and label it *A*.

I. Draw ray *AC*.

7 Which letter of the alphabet is a reflection of the letter b? (16-4)

   A. The letter d or the letter p

   B. The letter d or the letter q

   C. Only the letter p

   D. Only the letter d

8 Which view is shown of this solid? (16-11)

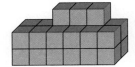 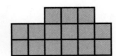

Solid   View

   F. Front view

   G. Top view

   H. Side view

   I. The view is not of this solid.

9 Which statement would NOT be used in an explanation of how the drawing shows that $\frac{2}{3} = \frac{4}{6}$? (16-12)

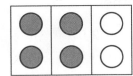

   A. 2 of the 3 rectangles are filled with shaded circles.

   B. 4 out of the 6 rectangles are shaded.

   C. Both $\frac{2}{3}$ and $\frac{4}{6}$ describe the part that is shaded.

   D. In the rectangles, 4 out of the 6 circles are shaded.

10 What is the new position of this shape after it makes a 180° rotation? (16-6)

   F.

   G.

   H.

   I.

11 Which solid's net would be made with 1 square and 4 triangles? (16-10)

   A. Rectangular prism

   B. Triangular prism

   C. Square pyramid

   D. Triangular pyramid

12 How many edges does this triangular prism have? (16-9)

13 Which solid's net would be made with 6 squares? Explain how you know. (16-10)

THINK
SOLVE
EXPLAIN

Set A, pages 328–331

You can use benchmark angles to classify angles.

A 90° angle makes a square corner.

A 45° angle is open half as much as a 90° angle.

A 180° angle forms a straight line.

Use a protractor to draw a 45° angle.

Draw ray BC. Place the middle of the protractor on endpoint B. Find the 45° mark and place a point. Label it A. Then draw ray BA.

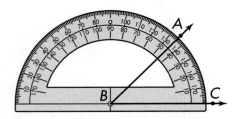

The measure of angle ABC is 45°.

Remember that an angle can be between benchmark angles.

Describe the angles below using benchmarks.

1. 2.

3. 4.

Use a protractor to draw each angle.

5. 45°   6. 360°

7. 180°   8. 90°

9. An angle that is greater than 90° but less than 180°.

10. An angle that is greater than 180° but less than 360°.

Set B, pages 332–335, 338–339

How can you move a shape on a plane?

A translation moves a figure in a straight direction.

A reflection of a figure gives its mirror image.

A rotation of a figure moves it about a point.

These figures could be related by a translation, a rotation, or a reflection.

Remember that two figures can be related by more than one manipulation.

Tell one way the two figures are related to each other.

1.   2.

3.    4.

5.    6.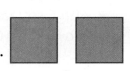

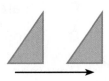

Set C, pages 336–337

How many lines of symmetry does the figure have?

Fold the figure along the dashed line. The two halves are congruent and fit one on top of the other.

It has 1 line of symmetry.

Fold along any of the dashed lines. The two halves are congruent and fit one on top of the other.

It has 4 lines of symmetry.

This figure has no dashed lines.

It has no lines of symmetry.

Remember that figures can have many lines of symmetry.

Tell if each line is a line of symmetry.

1. 2. 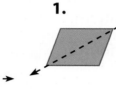 3.

Draw the lines of symmetry for each figure.

4. 5. 6.

Set D, pages 340–341

What is the least angle measure that will rotate the figure onto itself?

This figure can be rotated 90° to land on itself.

This figure can be rotated 180° to land on itself.

This figure can be rotated 90° to land on itself.

Remember, a figure has rotational symmetry if it can rotate onto itself in less than 360°.

Does the figure have rotational symmetry? Write yes or no. Give the least angle measure that will rotate the figure onto inself.

1. S 2.

3. E 4.

5. 6.

Set E, pages 342–344

Do rectangles tessellate?

Rectangles make a tessellation. There are no gaps or overlaps in the pattern.

Shapes can be combined to form a tessellation.

Start with a trapezoid and an equilateral triangle.

Use reflection to get other trapezoids and equilateral triangles.

Use rotation to get other triangles around the trapezoids.

Use translation to tessellate the pattern.

Remember that translations, reflections, and rotations can be used to make a tessellation.

Tell if each shape tessellates. If yes, trace the shape and draw the tessellation.

1.  2.

Use each shape to draw a tessellation.

3.   4.

Describe the transformation(s) used to tessellate the shapes.

5.   6.

Set F, pages 346–347

How many faces, edges, and vertices does this solid have?

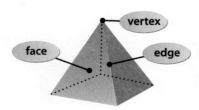

The solid has 5 faces, 8 edges, and 5 vertices.

Remember that the flat surface of a solid is the face.

	Solid	Faces	Edges	Vertices
1.	Triangular prism	5		
2.	Rectangular pyramid			5
3.	Cube		12	
4.	Rectangular prism	6		

Set G, pages 348–350

Tell which solid can be made from the net below.

When folded and taped together, the net would form a cylinder.

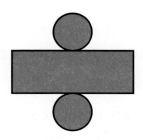

Remember some solids have more than one net.

Name the solid that can be made.

1. 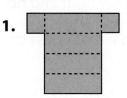 **2.**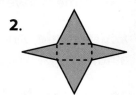

3. Draw two different nets for a triangular prism.

Set H, pages 352–353

Draw the front, right side, and top views of this solid.

Here is the front view of the solid.

Here is the right side view of the solid.

Here is the top view of the solid.

Remember to consider blocks that might be hidden from your view in the drawings.

Draw the top, right side, and front views of each solid figure.

1.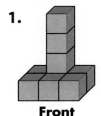

Front

2.

Front

Set I, pages 354–356

Suppose a square is cut as shown. Is each section $\frac{1}{4}$ of the square?

What do I know?   The square is cut into 4 pieces.

What am I asked to find?   Does each section represent $\frac{1}{4}$ of the square?

If each part is $\frac{1}{4}$, then the whole is divided into 4 equal parts. The parts are not the same size. Each section is not $\frac{1}{4}$ of the square.

Remember to explain your answer.

Write to explain.

1. Peter says that $\frac{3}{4}$ of a pizza is always the same as $\frac{6}{8}$ of a pizza. Nadia says that while they are equivalent fractions, $\frac{3}{4}$ and $\frac{6}{8}$ of a pizza could represent different amounts. Who is correct?

Glossary

A

A.M. Time between midnight and noon.

acute angle An angle that is less than a right angle.

acute triangle A triangle with three acute angles.

addends The numbers that are added together to find a sum.
Example: 2 + 7 = 9

Addends

algebraic expression A mathematical phrase involving a variable or variables, numbers, and operations.

analog clock Shows time by pointing to numbers on a face.

angle A figure formed by two rays that have the same endpoint.

area The number of square units needed to cover a region.

array A way of displaying objects in rows and columns.

Associative Property of Addition Addends can be regrouped and the sum remains the same.

Associative Property of Multiplication Factors can be regrouped and the product remains the same.

B

bar graph A graph using bars to show data.

benchmark fractions Fractions that are commonly used for estimation: $\frac{1}{4}$, $\frac{1}{3}$, $\frac{1}{2}$, $\frac{2}{3}$, and $\frac{3}{4}$.

base Flat surface or surfaces of solid figures that may have some curved surfaces.

breaking apart Mental math method used to rewrite a number as the sum of numbers to form an easier problem.

C

centimeter (cm) A metric unit of length. 100 centimeters = 1 meter

common factor A factor that two or more numbers have in common.

Commutative Property of Addition Numbers can be added in any order and the sum remains the same.

Commutative Property of Multiplication Factors can be multiplied in any order and the product remains the same.

compatible numbers Numbers that are easy to compute mentally.

compensation Choosing numbers close to the numbers in a problem to make the computation easier, and then adjusting the answer for the numbers chosen.

cone A solid figure with one circular base. The points on the circle are joined to one point outside the base.

congruent Figures that have the same shape and size.

counting on Counting up from the smaller number to find the difference of two numbers.

cube A solid figure with six congruent squares as its faces.

cylinder A solid figure with two congruent circular bases.

data Pieces of collected information.

day A unit of time equal to 24 hours.

decimal point A dot used to separate ones from tenths in a number.

degree (°) A unit of measure for angles.

denominator The number below the fraction bar in a fraction. The total number of equal parts in all.

difference The answer when subtracting two numbers.

digits The symbols used to write a number: 0, 1, 2, 3, 4, 5, 6, 7, 8, and 9.

Distributive Property Breaking apart facts into two simpler problems. *Example*: $8 \times 4 = (8 \times 2) + (8 \times 2)$

divide An operation to find the number in each group or the number of equal groups.

dividend The number to be divided.

divisibility rules The rules that state when a number is divisible by another number.

divisible Can be divided by another number without leaving a remainder. *Example*: 10 is divisible by 2.

divisor The number by which another number is divided. *Example*: $32 \div 4 = 8$

Divisor

edge A line segment where two faces of a solid figure meet.

←Edge

equation A number sentence that uses the equal sign (=) to show that two expressions have the same value.

equilateral triangle A triangle in which all sides are the same length.

equivalent Numbers that name the same amount.

equivalent decimals Decimals that name the same amount as another decimal. *Example:* 0.7 = 0.70.

equivalent fractions Fractions that name the same region, part of a set, or part of a segment.

expanded form A number written as the sum of the values of its digits. *Example:* 2,000 + 400 + 70 + 6

face A flat surface of a solid that does not roll.

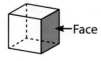←Face

fact family A group of related facts using the same set of numbers.

factors The numbers multiplied together to find a product. *Example:* 3 × 6 = 18

Factor

foot (ft) A customary unit of length. 1 foot = 12 inches

fraction A fraction is a symbol, such as $\frac{2}{3}$, $\frac{5}{1}$, or $\frac{8}{5}$, used to name a part of a whole, a part of a set, a location on a number line, or a division of whole numbers.

generalization A general statement.

hexagon A polygon with 6 sides.

hour A unit of time equal to 60 minutes.

hundredth One part of 100 equal parts of a whole.

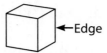

Identity Property of Addition The sum of any number and zero is that number.

Identity Property of Multiplication The product of any number and one is that number.

improper fractions A fraction in which the numerator is greater than or equal to the denominator.

inch (in.) A customary unit of length. 12 inches = 1 foot

inequality A number sentence that uses the greater than sign (>) or the less than sign (<) to show that two expressions do not have the same value.

intersecting lines Lines that cross at one point.

inverse operations Operations that undo each other.
Examples: Adding 6 and subtracting 6 are inverse operations. Multiplying by 4 and dividing by 4 are inverse operations.

isosceles triangle A triangle that has at least two equal sides.

kilometer (km) A metric unit of length. 1 kilometer = 1,000 meters

line A straight path of points that goes on and on in two directions.

line of symmetry A line on which a figure can be folded so that both halves are congruent.

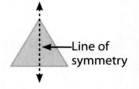

line segment A part of a line that has two endpoints.

meter (m) A metric unit of length. 1 meter = 100 centimeters

mile (mi) A customary unit of length. 1 mile = 5,280 feet

millimeter (mm) A metric unit of length. 1,000 millimeters = 1 meter

minute A unit of time equal to 60 seconds.

mixed number A number that has a whole number and a fraction.

month One of the 12 parts into which a year is divided.

multiple The product of any two whole numbers.

net A pattern used to make a solid.

Example: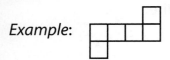

number expression An expression that contains numbers and at least one operation. A number expression is also called a numerical expression.

numerator The number above the fraction bar in a fraction.

obtuse angle An angle whose measure is between 90° and 180°.

135°

obtuse triangle A triangle in which there is one obtuse angle.

octagon A polygon with 8 sides.

P.M. Time between noon and midnight.

parallel lines In a plane, lines that never intersect.
Example: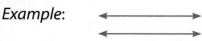

parallelogram
A quadrilateral in which opposite sides are parallel.

partial products Products found by breaking one factor in a multiplication problem into ones, tens, hundreds, and so on and then multiplying each of these by the other factor.

pentagon A plane figure with 5 sides.

percent A number that shows a comparison to 100. Percent means per hundred. The symbol for percent is %. 50% means 50 per 100, or 50 out of 100, and can also be written as $\frac{50}{100}$ or 0.50.

perimeter The distance around a figure.

period In a number, a group of three digits, separated by commas, starting from the right.

perpendicular lines Two intersecting lines that form right angles. *Example:*

point An exact location in space.

polygon A closed plane figure made up of line segments.

pound (lb) A customary unit of weight. 1 pound = 16 ounces

product The answer to a multiplication problem.

protractor A tool used to measure and draw angles.

pyramid A solid figure whose base is a polygon and whose faces are triangles with a common vertex.

quadrilateral A polygon with 4 sides.

quotient The answer to a division problem.

ray A part of a line that has one endpoint and continues endlessly in one direction.

rectangle A quadrilateral with 4 right angles.

rectangular prism A solid figure whose faces are all rectangles.

rectangular pyramid A solid figure with a rectangle for its base and triangles for all other faces.

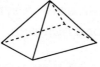

reflection Gives its mirror image.

rhombus A quadrilateral in which opposite sides are parallel and all sides are the same length.

right angle An angle that forms a square corner.

right triangle A triangle in which there is one right angle.

rotation Moves a figure about a point.

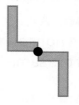

rotational symmetry A figure has rotational symmetry when it can rotate onto itself in less than a full rotation.

rounding Replacing a number with a number that tells about how many or how much.

scalene triangle A triangle in which no sides are the same length.

second A unit of time. 60 seconds = 1 minute

side Each of the line segments of a polygon.

simplest form A fraction in which the numerator and denominator have no common factors other than 1.

solid figure A figure that has length, width, and height.

solution The value of the variable that makes an equation true.

solve Find a solution to an equation.

sphere A solid figure that includes all points the same distance from a center point.

square A quadrilateral with 4 right angles and all sides the same length.

square pyramid A solid figure with a square base and four faces that are triangles.

standard form A way to write a number showing only its digits. *Example*: 2,613

straight angle An angle that forms a straight line.

sum The result of adding numbers together.

symmetric A figure is symmetric if it can be folded into two congruent halves that fit on top of each other.

tenth One of ten equal parts of a whole.

tessellation A repeating pattern that has no gaps or overlaps.

thousandth One out of 1,000 equal parts of a whole.

translation A change in the position of a figure that moves it up, down, or sideways.

trapezoid A quadrilateral with only one pair of parallel sides.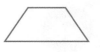

triangle A polygon with 3 sides.

triangular prism A solid figure with two bases that are triangles and the other three faces are rectangles.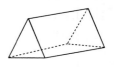

underestimate An estimate that is less than the exact answer.

variable A symbol or letter that stands for a number.

Venn diagram A diagram that uses circles to show the relationships between groups of data. *Example*: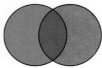

vertex (plural, vertices) The point where two rays meet to form an angle. The points where the sides of a polygon meet. The points where three or more edges meet in a solid figure that does not roll. The pointed part of a cone.

week A unit of time equal to 7 days.

word form A number written in words.
Example: Four thousand, six hundred, thirty-two.

yard (yd) A customary unit of length.
1 yard = 3 feet

year A unit of time equal to 365 days or 52 weeks or 12 months.

Zero Property of Multiplication
The product of any number and zero is zero.

Illustrations

Cover: Luciana Powell; 7, 49, 60, 124, 162, 163, 178, 236, 260, 305-307, 314, 320, 328 Leslie Kell; 10, 12 Dick Gage; 38 Kenneth Batelman; 200 Neil Stewart.

Photographs

Photo locators denoted as follows: Top (T), Center (C), Bottom (B), Left (L), Right (R), Background (Bkgd)

2 (BL) Earth Imaging/Getty Images, (BR) Russell Gordon/Danita Delimont, Agent; 3 (CL) Bettmann/Corbis, (CL) Getty Images; 9 (BR) Getty Images; 14 Getty Images; 22 (T) ©Mark Sykes/Alamy; 28 (TL) Andrew J. Martinez/Photo Researchers, Inc., (TL) Georgette Douwma/Nature Picture Library, (TL) Getty Images, (B) Jupiter Images; 29 (BL) Hideki Yoshihara /Jupiter Images, (T) Mary Evans Picture Library/Alamy Images; 35 (T) Jupiter Images; 37 (BR) Mary Evans Picture Library/Alamy Images; 39 (BR) Hideki Yoshihara /Jupiter Images; 46 (T) ©Royalty-Free/Corbis, (TC) PHONE Labat J.M./Peter Arnold, Inc.; 47 (T) Acc. #I-20828/Phoebe A. Hearst Museum of Anthropology; 61 (BR) Jupiter Images; 68 (CR) Getty Images, (BC) Purestock/Getty Images, (BL) Roger Harris/Photo Researchers, Inc.; 69 (L) ©Alex Steedman/Corbis; 71 (BR) ©Jeff Greenberg/Alamy Images; 77 (BR) ©Steve Vidler/SuperStock; 88 (TC) Imaginary recreation of an Aztec Sun Stone calandar, Late post classic period, Aztec/Jean-Pierre Courau, Private Collection/Bridgeman Art Library, (BC) Marc Muench/Corbis; 89 (CL) Marianna Day Massey/Corbis, (TL) Mike Hill/Alamy Images; 92 (B) Alain Dragesco-Joffe/Animals Animals/Earth Scenes; 95 (BR) ©tbkmedia. de/Alamy; 103 (R, L, CR, CL) ©Royalty-Free/Corbis; 107 (T) ©Yann Arthus-Bertrand/Corbis, (B) Tracy Morgan/©DK Images; 114 (B) Louie Psihoyos/Getty Images, (TL) SSPL/The Image Works, Inc.; 115 (BL) Oliver Eltinger/Corbis, (TL) Rubberball/Getty Images; 132 (TL) AP/Wide World Photos, (B) Stan Osolinski/PhotoLibrary Group, Ltd.; 133 (TL) ©Daniel Joubert/Reuters/Corbis; 139 (BR) ©Cameron Davidson/Jupiter Images; 143 (BR) ©Daniel Joubert/Reuters/Corbis, (BR) AP/Wide World Photos; 150 (BC) Andy Holligan/DK Images, (TL) Getty Images, (CL) John Gress/Corbis; 151 (BC) Douglas Peebles/Corbis, (T) image100; 156 Getty Images; 170 (TL) ©Nicholas Veasey/Getty Images, (T) Adam Jones/Alamy Images, (TR) DK Images; 171 (B) ©Nicholas Veasey/Getty Images, (T) Damian Dovargnes/AP/Wide World Photos, (T) Jupiter Images; 173 (CR) ©Rolf Nussbaumer/Animals Animals/Earth Scenes; 174 (T) Nigel Hicks/©DK Images; 175 ©Nicholas Veasey/Getty Images; 185 (BR) ©Andre Seale/Alamy Images, (T) One Mile Up, Inc.; 190 (TL) Getty Images, (B) VEER Gib Martinez/Getty Images; 191 (T, C) ©Inga Spence/Getty Images, (TL) Pablo Martinez Monsivais/AP Images; 205 (BR) ©Mark E. Gibson Stock Photography; 209 (T, C, B) ©Tony Kwan/Alamy; 214 (TL) Courtesy of Air Tractor, Inc., (TL) Don Klumpp/Getty Images; 215 (BL) Iconica/Getty Images, (TL) NASA/ Science Faction/Getty Images; 230 (T) Eddie Gerald/Alamy Images, (TC) Nature Picture Library, (TL) Scott T. Smith/Corbis; 254 (TL) Geosphere/Planetary Visions/Photo Researchers, Inc., (BC) Keren Su/Corbis; 255 (TL) Courtesy of New Bremen Giant Pumpkin Growers, (T) Summerhayes, Soames/Photo Researchers, Inc.; 276 (T) Momatiuk - Eastcott/Corbis, (TL) The Granger Collection, NY; 277 (T) ©Charles E. Rotkin/Corbis, (T) ©Prof. Yves Roisin/Museum des Sciences Naturelles, Bruxelles, Belgium; 302 (B) Getty Images; 303 (TL) Clay Jackson/AP Images, (CR) Rusty Gaul; 320 Getty Images; 326 (B) ©Joseph Sohm; Visions of America/Corbis, (T) Robert F. Bukaty/AP Images; 327 (BL) M. C. Escher's "Symmetry Drawing E78"/©The M. C. Escher Company, Baarn, Holland. All rights reserved., (TL) Max Alexander/©DK Images; 331 (B) Jupiter Images; 337 (B) ©Digital Vision Ltd./SuperStock; 339 Digital Vision, (C) Getty Images, (BC) Stockdisc; 344 (TR) Jupiter Images; 350 (C) Jupiter Images.

Nets, 348–350

Number lines
decimals, 238–239, 284–286, 290–291
fractions, 284–286
mixed numbers, 290–291

Number patterns, 345

Number Sense
addition and multiplication, 59
bar graphs, 257
common factors, 259
common multiples, 261
completing a numeric expression, 123
division, 12
fact family, 55, 61
fractions and decimals, 282
multiplication, 79, 95, 103, 237, 335
percents, 292
perimeter and area, 319
place value, 6
rounding decimals, 242
rounding whole numbers, 19, 31, 184
subtraction, 222, 223
Venn Diagrams, 243, 261
writing greater numbers, 16
writing number sentences, 141

Numeration
decimal point, 233, 235
decimals, comparing, 244–245
decimals, ordering, 246–247
Egyptian number system, 7
estimating relative amounts and distances, 10–12
estimating sums and differences, 20–21
expanded form, 4–9
millions, 8–9

numerical patterns, 345
period, 4
place value in decimals, 232–237
place value in whole numbers, 4–6, 8–9
standard form, 4–9
thousands, 4–6
whole numbers, comparing and ordering, 14–17
whole numbers, rounding, 18–19
word form, 4–9

Ordering. *See also* Number lines.
decimals, 246–247
whole numbers, 14–17

Partial products, 75, 90–92, 94–95, 134–139

Patterns
Look for a Pattern, 198–199
multiplying multiples of 10, 100, and 1,000, 70–73, 116–118, 120–121, 140–141, 152–153, 158–159
numerical, 345
skip counting, 30–31
using rules to complete tables, 194–197, 203

Percents, 292–294

Perfect Squares, 119

Perimeter, 316–319

Period, 4

Perspectives, 352–353

Place value
decimals, 232–237
whole numbers, 4–6, 8–9

Prisms, 346–350

Problem Solving
Draw a Picture, 22–23, 40–41, 62–63, 248–249
Exact Answer or Estimate, 182–184
Look for a Pattern, 198–199
Make a Table, 206–208, 266–267
Make an Organized List, 160–161
Make and Test Generalizations, 270–271
Missing or Extra Information, 106–108
Multiple-Step Problems, 126–127, 164–165
Problem-Solving Handbook, x–xxi
Reasonableness, 80–82
Selecting Appropriate Measurement Units and Tools, 320–321
Solve a Simpler Problem, 206–208, 310–311
Try, Check, and Revise, 100–101
Two-Question Problems, 144–145
Use Objects, 266–267
Use Reasoning, 296–297
Work Backward, 224–225
Write an Equation, 22–23, 40–41, 62–63
Writing to Explain, 354–356

Properties
Commutative Property of Multiplication, 32–33
Distributive Property, 34–35
Identity Property of Multiplication, 32–33
Zero Property of Multiplication, 32–33